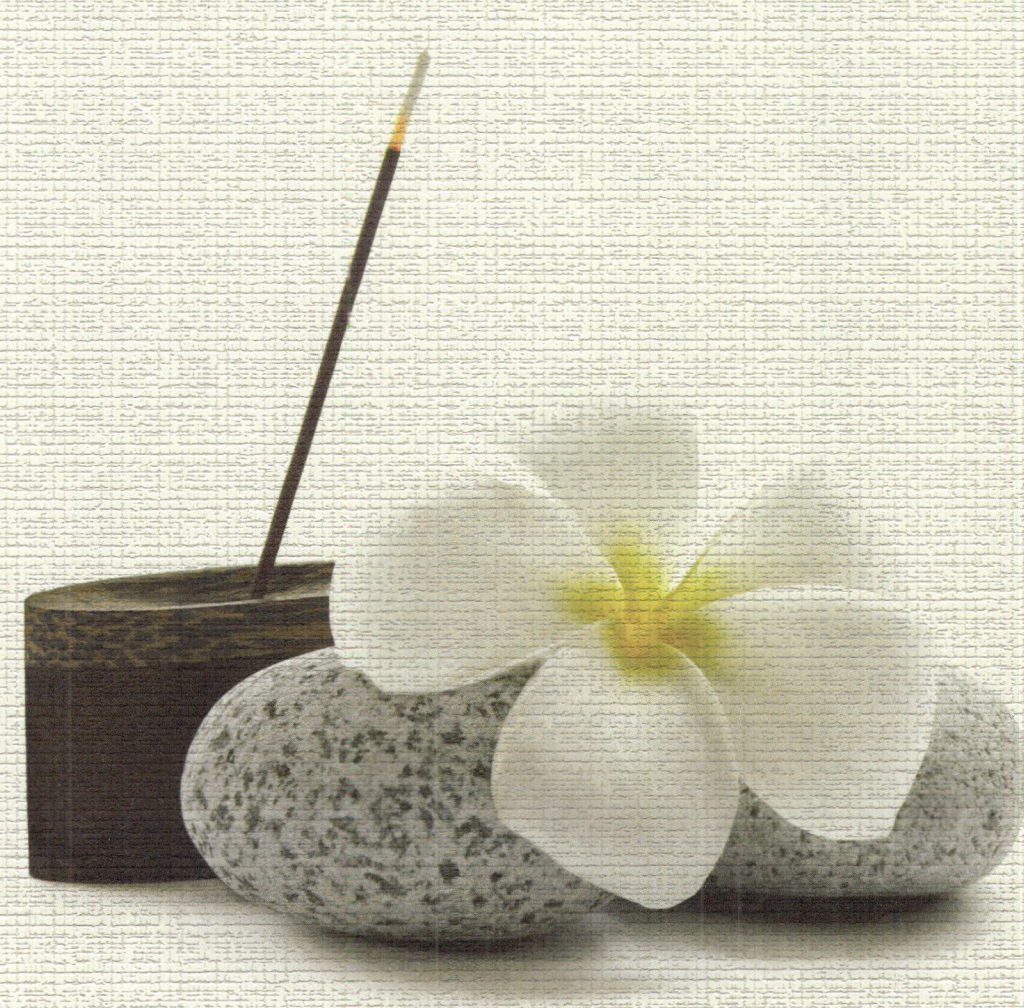

SPECTACULAR HOMES
of the Pacific Northwest

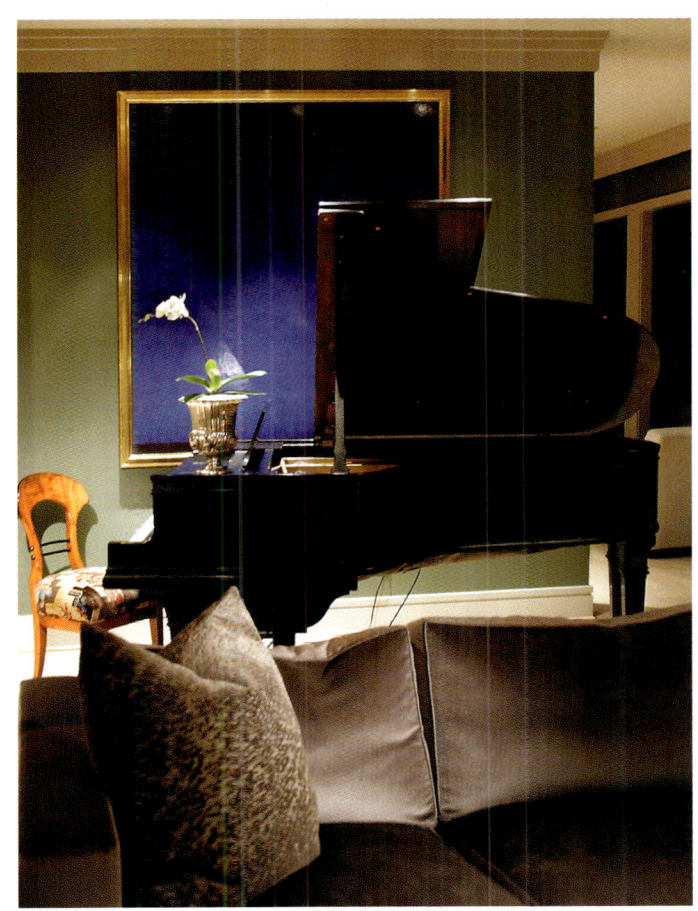

AN EXCLUSIVE SHOWCASE OF THE FINEST DESIGNERS IN WASHINGTON AND OREGON

Published by

PANACHE
PARTNERS LLC

13747 Montfort Drive, Suite 100
Dallas, Texas 75240
972-661-9884
972-661-2743
www.panache.com

Publishers: Brian G. Carabet and John A. Shand

Editor: Shanna Germain
Designer: Mary Elizabeth Acree

Copyright © 2006 by Panache Partners, LLC.
All rights reserved.

No part of this book may be reproduced or transmitted in any form or by any means, electronic or mechanical, including photocopying, recording, or by any information storage or retrieval system, except brief excerpts for the purpose of review, without written permission of the publisher.

All images in this book have been reproduced with the knowledge and prior consent of the designers concerned and no responsibility is accepted by the producer, publisher, or printer for any infringement of copyright or otherwise arising from the contents of this publication. Every effort has been made to ensure that credits accurately comply with the information supplied.

Printed in Malaysia

Distributed by Gibbs Smith, Publisher
800-748-5439

PUBLISHER'S DATA

Spectacular Homes of the Pacific Northwest

Library of Congress Control Number: 2004117268

ISBN 13: 978-0-9745747-4-5
ISBN 10: 0-9745747-4-0

First Printing 2006

10 9 8 7 6 5 4 3 2 1

Previous Page: Ted Tuttle, Ted Tuttle Interior Design
See page 89   Photo by Scott Van Dyke

This Page: Dana Foster, DTF Design, Inc.
See page 39   Photo by Michael Walmsley

This publication is intended to showcase the work of extremely talented interior designers, designer's and decorators. The Publisher does not require, warrant, endorse, or verify any professional accreditations, educational backgrounds or professional affiliations of the individuals or firms included herein. All copy and photography published herein has been reviewed and approved as free of any usage fees or rights and accurate by the individuals and/or firms included herein.

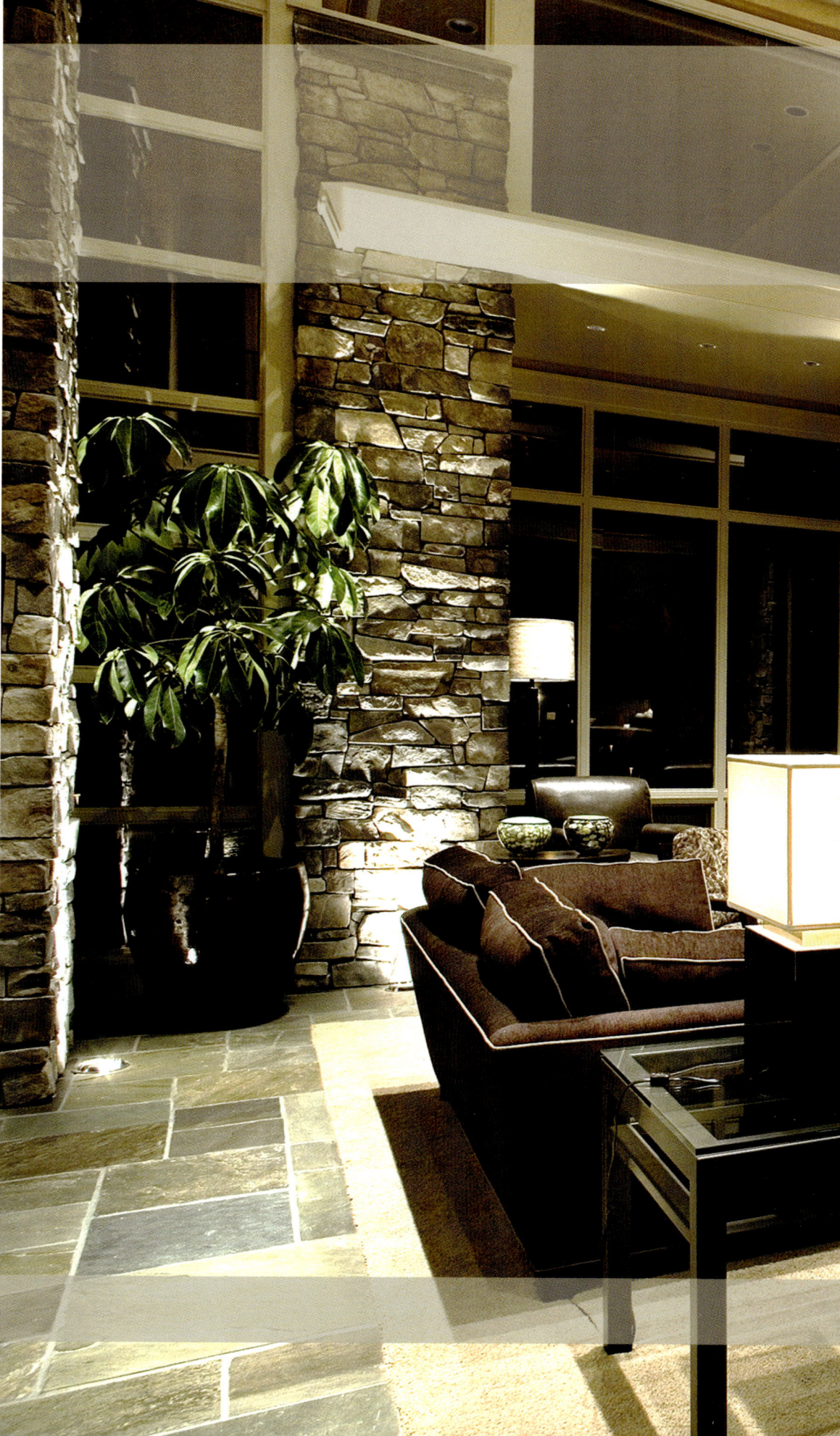

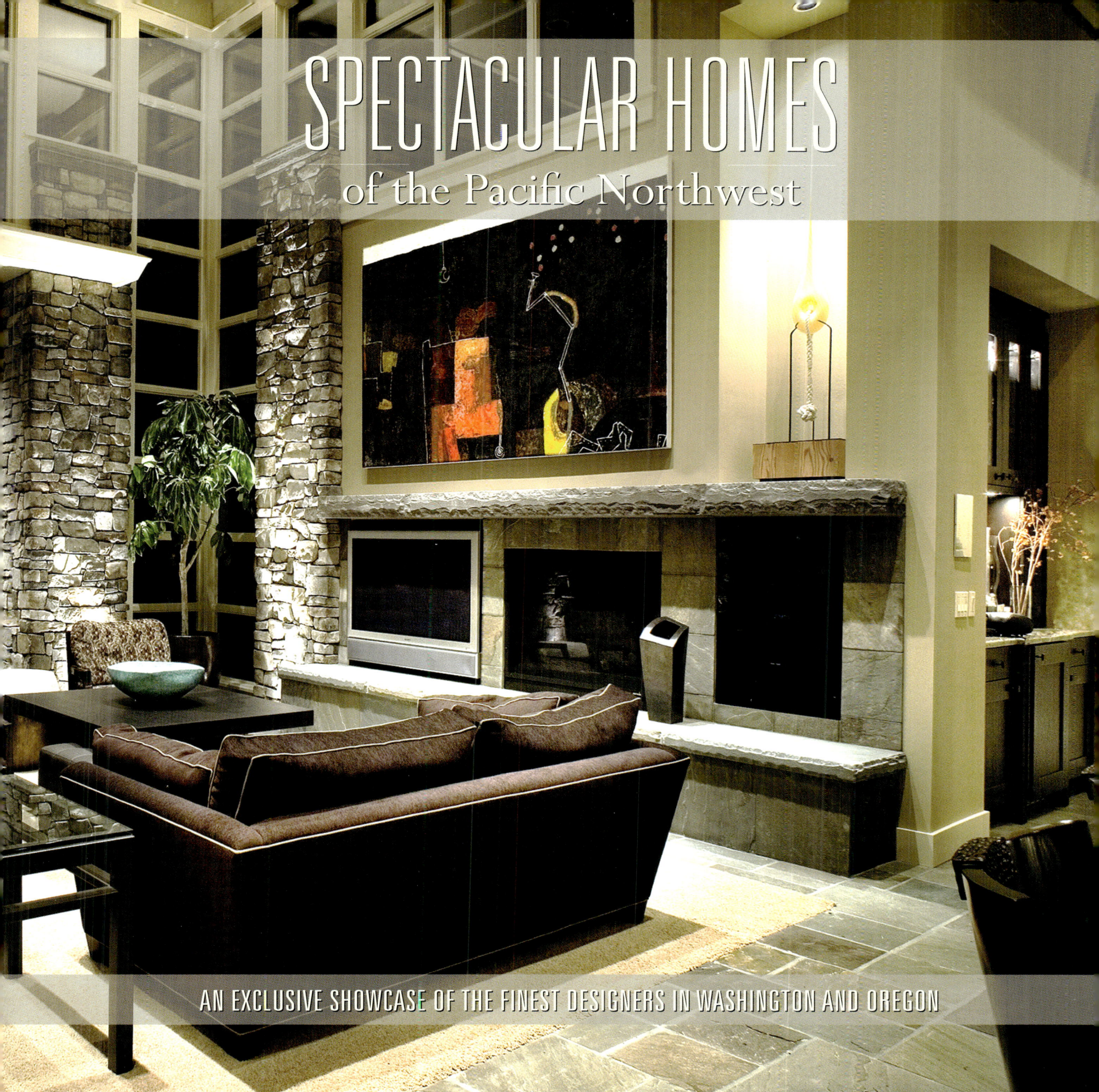

SPECTACULAR HOMES
of the Pacific Northwest

AN EXCLUSIVE SHOWCASE OF THE FINEST DESIGNERS IN WASHINGTON AND OREGON

DESIGNER ERIN DAVIS, ARLENE LORD & STEPHANIE NESS, MOSAIK DESIGN, page 131

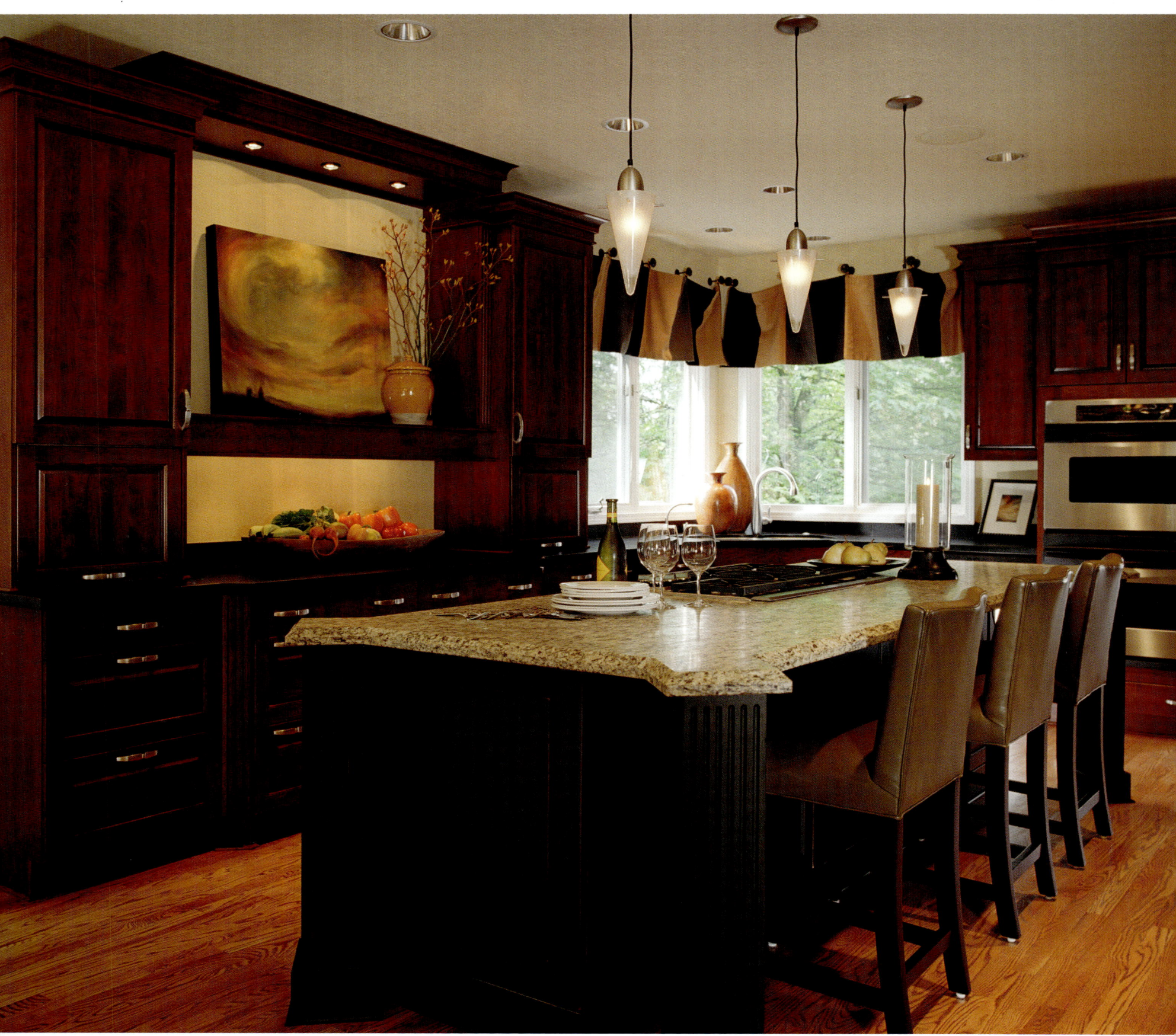

INTRODUCTION

The Pacific Northwest is a land of beauty. From the snowy-peaked Cascade mountains and expanses of old-growth forests to the craggy high deserts, meandering rivers and the soft swell of the Puget Sound, this area's gorgeous natural landscape awes and attracts individuals from around the world. Many come just to visit and to partake in the wonder, but many others choose this area as home—a place to live, work, raise a family and buy a home.

Those who live in the Pacific Northwest know that the interior of any home has to be incredibly stunning to compete with the mountains, rivers, forests and ocean that peek through the windows. The designers featured in Spectacular Homes of the Pacific Northwest understand that—thus, they strive capture the incredible beauty of this area in each and every home. They accomplish this by listening to their clients, making the best use of spaces, colors, fabrics and furniture, and by designing with talent, creativity and passion.

Within the pages of this book, you will see some of the most truly spectacular homes of the Pacific Northwest, homes that rival the comfort, sophistication and spirit of those anywhere in world. Some of these homes have been designed for work, others for play, some for a bit of both. In others, the designer created a warm, welcoming refuge for their busy clients. Still other homes are designed as showrooms, places that are comfortable to live in while also showcasing personal art collections, antiques and other treasured possessions. Some are near-perfect recreations, evoking an era long-past, while others feature the best in contemporary technologies and sophistication. The one thing that each of these homes has in common is that each has been lovingly created by a talented designer specifically to reflect their client's lifestyle and passion.

In today's busy world, we all need a place to find refuge and quiet, to share food and joy with friends and family, a home that reflects both who we are and the world around us, and that reminds us of the beauty everywhere. I hope that as you view these homes, and read the stories of the designers who created them, that you will be inspired and guided by each one's creativity, passion and sense of wonder.

May your life always be filled with beauty, and may your home always be spectacular.

Welcome home,

Shanna

DESIGNER KATHLEEN WILLIAMS, DESIGN BY KATHLEEN WILLIAMS, INC., page 105

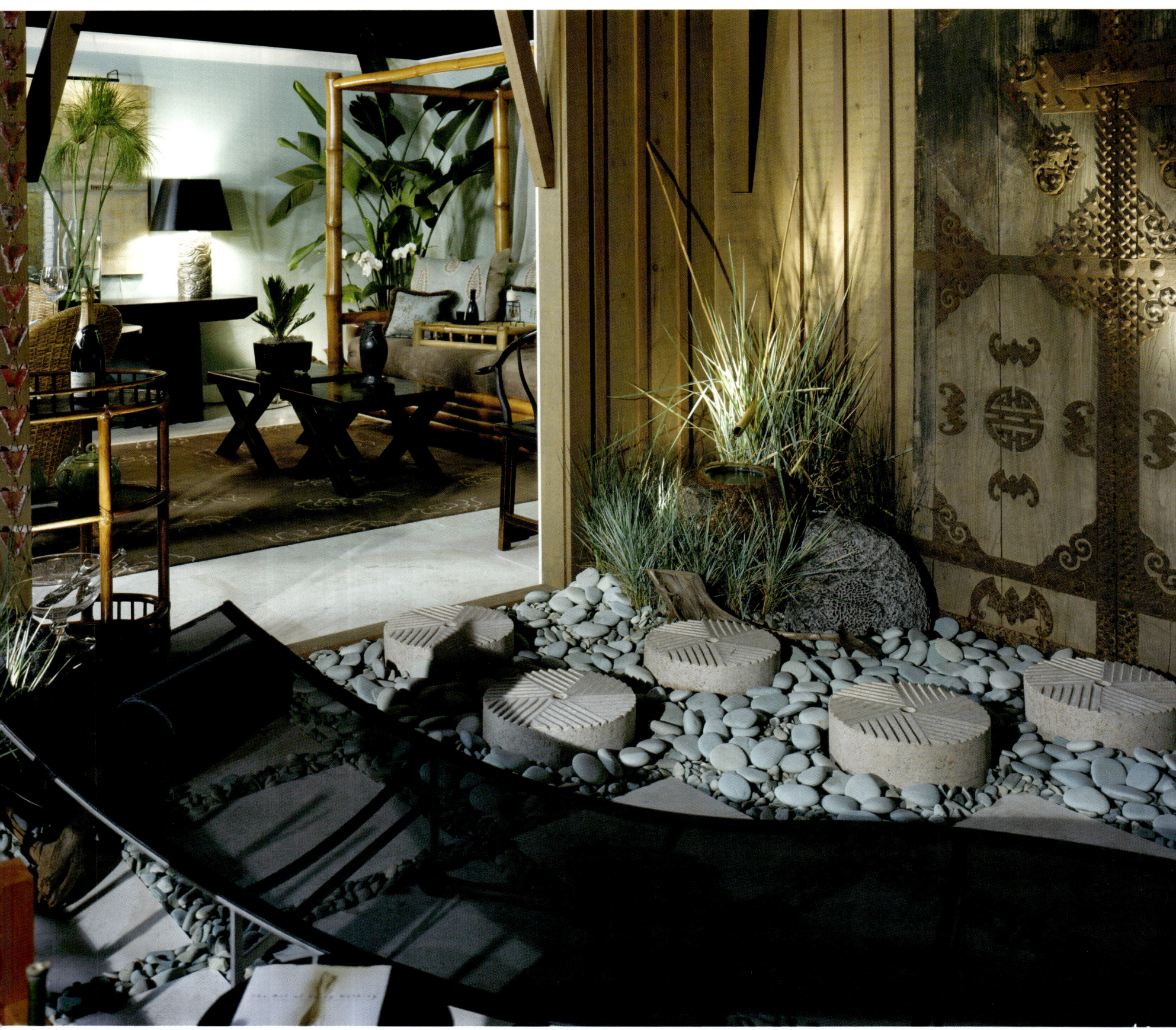

Table of Contents

WASHINGTON

Christine Archer
Christine Archer Interiors	11
Kathleen Bohlken
Kathleen Bohlken Interior Design	17
DeAnne Brenneis
The John Brenneis Architects, Inc. P.S.	21
Debbie Cahill
Debbie Cahill Interior Design, LLC	23
Gregory Carmichael
Gregory Carmichael Interior Design	27
Bonnie K. Crawford
BCDG Bonnie Crawford Design Group	29
Michelle Dahl & Sandy Holstead
Belle Grey Interior Design, LLC	35
Dana T. Foster
DTF Design, Inc.	39
Ann Gordinier
A. Gordinier Interiors, Inc.	43
Mary Hanson
LIBERTY 123, LLC	47
Fran M. Hazel
Fran M. Hazel Design Interiors	53
Michèle Heidt
Heidt & Oldfield Design	55
Larry Hooke
Larry Hooke Interior Design	59
Tami Jones
Tami Jones Interior Design	65
Cynthia Mennella
Cynthia Mennella Design	67
Cheryl K. Monroe
Monroe Design & Development Co.	71
Craig Norberg
Norberry Tile	75
Linda Schoener
Schoener's Interiors	77
Kylee Shintaffer
Kylee Shintaffer Design	83
Ted Tuttle
Ted Tuttle Interior Design	89
Diane Wainhouse & Val Scalzo
Heartland Interiors, Inc.	95
David Weatherford
Weatherford Antiques & Interiors	99
Kathleen Williams
Design by Kathleen Williams, Inc.	105
Ann Jones-Wilson
Jones-Wilson Designs	111

OREGON

Carolyn Allman
C. Allman Design Group	119
Lori Brock
Brock Designs	125
Erin Davis, Arlene Lord & Stephanie Ness
Mosaik Design	131
Keri Davis
Keri Davis Design	133
Melody Emerick
Emerick Architects P.C.	137
Kathie Pozarich
KP Design Group	143
Carol Williamson
Carol Williamson + Associates	149

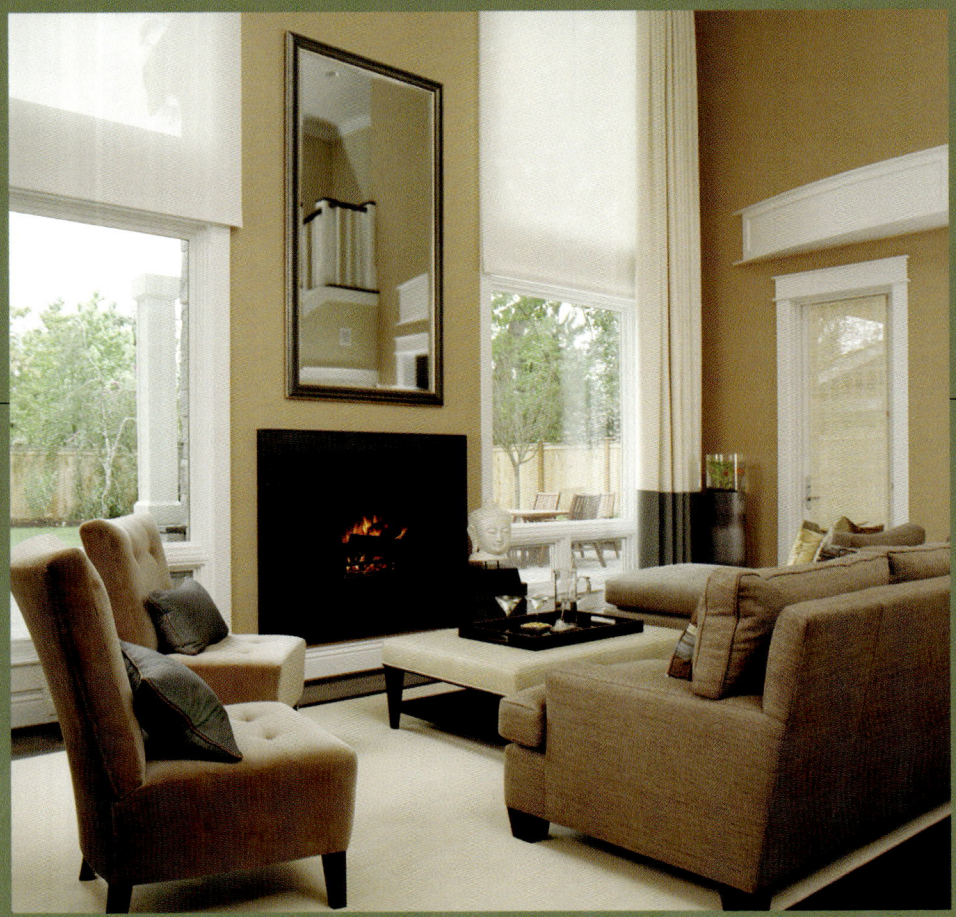

DESIGNER MARY HANSON, LIBERTY 123, LLC, page 47

WASHINGTON

AN EXCLUSIVE SHOWCASE OF THE PACIFIC NORTHWEST'S FINEST DESIGNERS

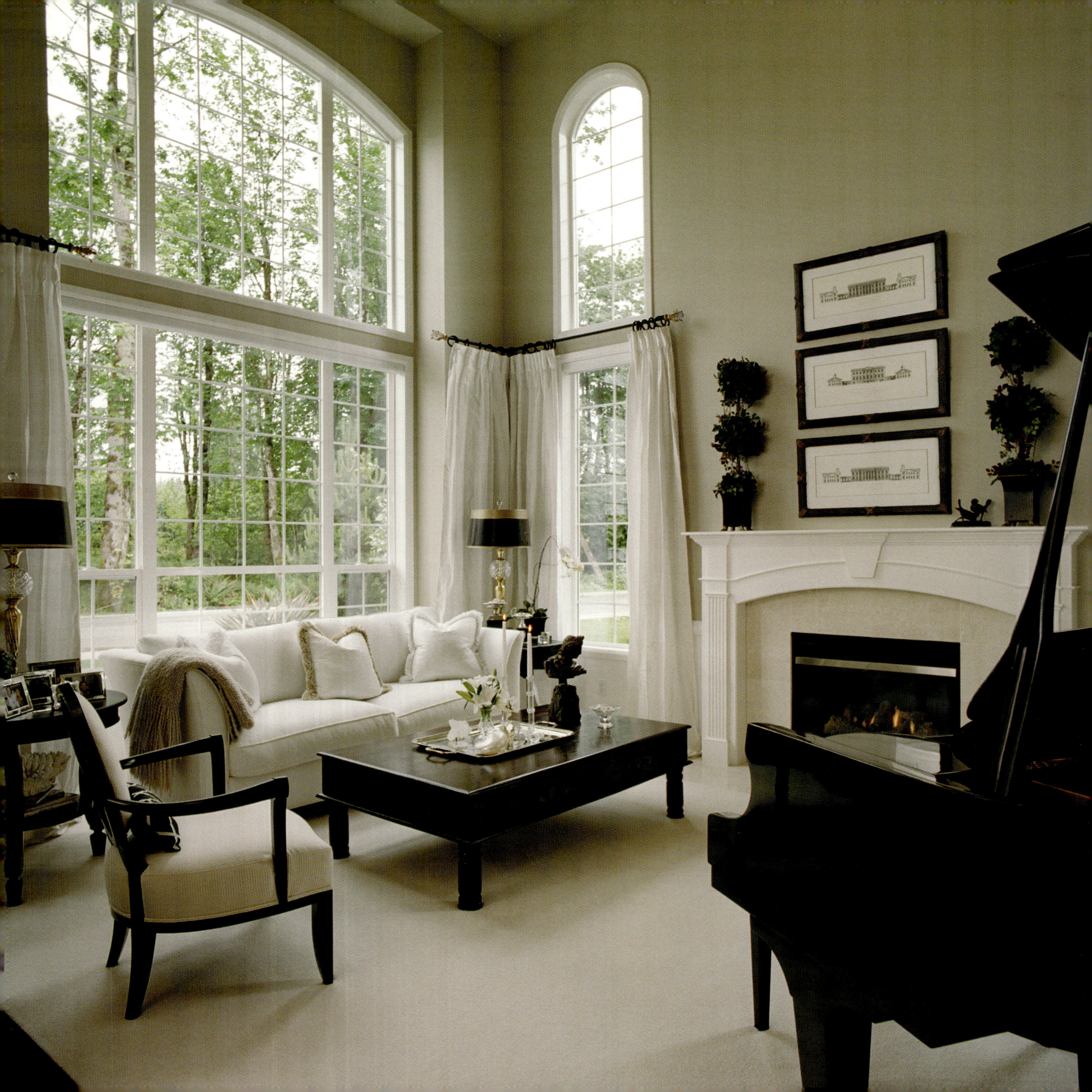

CHRISTINE ARCHER

Christine Archer Interiors

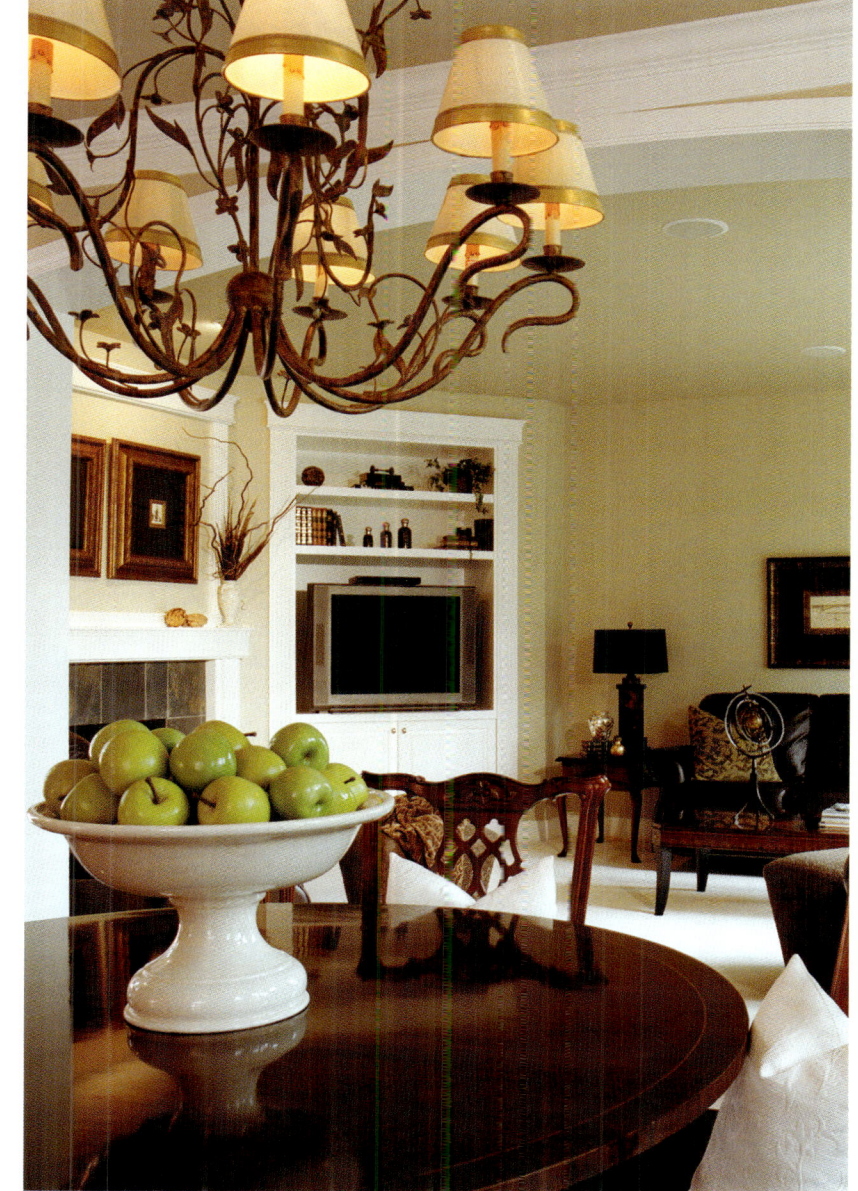

Ask Christine Archer why she's a designer, and she'll admit she doesn't have a choice. As someone who "lives, breathes and sleeps" design, Christine has been designing homes in her head since she was 12 years old. Soon after, she moved on to planning rooms in her parent's basement and dressing up her mom's furniture.

Born with a gift for interior design, it wasn't long before Christine had the opportunity to put her talents to work. A designer and the owner of her own firm for the past eight years, Christine caters primarily to residential clients, although she occasionally dabbles in commercial work for variety.

With her passion for design, garnering the attention of the media was all in a day's work. Christine has been a twice featured guest on Seattle's KCMO television show, "Northwest Afternoon," and her projects have been showcased on local television in Charlotte, N.C.

Christine begins each project by getting to know her clients and their design needs. Her clients say they love Christine's ability to walk into a room and know exactly what it can become. She prides herself on keeping abreast

LEFT
A two-story living room with arched windows, baby grand piano and a contrast of black and white shows off the grand architecture.

RIGHT
View from the kitchen eating area into an inviting, brown-hued family room.

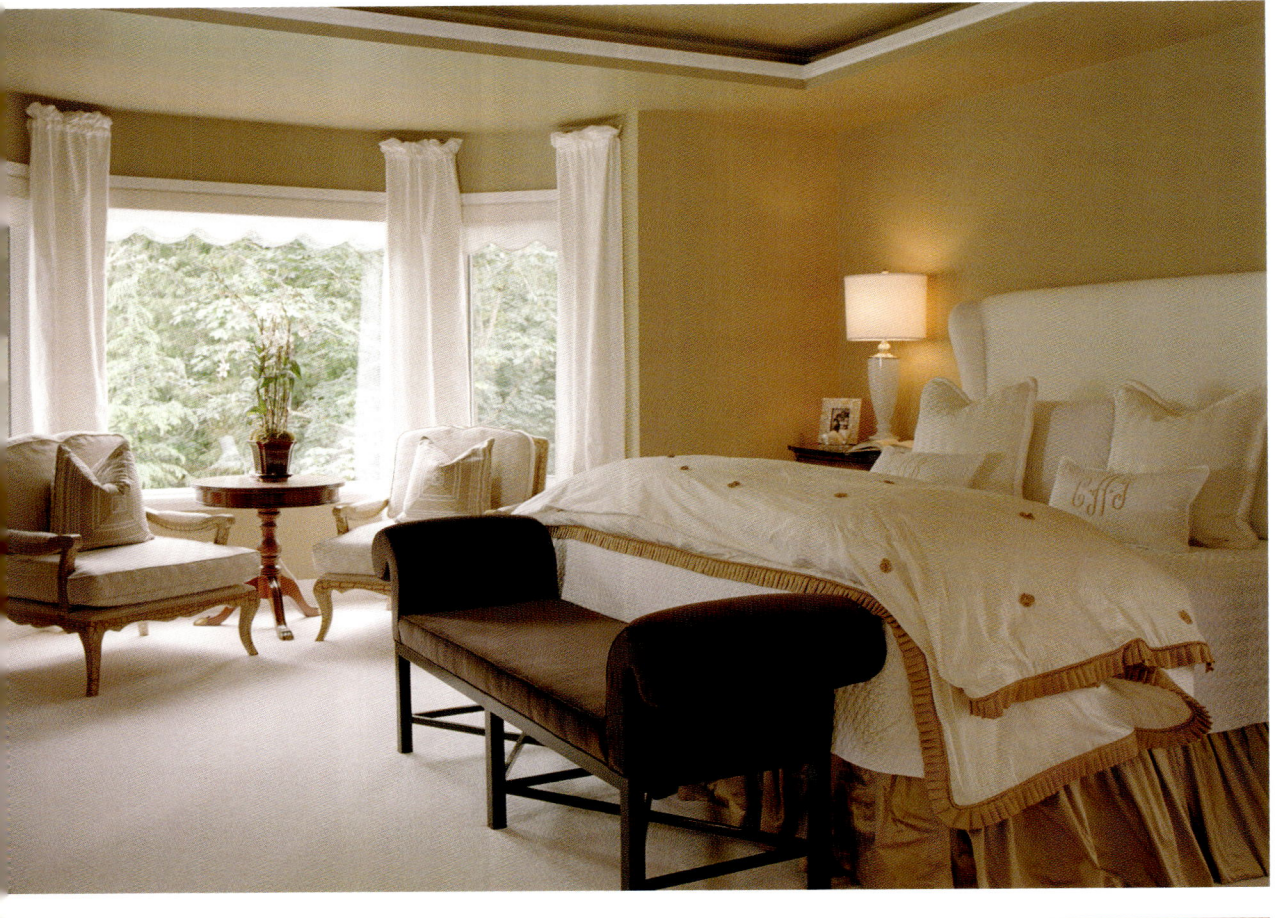

of all the newest design developments and on collaborating with talented partners who handle additional design services, including painting, sewing, hardware and delivery, and set up of furniture.

Although Christine's personal preference leans toward traditional design, she always adds whimsical, cutting-edge pieces as accents. A great example is a Thomas Pheasant bowl atop an old antique sideboard.

For Christine, materials can make or break a space. She even admits to "salivating over fabrics," especially when she finds perfect silk or taffeta for a room. Gorgeous fabrics used in window treatments, pillows and upholstered furniture are her piece de resistance.

As a Northwest designer, Christine finds that windows are especially important in her work. Not only are windows the perfect opportunity to bring in the slanted sunlight and the beautiful Northwest view, in Christine's hands they even become art. In every home, she works to "capture the view and light and frame it in a beautiful way."

While Christine's first love is designing, her second is getting to know her clients and their families. Often, she says, it's sad when a project ends. Her goal with every project is to "share my work with others to inspire them to decorate their homes and love them as much as I do."

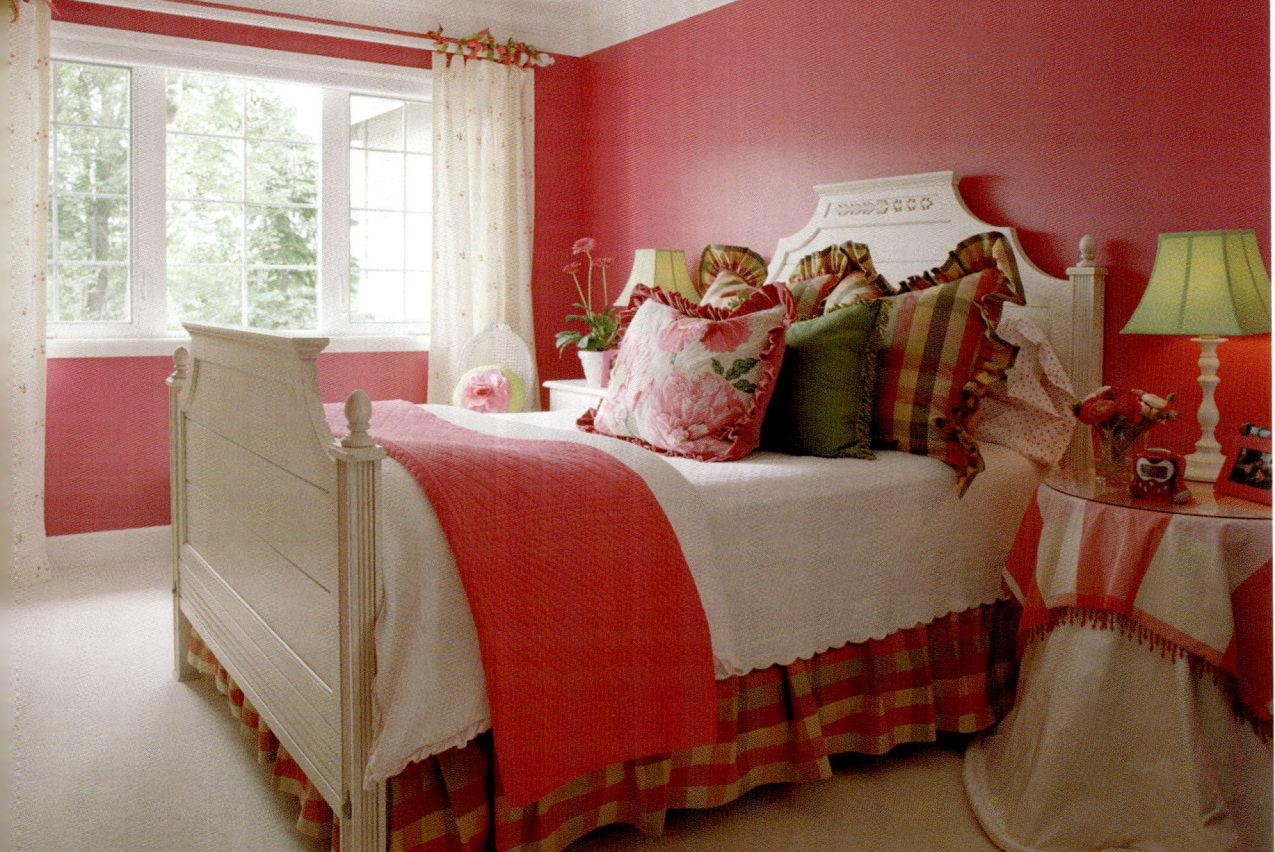

TOP
Serene bedroom, striving for a simple and elegant look. Headboard custom designed by Christine Archer.

BOTTOM
The fresh watermelon pink walls and striking fabrics are a great play of color and textures.

FACING PAGE RIGHT
Daylight basement, with large game table and black-felt pool table—perfect for entertaining.

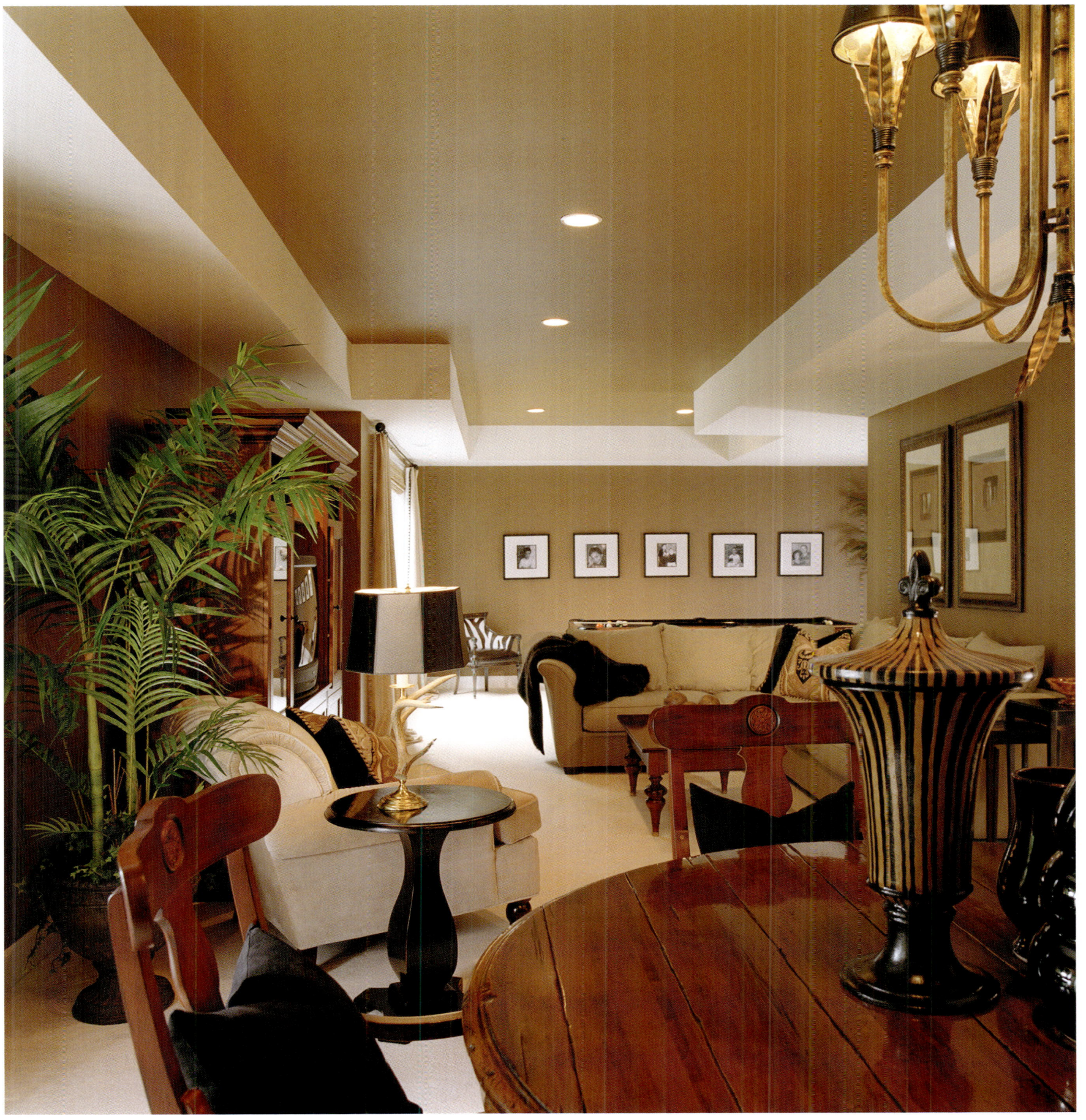

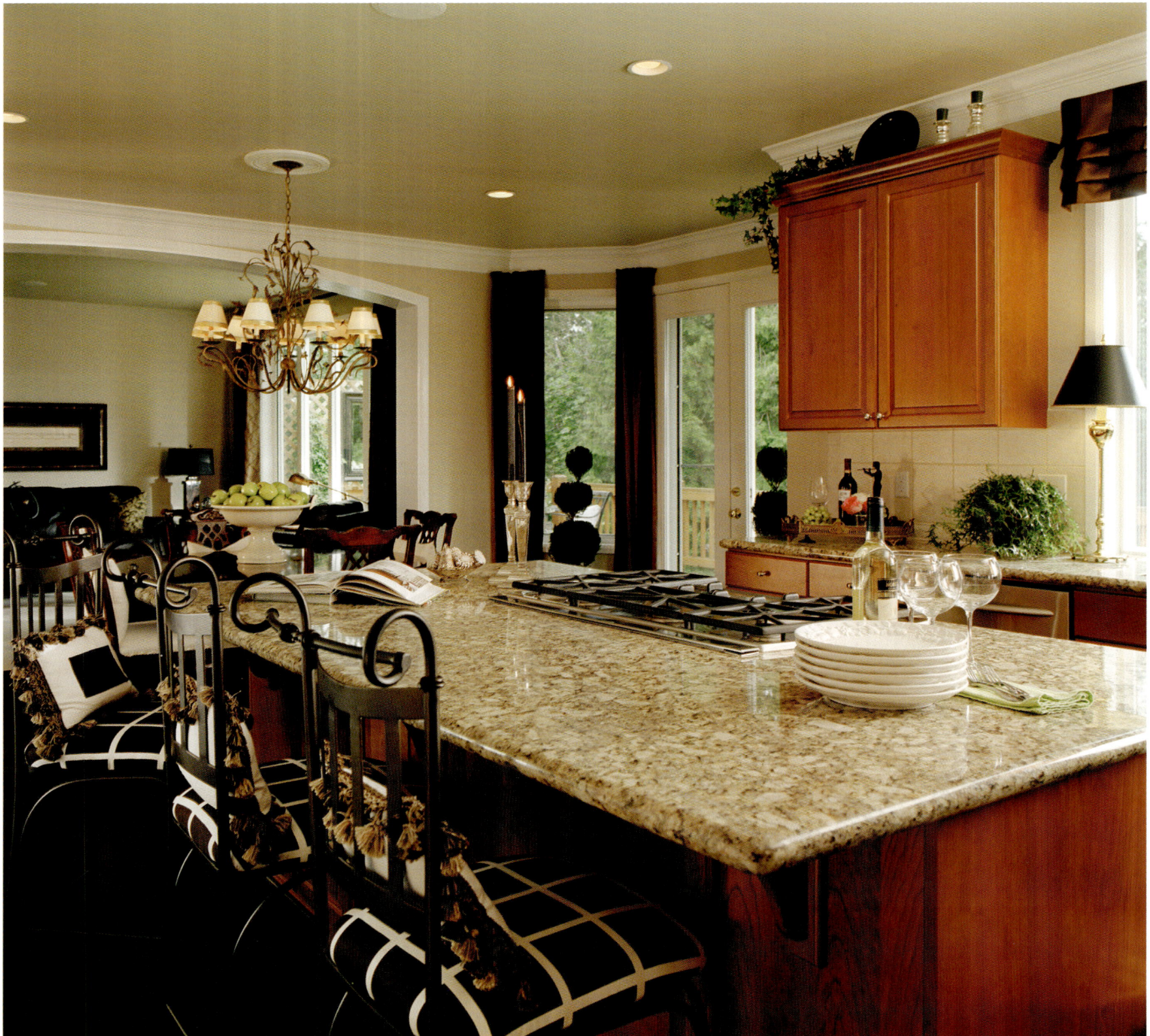

ABOVE
This kitchen view shows off the beautiful chocolate fabrics that accent the ebony floor and rich granite slabs.

FACING PAGE RIGHT
The round mirror and iron sconces add a bit of drama to the bar area in another part of the daylight basement.

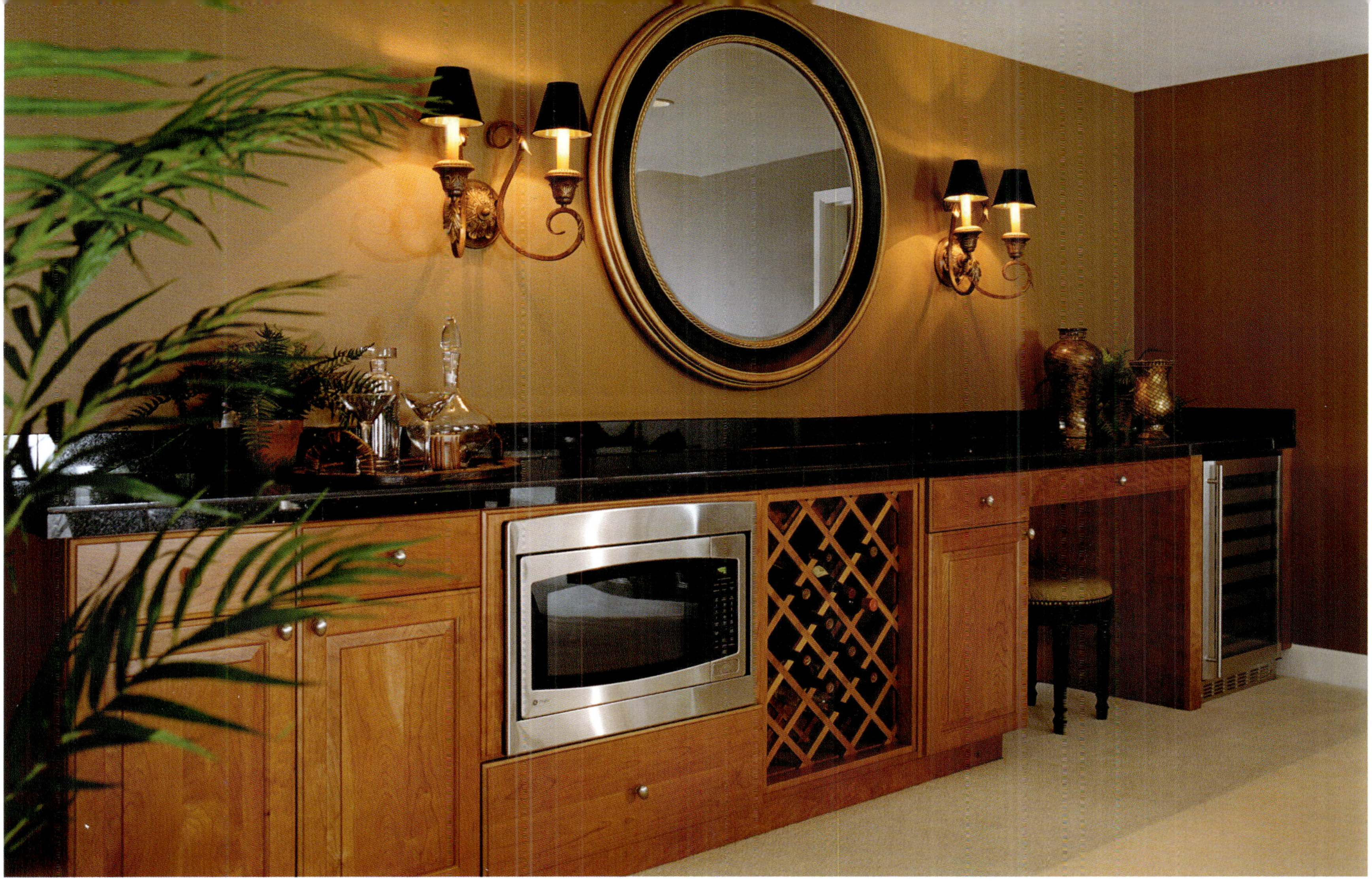

More about Christine…

WHAT PERSONAL INDULGENCE DO YOU SPEND THE MOST MONEY ON?

Fabrics. For her, nothing is better than seeing a stunning silk window treatment. It's the same feeling she gets when she sees a gorgeous diamond.

WHO HAS HAD THE BIGGEST INFLUENCE ON YOUR CAREER?

Her family. Even as a small child, she would dream about what kind of house she would live in and how she would decorate it. Her family always encouraged those talents. Professionally, Barbara Barry has been a real inspiration.

WHY DO YOU LIKE DOING BUSINESS IN THE PACIFIC NORTHWEST?

The people in the Northwest are the most genuinely nice people Christine knows. She feels fortunate to have such wonderful clients.

WHAT'S ONE THING THAT MOST PEOPLE DON'T KNOW ABOUT YOU?

Her house is impeccably clean, but her cars are a mess, full of samples, fabrics and books.

WHAT ARE YOU READING RIGHT NOW?

Every decorating magazine under the sun. She treasures the mornings when she can read her magazines and drink her coffee before she goes to work.

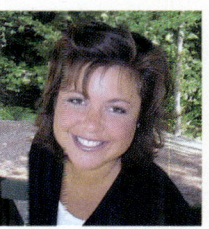

Christine Archer Interiors
Christine Archer
Allied Member ASID
25818 NE 4th Place
Sammamish, WA 98074
425.898.7789

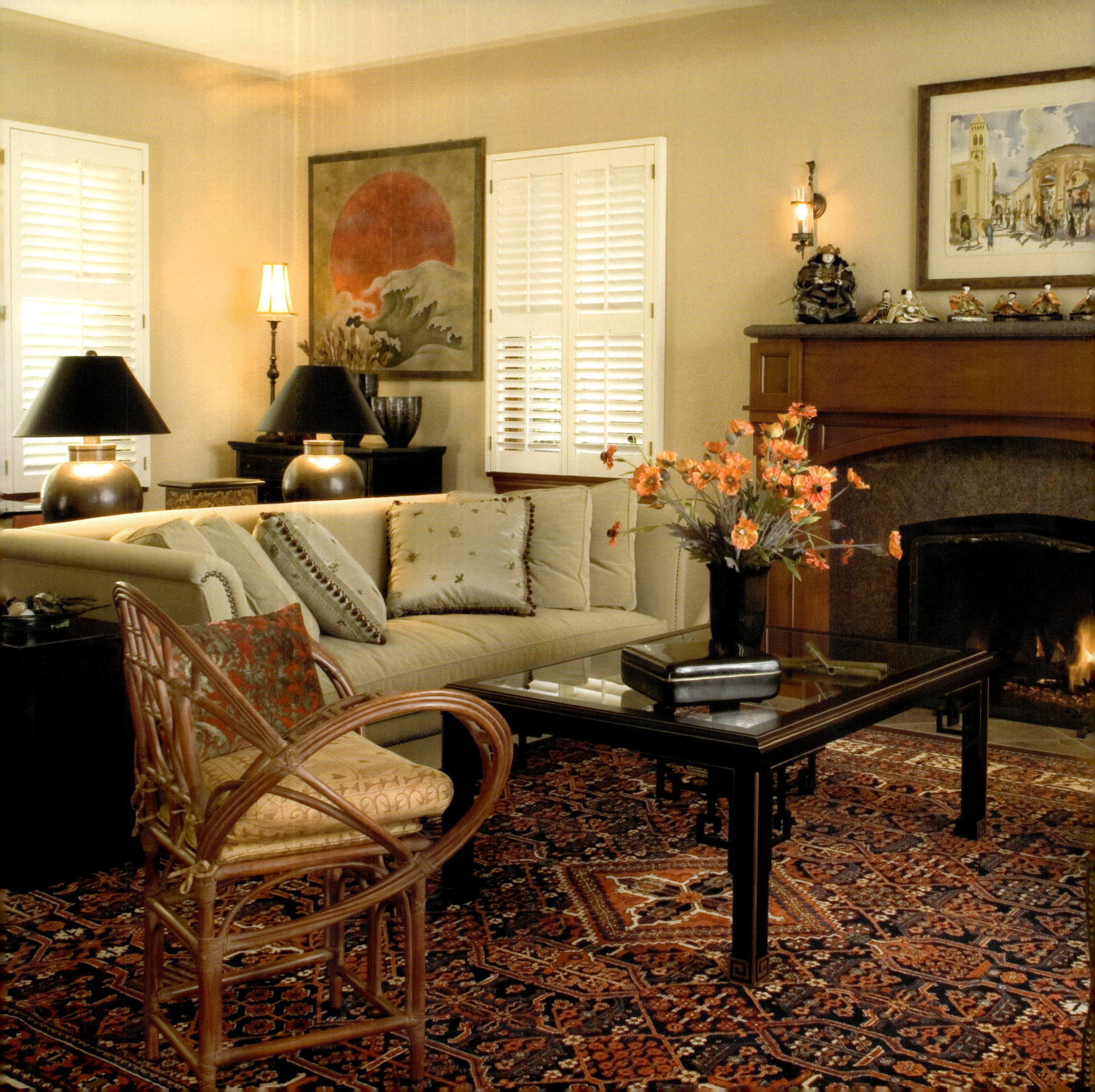

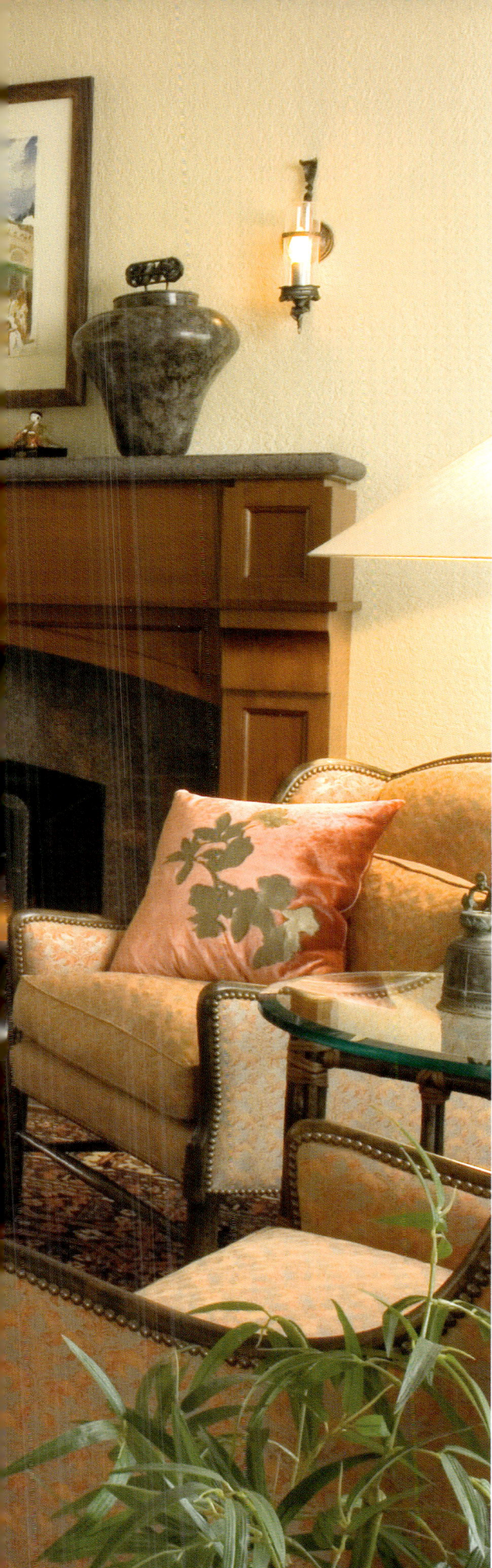

Kathleen Bohlken

Kathleen Bohlken Interior Design

The architect Le Corbusier is believed to have said that "God is in the details," meaning that even the grandest of projects depends on the success of the smallest components.

Kathleen Bohlken, an interior designer with more than 20 years of experience, believes design is also in the details. Kathleen specializes in turn-key designs, where she not only does all of the planning and design work, but she also chooses and purchases everything down to the last detail, including silverware, cookbooks, bedding and even planted pots on the deck. "I work with every aspect of the design," she says. "Every detail is totally integrated into either the room or the whole project to create a design that is thoroughly planned and pulled together."

This attention to detail has earned Kathleen residential and commercial clients from around the globe. Recent commercial projects include spas and salons, yoga centers, churches and local restaurants. She has completed turn-key vacation homes in Manhattan, Sun River, Portland, Palm Desert, Sun Valley, Alaska and Japan. Her stunning design work has also earned her placement in such prestigious publications as *Seattle Homes & Lifestyles* and *Better Homes & Gardens*.

LEFT
This beautiful Northwest Living Room is complemented by: Baker Tuxedo sofa and chest, a Kravet Hunan cocktail table and pillows, shutters from Shutters Northwest, East West Room lamp, Jennifer West silk pillows, McGuire butterfly chair, tripod table and brass lamps. The Minton-Spidell wing chairs use Fortuny fabrics from Italy. Accessories and antique screen from Lawrence and Scott.

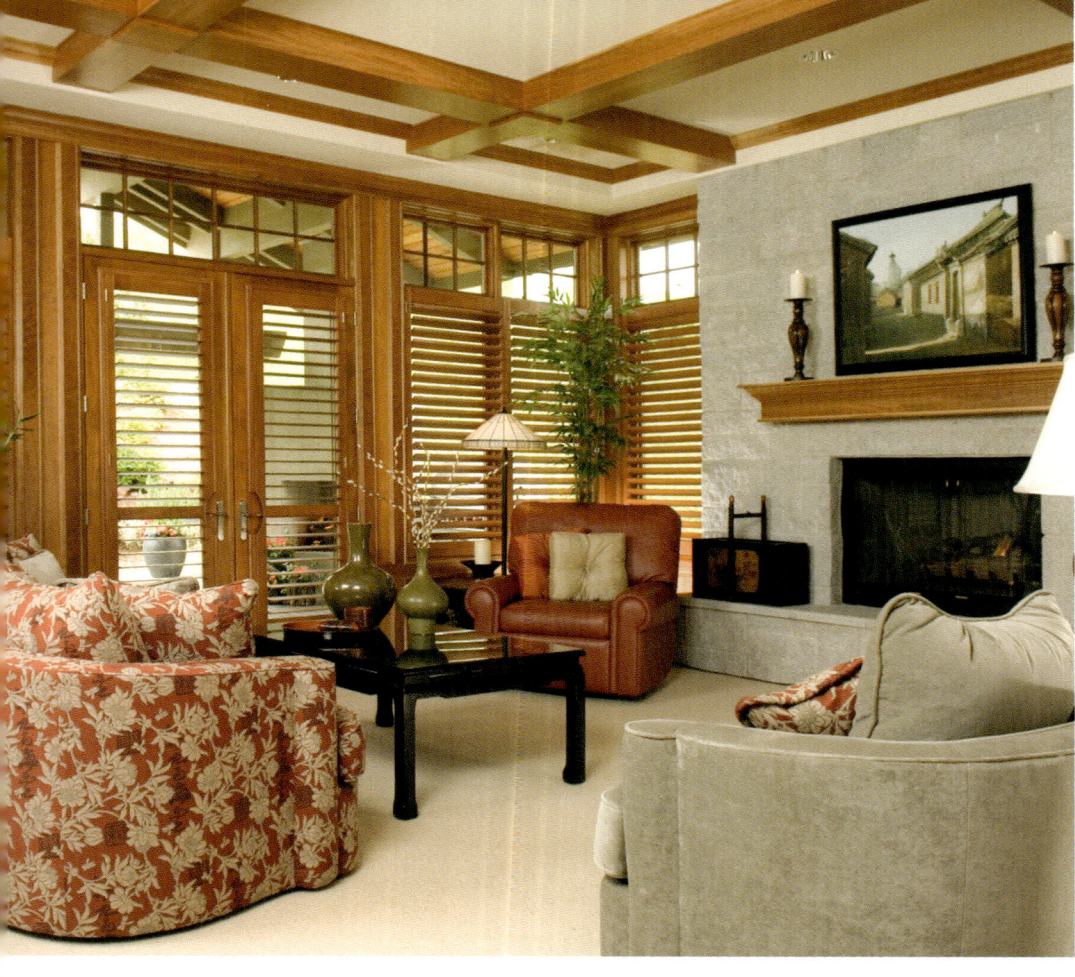

Kathleen, who grew up in the furniture business, says design has always come naturally to her. "I feel very blessed to be in this business and to have found my niche," she says. "Anybody that's around me knows that I love design and my clients more than I can express."

Kathleen works in styles that range from Asian to contemporary. Due to her background teaching meditation for eight years, and her extensive work with spas and yoga centers, all of her designs carry an element of spirituality and peacefulness. "I love to work in all styles," she says. "It really just depends on the client—I enjoy helping them see what they have and discovering what it is that works best for them."

Hand-in-hand with Kathleen's love of design is her love of art. She is also an art consultant, introducing art to design showrooms and commissioning work for her residential and commercial clients.

Kathleen works closely with The Artizan Group, Inc., a construction firm in Seattle, and with her daughter-in-law, Stephanie Sullivan. She has two children and five grandchildren, all of whom live within 20 minutes of her.

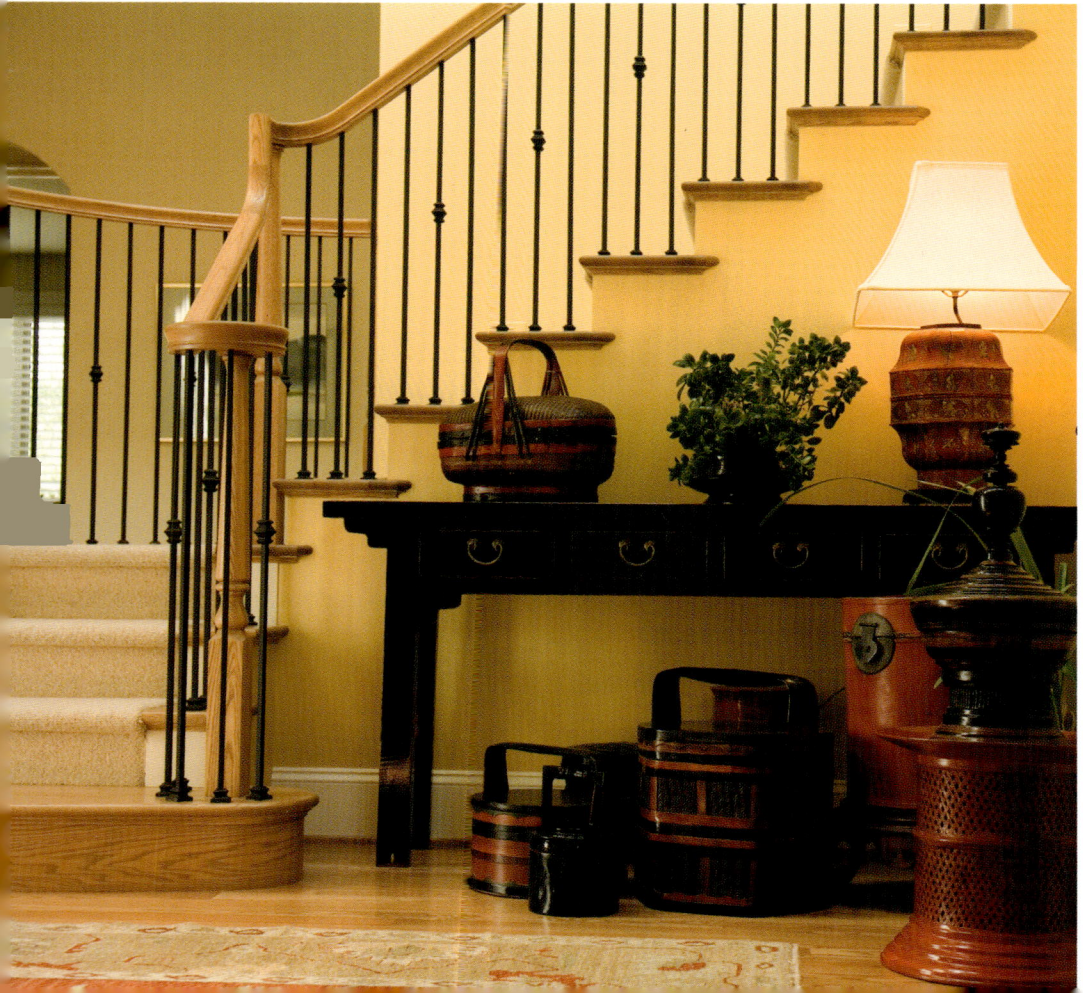

TOP
This classic contemporary living room is framed with cherry wood shutters from Shutters Northwest, with a Chinese oil painting over the fireplace, Bernhardt fabric sofa and chairs, Rosebank cocktail tables, American Leather chair and Jane Piper Reed accessories to create an inviting atmosphere.

BOTTOM
This classic Tufenkian rug, Asian antique lamp and accessories surround the sofa table, all by Jane Piper Reed, at the entry of this inviting Northwest contemporary home.

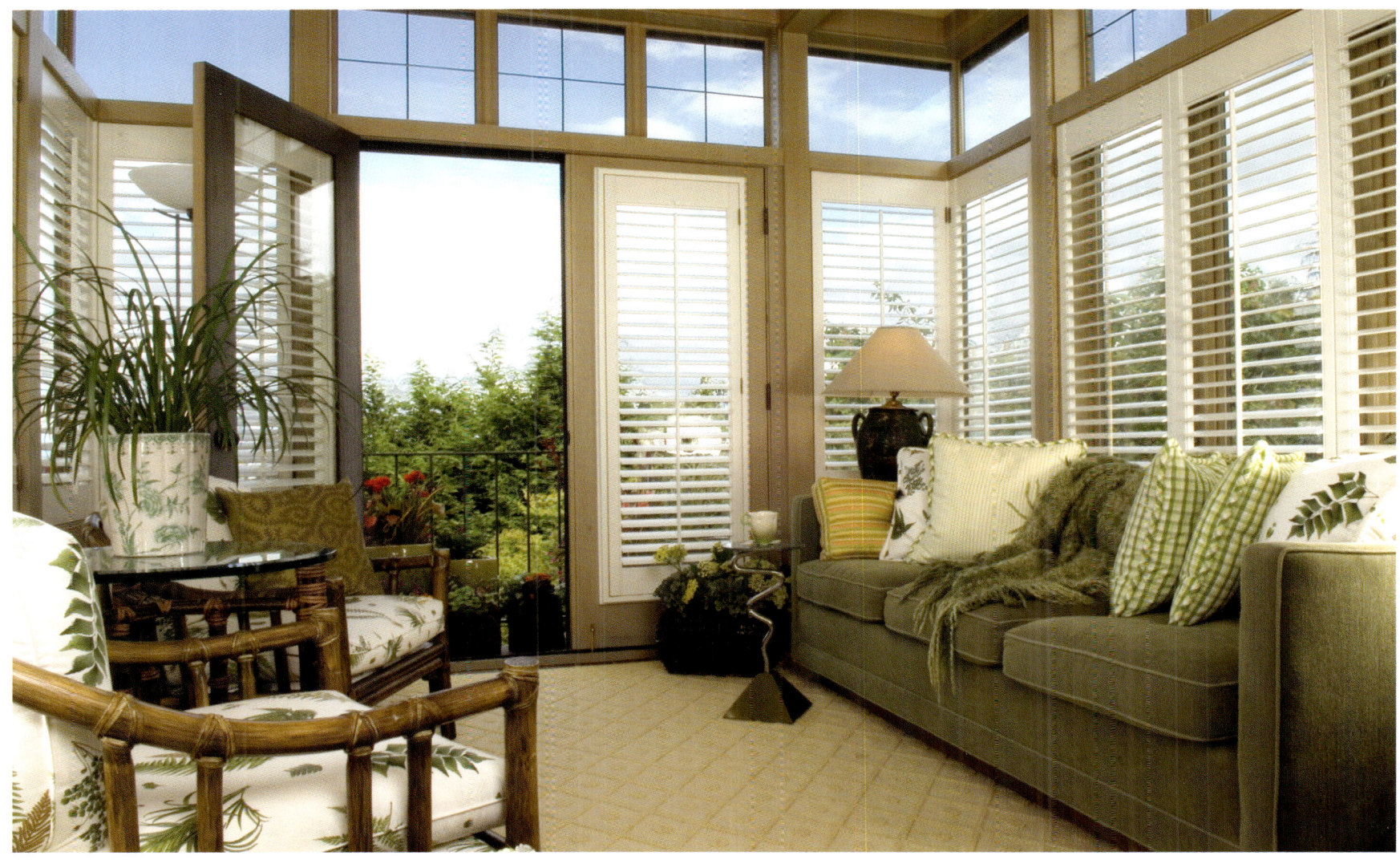

ABOVE
This lovely sunroom is surrounded with shutters by Shutters Northwest, creating a cozy atmosphere along with a colorful yellow Stark area rug, a squiggle table from Terris-Dreheim and an antique Turkish olive jar lamp from East West Room along with McGuire chairs and tripod table, complemented by Brunswick and Fee fabrics.

More about Kathleen…

YOU WOULDN'T KNOW IT, BUT MY FRIENDS WOULD TELL YOU I WAS…

Enthusiastic, energetic, positive, always the planner, the one who pulls everyone together, they have nicknamed me "the gatherer."

NAME ONE THING MOST PEOPLE DON'T KNOW ABOUT YOU.

I have developed a line of purses called KB Bags, as well as a toddler line called Ladybug Bags. My new line, the Pillow Purse Collection, takes its inspiration from the interesting combinations of fabrics that I use for pillows and bedding in my interior designs.

WHO HAS HAD THE BIGGEST INFLUENCE ON YOUR CAREER?

My family. I grew up in the furniture business: my grandparents, father and uncle all had stores in the Midwest. I was at my first furniture market in Chicago at the age of three and a half years old.

Kathleen Bohlken Interior Design
Kathleen Bohlken, Allied ASID
2054 Newport Way NW
Issaquah, WA 98027
425.391.9088
Fax 425.313.9488
www.kathleenbohlken.com
The Artizan Group, Inc.
206.419.1760

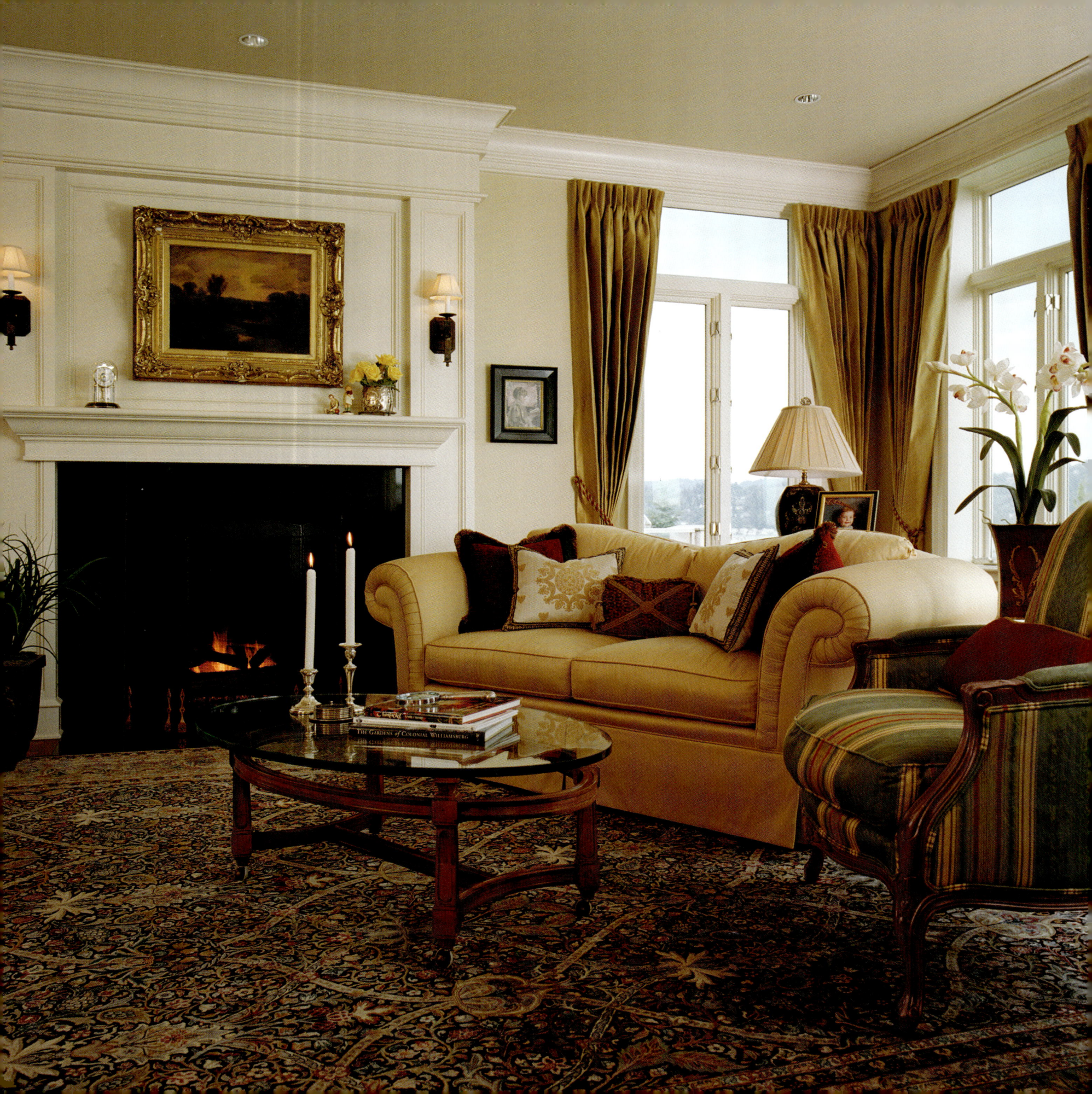

DeAnne Brenneis

The John Brenneis Architects, Inc. P.S.

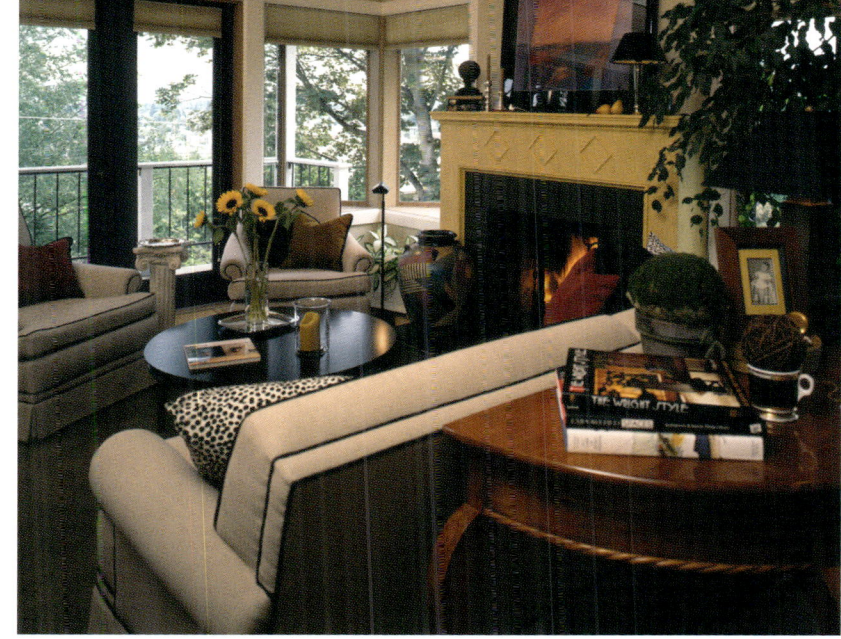

LEFT
Sumptuous fabrics, exquisite artwork and fine furnishings combine to create this traditional and formal living room.

RIGHT
An eclectic mixture of styles from classic to contemporary, combined with a colorful palette create this inviting living room space.

DeAnne Brenneis doesn't have a signature style–and she doesn't want one. Instead, this accomplished designer prides herself on being able to move among many design vernaculars, and loves the challenge of creating spaces that reflect each client's unique personality.

As a style chameleon, DeAnne gets a feel for her clients' tastes almost intuitively by visiting their home and getting to know them. She then creates design proposals which are specific to their individual style and needs. For this reason, each of DeAnne's projects are uniquely different.

Is there any common thread in DeAnne's body of work? Color. DeAnne encourages the use of color. Most people will tire of a "safe" neutral palette more quickly than one with color. DeAnne believes that "a well-conceived color scheme with contrast in all the right places is the key to any successful interior."

As the daughter and wife of architects, DeAnne has a thorough understanding of every aspect of the construction process from design conception to the finished project. Having gained the respect of many local contractors and architects, DeAnne enjoys working with a wide array of design and construction professionals.

A designer since 1982, DeAnne works primarily with residential clients, but has also completed many commercial spaces. DeAnne's ability to find the individual design comfort zone of each and every client, and then create a space that's a perfect match, makes her unique in the design community.

The John Brenneis Architects, Inc. P.S.
DeAnne D. Brenneis, IIDA
6064 Second Avenue Northwest
Seattle, WA 98107
206.784.3626

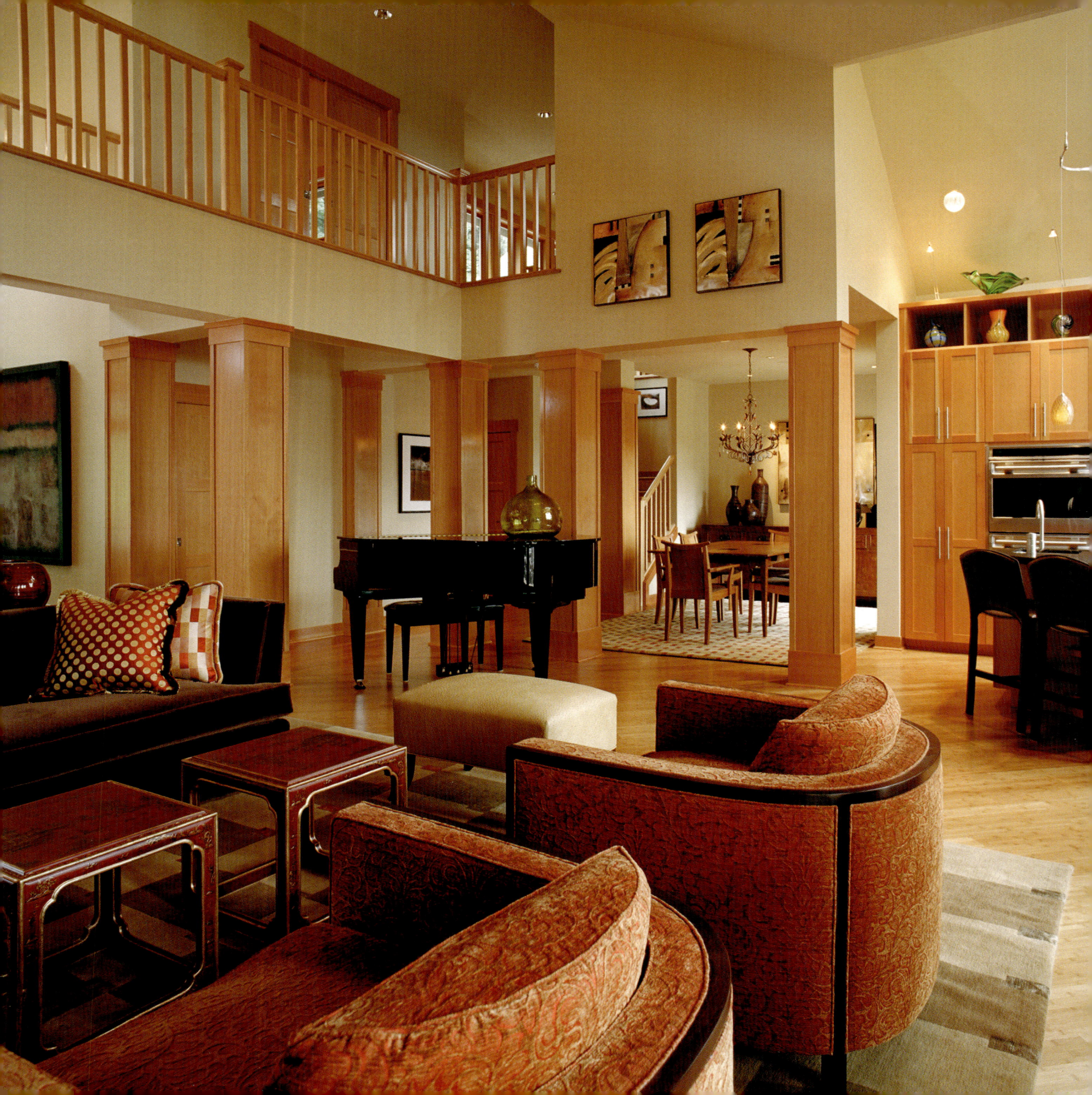

DEBBIE CAHILL

Debbie Cahill Interior Design, LLC

Every career test she's ever taken has pointed Debbie Cahill in one direction: interior design.

Still, Debbie wasn't convinced that design was the way she wanted to go. Instead, she headed toward college and a Political Science degree, all with the intention of going to law school. It wasn't until she started traveling the world—eventually landing in Japan—that she realized that she really did want to be a designer after all. Soon after, she enrolled in interior design school.

Debbie graduated in 1993 and has been working as a designer in the Pacific Northwest ever since. Two years ago, she opened Debbie Cahill Interior Design, LLC.

Thanks to her family's building materials export company, Debbie has been around the industry most of her life and is very familiar with the construction process. She speaks the same language as contractors and subcontractors and says they are often "shocked" by the extent of her building construction knowledge.

Debbie often conducts projects from the architectural planning through the construction process. Along the way, she says she, "pretty much puts my hands all over everything," specifying all materials in the project from the exterior and all interior finishes and details.

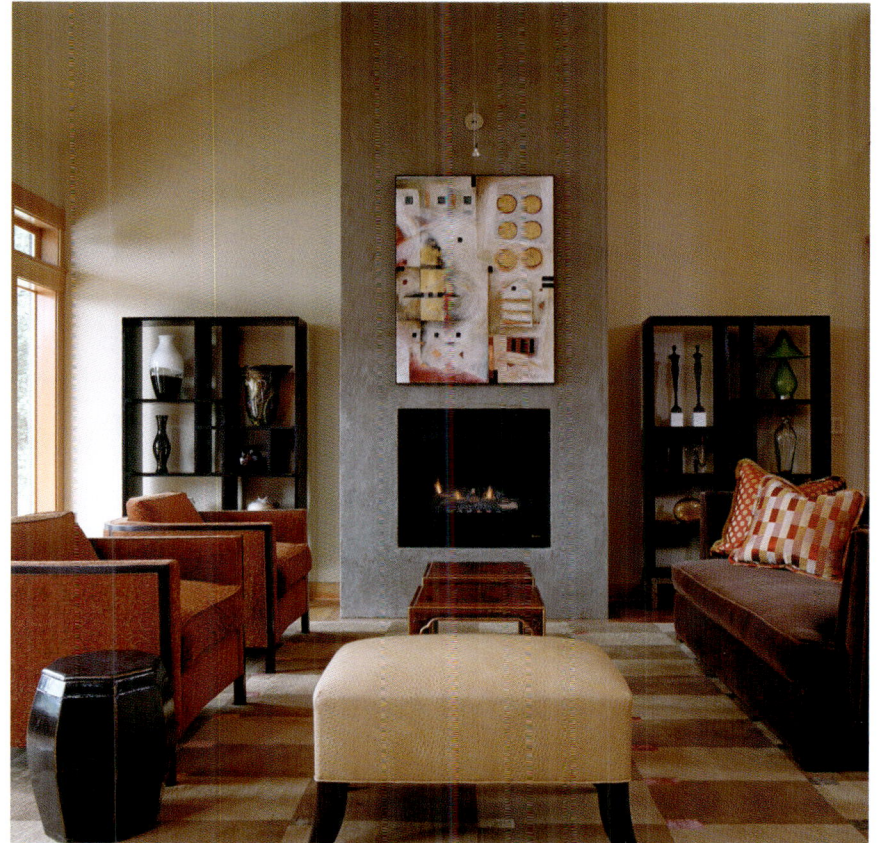

ABOVE
Fall City living room. Milestone fireplace.

LEFT
Two-story living room looking through to the dining room.

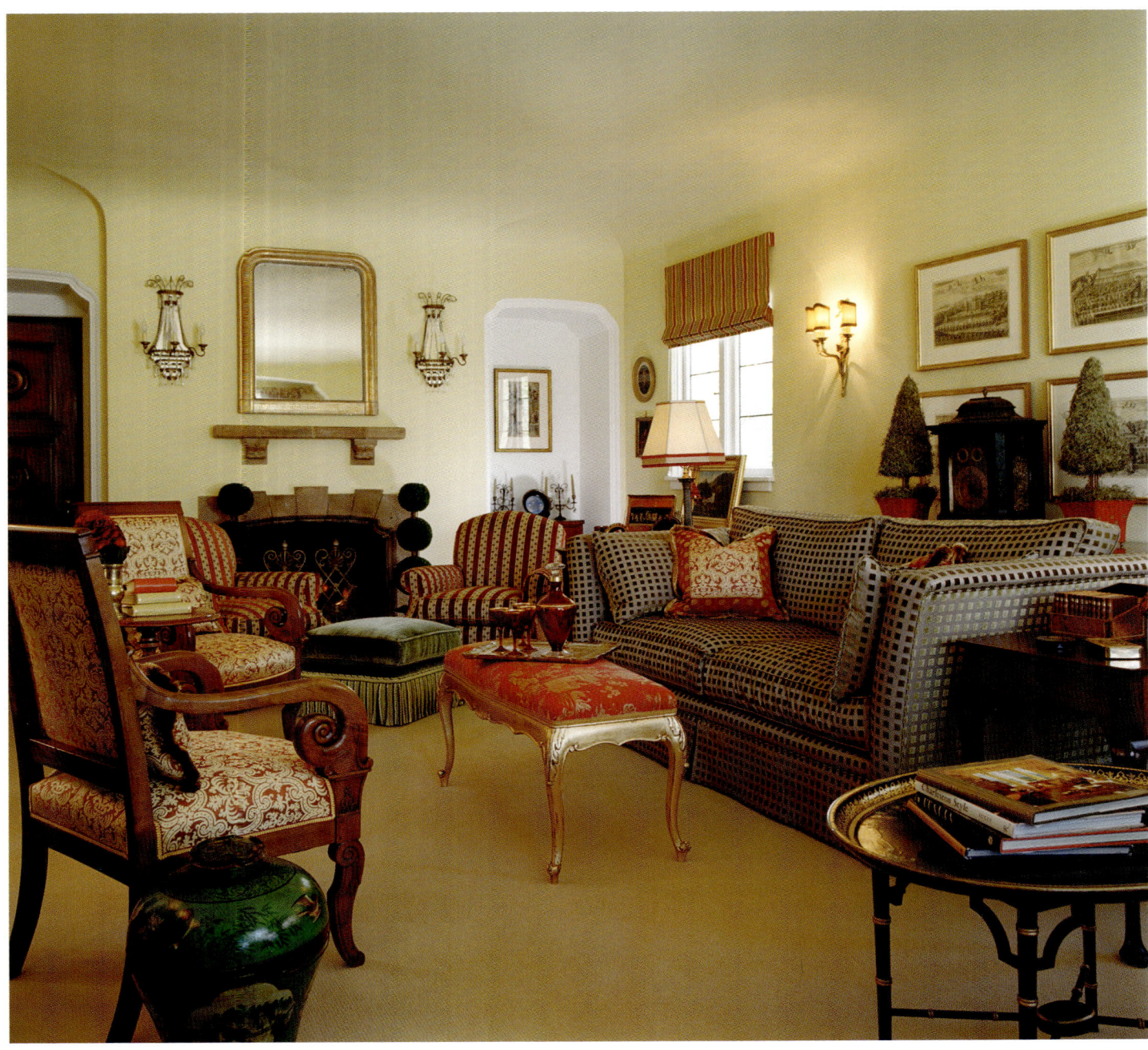

Debbie also has the special talent of being a liaison between client and crews. Not only can she "translate" from the clients to the contractors and back, she has the knowledge to get the most from contractors. Sometimes a contractor will say, "Oh we can't do that," and Debbie fires right back with, "Oh yes you can, if you do this and this." It isn't long before the contractors are agreeing with her and helping her deliver up exactly what the client ordered.

To help clients decide what they'd like—and then make sure they get it—Debbie begins by having each client fill out a questionnaire and then has them put together a notebook, which details everything from the floor plan to a photo of the lighting fixtures they've chosen. During the process, she and the client can refer back to the notebook to make sure everything's moving forward as planned. Photos and color swatches are an important part of this, she says, because "you don't all speak the same language–everyone's version of green is different."

In her work, Debbie's preference is for a mix of old and new. Rather than stick with one period, she gives pieces an unexpected edge by mixing new and old. Antique settees with modern fabrics, contemporary sofas surrounded by antiques—design choices like these allow each piece to make a statement and create its own story rather than become part of a set. As Debbie says with a laugh, "I don't do any matchy-matchy."

Debbie's favorite material is Milestone Hybridized Portland Cement, a cement-based product that she believes is the "coolest design material ever." After adding pigment and texture to Milestone, Debbie uses it to create mantels, counter tops, built-in niches and to cover out-dated elements such as brick walls.

If there's one thing that influences Debbie's work on a continual basis, it's her love of traveling. Everywhere she goes, she is inspired by what she sees around her. A perfect example is her yearly trek to Italy, which she calls inspirational. "In the Tuscan countryside, they can't buy land and build a home, so they must find an old estate and restore it," she says. "They update it with modern conveniences while trying to preserve the integrity of their buildings. I think that is something we as designers should try to do more often."

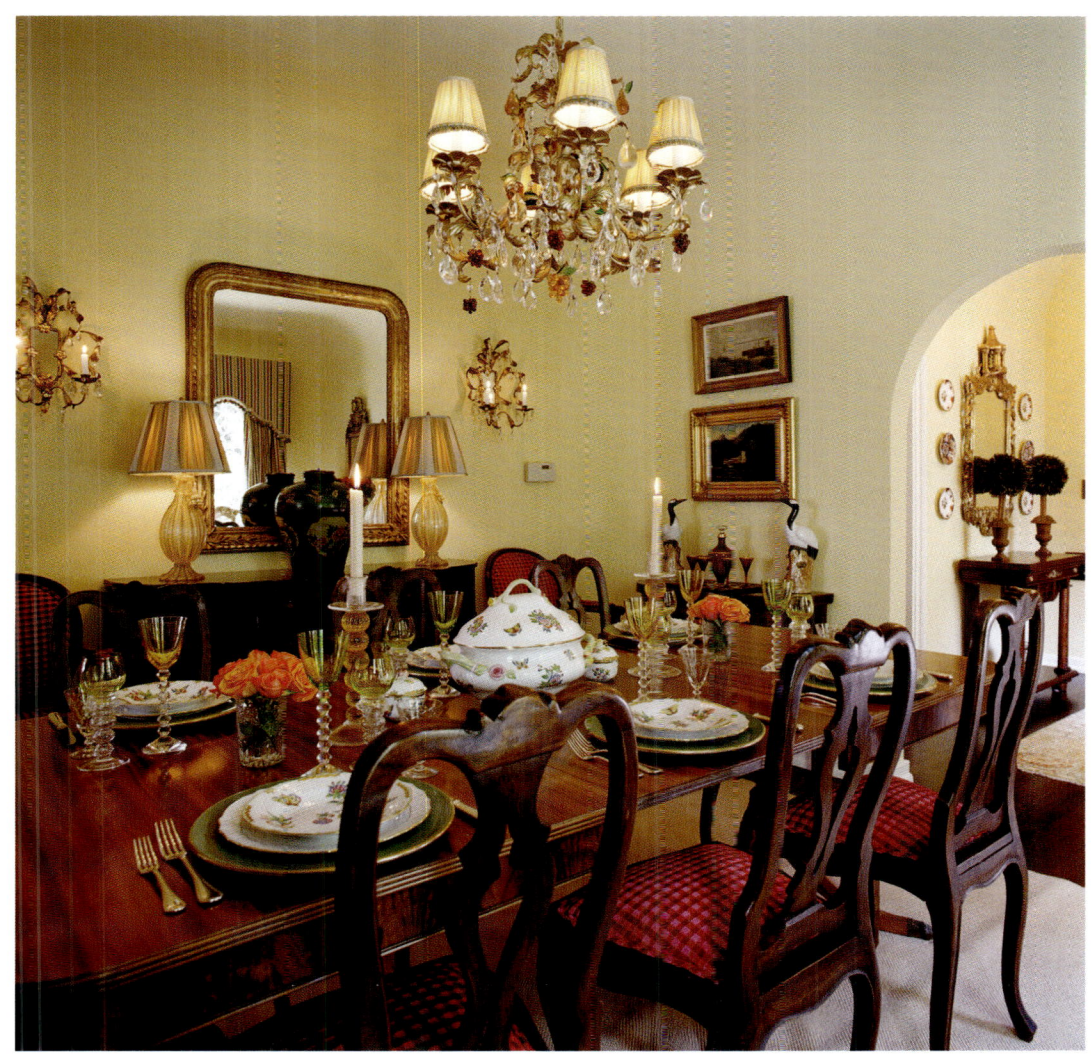

ABOVE
19th century Louis Phillipe mirror over a flame mahogany Hepplewhite sideboard.

LEFT
19th century Louis Phillipe mirror with Greek key design is flanked by 19th century crystal and brass sconces.

More about Debbie…

WHAT PERSONAL INDULGENCE DOES SPEND THE MOST MONEY ON?
Shoes. She loves shoes!

WHAT COLOR BEST DESCRIBES DEBBIE AND WHY?
Orange. It is a fun sassy color. Not something you see every day.

YOU CAN TELL SHE LIVES IN THE PACIFIC NORTHWEST BECAUSE:
She wears jeans constantly. When meeting clients, she dresses casually. She wants clients to be comfortable and she visits construction sites a lot—and who wants to go to the dry cleaners every day?

YOU WOULDN'T KNOW IT, BUT DEBBIE'S FRIENDS WOULD TELL YOU:
She was very funny and easygoing. She has a great sense of humor, which she believes is essential for this business.

Debbie Cahill Interior Design, LLC
Debbie Cahill
Debbie Cahill Interior Design, Allied Member ASID
2212 Queen Anne Ave N #320
Seattle, WA 98109
206.617.2126
Fax 425.251.3700

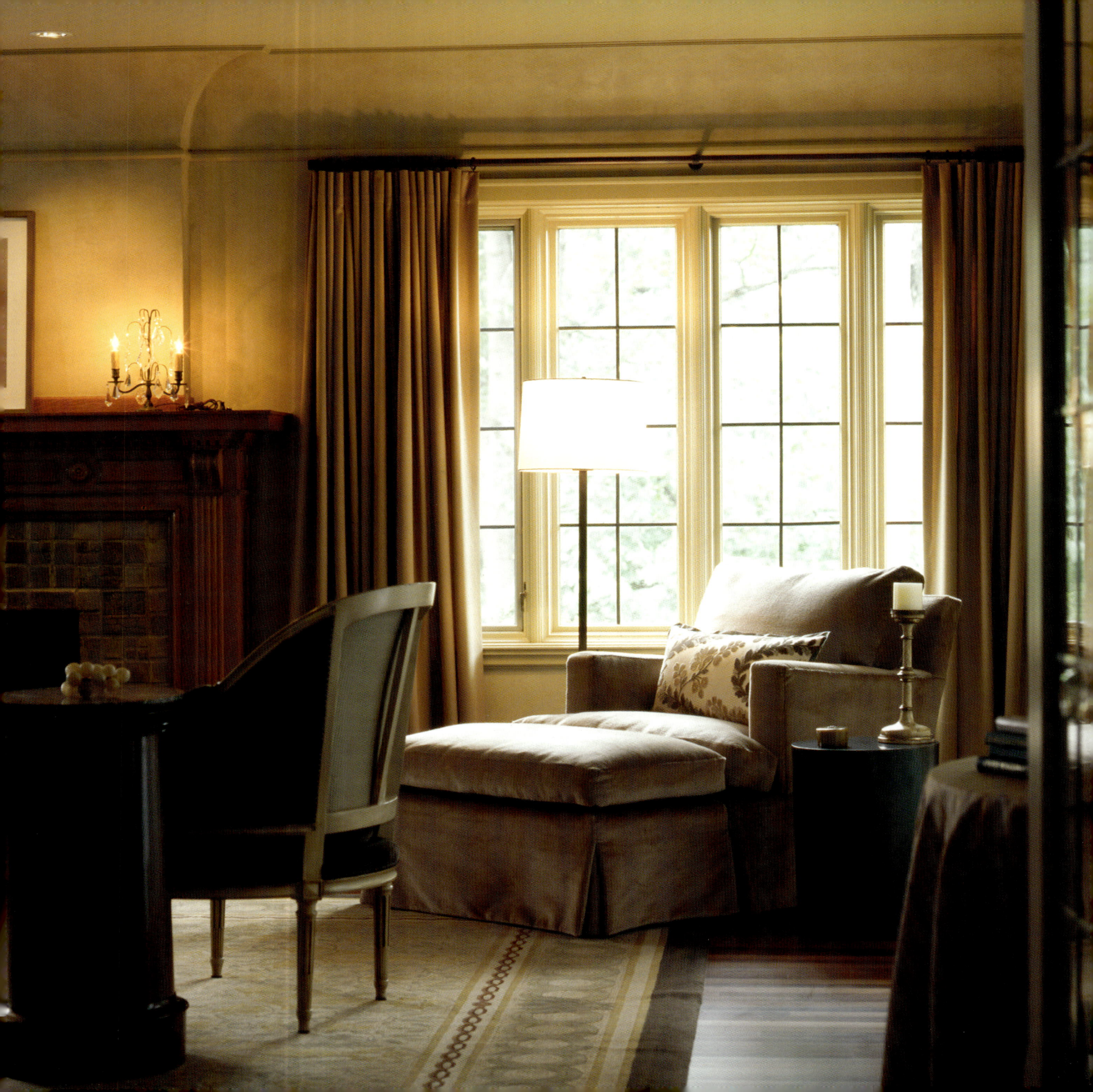

GREGORY CARMICHAEL

Gregory Carmichael Interior Design

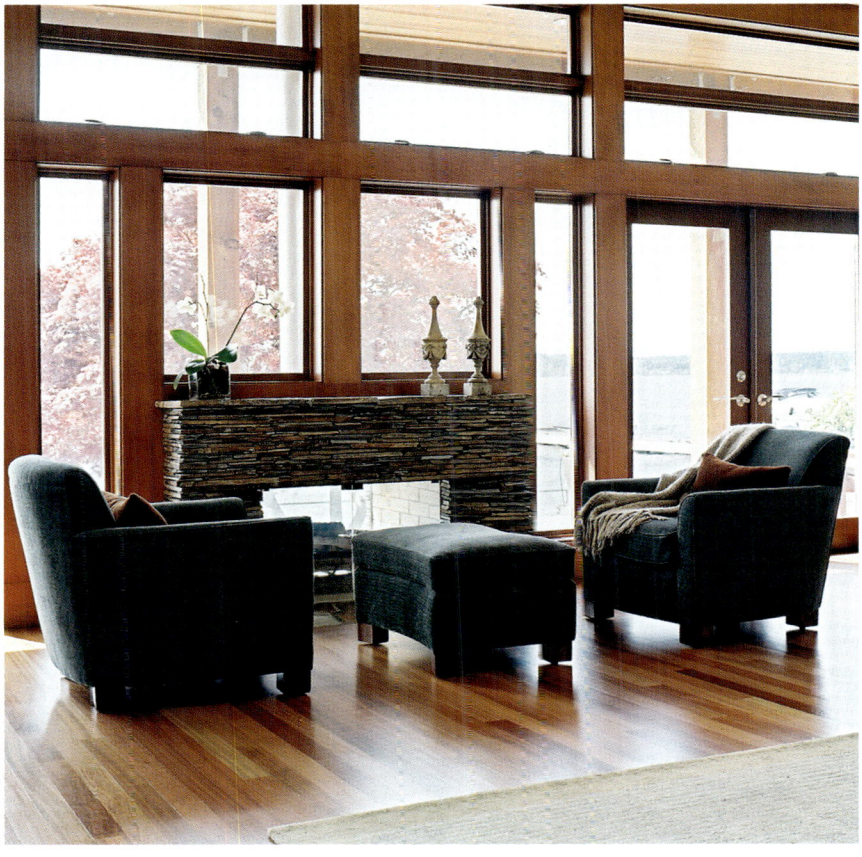

ABOVE
Living room in Lakeside Home with Stacked Stone fireplace open on two sides (living room and terrace). Brazilian cherry wood flooring.

LEFT
Formal living room in landmark turn of the century Spokane home. Custom upholstery pieces and custom-designed rug blend with antiques, original mantle piece and fireplace tiles.

Gregory Carmichael has a theory about design: it's all about paying attention. He makes a point of paying attention to everything, but especially to every single detail of his designs. "To me, the finished project is a collection of minute details that create the feeling and emotional response of a place," he says. "Every little part is equally important."

Gregory extends this detail-oriented philosophy to his clients as well. "We spend a lot of time talking with clients early on and taking our cues from them," he says. "A lot of it is detective work, trying to decipher what someone really wants."

Collaboration is another key component in Gregory's design process "Good design is a collaboration and combination of clients, design, space and the environment," he says. "And all of our best projects have been the result of teaming up with our clients and architects and other design professionals."

This native Northwesterner says his projects are often steered by the region. "I feel lucky to be from here," he says. "I believe there is definitely an influence and that it makes me more in tune to the area's natural beauty."

Not surprisingly, Gregory's focus on detail and his creativity don't end with design. Although most people don't know it, Gregory is also a classically trained pianist who continues to study music and give occasional concerts.

Gregory Carmichael Interior Design
Gregory Carmichael
5953 California Ave SW Suite 100
Seattle, WA 98136
206.623.2002
Fax 206.623.3104
www.gcid.com

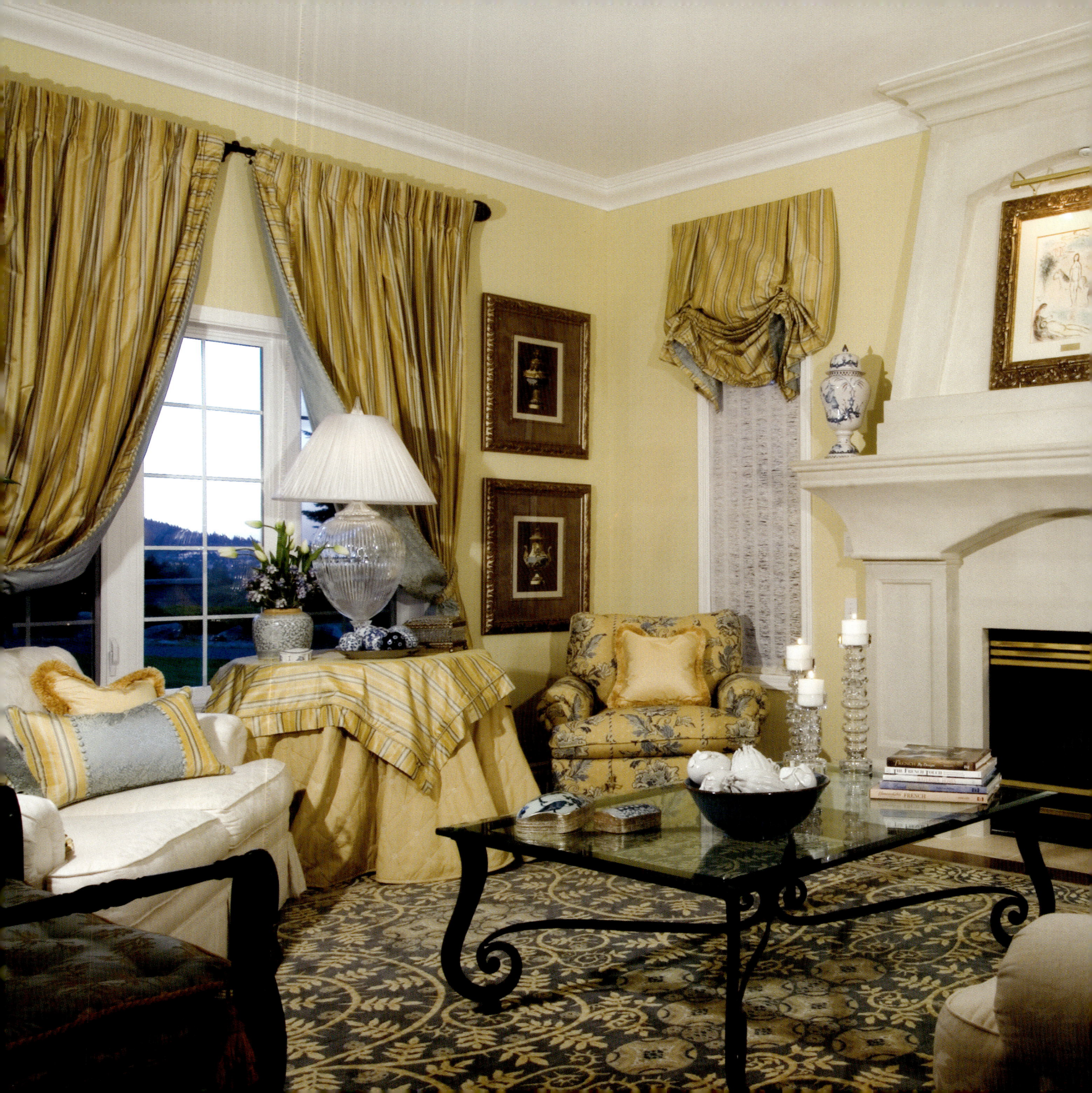

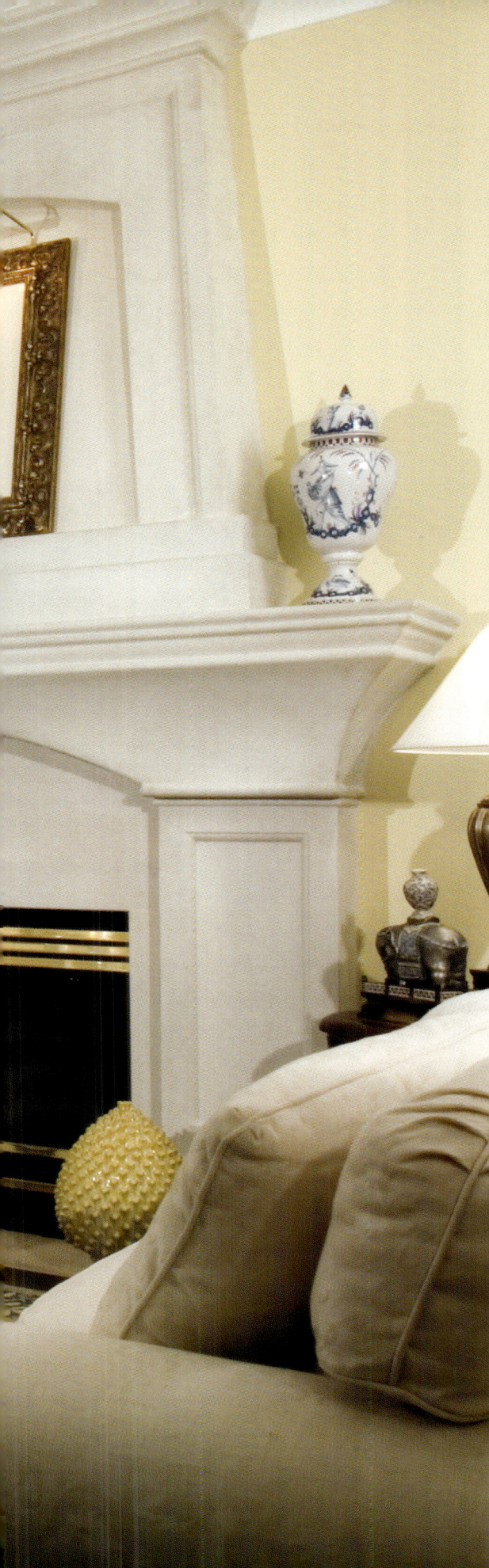

BONNIE K. CRAWFORD

Bonnie Crawford Design Group

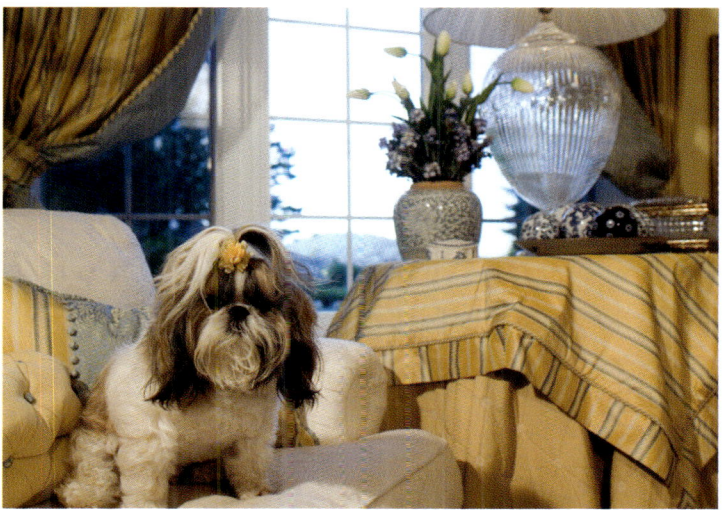

Bonnie came to her mature predilection for culture, fine art and the performing arts via her family heritage. Prominent in art and literature, her family includes a repertoire of fine artists, vocalists, poets, authors, musicians, antique dealers and educators. Although, Bonnie did inherit some of these family talents, she knew at a very young age that she was destined to expand the imaginative and creative family tree by focusing on interior design. Since childhood, Bonnie's creativity was influenced by the people who surrounded her.

Bonnie's grandmother, in particular, a concert pianist, and nouveau artist, instilled deep within her the ability to visualize the world around her through the eye of an artist. This was a renowned career woman, that in her day defined her own sophisticated and classic style that was reflected in her published poetry, music art, dress and surroundings. Spending time in her studio with its etchings and furnishings selected from around the globe, richly influenced Bonnie's personal genesis of creative independency, and the place where her predilection to interior architectural design took root.

Before Bonnie graduated from college, she won 1st place in an national design and lighting competition and had built a resume that encompassed ASID Student Chapter President,

LEFT
The custom fireplace recalibrates the room's 10-foot high stature, while dramatizing the space and drawing you into the ambiance of this "French salon" interpretation. Detailed window treatments visually raise the existing window height, while rich fabrics, furnishings and accessories complete the look.

ABOVE
"Muffin" poses among the French details in pillows and dressings. An intentionally oversized crystal lamp balances the room's height and adds a dramatic touch.

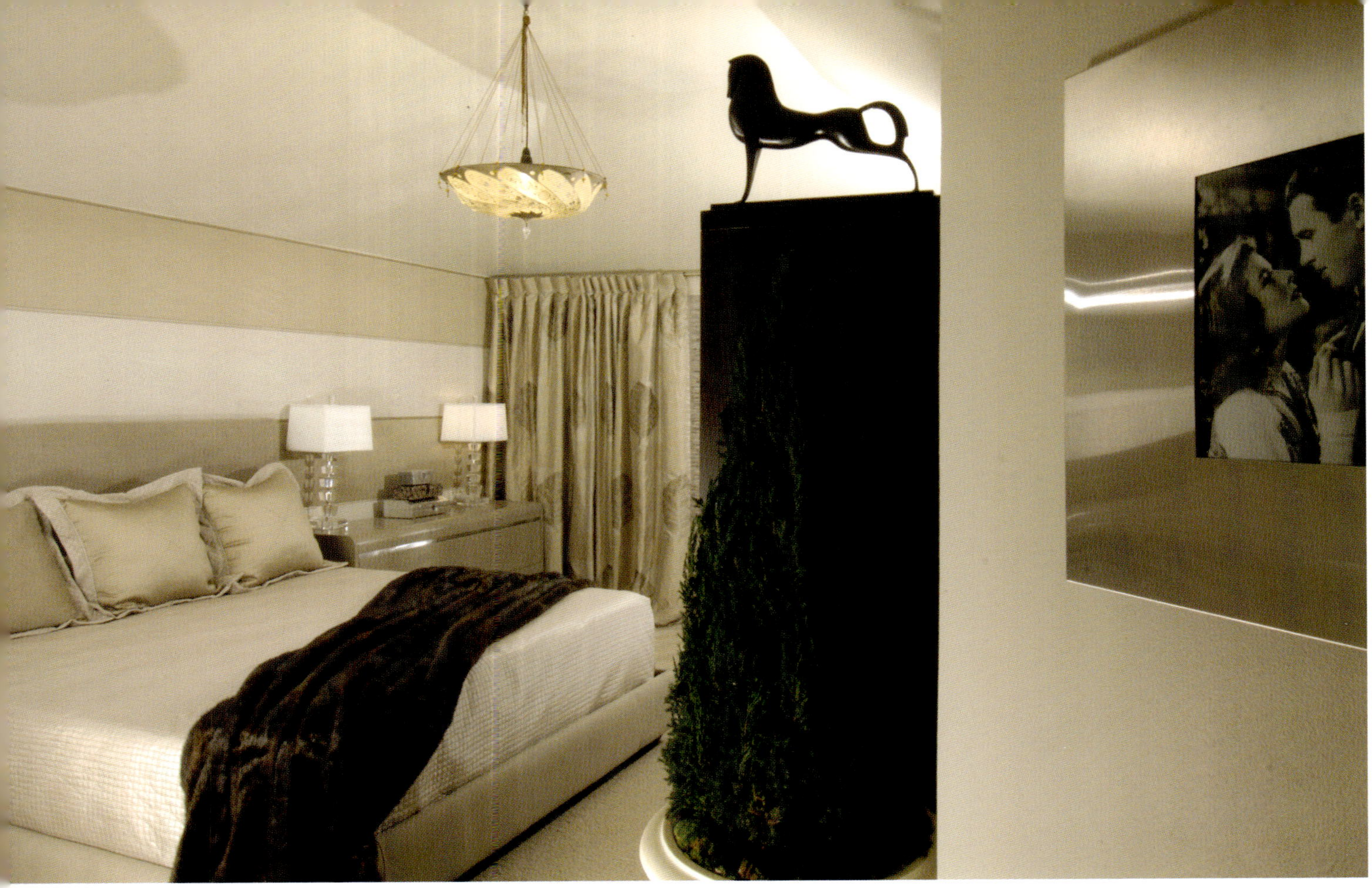

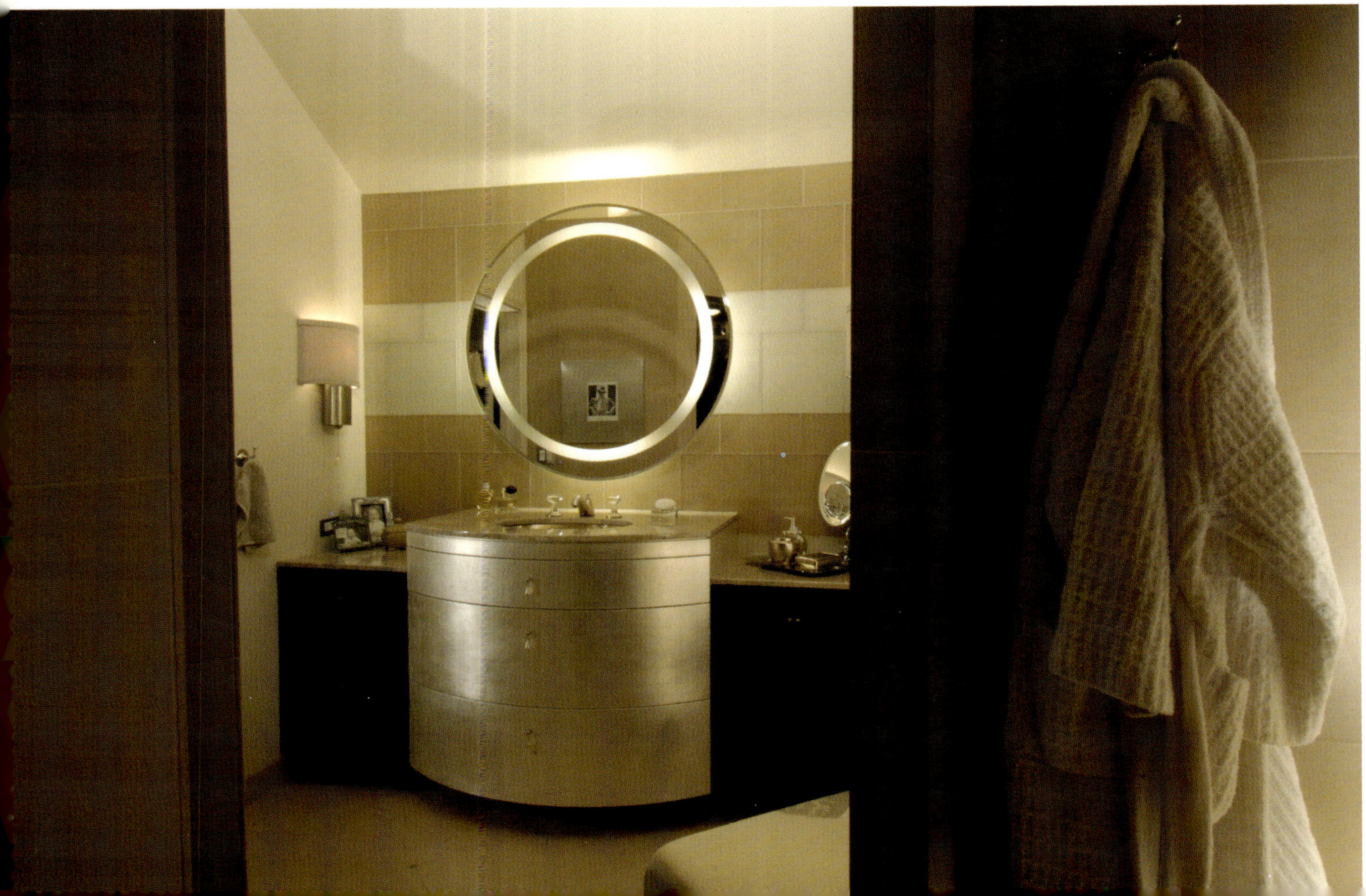

TOP
Luminous, sleek, silk and fur offer femininity, yet broad-seated furnishings in wool suiting contrasted with deep walnut woods presents equal opportunity for masculine appeal. The unfussy Fortuny chandelier and Bronze Trojan Horse lend character signatures to this artfully engineered design, that's equitably fitting to both sable and cigar.

LEFT
Setting a new standard for luxury, clean, modern lines embody the "film noir" ambience of old Hollywood, but reinterpreted in contemporary terms. Frosted glass tile wraps the perimeter walls restating the silk upholstered bedroom version of the same bold horizontal stripes. Enormous storage capacity is concealed in this custom floating vanity of espresso walnut and silver leafing.

FACING PAGE RIGHT
Pedestal tub reclines upon porcelain tile that also clads the partition walls, [and] ceilings of the sky-lit walk-in shower and water-closet sections (not shown). Dividing them, an angled wall (just out of view) glitters in polished marble mosaic adding the toniest of juxtaposition to this well-heeled space. Solid crystal egg hardware, polished nickel and hand-applied silver leafing, create a flawless finish to this luxurious spa/bath suite.

President's Honor Roll and First in her class. She has continued active leadership rolls in Interior Design, Hospitality and Real Estate organizations as well as other Civic and Community organizations. Her firsthand knowledge of real estate appraisal, architectural, commercial, retail and institutional design is value added to her design projects.

Her professional practice has spanned over two decades. BCDG Interiors focuses on tailor-made environments, customized to the residential and commercial clients needs and wants. With extensive experience in all aspects of design, Bonnie refuses to allow herself to become pigeonholed by one particular look, rather, she personifies her clients' uniqueness with passion and style. "The process of a good design is a unique one that I am fortunate in sharing with each client," says Bonnie. "Listening is the foundation and first step in any project." She is constantly inspired by her clients, their interests and tastes. She brings it all together into a structure that she describes as a three-dimensional art form. She then takes it to another level that she terms "Four-dimensional Design." She describes that as a design format that evokes an experience perceived via the senses and emotions. "Clients may start out with a desire to know how to make a place their own, for living or working, but over the years, I've found that people drawn to my work are generally those who long to be able to do it with a measurable sense of style, of comfort, of drama or grace. I love to help them make that happen!"

Bonnie's accomplishments run the gamut of residential, commercial, small medical, mixed-use, retail, institutional and hospitality design. Her work has been featured in local and national news and trade media. This year alone, Bonnie was awarded "1st Place Bathroom Design," "1st Place Bedroom Design, and 1st place in "Best of Contemporary Design" at the Regional, NW Design Awards. A recent shelter publication has named her firm, Bonnie Crawford Design Group, as #3 of the top 25 designers in its yearly listing.

When not at work, you will find Bonnie landscape gardening or gourmet cooking for her family and friends. Her favorite night out is enjoying the Pacific Northwest Ballet. Bonnie, a former dancer, likens the ballet to her design work. "The synergy among the different disciplines that come together in lighting, set design, costuming, orchestra and dance movement sets the stage for transforming the performance into a personal 'experience'... that fourth dimension. "She says, "My goal is that every project concept I develop, finish as an inspired experience for everyone who enters that finished space.

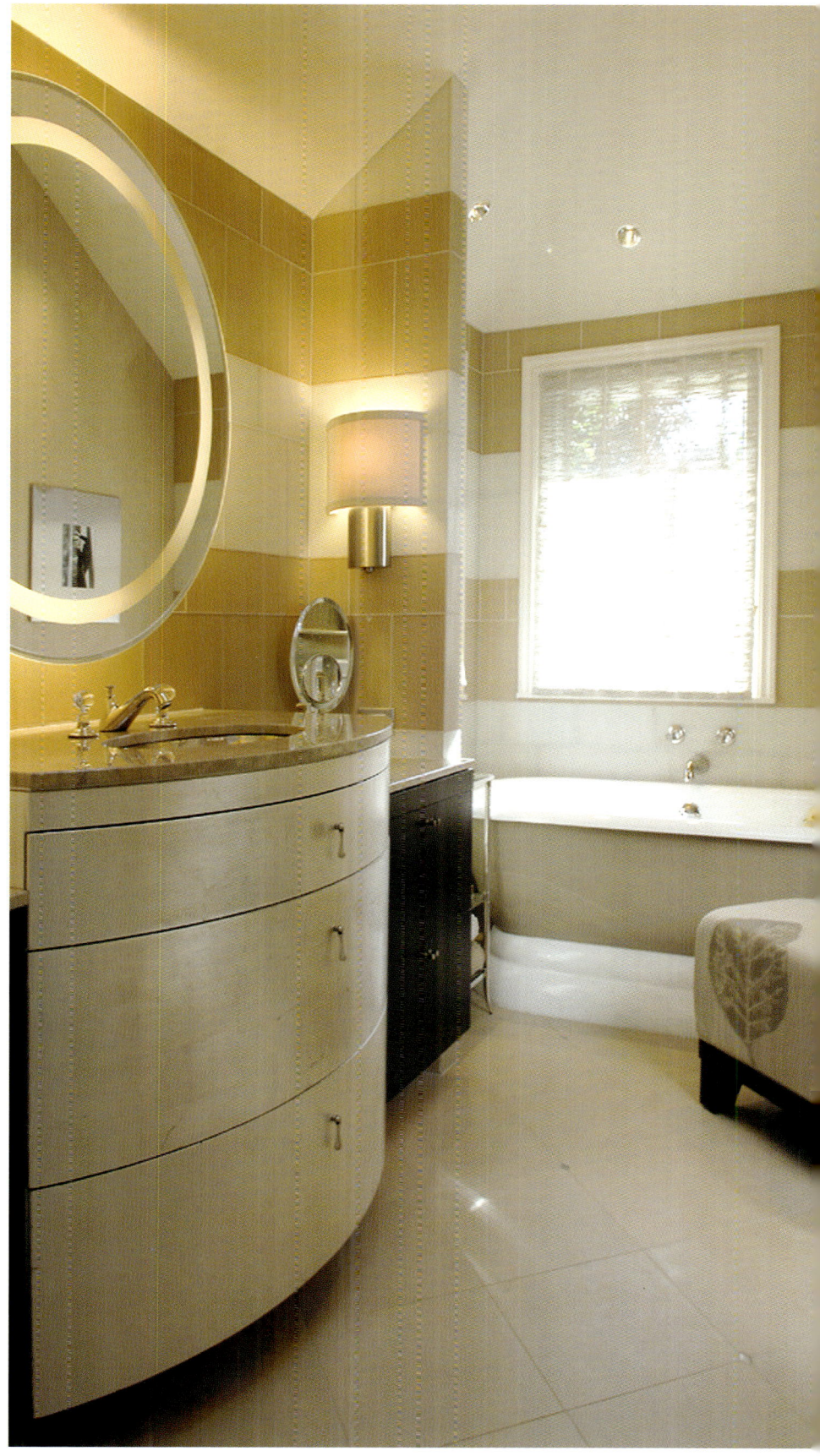

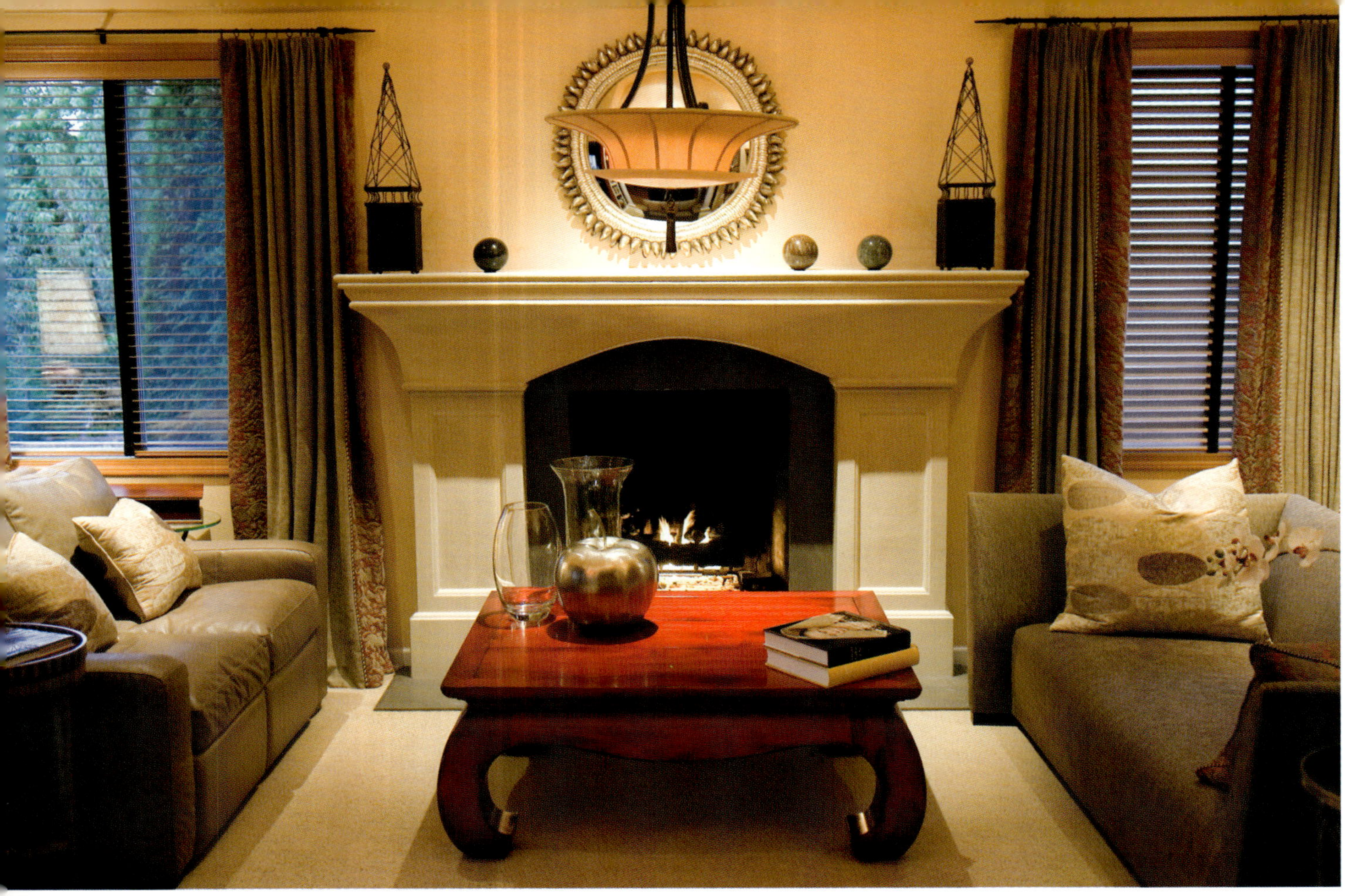

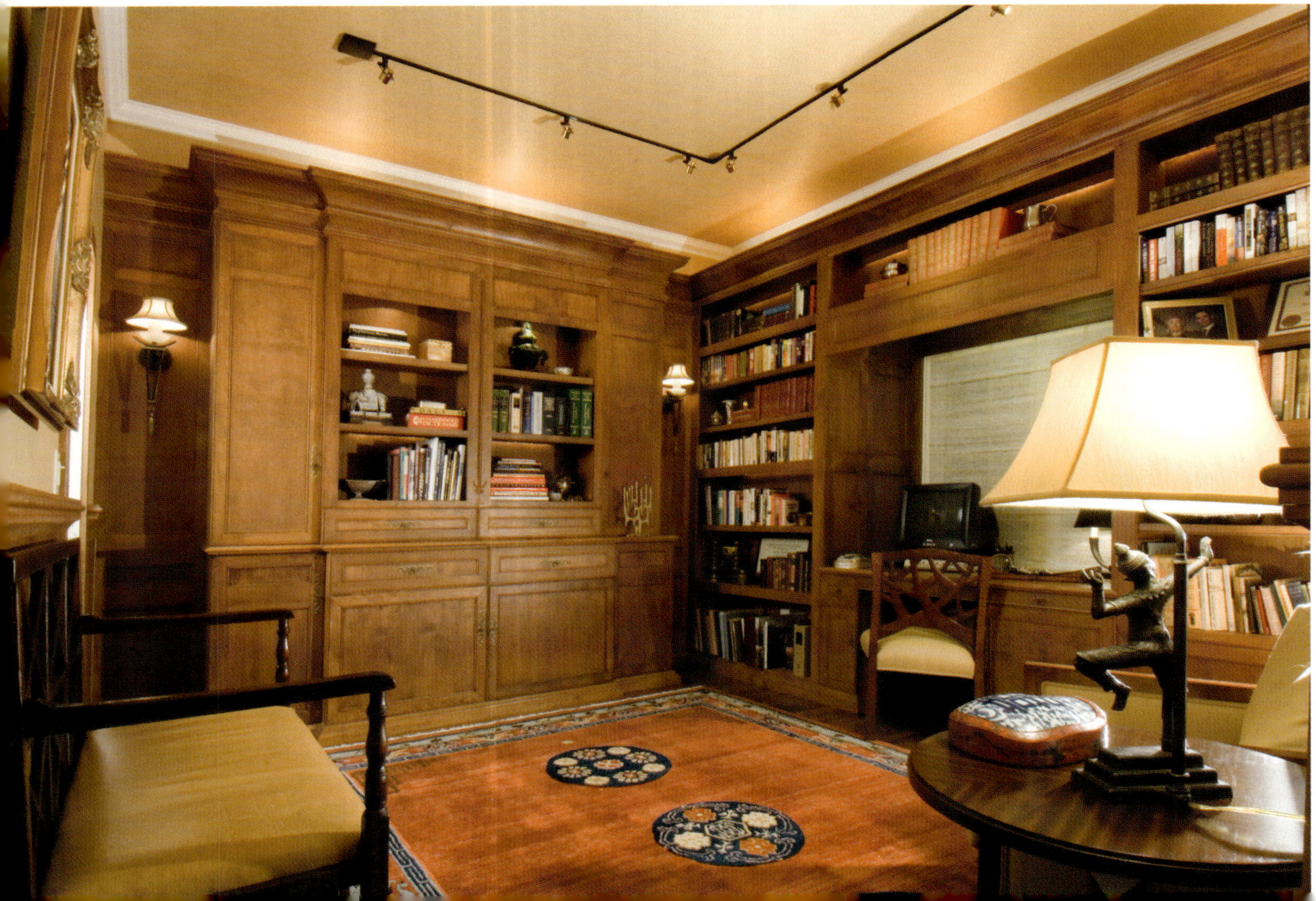

TOP
Replacing a dowdy all-brick ill-proportioned model with bulky hearth, this dynamic 6-foot tall fireplace captures the center of attention for sipping brandies by the fire or cozy family friendly conversation. Switching focus to the custom built-in media wall (not shown) allows relaxed viewing from Donghia Chaise and motorized, leather sofas, that function as theatre seating for movie time.

LEFT
Custom cabinetry reinvents this former empty room to exacting to client's needs in transforming it into his dream library. All equipment and office paraphernalia are conveniently stored out of sight. Seven separate lighting sources were implemented for both task lighting and ambience.

FACING PAGE RIGHT
Silk chandeliers and an Indonesian bench paired with pine table and silk plaid draperies combine French Country styling with Asian touches. When lowered, sheer Roman shades of silk with metallic bronze, interwoven with jute string, veil the saltwater view and sparkling city nightscape with warmth and gentle luster.

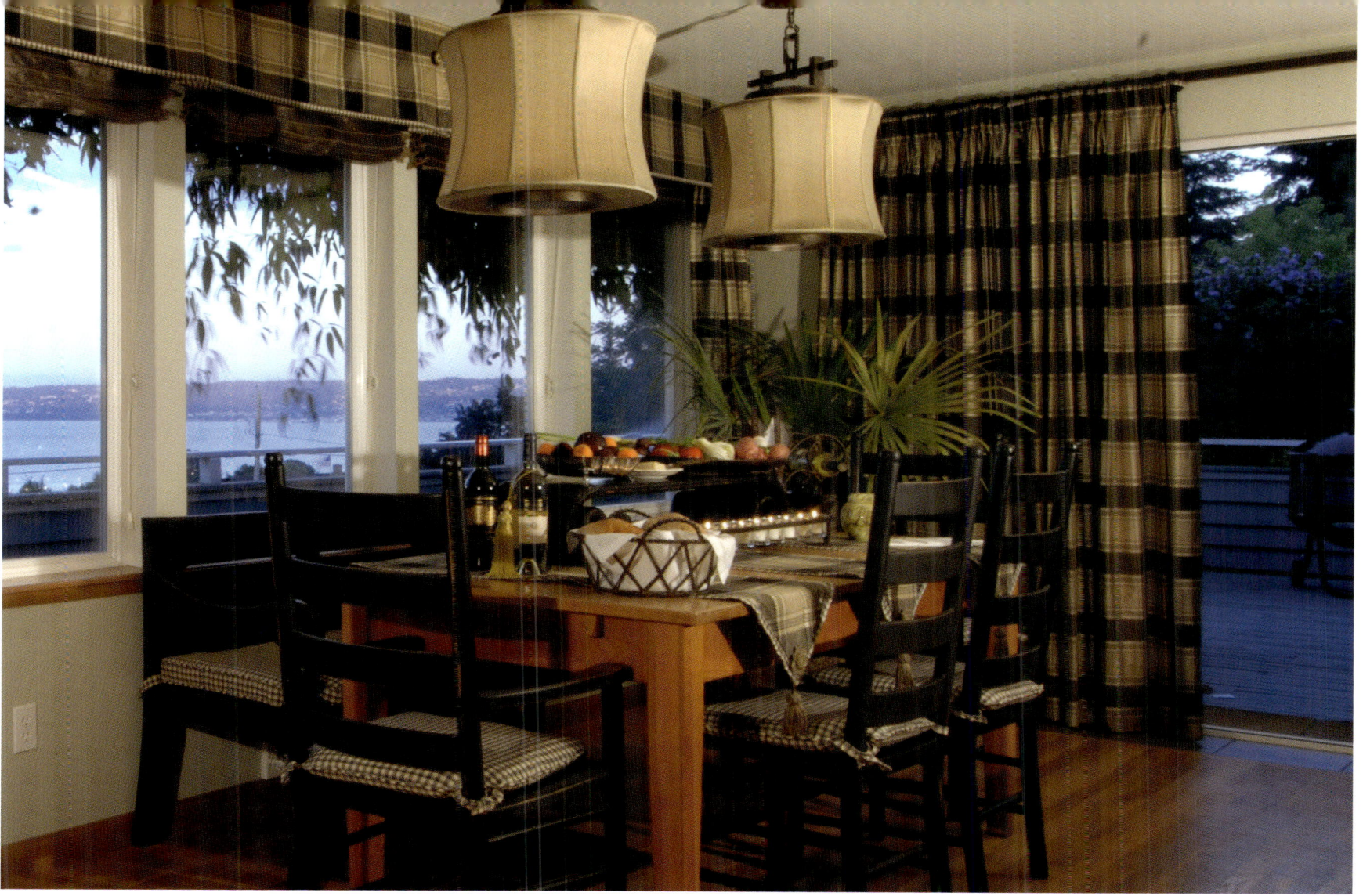

More about Bonnie...

WHAT ARE YOUR FAVORITE DESIGN TRENDS?

Historically, trends are a fact of life. Always with us, they evolve and revolve. We, as designers, somehow sense what's going to be the preferences for the next 5-10 year span, as they have already taken root within us on a personal level. I love to do "trendy" places with hip clients on the cutting edge. However, equally valid is the client who appreciates current trends, but prefers the fusion of various trends over time, melded together into an art form that will not only stand shoulder-shoulder with the latest couture, but will also be perceived as timeless.

WHAT DO YOU LIKE BEST ABOUT BEING IN THE DESIGN BUSINESS?

"Working with my clients; creating that relationship of imagination and creation. Secondly, being able to participate in industry supported organizations such as ASID to increase public awareness of what the business of true professional interior design is all about."

WHAT GOAL DOES ALL OF YOUR DESIGN PROJECTS SHARE?

"Designing a space that encompasses an atmosphere that appeals to my clients' lifestyle and good sense as well as, to their sensory and emotional experience within it. BCDG Interiors has a motto, "Interior Design–A Three Dimensional Art Form, Inspired Design–A Fourth-Dimensional Experience." Although I love to hear my projects described by others as "art in the third dimension" my greatest satisfaction comes from knowing my clients encounter the "magic" of that experience every time they cross the threshold into their newly completed space.

(BCDG) Bonnie Crawford Design Group
Bonnie K. Crawford, ASID
Seattle Design Center
5701 Sixth Avenue South
Suite 252
Seattle, WA 98108
206.328.4340
Fax 206.763.5795

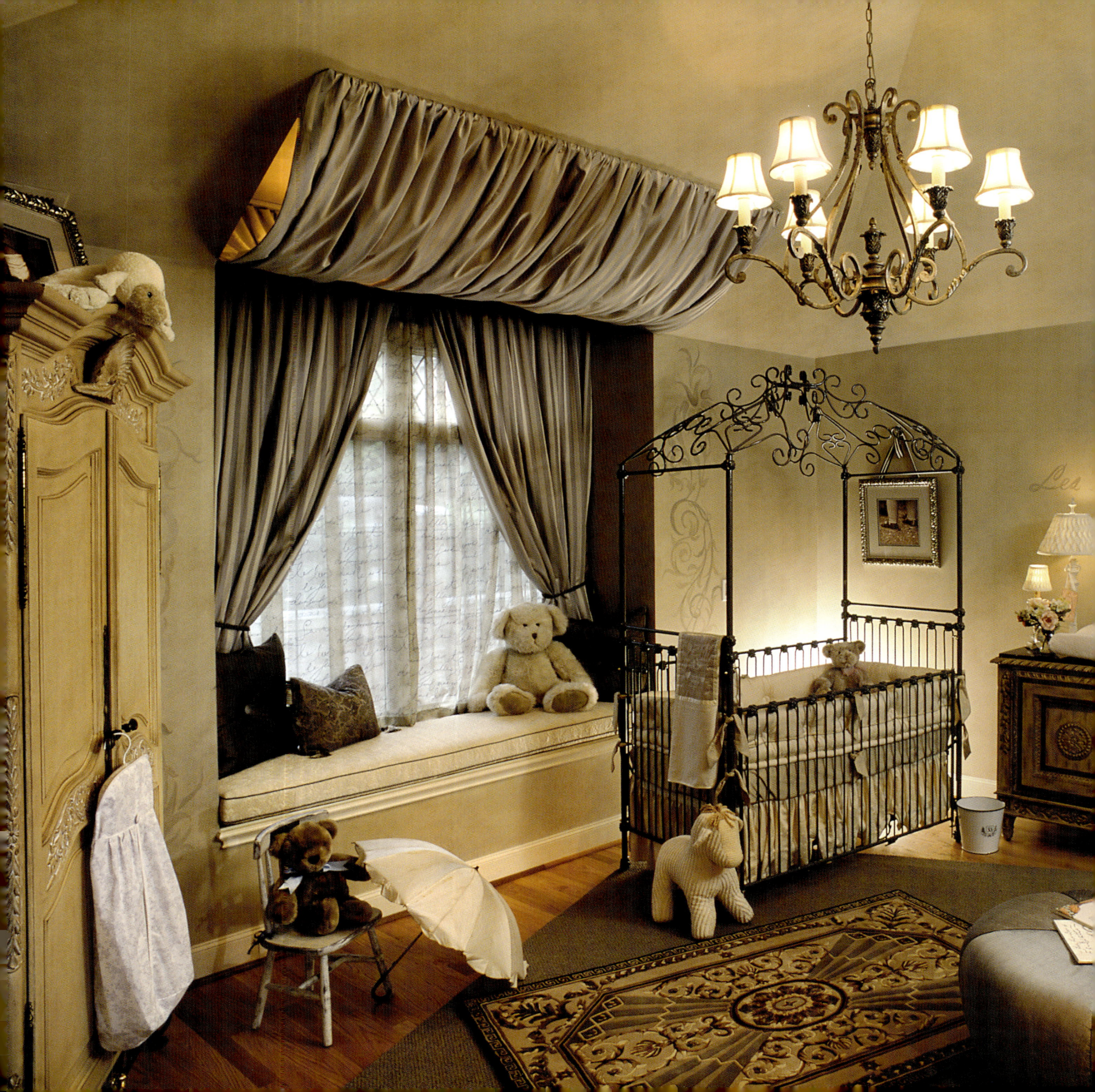

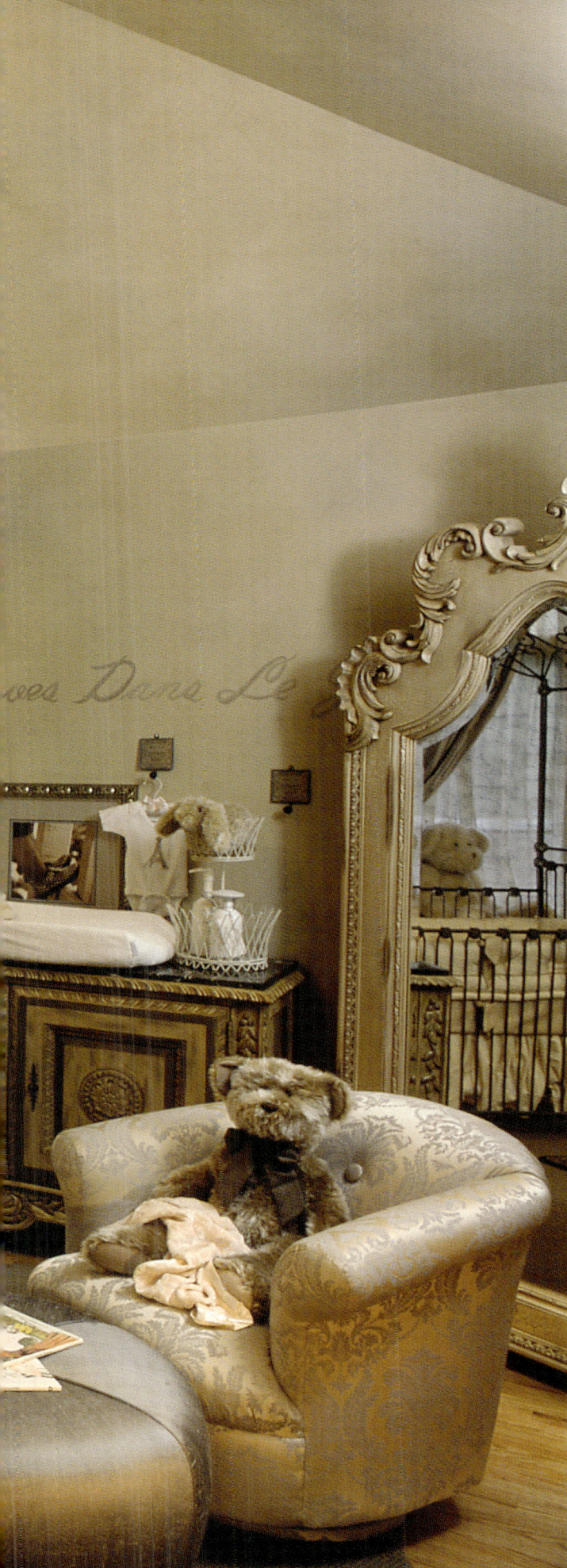

MICHELLE DAHL & SANDY HOLSTEAD

Belle Grey Interior Design, LLC

Michelle Dahl and Sandy Holstead are truly a dynamic duo of style. Whether they're designing second homes or planning their outfits, these designers believe in doing everything with style and flair.

With 12 years of design experience between them, Michelle and Sandy love designing in the Pacific Northwest because of the opportunity to do a variety of styles, everything from Mediterranean to lodge to classic waterfront. Together, they have designed dramatic residential spaces in the Northwest, as well as in Hawaii, Phoenix and Sun Valley. But don't let their high profiles and glamorous interiors fool you; Michelle and Sandy are true Northwesterners, combining their professionalism with an approachable non-intimidating presentation.

This duo believes in pushing the design envelope as far as their clients will let them. They have an innate ability to understand what their clients want and then articulate it in clear, simple language. For Michelle and Sandy, the biggest compliment is when a client says, "I didn't even know how to explain what I wanted but you were able to create exactly what I was looking for."

LEFT
French-inspired nursery with French writing on the wall and sheers.

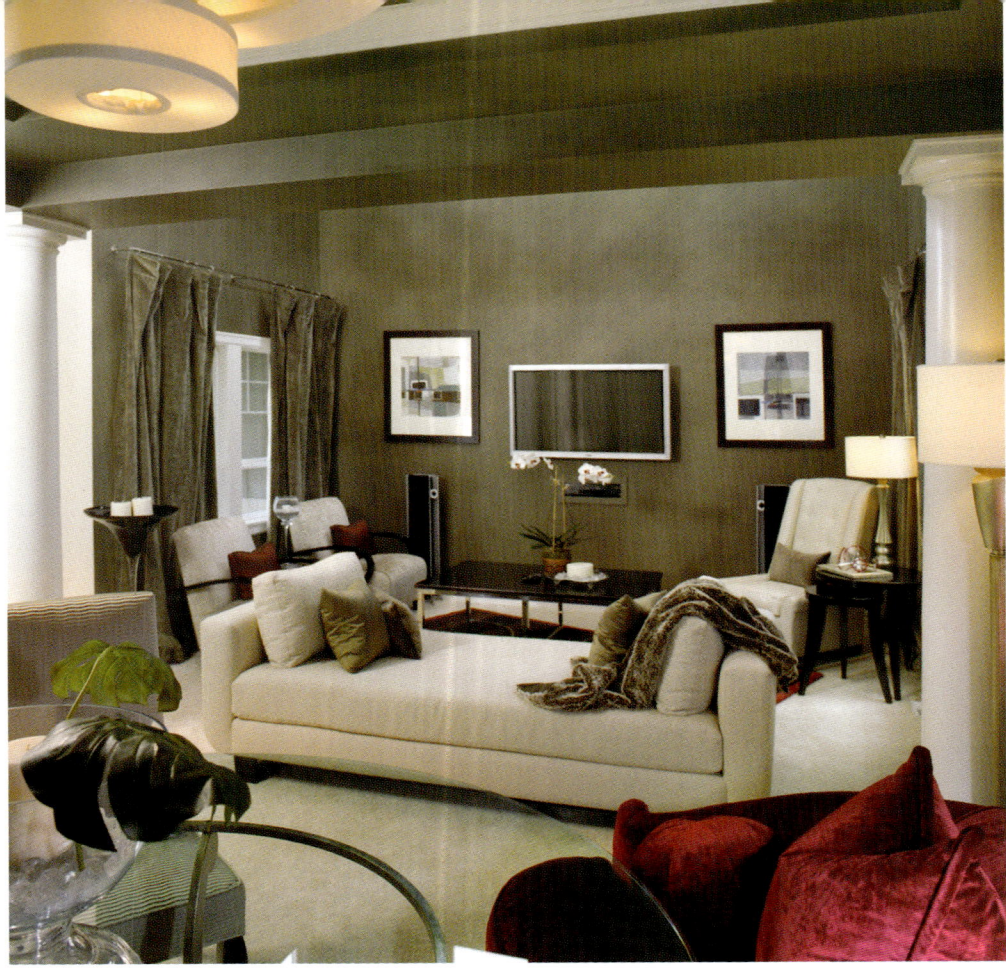

Michelle and Sandy both have an eye toward monochromatic with a "wow." For this design team, that means letting rooms pop with lots of rich, dramatic textures or soft, sophisticated patterns. Color is used sparingly in accessories and art to create focal points that can be changed through the years. Their ideal design has just enough "spice and sass" to grab everyone who walks in the room.

Even the name of their company shows their unique take on design, combining the duo's love of both belle—an ornate, feminine style—and grey—a color they find sleek and stylish.

For both Michelle and Sandy, their style sense started at home. This is especially true of Michelle, who says her mom encouraged her to go her own way, whether it was painting a huge red stripe around her room at 3 am or painting the keys of her piano different colors.

The duo has been honored for their work, garnering awards such as the Seattle Design Center Award—twice—and being published in *Seattle Homes and Lifestyles*.

For this style-forward team, there is nothing they love better than "the reveal"—that day when "families cry tears of joy and otherwise private clients hug their interior designer, when it all comes together and you can sit back and be proud."

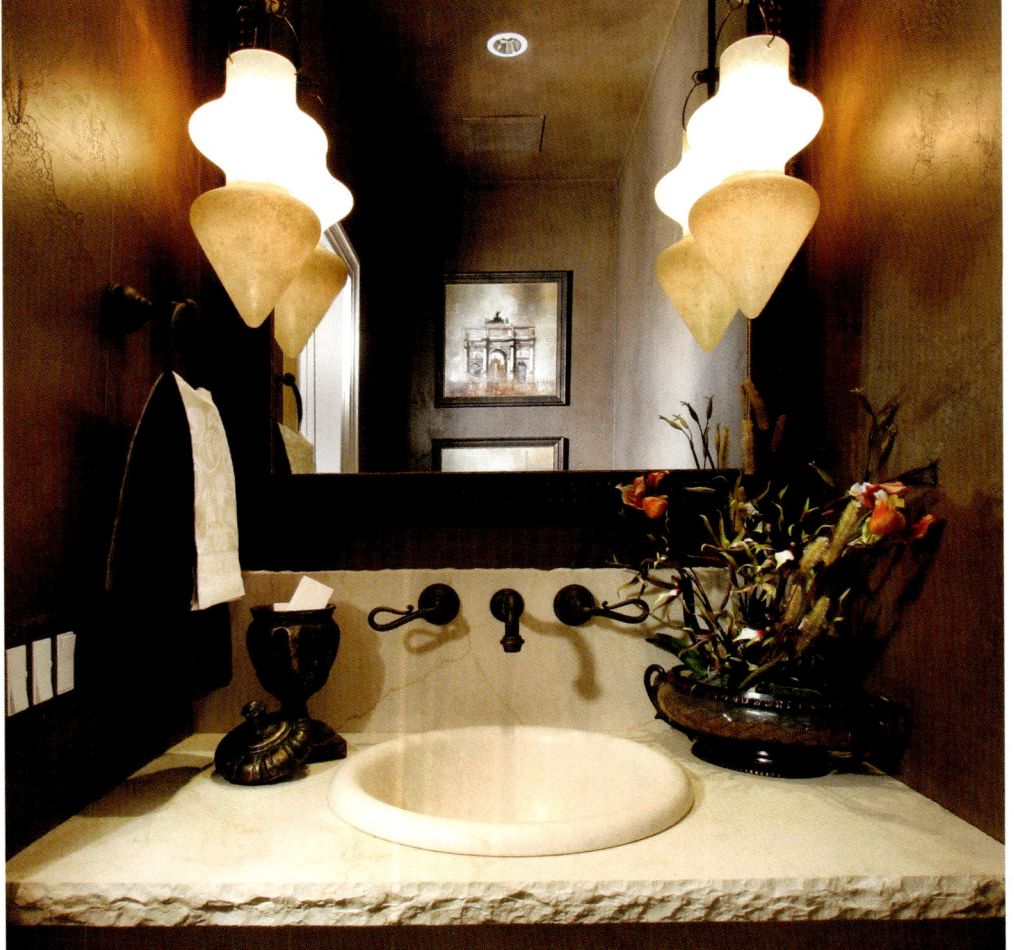

TOP
Monochromatic bachelor's residence, faux painting by Tara Whited.

BOTTOM
Tuscan-inspired powder room with plaster walls and chipped-edge floating marble sink.

FACING PAGE RIGHT
Kitchen remodel, custom cabinets by Stark Contractors.

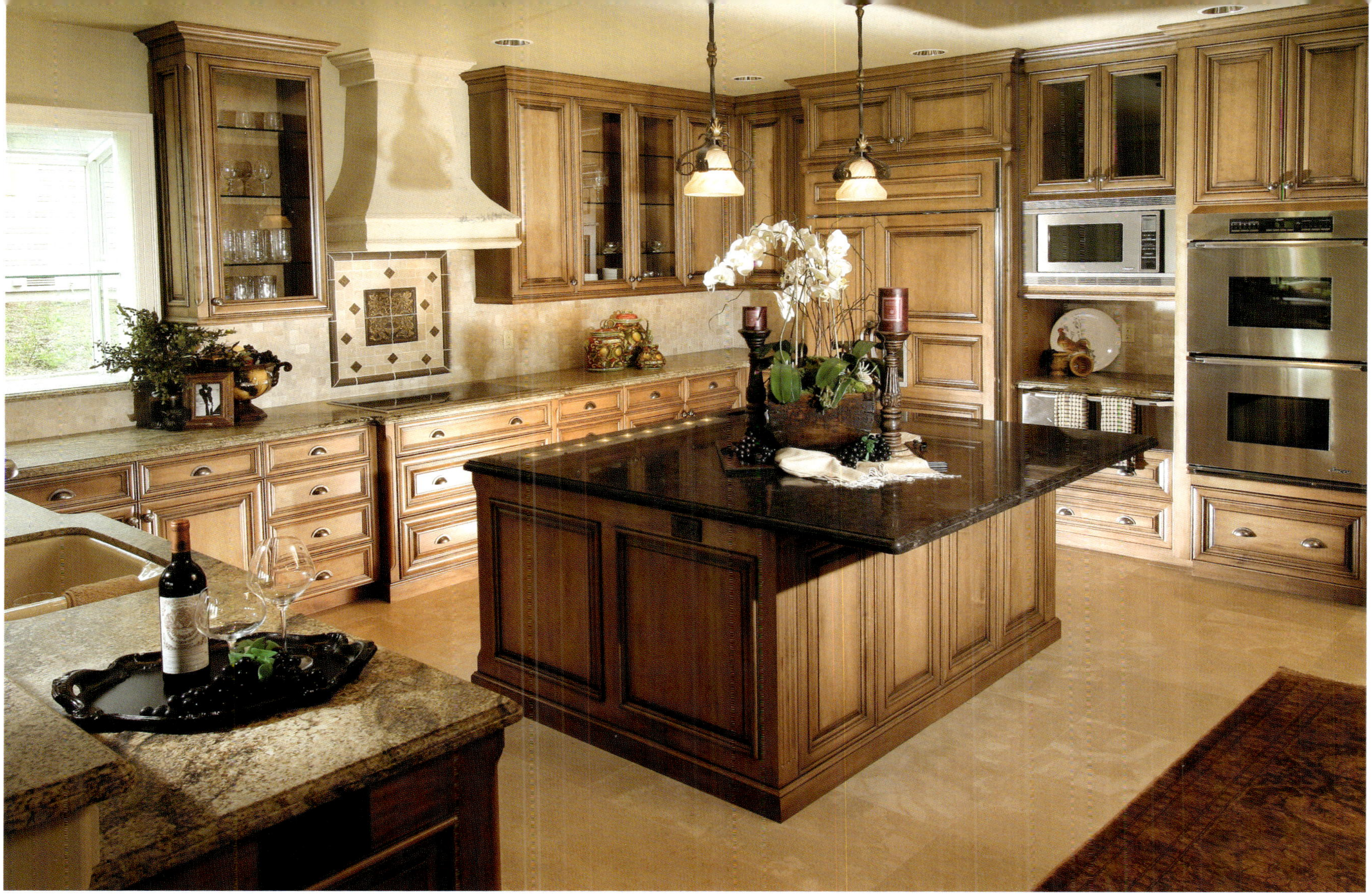

More about Michelle & Sandy...

WHAT PERSONAL INDULGENCE DO MICHELLE AND SANDY SPEND MONEY ON?

Clothes and shoes. Luckily, they have the same tastes so sometimes an "accessory shopping afternoon" needs to turn into a trip to the closest boutique.

WHAT COLOR BEST DESCRIBES MICHELLE AND SANDY?

Grey—it's such an ambitious color. It can be strong and sexy or soft and cozy. It is the color they feel the best in and it has become such a part of their environment with many days being grey.

YOU CAN TELL THEY LIVE IN THE PACIFIC NORTHWEST BECAUSE...

They have an umbrella to match every purse.

WHAT IS THE SINGLE THING MICHELLE AND SANDY WOULD DO TO BRING A DULL HOUSE TO LIFE?

Artwork!

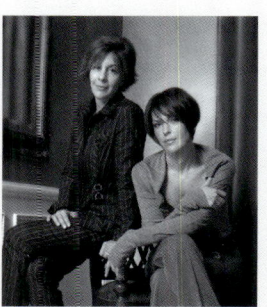

Belle Grey Interior Designs, LLC
Michele Dahl and Sandy Holstead
7900 SE 28th Street
Mercer Island, WA 98040
206.230.5800

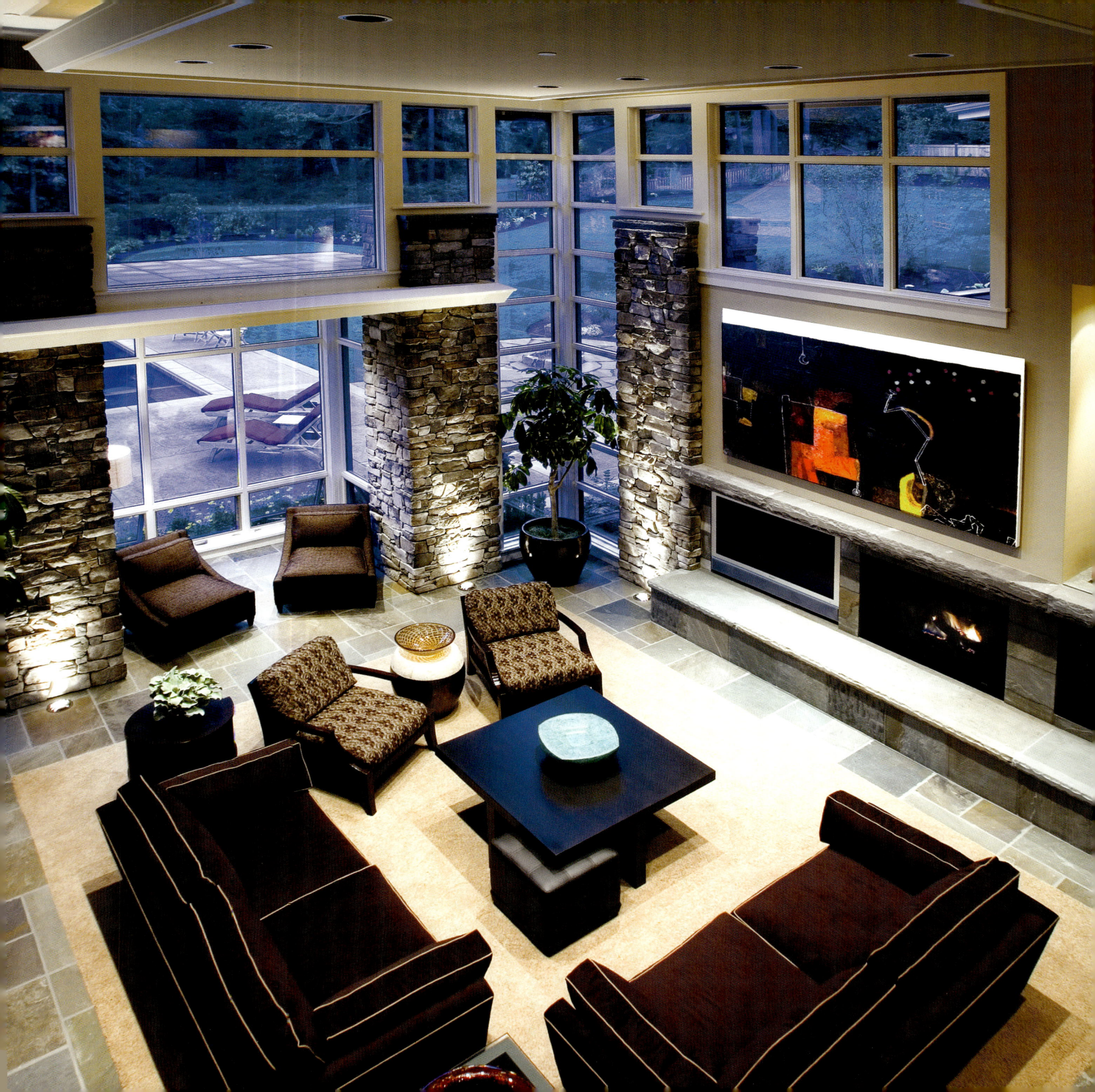

Dana T. Foster
DTF Design, Inc.

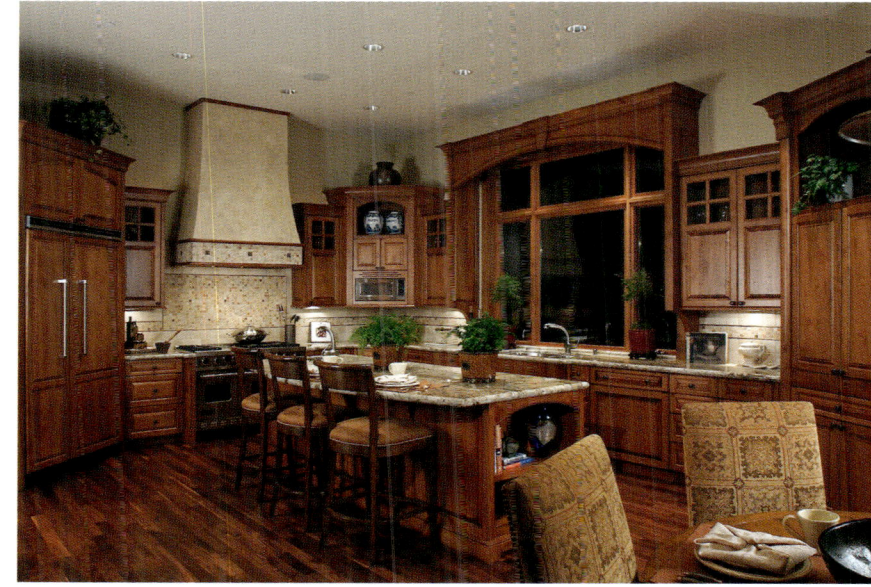

LEFT
Lighted stone columns wrap inside to outside; Pennsylvania Blue Stone flooring; many local artists including an abstract painting by Reilly Jensen above the fireplace.

RIGHT
Custom, distressed alder cabinetry; plaster covered hood incorporating antique biblical mosaic stone tiles and metal tile accents; black walnut hardwood floors.

Dana Foster's flourishing design business is a testament to her ability to create artful, elegant interiors that capture a more casual lifestyle. She is a graduate of Arizona State University's prestigious five year FIDER accredited Interior Design program with architectural emphasis. One look at her residential and commercial creations and it is easy to see why Dana's clients return to her project after project.

Dana Foster grew up surrounded by construction and the process that went into building structures—both her father and brother work in the construction industry. Her ability to navigate the landscapes of both design and construction provides Dana with a high level of comfort on any job site and allows her to work closely with contractors. "I speak their language, which matters because the relationship that I have with the builder is as important as the relationship I have with the client," Dana says. "I also understand the building process, so I provide realistic design solutions that can be built."

In fact, Dana can often be found at the job site in jeans and boots, chalking various layouts on the plywood sub floor. It is this accessibility and ability to connect with people, coupled with her extraordinary vision and versatility that Dana's clients love about her. "My ability to connect with people and understand their needs and design objectives is often what lands me the job," she says. "I have many clients that come back year after year because I've created that special connection." She often continues to spend time with her clients socially after she's completed their homes. "I like to be part of their family and to know that we have a relationship that will last," she says.

The intricate process by which Dana discovers her clients' design preferences is paramount to begin the design process and offer design solutions that are based on the client. She asks a lot of questions about the clients' lifestyle and family, their values and interests and backgrounds including how they entertain, cook, spend

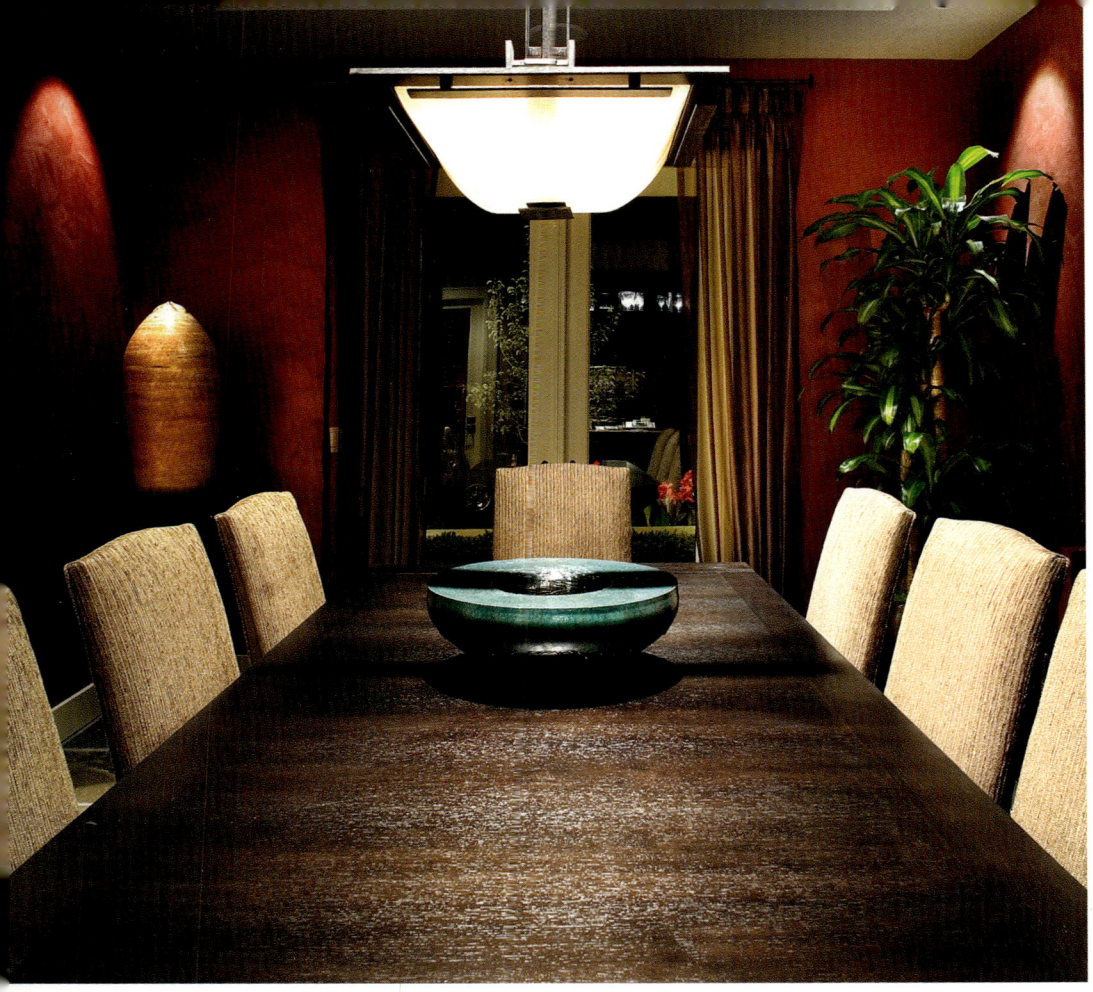

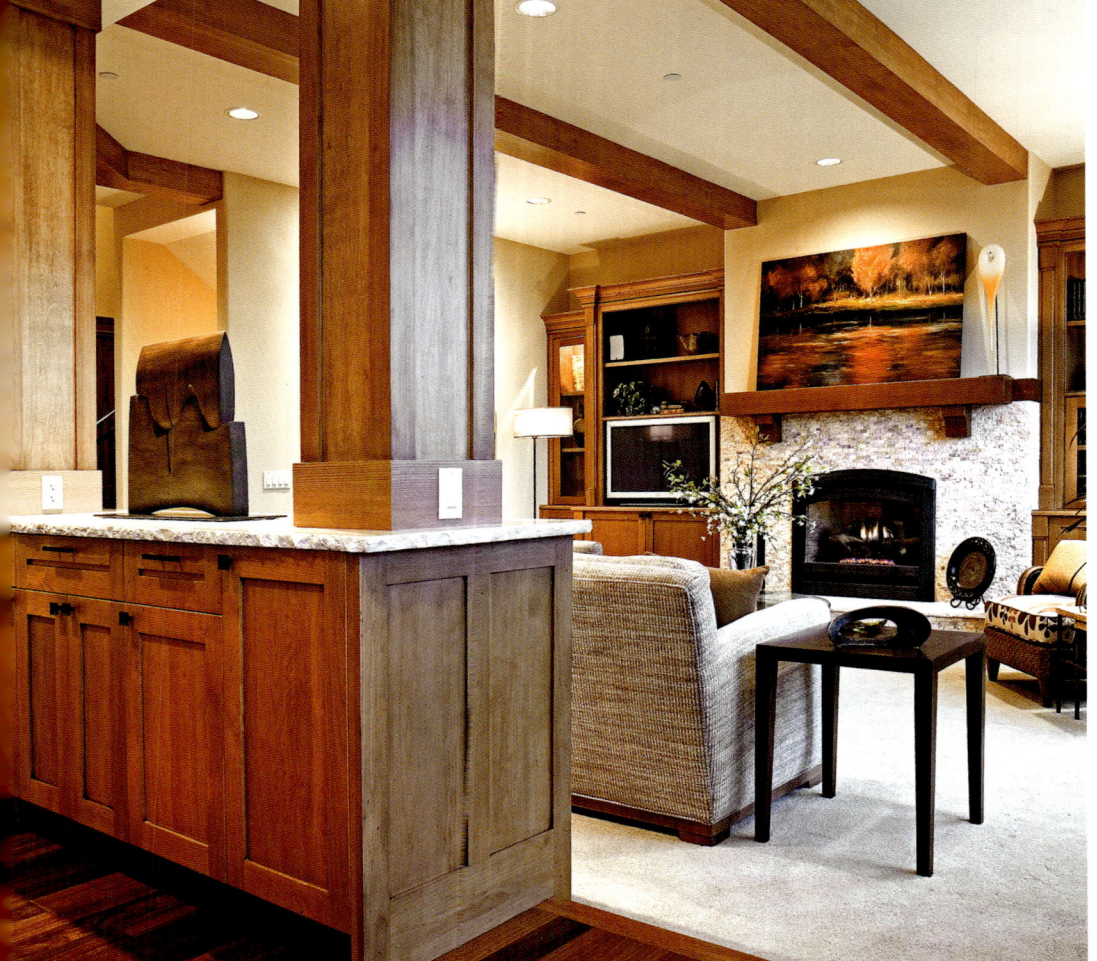

their weekends, and live day to day. "I try to understand and relate to their personal lifestyle right away and figure out who they are as people before I even begin the creative design process," she says.

Detail- and solution-oriented, Dana drafts a drawing of each design as she envisions it. These drawings enable clients and builders to understand her vision while also providing the opportunity to make revisions on paper prior to the construction or redesign, saving both time and money. "It's so critical to have a visual representation of the design concept, to show clients how I envision the space," she says.

While many designers focus on furniture or accessories, Dana's true passion is for creating the architectural shell of the home. She artfully blends colors, textures and materials, including: flooring materials and accents, tile and stone layouts, lighting, specialty paint, custom hardware and cabinetry. This allows her to create a solid base in the fixed parts of the home before she moves on to create rich, warm, timeless interiors.

A strong advocate of designing for the climate, Dana often finds inspiration from the beauty of the Northwest. For her, this means incorporating colors, textures and sounds from the surrounding environment such as natural stone and wood, water, and earth tones. She is skillful creating elegant palettes of earth tones of olives, caramels, chocolates, creams and golds.

When she is not designing beautiful environments for the Northwest, Dana is often found exploring the area in which she lives. A big fan of Seattle's art and cultural offerings, she also enjoys hiking, camping, boating, snowshoeing, and snowmobiling in the greater Pacific Northwest.

TOP
Lusterstone walls in deep oxblood red; handcrafted mahogany table. Glazed ceramic sculpture by Ann Mallory.

BOTTOM
Craftsman detailing; chiseled limestone countertop; forged iron hardware; cumaru hardwood floors.

FACING PAGE RIGHT
Warm, rich colors; textural stone mosaics; hand-blown glass sculpture by northwest artist Chuck Lopez.

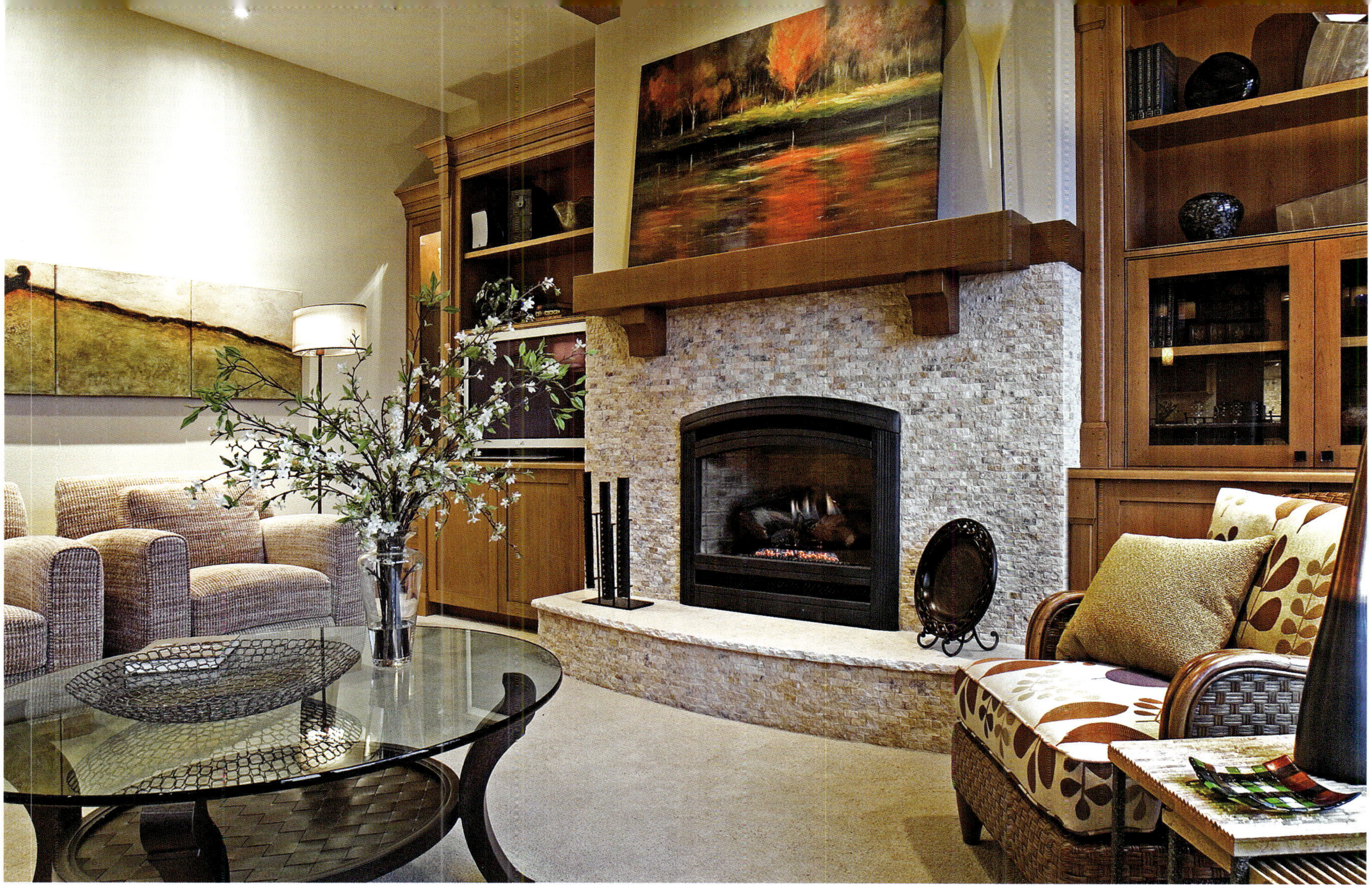

More about Dana…

WHAT IS THE BEST PART OF BEING AN INTERIOR DESIGNER?

My favorite part is feeling the satisfaction and reward from seeing happy clients throughout the project and knowing they trust and respect my guidance and recommendations.

WHAT ONE ELEMENT OF STYLE OR PHILOSOPHY HAVE YOU STUCK WITH FOR YEARS THAT STILL WORKS FOR YOU TODAY?

The element of style that I have applied for years is incorporating colors, materials and textures that are indigenous to the area and therefore creating interior environments that are appropriate to the architecture, the setting, and the needs and styles of each client.

My design philosophy has always been to listen and relate to each client and provide design solutions that meet their design style, personal needs, and lifestyle. I commit myself to building and maintaining strong relationships with clients, builders, architects, and vendors.

WHAT DO YOU LIKE BEST ABOUT DOING BUSINESS IN THE PACIFIC NORTHWEST?

I love working with clients in the Northwest because they are usually down to earth, hardworking, warm people who truly appreciate and respect the natural beauty of our area and who feel blessed to be building their dream home or improving their interior environment.

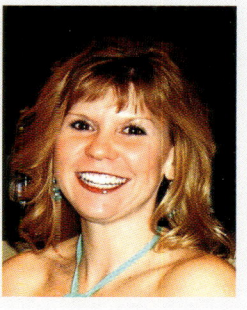

DTF Design, Inc.
Dana Foster
Sammamish, WA 98074
425.961.0305
Fax 425.961.0306
www.dtfdesign.com

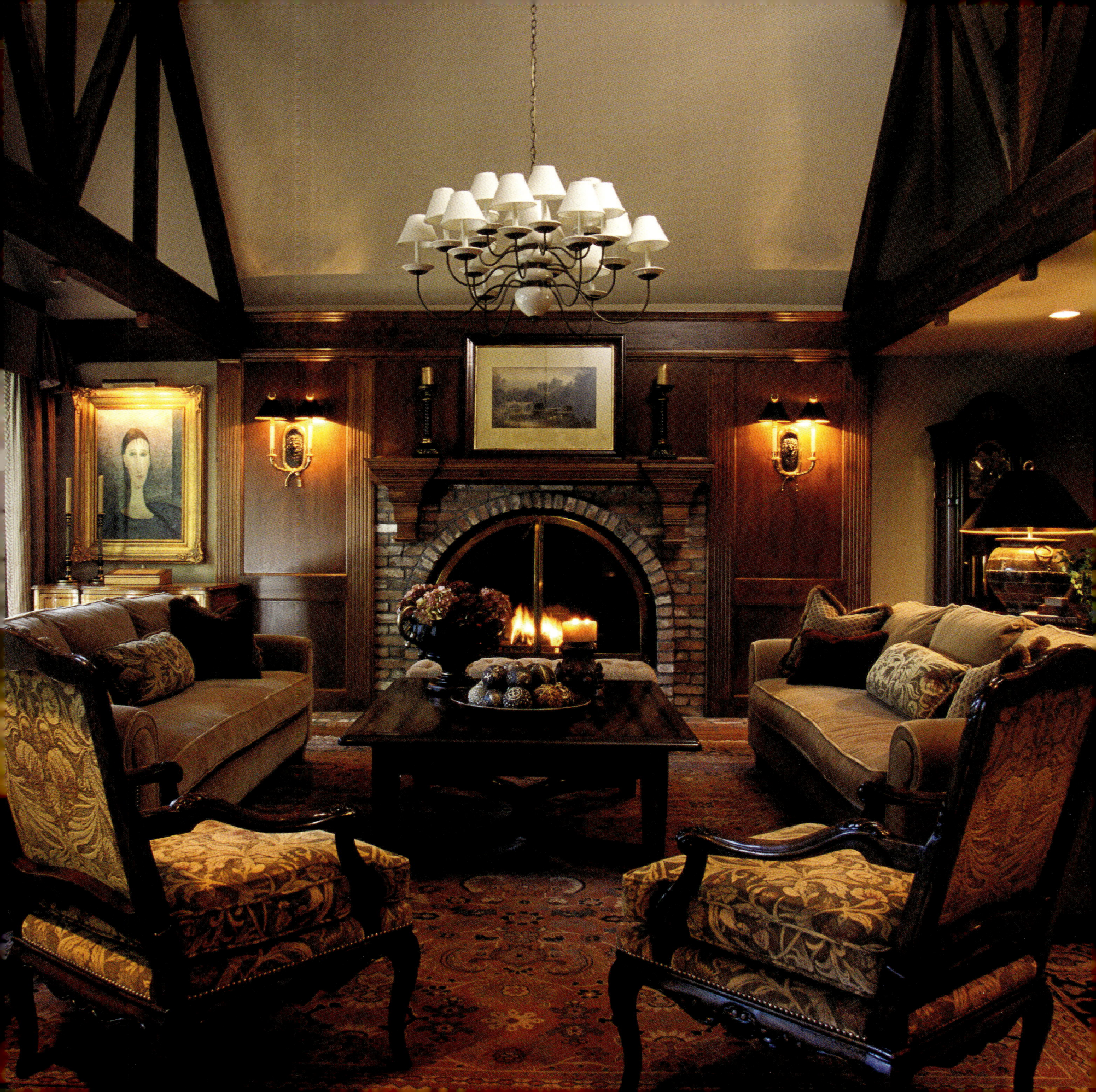

ANN GORDINIER

A. Gordinier Interiors, Inc.

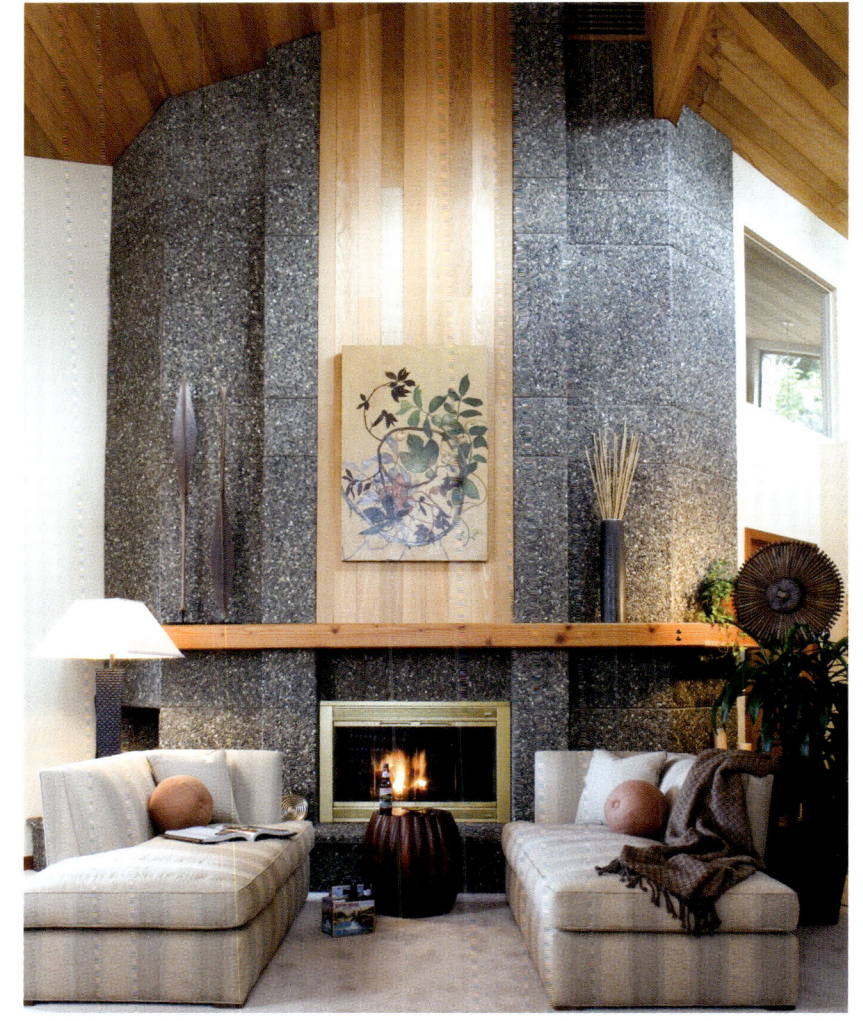

Ann Gordinier and Associates have been creating award-winning designs since 1978. Her firm, Gordinier Interiors has garnered a range of awards from professional organizations including the Seattle Home and Garden Show, The Seattle Interior Show and the prestigious Marjorie Siegel Award for contributions to the design community, to name just a few. She was on the board of American Society of Interior Designers (ASID) and has been active in many other community charities.

Ann has a following of an amazingly loyal clientele that not only recognizes her uncanny ability to visualize a beautiful, yet comfortable room, but also her charming sense of humor. She is a meticulous professional with an eye for detail and a sense of perfection but balanced with a zest for life and laughter.

Since college, Ann has stunned people, from her beginnings in the fashion world as a magazine editor to her transition into the interior design field. She has an innovative way of combining color, fabric and styles into her work. After completion of design school, she established her own firm and maintains clients throughout the United States and Canada.

RIGHT
A commanding officer at Camp David under two Presidents, this Navy family finally has settled in a home of their own. Simple furnishings where chosen to complement the interesting architecture and the city view. With commissioned art pieces completing the room.

LEFT
Custom wood paneling brings warmth and a counterbalance to this Tudor-detailed living room. The soft earthy palette creates an Old World ambiance, complete with fine art.

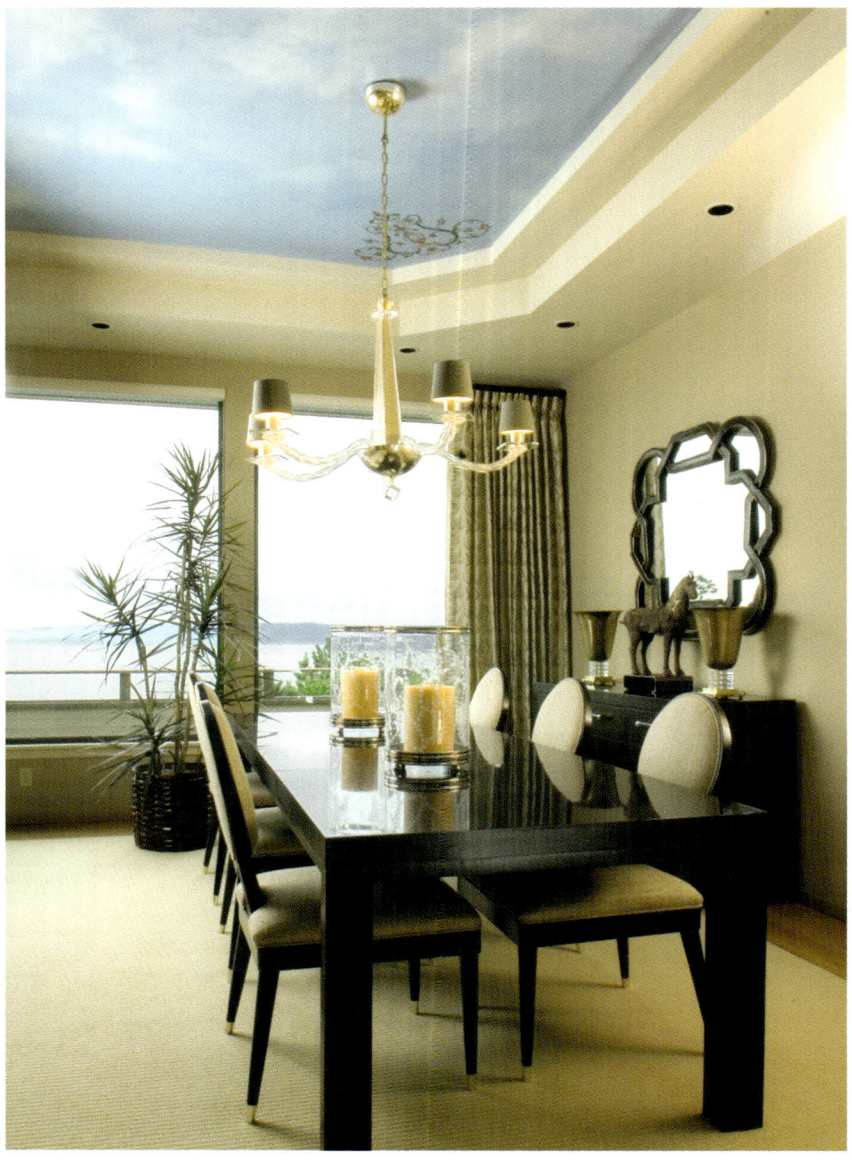
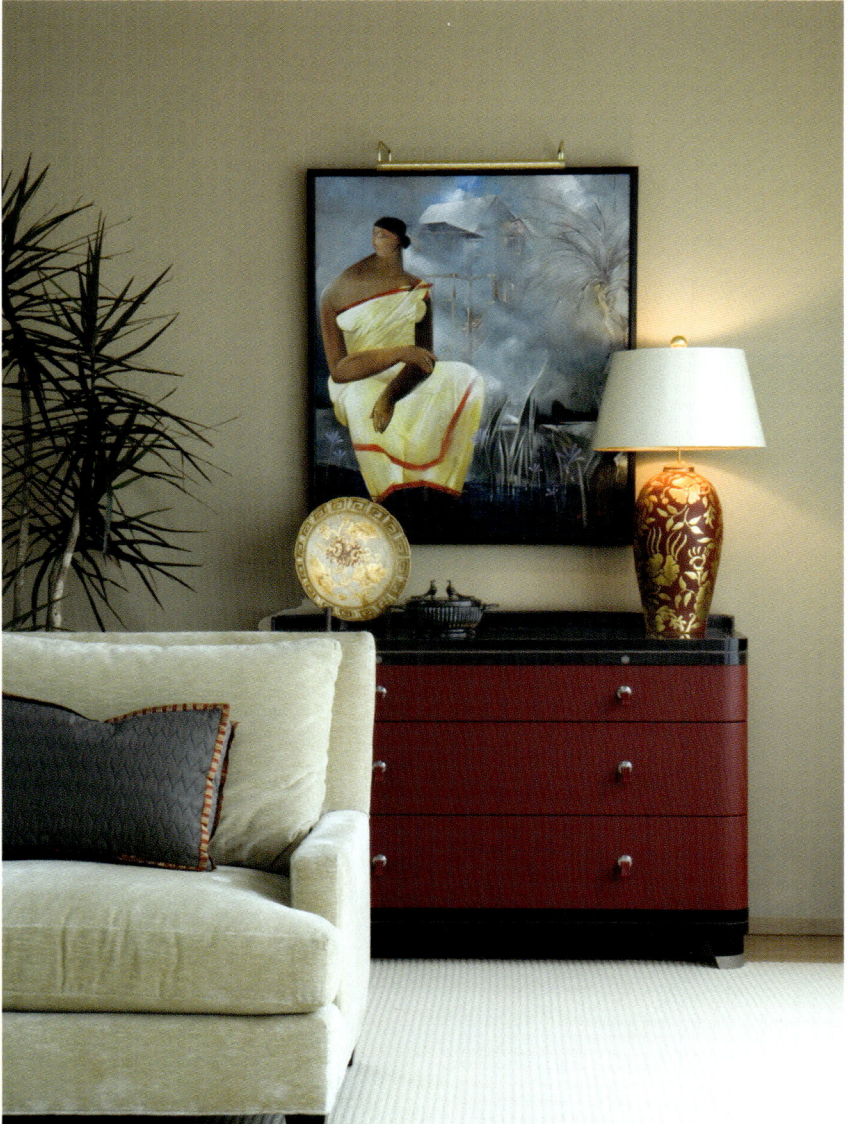

LEFT
Simplicity of furnishings allows full focus on the sculptural Donghia chandelier and magnificent view of Puget Sound. Hand-painted sky with Indian scroll motif reflects the owner's heritage.

RIGHT
This vignette is from the same view home. The unusual red leather dresser anchors the original art above as well as showcasing the antique collectibles.

Although proficient in many styles, her world travels have left her with a love for classic design influenced by France, England and of course, Italy, always with a timeless integrity. Ann finds great satisfaction when combining the new classic aesthetic with old world charm. "I love the chance to try out new ideas and products and be creative on my clients' behalf. The design field is ever changing and I love that."

Ann's East Coast upbringing along with her mother's Saturday antiquing adventures helped shape her love of collecting and incorporating antiques into her interior design. "There is nothing that adds warmth, character and individuality to a room more than an antique, no matter how great or small."

Ann's theory is that a room should be exciting, varied in scope, yet comfortable and inviting, with a touch of whimsy, but most of all, it should be a fun journey… surpassing all your expectations.

More about Ann…

WHAT PERSONAL INDULGENCE DO YOU SPEND THE MOST MONEY ON?

Travel! I must have at least one major trip a year. It inspires me and gets my "juices" flowing... the minute I return I start thinking about the next country I want to explore

IF YOU COULD ELIMINATE ONE DESIGN/ARCHITECTURAL/BUILDING TECHNIQUE OR STYLE FORM THE WORLD, WHAT WOULD IT BE?

Hard-edged modernism. I appreciate this style, but wouldn't want to live in it. I need warmth and the coziness of fabric, color and soft edges.

WHAT SINGLE THING WOULD YOU DO TO BRING A DULL HOUSE TO LIFE?

Of course, color! It does more, for less, than any one element.

WHAT DO YOU LIKE MOST ABOUT DOING BUSINESS IN YOUR LOCALE?

The attitude of the Northwestern people... friendly, helpful and open to new ideas.

WHO HAS HAD THE MOST INFLUENCE ON YOUR CAREER?

My dear mother, who was adventurous and ahead of her time in color, fabric and design, and incorporated antiques in every room.

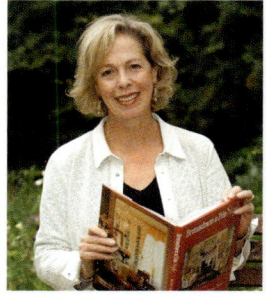

A. Gordinier Interiors, Inc.
Ann Gordinier
5701 6th Avenue South
Seattle, Washington 98108
206.764.1949
Fax 206.766.8273

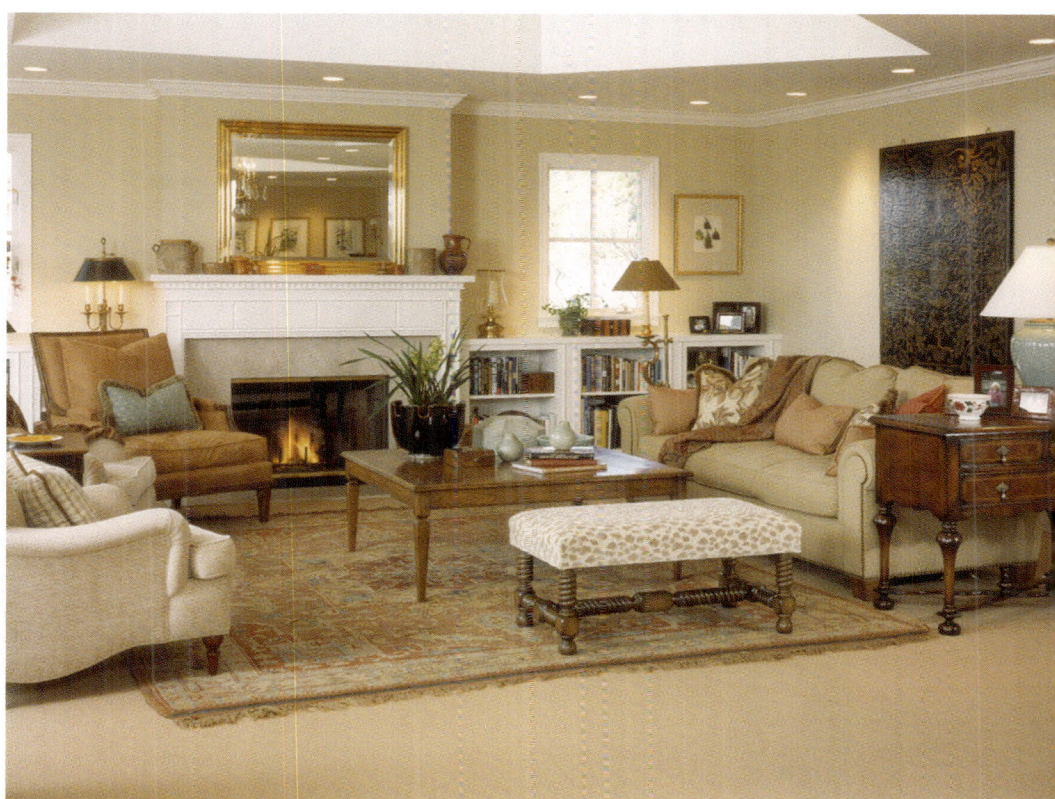

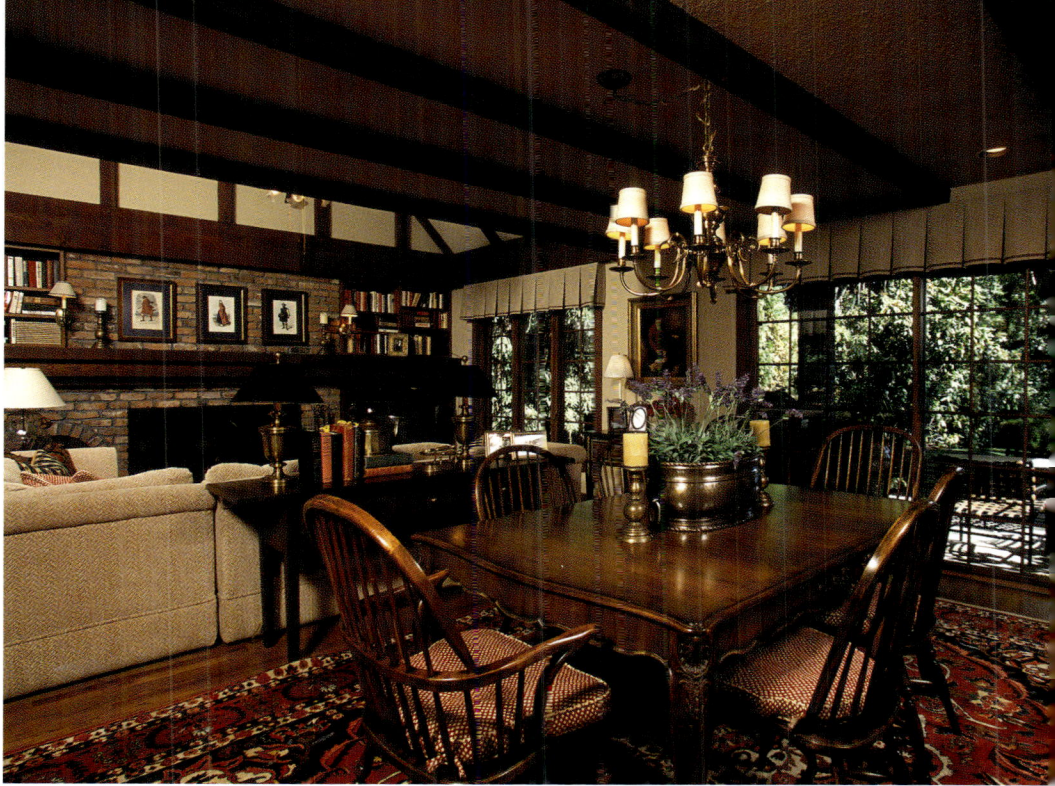

TOP
Timeless, yet stylish, reflecting the owner's sophisticated taste.

BOTTOM
The great room adjoins the kitchen and is truly the core of this home. Remodeled for a lively family, this living room was designed to be cozy, yet accommodate a large group.

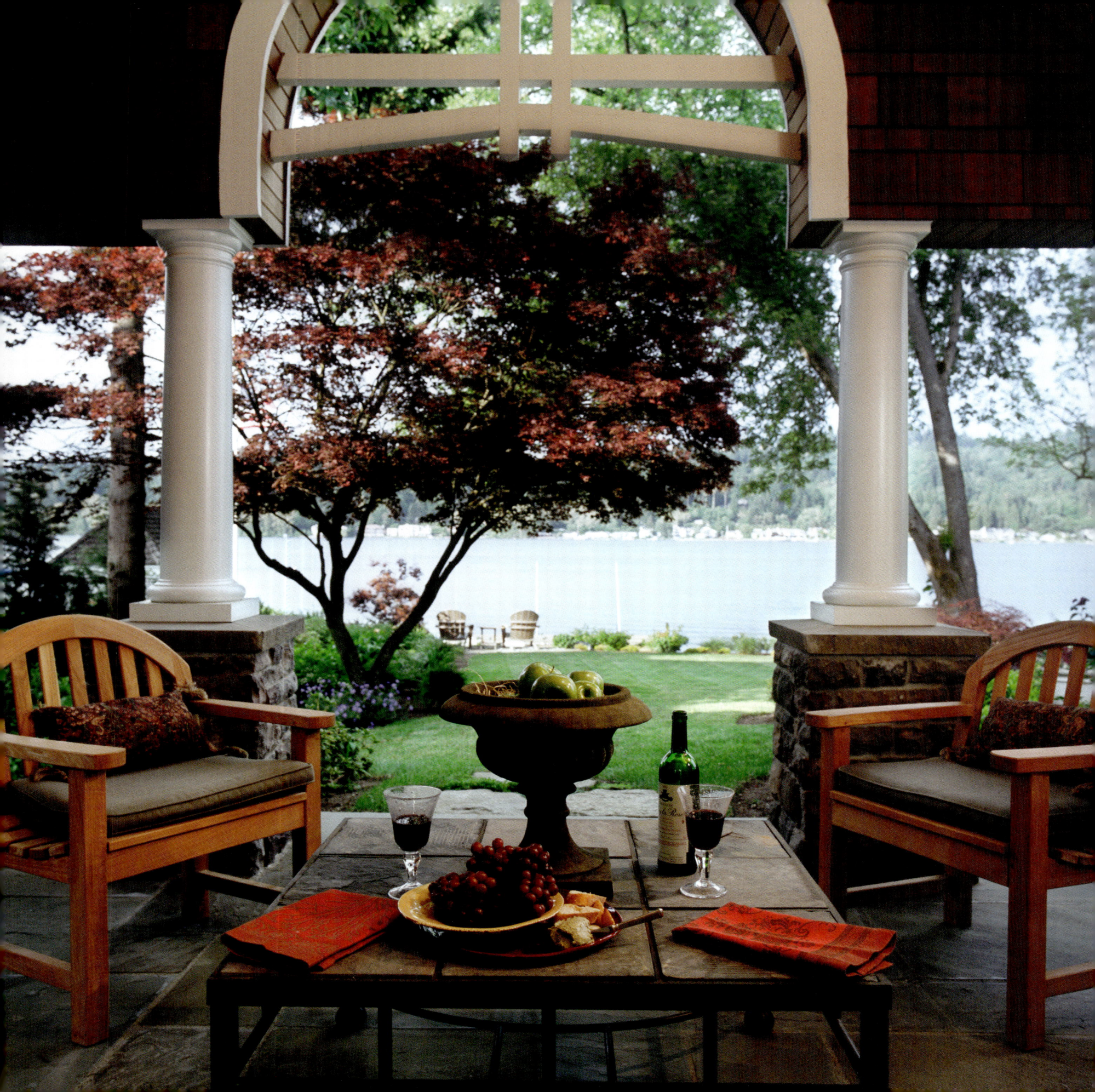

MARY HANSON
LIBERTY 123, LLC

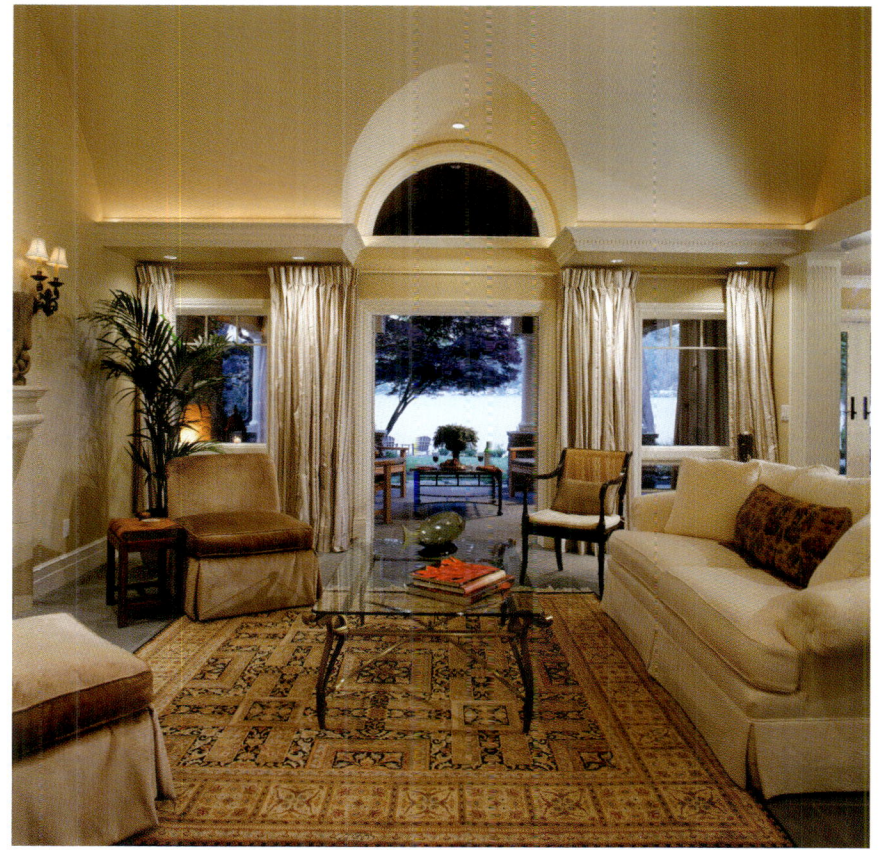

Mary Hanson's booming design business is a testament to her creative vision and passion. By always focusing on how small details fit into the big picture, Mary seamlessly incorporates location, architecture and furnishings to create harmonious and wholly unique settings for her clients. Mary excels in all aspects of design, including new homes and remodels. "The range gives me the ability to assist the client on multiple levels, from building and furnishing a home, to taking care of the accessories," she explains.

But a keen eye for color is what really sets Mary's designs apart. "Color is what makes or breaks a space," she says. "I always use a creative palette to ensure my design flows effortlessly from room to room."

Mary admits to being strongly influenced by her mom's impeccable sense of style. "She was always able to create interesting and unique interiors on a shoestring budget," she says. "My mom just really had a knack for putting things together. And I was the perfect sponge, absorbing it all."

LEFT
Outdoor Room with wood burning fireplace is furnished with teak and custom iron and stone table. Chairs by Smith & Hawken, coffee table made by Custom by Ross Bendixen, accessories by LIBERTY 123.

RIGHT
This living room's architectural details include the double barrel vaulted ceiling and cove detailing with a view of the outdoor living room and gardens with lake beyond. Sofa by Beacon Hill fabrics, Regency side chair and ledger table from Michael Folks, window treatment fabric from Old World Weavers and coffee table by Ross Bendixen.

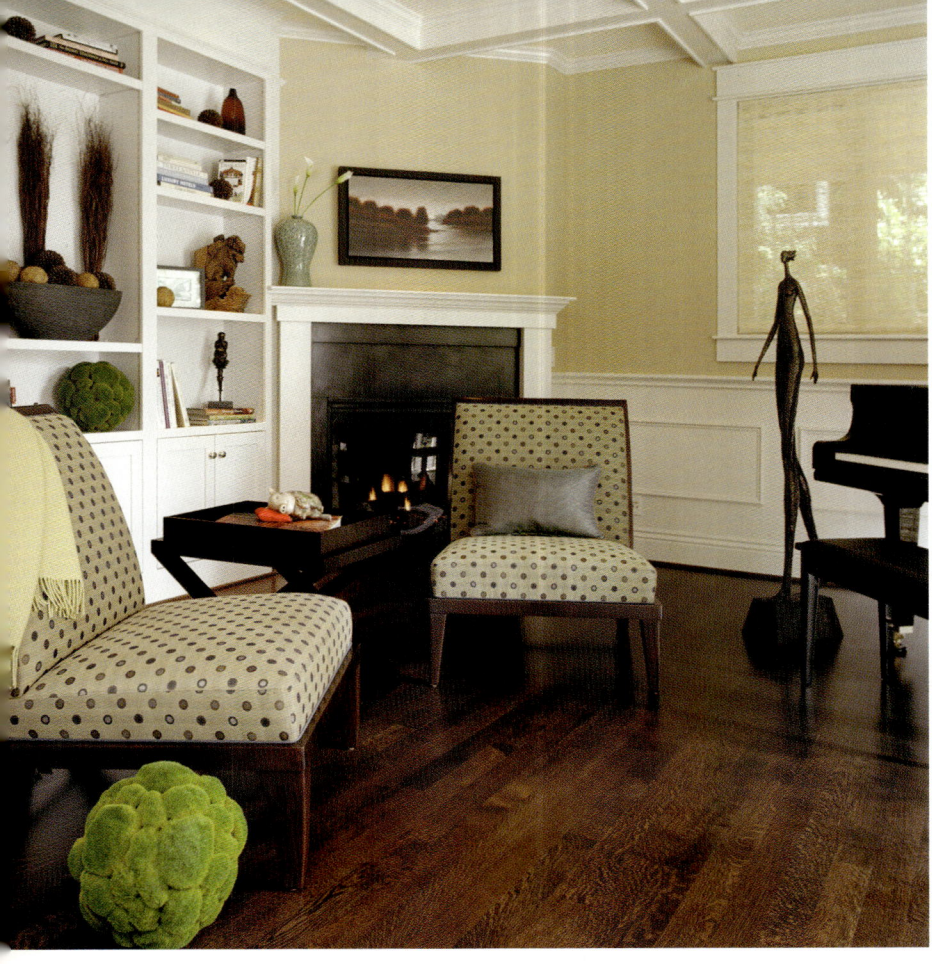

To pursue her interest in design, Mary attended Bellevue Community College Interior Design School. For the last 18 years, Mary has worked with clients around the world to create their dream homes. The quality of Mary's work is not only reflected in the accolades of her clients, but also through awards received and designs featured in nationally-syndicated publications. Mary has been honored with the Silver MAME Award for Street of Dreams, and her work has been showcased in *Sunset Magazine*, *Better Homes and Gardens*, *Seattle Times Pacific Magazine*, *Seattle Magazine*, *Northwest Home and Garden* and *Seattle Bride*.

In addition, Mary and her daughter, Liberty Hanson, own LIBERTY 123, a successful home furnishing boutique located in Kirkland, Washington. The two opened the store together five years ago, and in 2005, the boutique was chosen as one of *Northwest Home and Garden's* "Top Shops." LIBERTY 123 was also designated one of "Our 100 Favorite Shops for Cottage Style" by *Cottage Living Magazine*.

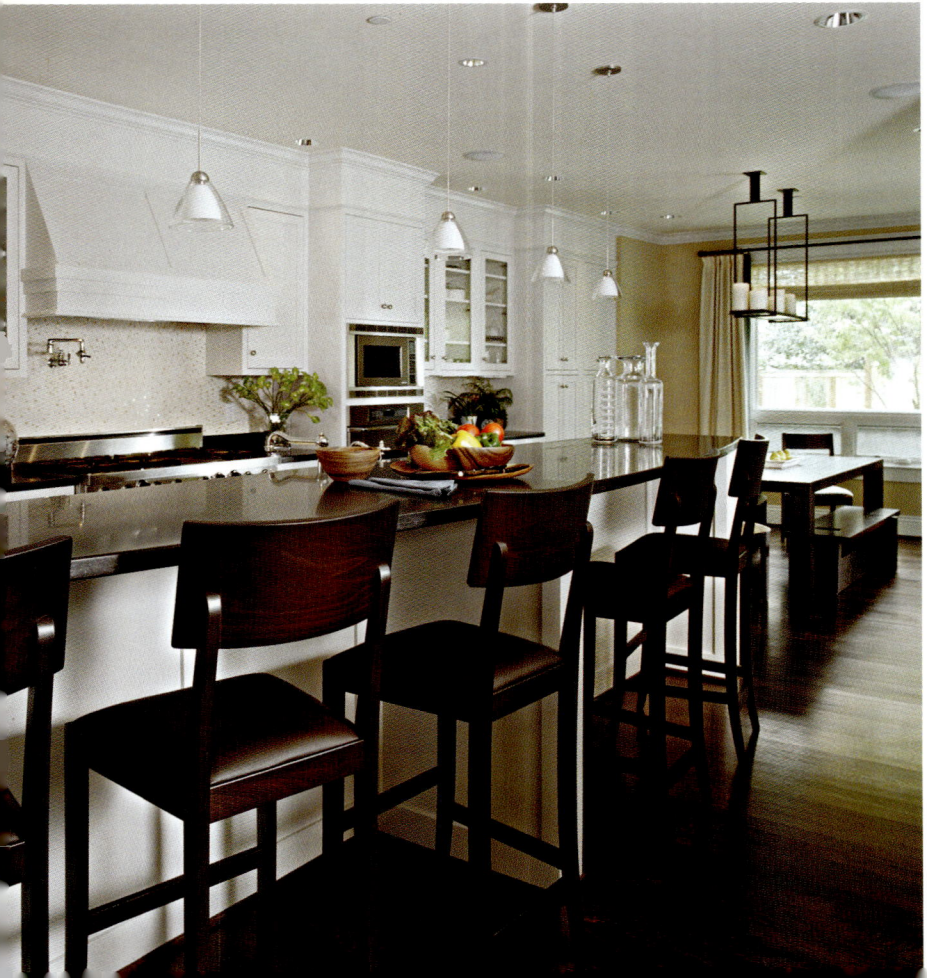

TOP
This beautifully detailed study with box ceilings is inviting to those musically inclined or anyone wanting a quiet retreat.

BOTTOM
This kitchen inlcudes a mile long island counter allows for an audience for the serious chef. Ann Sacks mosaic stone adds texture to the backsplash. Holly Hunt light and custom table and bench by Gulassa.

FACING PAGE RIGHT
Master bedroom includes a bed by Barbara Barry and Yves Delorme linens and accessories by LIBERTY 123.

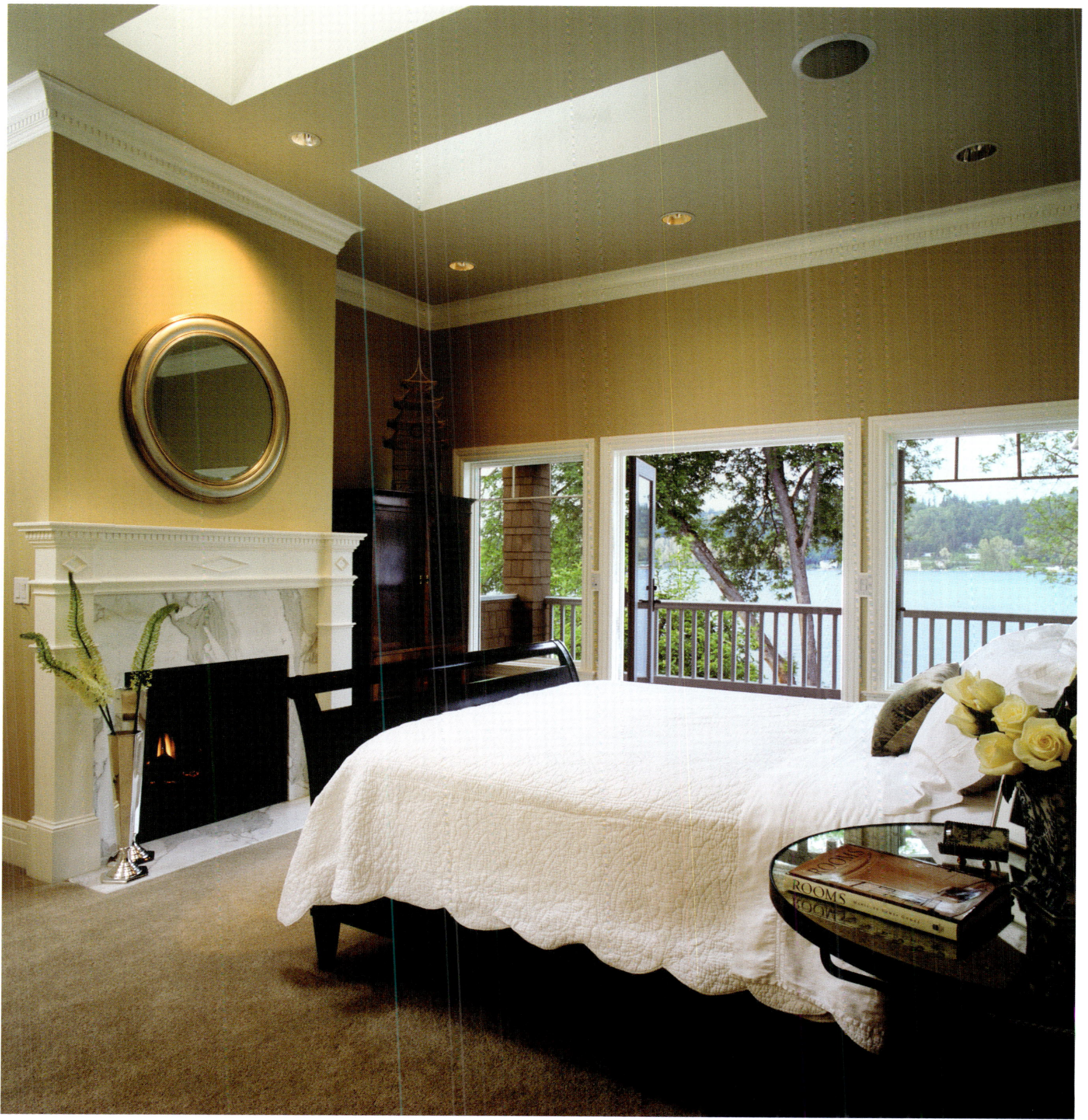

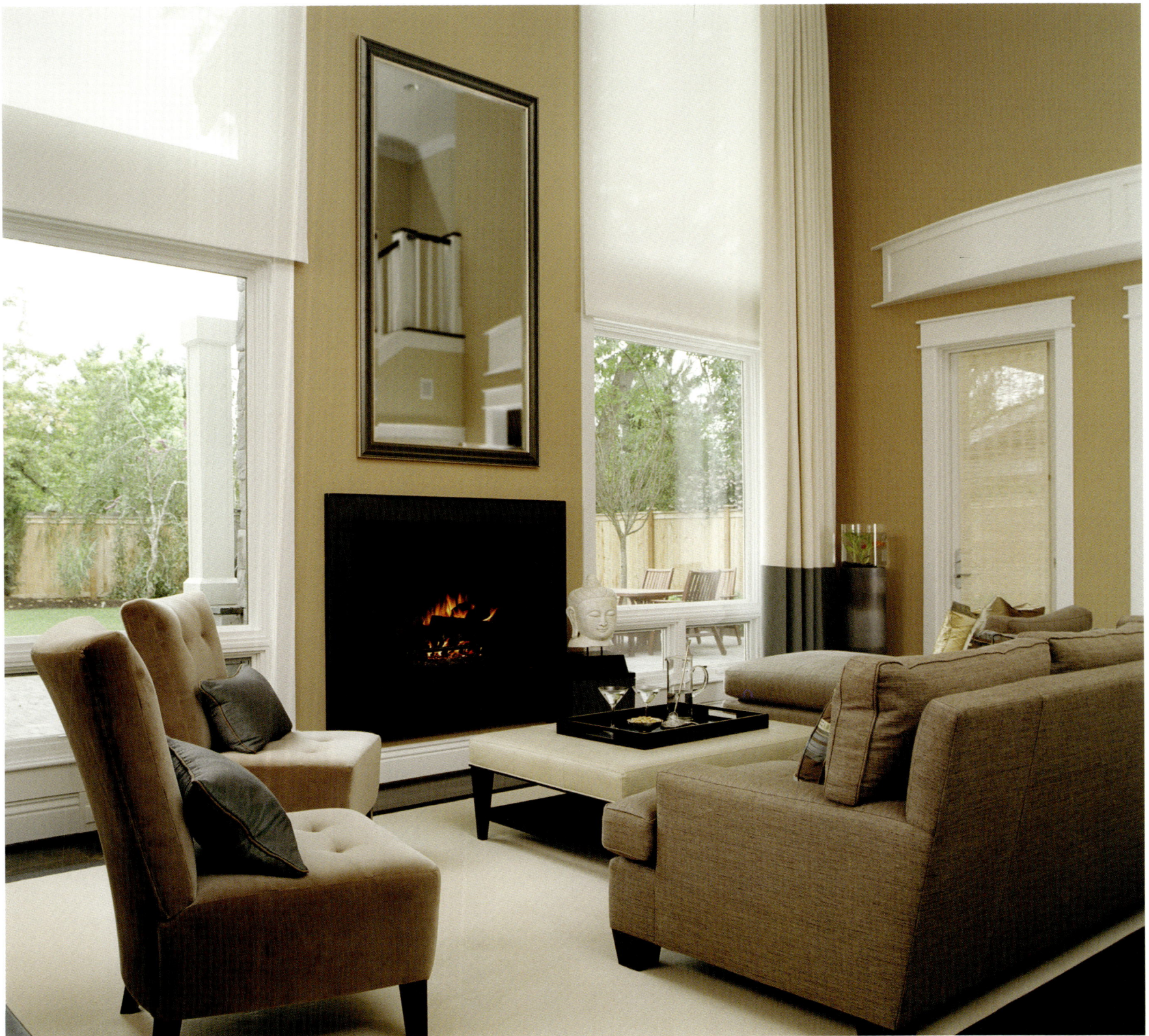

ABOVE
Dramatic 22-foot ceilings with two-toned drapes from floor to ceiling give this great room a stunning presence. Custom steel fireplace and textured furnishings by Baker, accentuate the contemporary architecture.

FACING PAGE LEFT
Indigo colored walls and Barbara Barry vanity detail this powder room.

FACING PAGE RIGHT
This guest bedroom is complemented with custom bed, Oly nesting tables, Yves Delorme linens and accessories by LIBERTY 123.

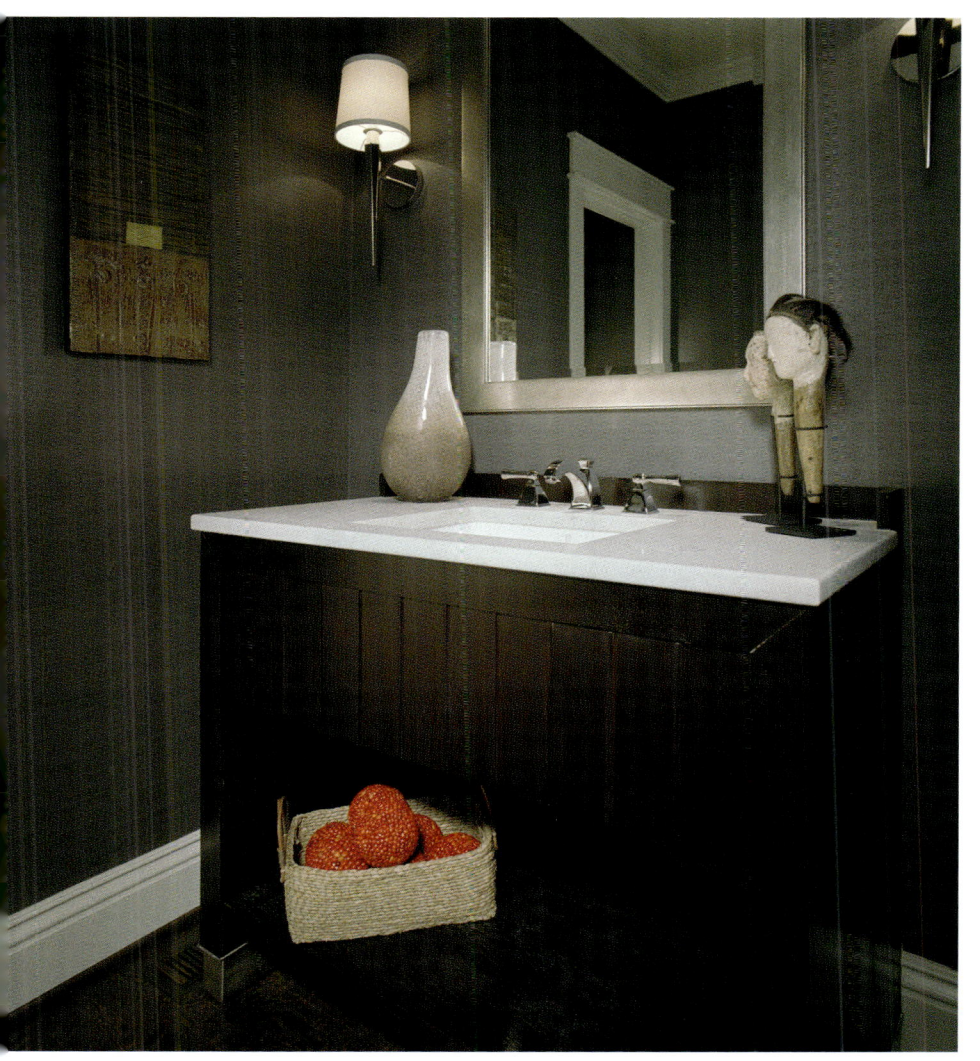
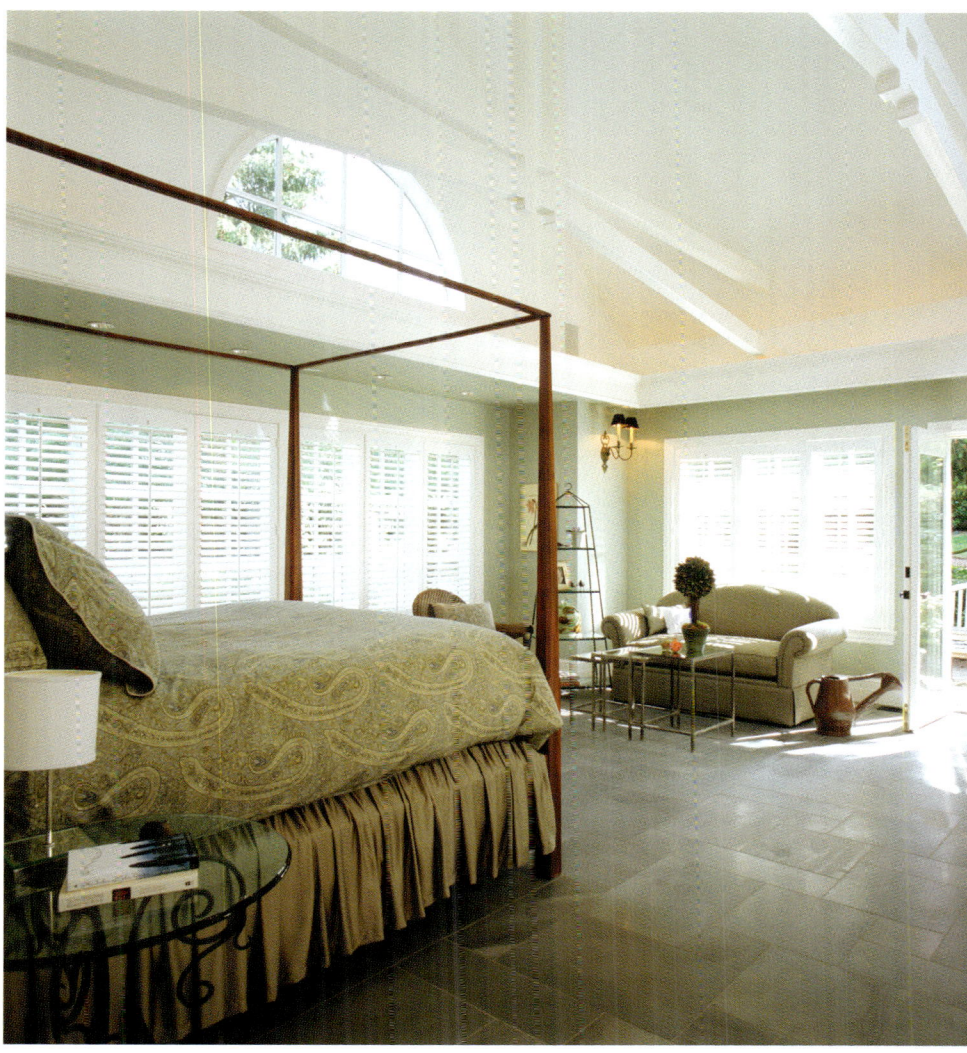

More about Mary...

WHAT COLOR BEST DESCRIBES YOU AND WHY?

The color green because of its ability to convey so many feelings with just the slightest variation of hue. I appreciate its versatility.

WHAT ONE ELEMENT OF STYLE OR PHILOSOPHY HAVE YOU STUCK WITH FOR YEARS THAT STILL WORKS FOR YOU TODAY?

Whatever the shape or size of the space, I always set out to enhance the best features of the architecture, just like a stylish person dresses and grooms to show off their individual strengths.

WHAT IS A SINGLE THING YOU WOULD DO TO BRING A DULL HOUSE TO LIFE?

The most important thing I can do for my clients is encourage them to show their personality through their home design.

Liberty 123, LLC
Mary Hanson
123 Park Lane
Kirkland, WA 98033
425.822.1232
Fax 425.889.9560

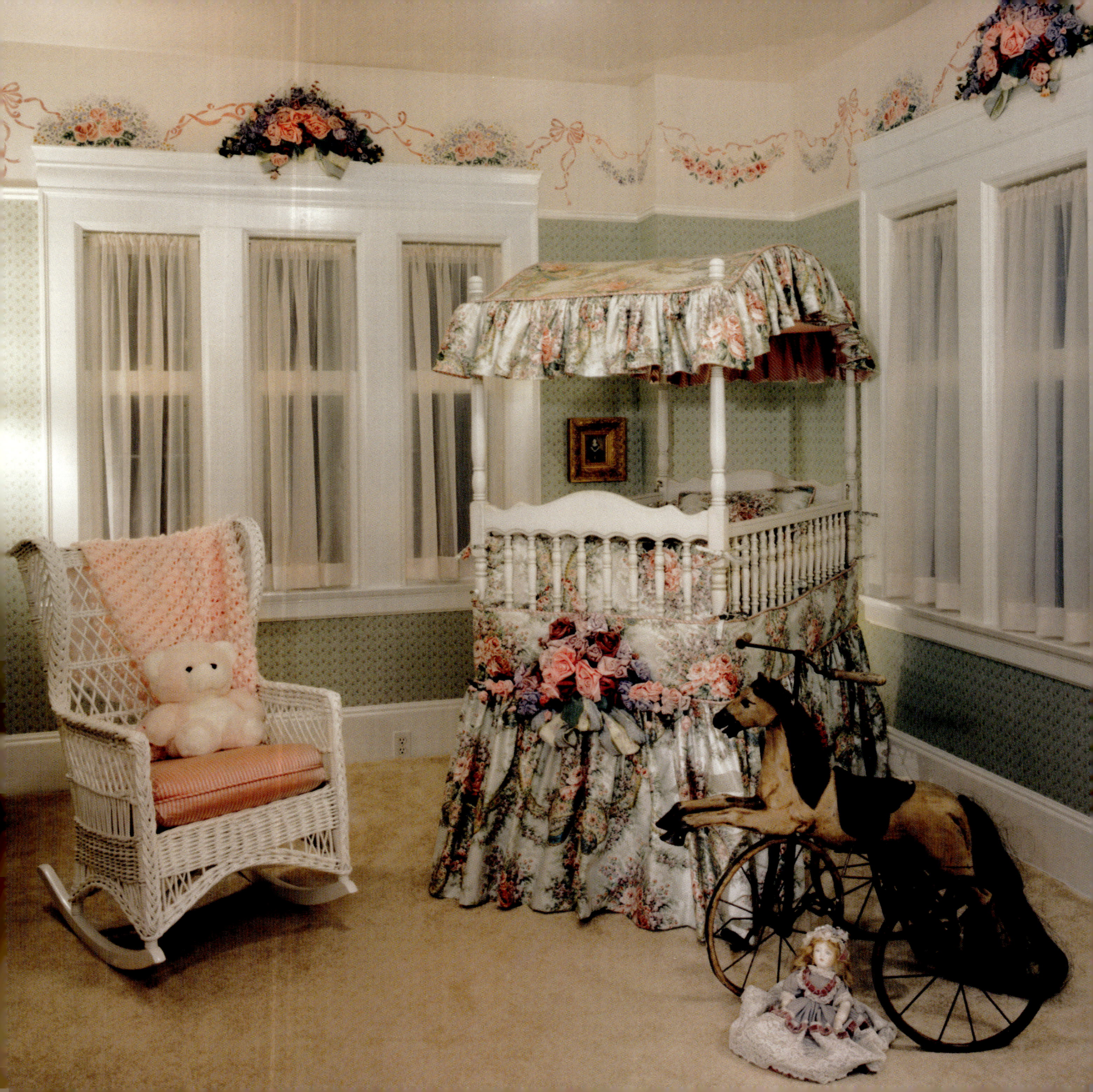

Fran M. Hazel

Fran M. Hazel Design Interiors

As a 20-year veteran of the design industry, Fran knows her stuff—and she is extraordinarily proficient at one of the most important design skills: listening.

"It sounds funny, but I listen with my ears and my eyes," she says. "I glean the most from my clients by looking at what they already have, at what they like to surround themselves with."

Fran's personal taste runs toward country cottage and contemporary. But one peek at her portfolio and it becomes clear that Fran is fluent in many design languages, including English, French, transitional and eclectic. "My personal style doesn't come into play when I design for a client," she says. "If I'm going to be worth my weight in gold as a designer, then I should know enough about design to be able to accomplish all styles."

One of Fran's favorite projects involved finding a creative way for her client to incorporate an antique stained-glass church window into her new home. Building codes would not allow the window to be on the outside of the building, so Fran devised an unusual and beautiful solution: she hung the window on a wall at the top of the staircase. "The backside of the wall was a walk-in closet, so we put up a little false wall in the back of the closet," Fran says. "Between the window and the false wall, we installed lights. Now when you go up the stairs, it looks like sunlight is coming through the window."

Grateful to have a career that she loves, Fran spends a lot of time in homes—when she's not designing someone else's, you can find her in her own home with her husband Geoff, her three children and her six kitties.

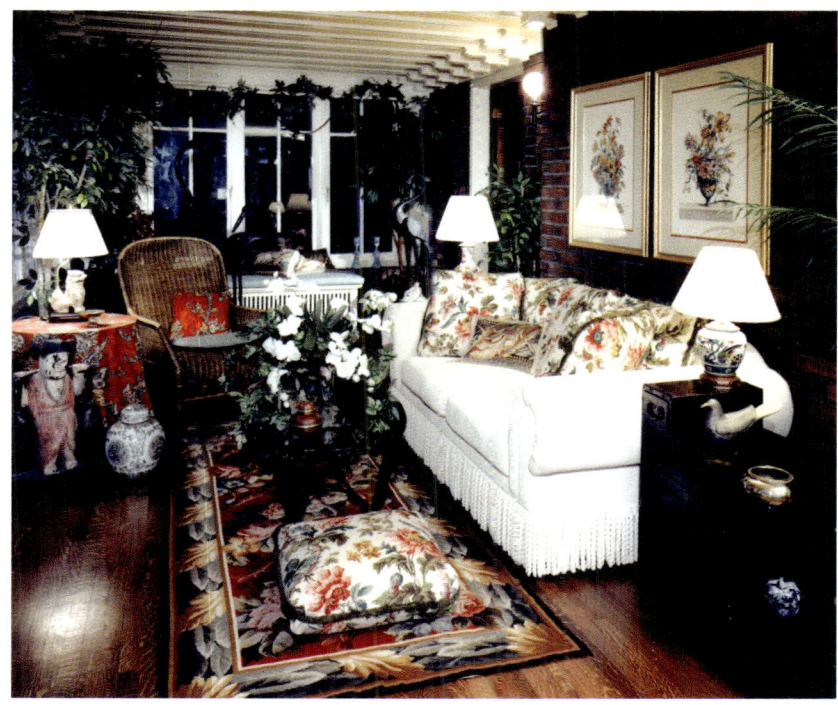

ABOVE
This Asian influenced garden room creates a cozy space to enjoy a 180 degree view of downtown Seattle.

LEFT
Pink and green with a mature flora allows this nursery to grow with Jenny.

Fran M. Hazel Design Interiors
Fran M. Hazel
2428 129th Ave. SE
Bellevue, WA 98005
425.641.0191
Fax 425.401.6554
www.franmhazeldesign.com

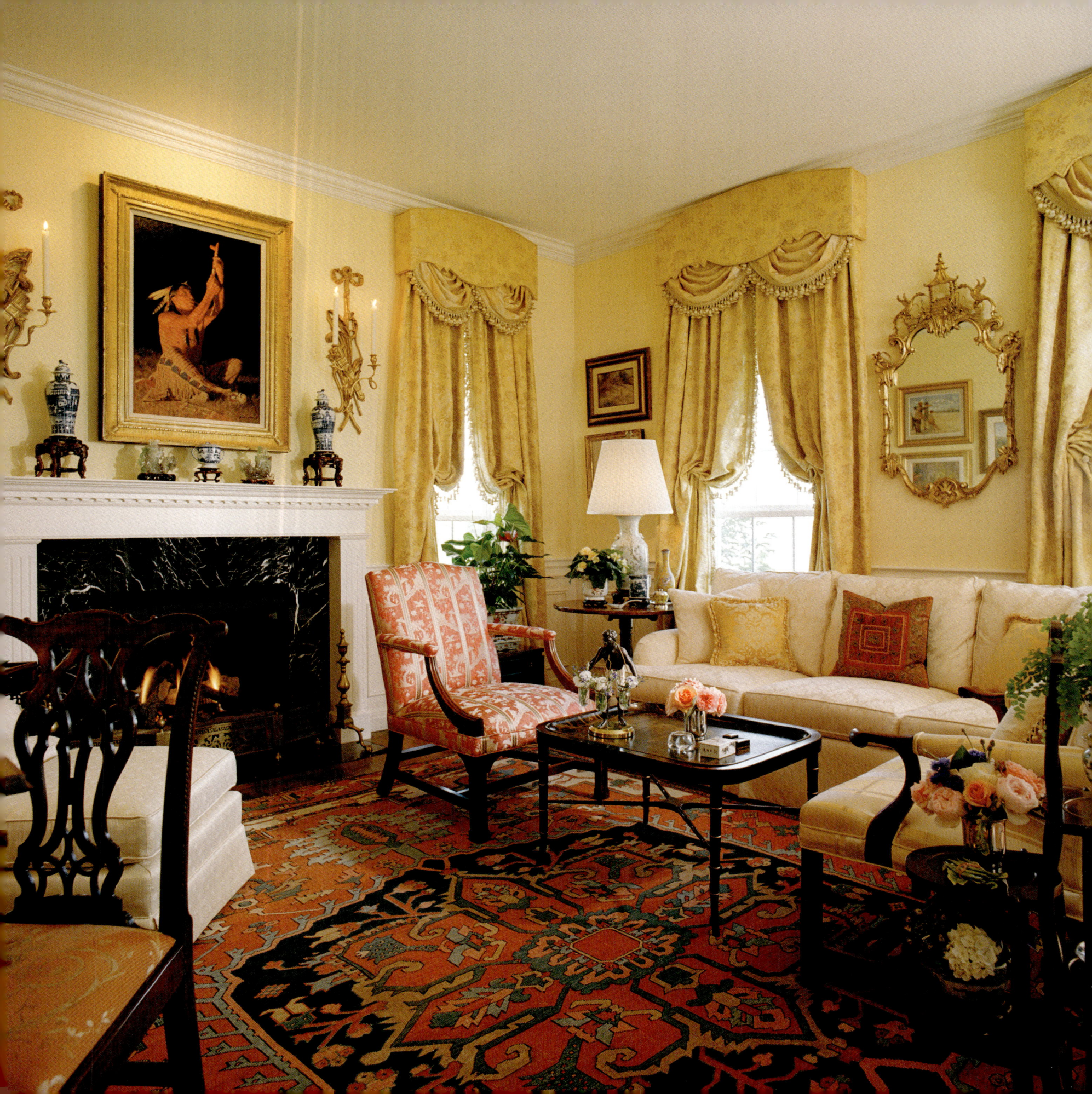

MICHÈLE HEIDT

HEIDT & OLDFIELD DESIGN

Sophisticated, serene, elegant and timeless—these are words that are often used to describe designer Michèle Heidt, but they also perfectly capture the feel of Michèle's residential designs.

"My design philosophy incorporates classical elements redefined for today's active families and lifestyles," Michèle says. "I am dedicated to integrity of design, balance and elegance. Fine craftsmanship and quality is paramount and is the hallmark of any room that I design, whether the design is traditional or contemporary. Each room should be able to age gracefully and be viewed as great design even 20 years from now."

Michèle entered the interior design business in 1989. She worked in Toronto, Santa Fe, Savannah and Florida before heading to Seattle, where she opened Heidt & Oldfield Design in 1999. "My business is based on very personal service and relationships with my clients," she says.

An Allied ASID member, Michèle serves on the advisory board of *Fine Interiors*, a national design magazine and publishes an article in each issue on theme table settings. She was published in *Northwest Home and Garden* in November 2005.

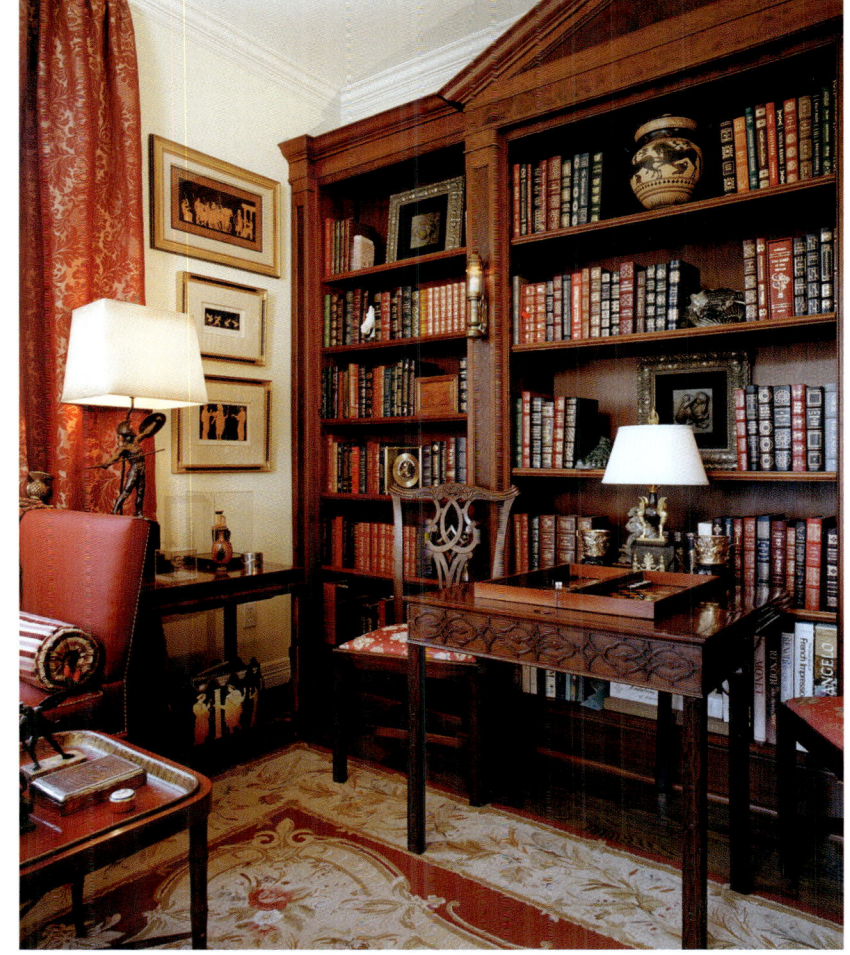

LEFT
Heidt selected a palette of yellow and red paired with an antique "Serapi" rug, English antiques, Scalamandre and Schumacher fabrics to create an elegant setting for a collection of American paintings using "Plains Indian" by David Mann as a focal point.

RIGHT
Library features a cherry and burl-madrona bookcase custom designed by Heidt and displays the owner's collection of antique Greek, Roman and Egyptian artifacts. Sir William Hamilton prints complement the collection.

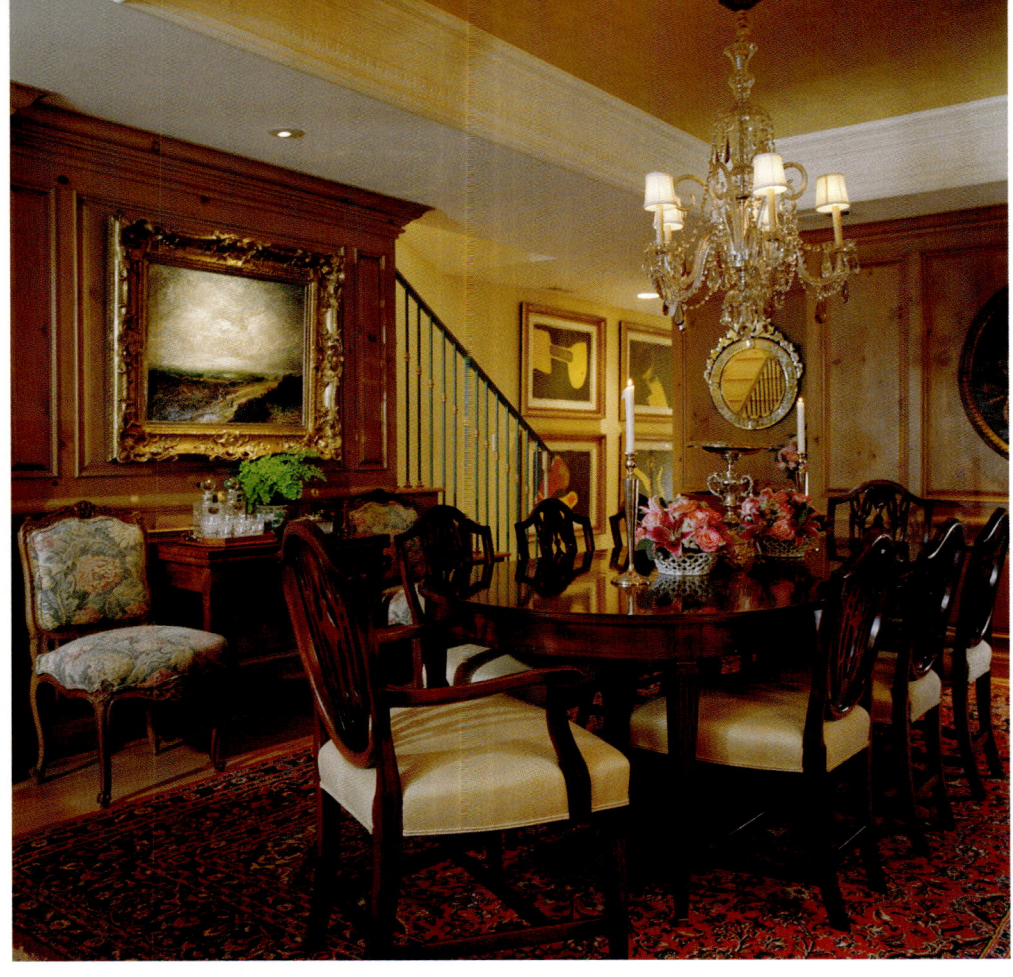

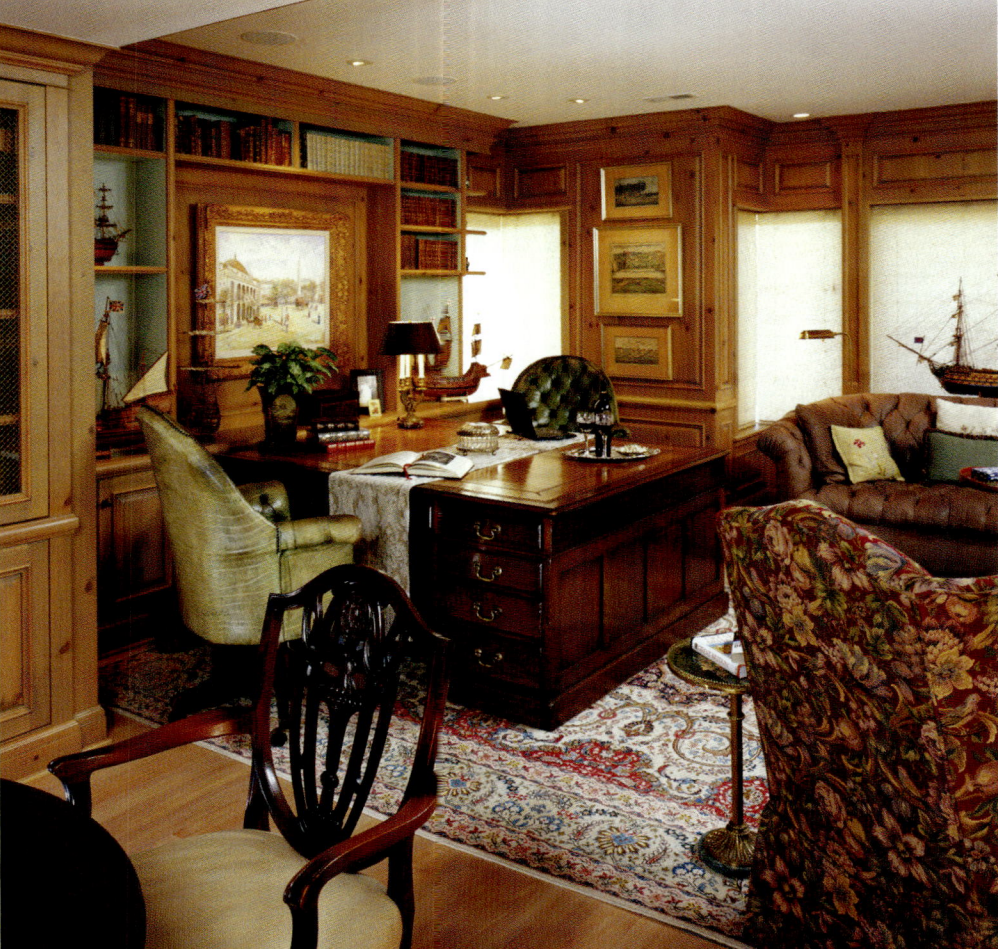

Talented and driven, Michèle loves to tackle a project from the ground up. On a recent condominium project, she completely reconstructed the condo by removing all interior walls and designing a new floor plan for the client, who was downsizing. To meet her client's needs, Michèle also relocated the kitchen and bathrooms, moved all of the heating, air-conditioning, electrical and electronics systems, and then designed the details and surfaces of the interior. "I love being the project manager for long-term projects like this," she says.

Michèle's clients benefit from her drive and knowledge in other ways as well: she always takes the time to help them develop their own personal style. She accomplishes this by showing clients how they can use existing art, furnishings and items of sentimental value to create a sophisticated, serene environment that reflects their personality.

While on trips, Michèle always keeps her clients in mind, and will often purchase a piece of art, a sculpture or other design element for them. "I believe that the best is not necessarily the most expensive, but the best is what is most appropriate," she says. "I give my clients good value by shopping creatively and finding those unusual pieces that are focused on detail and quality, just as I would for myself."

There's one other word that can be used to describe Michèle: Perfectionist. "It's the challenges and the results that drive me. I never leave a project half-finished and I strive to deliver more than what the client expects," Michèle says.

TOP & BOTTOM
This dining room and library are part of a complete 3-story condo remodel. To satisfy the client's request to have large dinner parties, both rooms were paneled in pine with a 7-step finish to give an aged patina. "When necessary, the table can extend into the library" says Heidt. The antique furniture mixed with old master (John Constable), French impressionist (Claude Pissarro) and contemporary art (Louise Hoeschen-Goldberg) enliven the space.

FACING PAGE RIGHT
"I loved creating this living room for a professional couple. It was to be used daily, reflect the clients' favorite colors of blue and yellow and be a sophisticated environment," Heidt remarks.

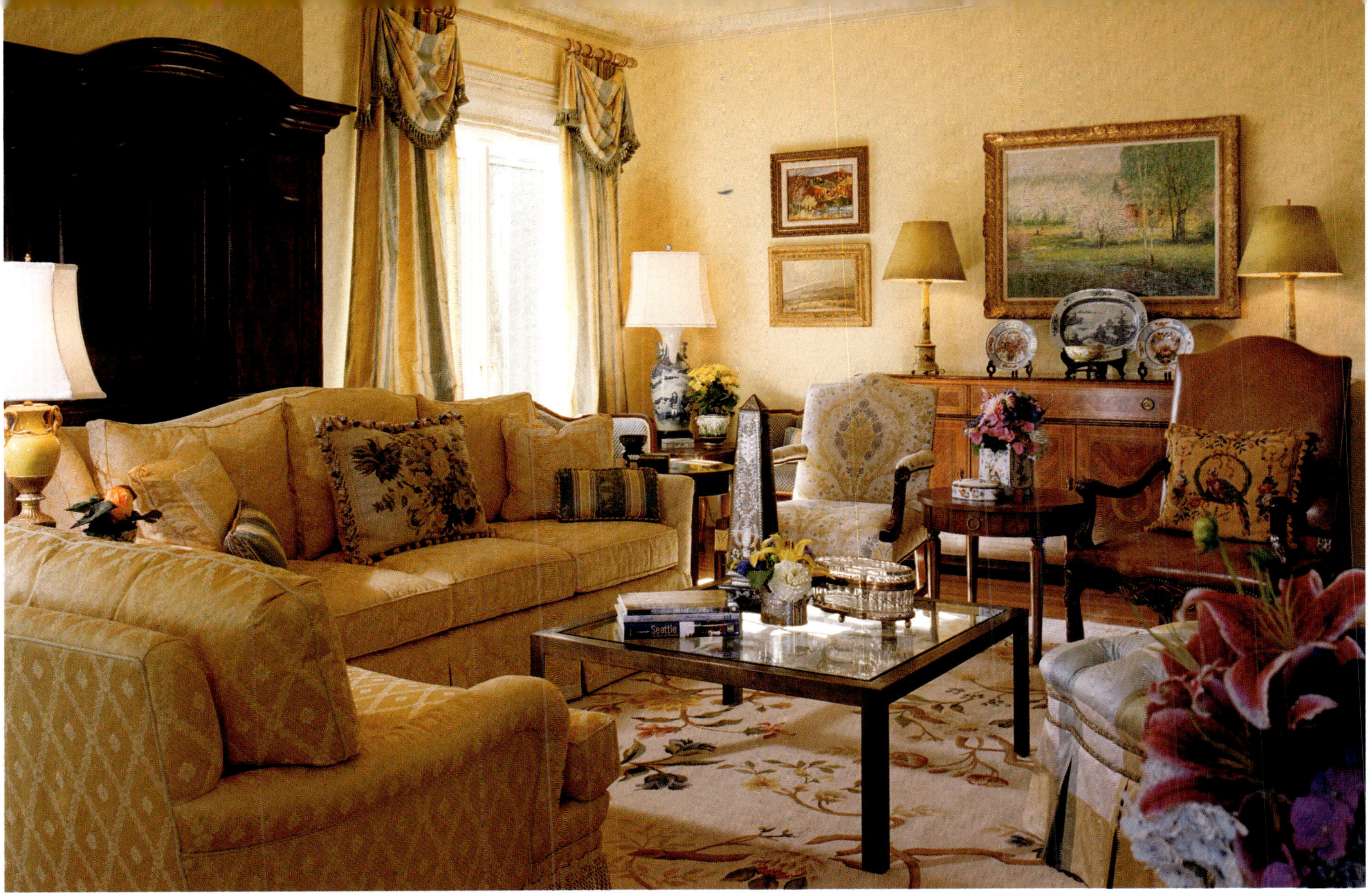

More about Michèle…

WHAT COLOR BEST DESCRIBES YOU AND WHY?

How can I select a favorite color when all colors are important to me? Each environment requires different colors in order to fulfill the design requirement. I often mix my own paint colors. My own home interior is various shades of yellow, because it reflects the light and gives the rooms life, especially in our somber winters.

WHAT SEPARATES YOU FROM YOUR COMPETITION?

I have lived and traveled extensively in many locales and in different cultures. My husband and I collect antiques and have an eclectic art collection as well as an extensive library on architecture, antiques and design. All this exposure is reflected in my design work. In addition, my extensive knowledge of construction techniques coupled with my creativity and understanding of human nature allows me to help clients achieve a mutually desired and exciting design concept focused on a common vision.

WHAT PERSONAL INDULGENCE DO YOU SPEND THE MOST MONEY ON?

I have a passion for collecting 18th century Chinese Blue and White porcelain, both Chinese export or those items made for the Chinese market.

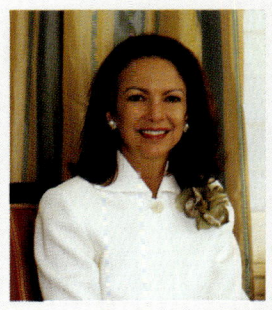

Heidt & Oldfield Design
Michèle Heidt, Allied Member ASID
4893 160th Court SE
Bellevue, WA 98006
425.401.6936
Fax 425.401.6936

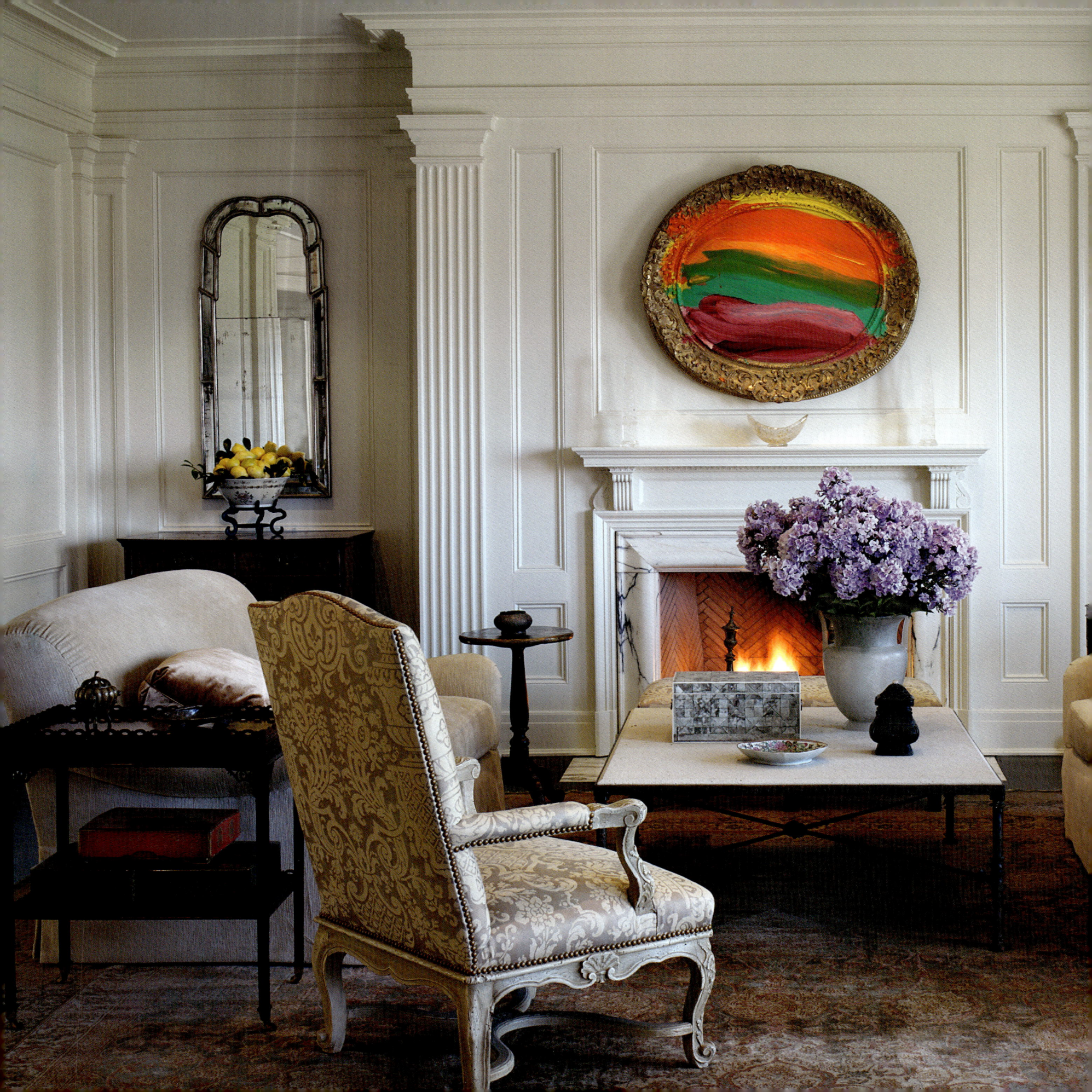

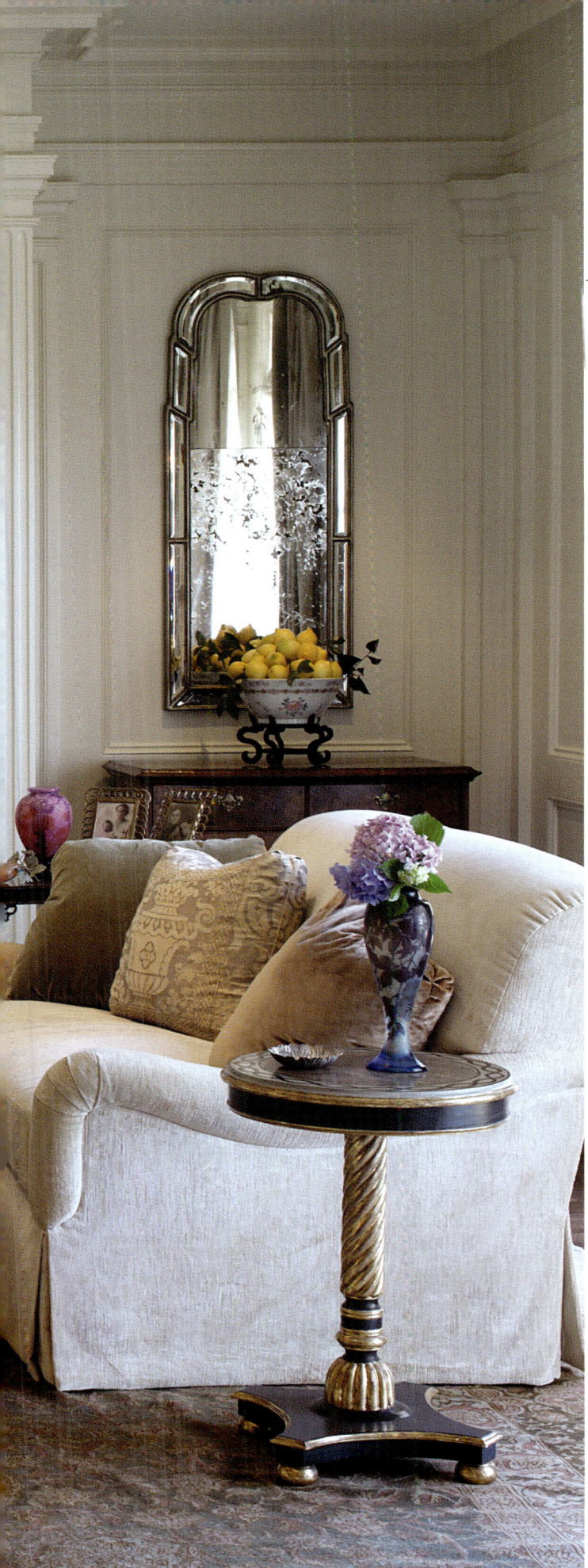

LARRY HOOKE

Larry Hooke Interior Design

For Seattle designer Larry Hooke, his design style is "traditional to transitional." This hard to define style is grounded in a traditional format or point of view, while keeping its orientation in a present day modern mentality. "I believe there is nothing more enduring or livable than good traditional design, with your feet planted firmly in the present," he says.

Every project begins with planning the practical aspects of client's rooms and their usage, as well as the color and fabric selections. The other major consideration are the clients themselves and their lifestyle. There is no greater compliment than to hear "it looks just like them!" "That to me is the ultimate compliment and measure of a successful interior project–besides, of course, that it is beautiful!" says Larry.

Almost all furniture and drapery treatments are custom designed to the specifications of the scheme with the priority being "old-world" quality and craftsmanship. "Beautifully made, comfortable furnishings endure and last, "trends come and go but when something is really great, it is always great-period!" Larry sources most of his antiques, accessories and art for projects out of town in cities such as San Francisco and New York.

"A period room recreation is never my intention because although you can draw inspiration from past styles, our modern times have so many great things to offer a home and our lifestyles."

LEFT
Howard Hodgkins "Out My Window" 1998 hangs over the mantle flanked by George I Walnut chests and custom-designed mirrors. A Giacommetti coffee table rests on an important signed Sivas rug with painted Regence armchairs covered in Fortuny.

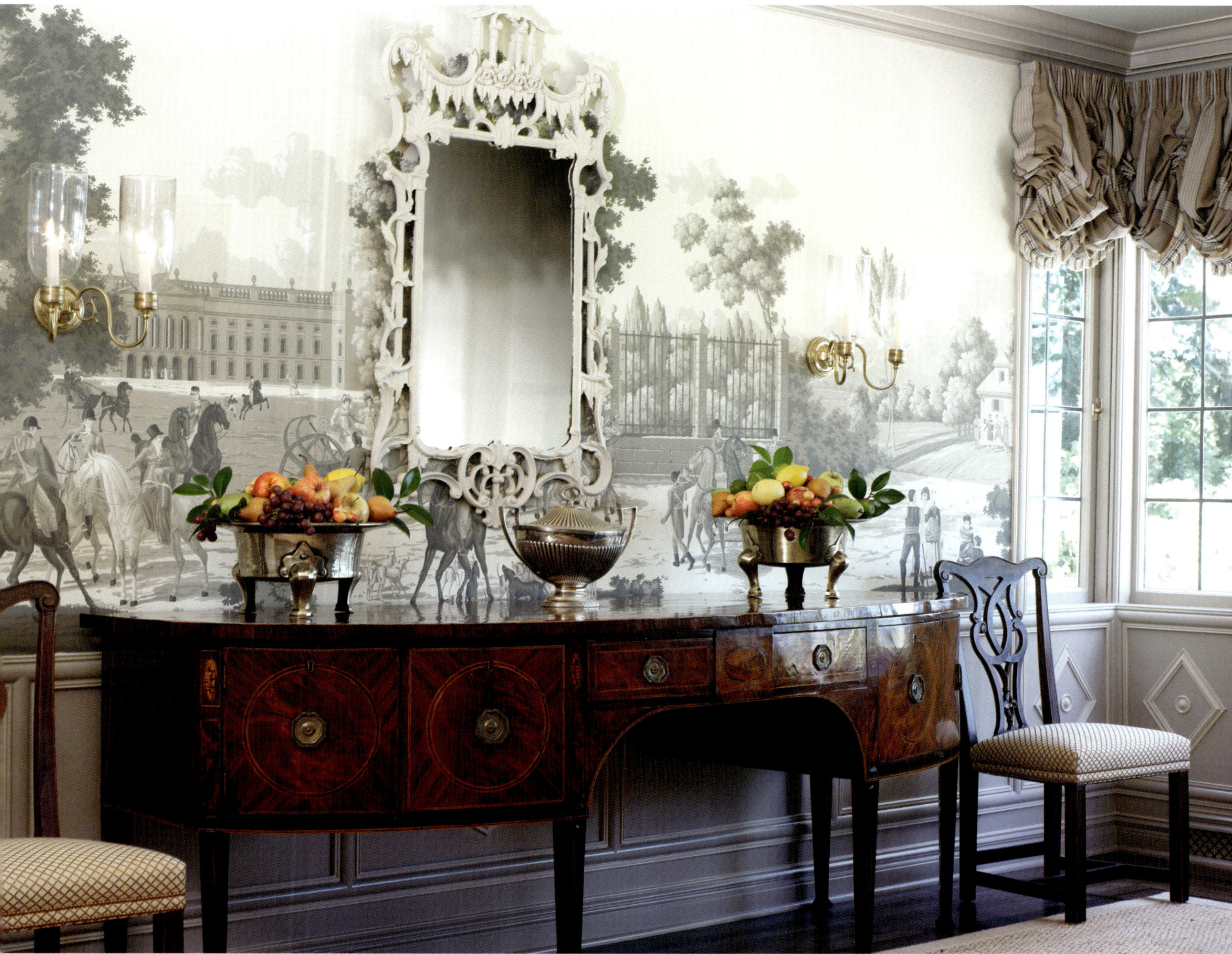

ABOVE
Custom-painted "La Chasse" Mural by deGournay of London sets the tone for a dining room with a painted Chippendale mirror and a Georgian sideboard formerly in the collection of Ann Landers.

FACING PAGE RIGHT
A rock crystal chandelier and candlesticks against a silver leafed wallpaper background add drama to a dining room with a Willem de Kooning painting of a nude and a massive Chinese Export punch bowl.

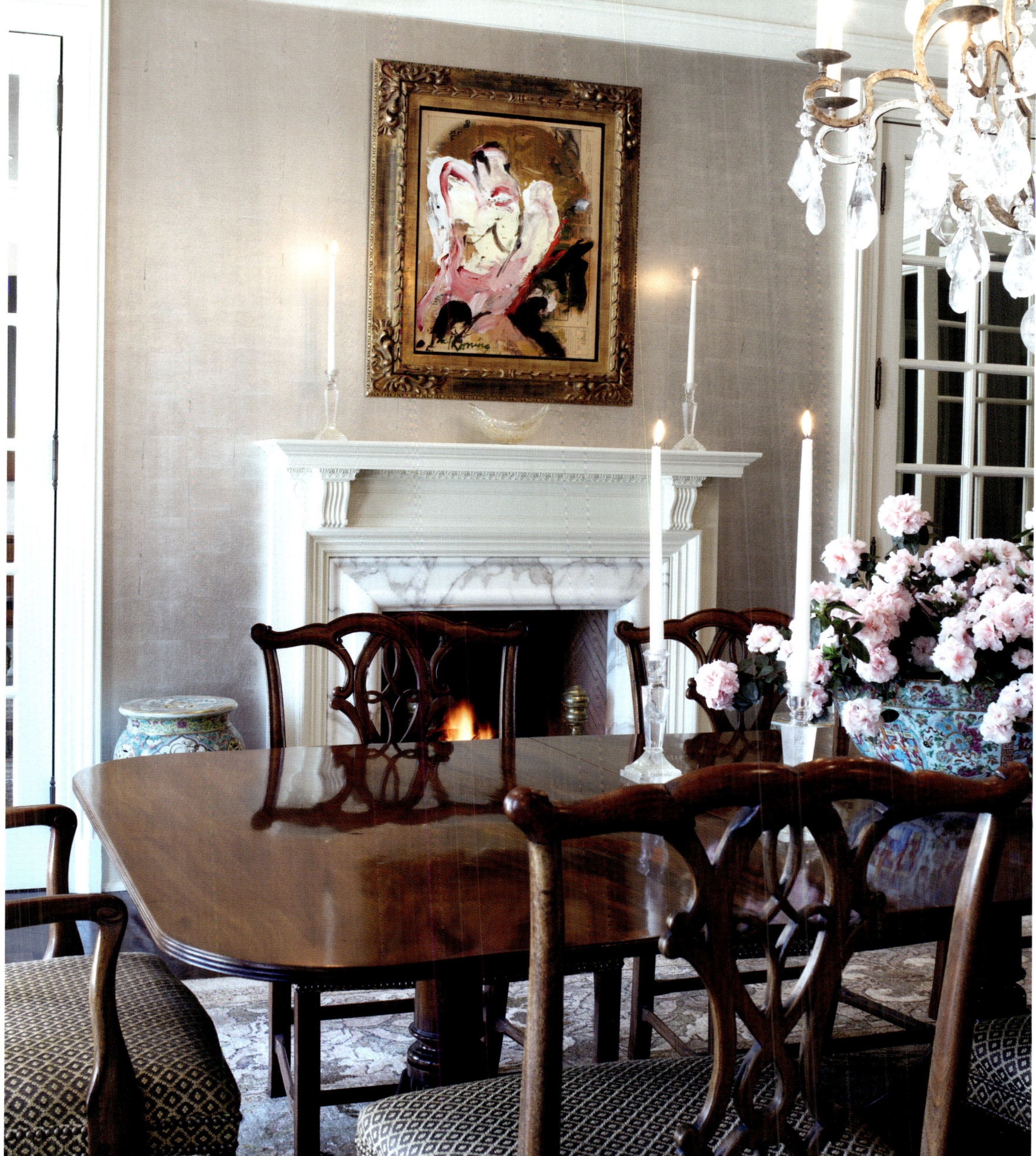

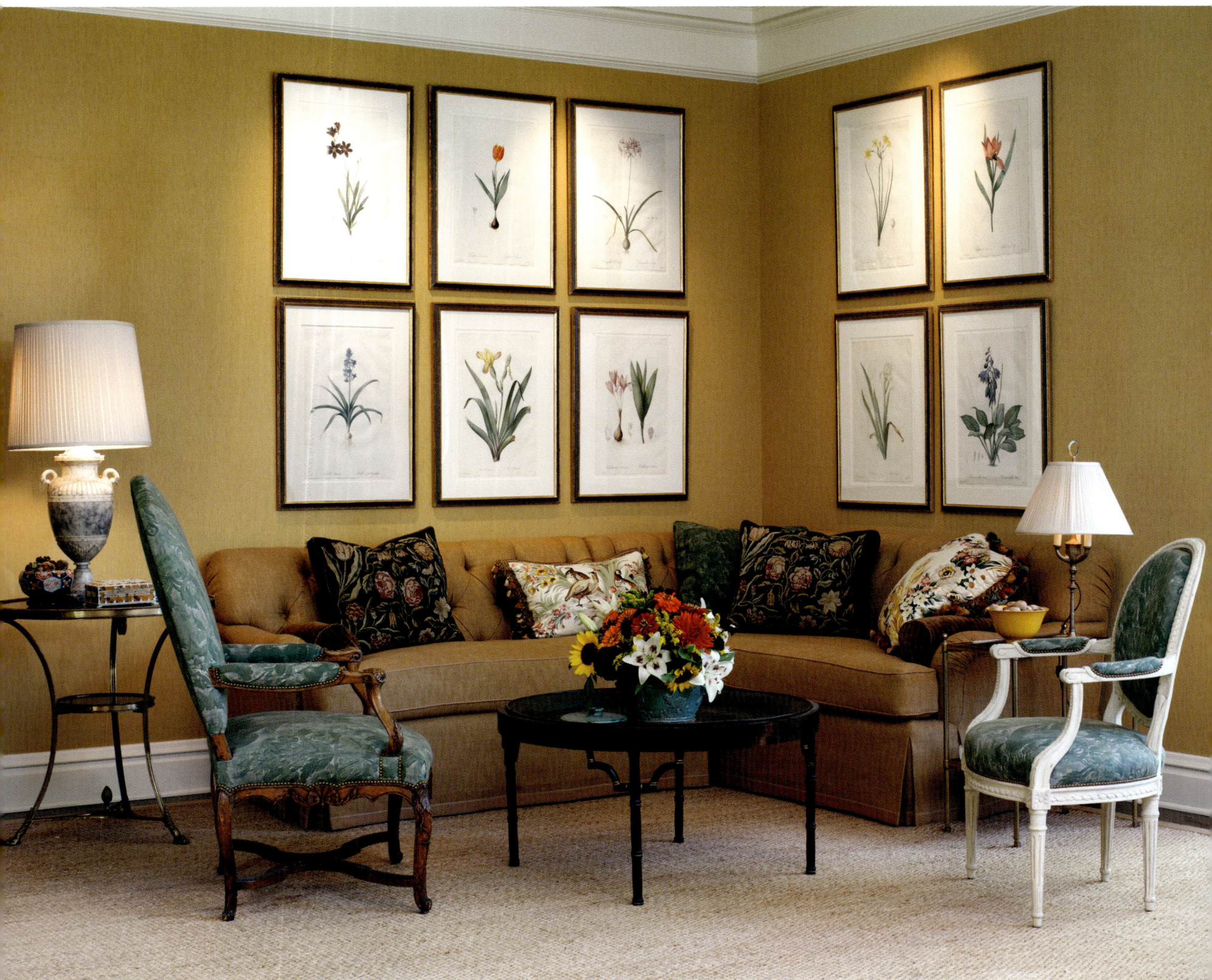

ABOVE
A set of ten late 18th century Redouté botanicals over a custom sectional anchor a living room corner with period French chairs covered in Fortuny and 17th century floral tapestry pillows.

FACING PAGE RIGHT
Louis XVI gilt fauteuils covered in Fortuny flank a silk mohair sofa in a subdued master bedroom.

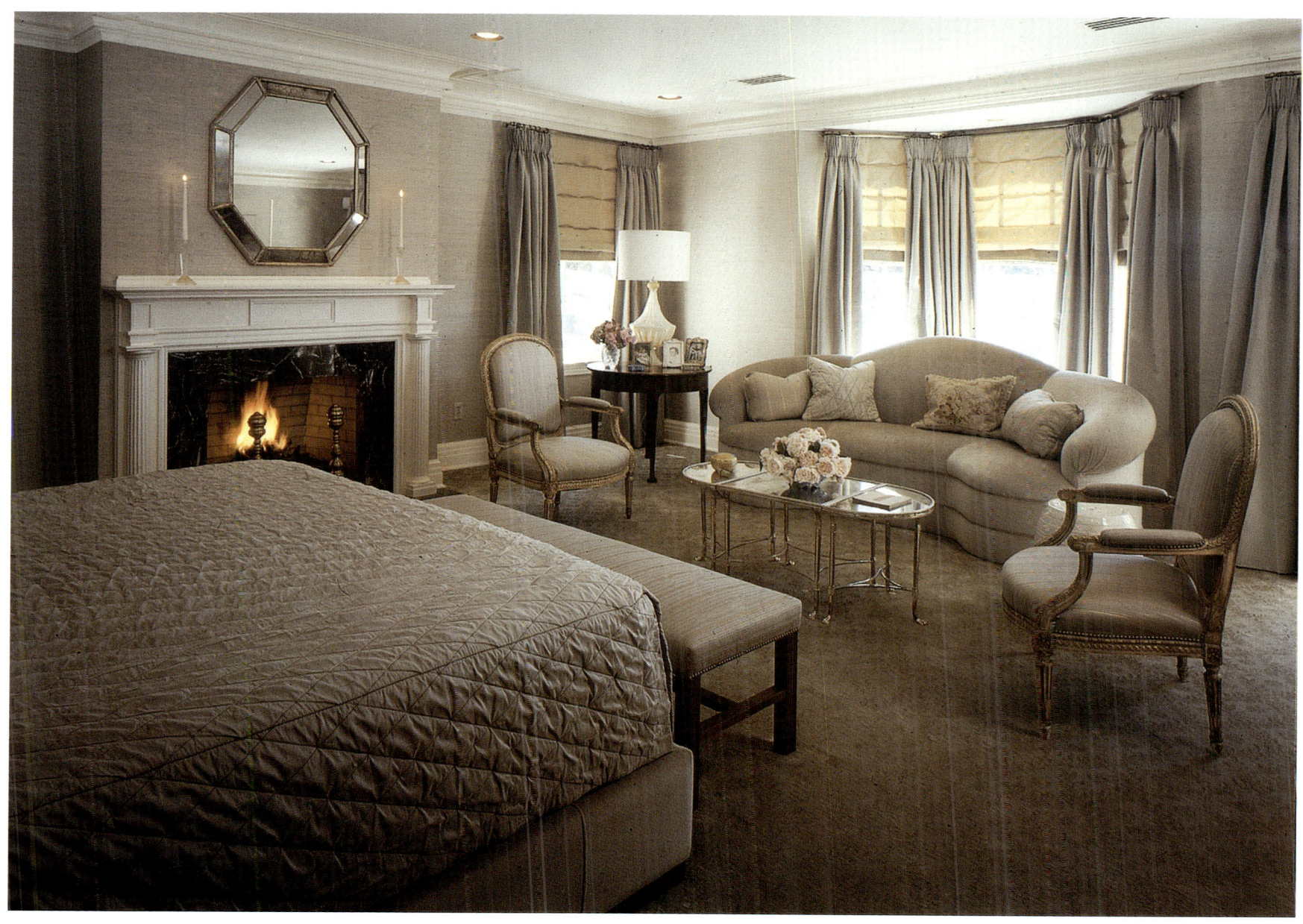

More about Larry…

WHAT PERSONAL INDULGENCE DO YOU SPEND THE MOST MONEY ON?

My collection of art and antiques.

WHAT ONE ELEMENT OF STYLE OR PHILOSOPHY HAVE YOU STUCK WITH FOR YEARS THAT STILL WORKS FOR YOU TODAY?

"Do it right the first time."

WHO HAS HAD THE BIGGEST INFLUENCE ON YOUR CAREER?

Rose Tarlow, Jean Jongeward and Michael Taylor.

WHAT IS A SINGLE THING YOU WOULD DO TO BRING A DULL HOUSE TO LIFE?

Quality.

Larry Hooke Interior Design
Larry Hooke
Seattle, WA
206-328-9290

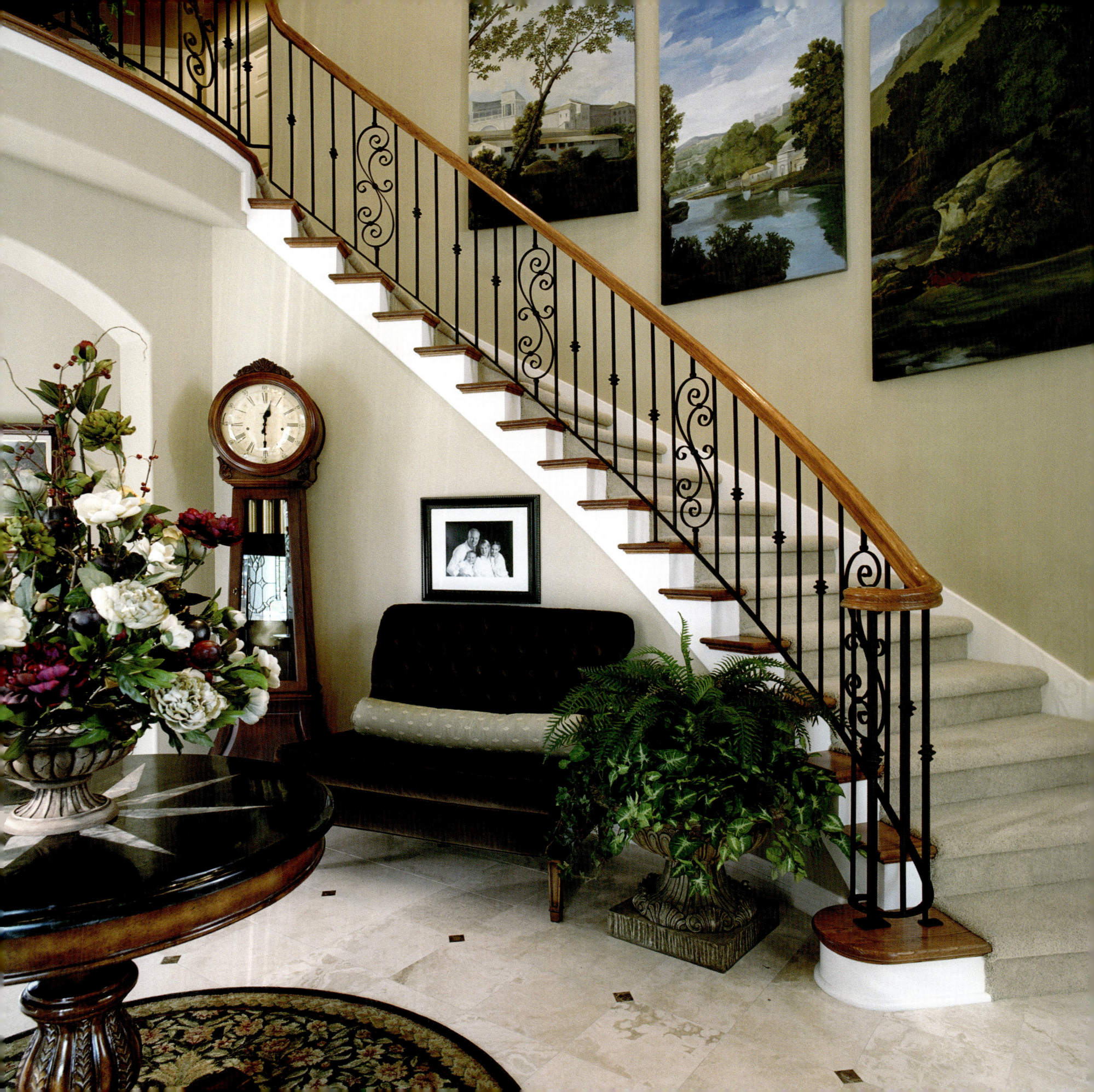

TAMI JONES
Tami Jones Interior Design

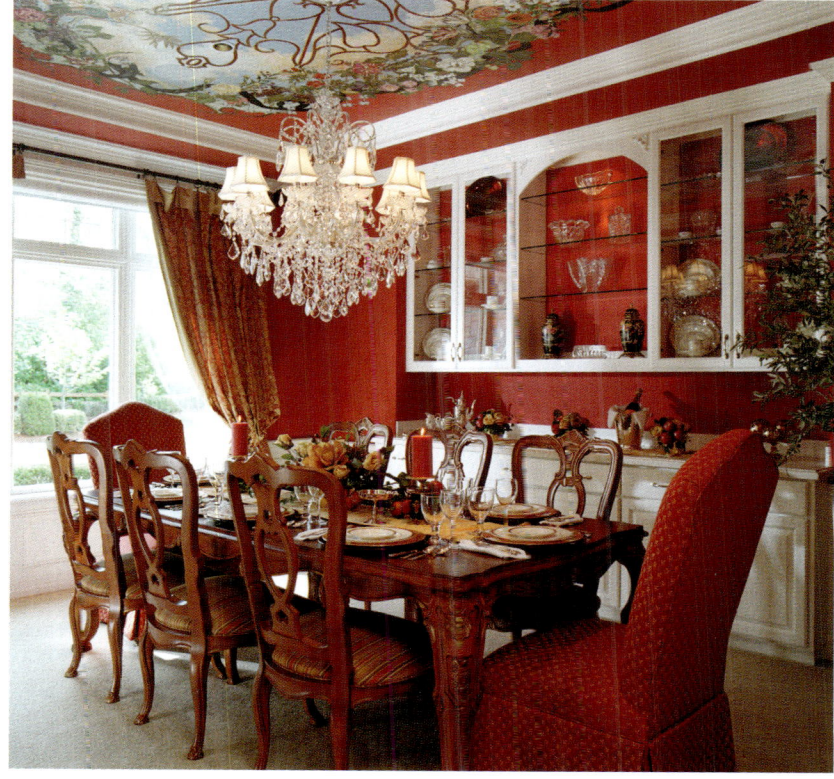

There's no doubt in Tami Jones' mind that she's in the right career. This talented young designer loves everything about what she does, from using beautiful fabrics and custom wall treatments to helping clients turn their space problems into space solutions.

Before entering the design world, Tami worked in the high-tech industry, a career that gave her a leg up in planning spaces and solving conceptual design problems. When she decided to do something else with her life, friends encouraged her to focus her talents on the design industry. It wasn't long before Tami had her degree from Bellevue Community College and a whole new career under her belt.

As a late-comer to design, Tami says she was inspired by another woman who also started her career in her mid-30s: world-renowned gourmet chef Julia Child. Like Julia, Tami may have found her dream job later than some, but she is quickly making up for lost time by rising to success in her field.

Never one to stop learning, Tami got involved with the International Interior Design Association early in her career, and has already been elected to serve a two-year term as VP of membership for the Northern Pacific Chapter of IIDA. She believes the opportunity to work with local and national design professionals has been invaluable to her own success.

For her personal style, Tami prefers clean lines, with old-world influences, but she prides herself on being able to design in a variety of styles. Whether she's creating a French country kitchen or a more contemporary space, she collaborates closely with her client to create the environment of their dreams.

ABOVE
View from entry into formal living room—custom florals created by Ambassador Imports, Inc., formal dining room with custom hand painted mural on the ceiling and custom design window treatments.

LEFT
Entryway, spiral stair case with original artwork. Custom florals by Ambassador Imports, Inc.

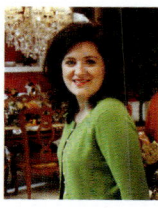

Tami Jones Interior Design
Tami Jones
PO Box 405
Fall City, WA 98024
425.260.1337

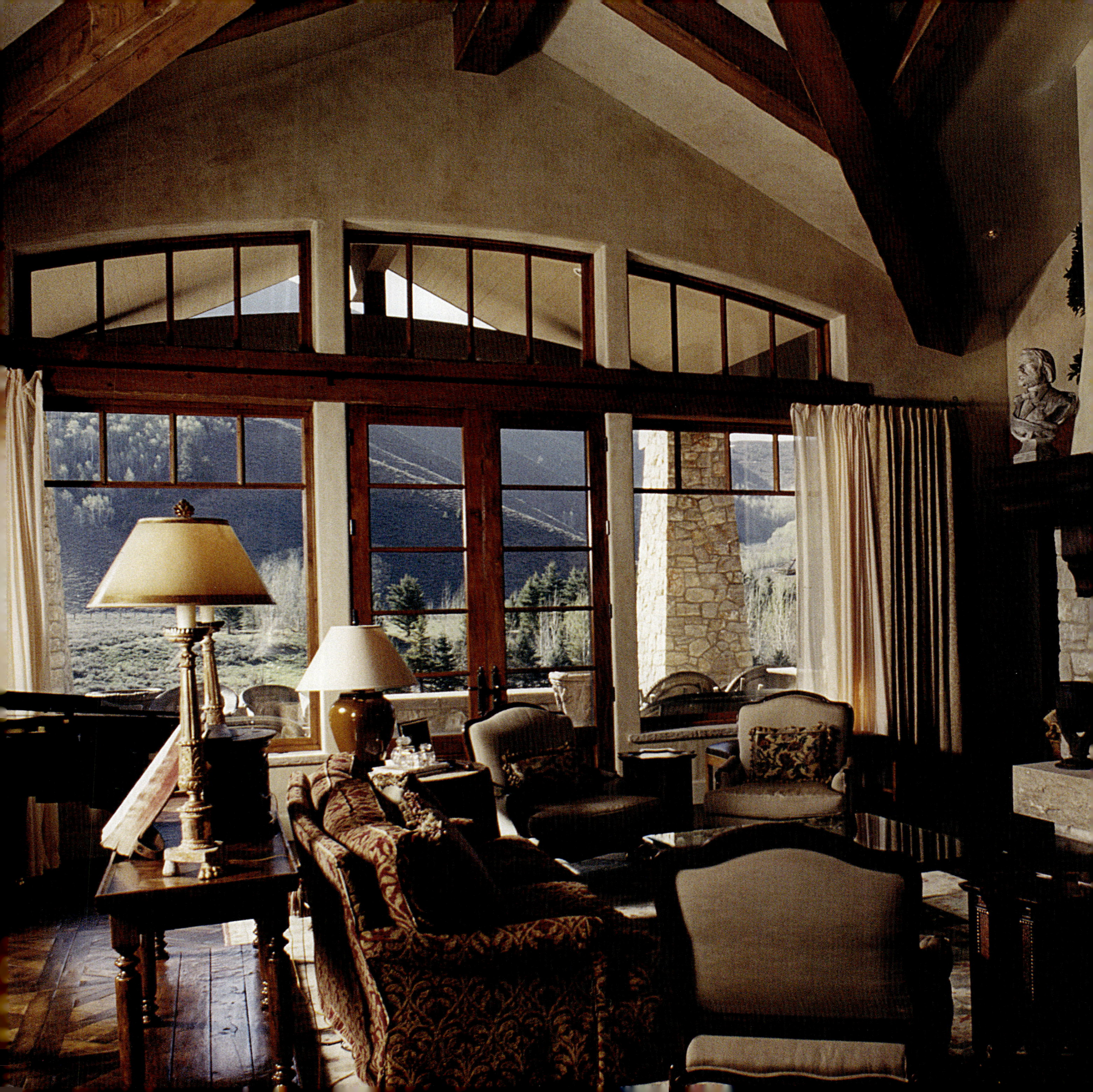

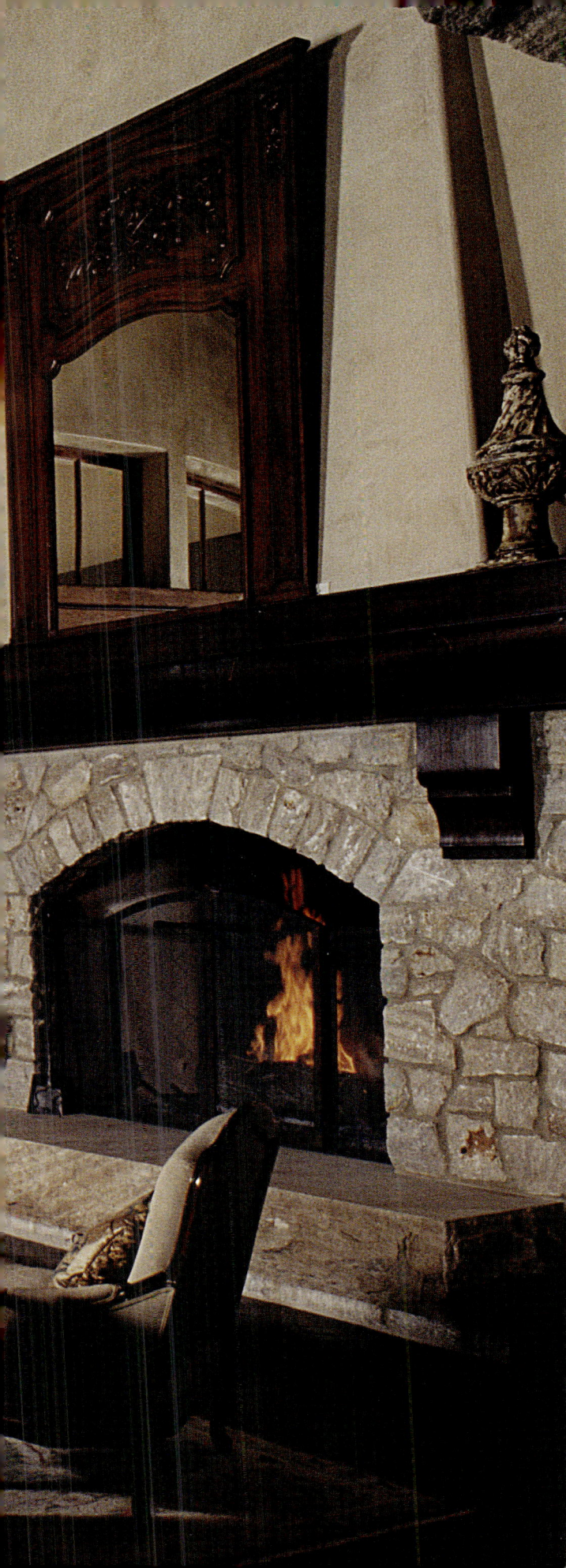

Cynthia Mennella

Cynthia Mennella Design

If you asked clients to describe what it's like to work with Cynthia Mennella, they would praise her straight-forward approach and style, her cooperative efforts, and her project leadership. And that's before they even get into her design expertise and her attention to detail. It's easy, then, to see why Cynthia's clients return to her time after time, trusting her to complete entire projects.

Cynthia likes nothing better than taking on new construction ventures, preferably as a charter member of the design team, along with the project architect and builder. "My involvement starts at the preliminary architectural phase," she says. "I'm deeply involved from the initial schematic design, through the construction build-out, to when we're installing the furniture."

The majority of Cynthia's clients are West Coast-based but that doesn't keep her from being on the go. Her clients request her design services on their primary high-end residences and secondary homes in places as diverse as Sun Valley, New York City, Los Angeles, London and St. Jean Cap Ferrat, France. Cynthia has also worked on private aircraft, helicopters and custom-designed yachts in Amsterdam.

LEFT
The architectural intent is a combination of Sun Valley Lodge style and French Country. It resonates European references, from Southern France to the high Alpine mountains. It is spacially rich in texture, form, and uses monochromatic tones which blend to the seasonal changes.

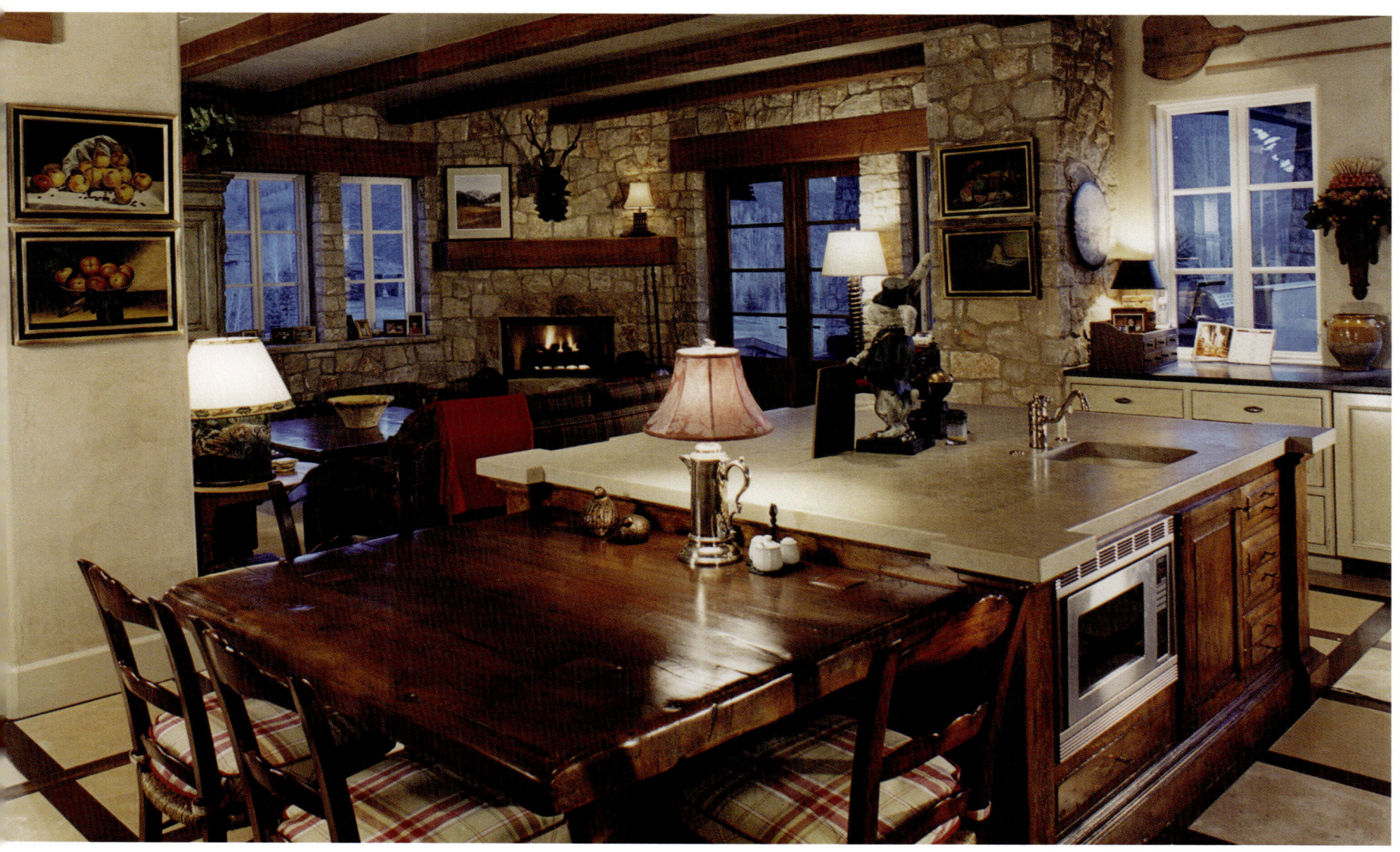

Choosing to study both art and interior design in college, Cynthia graduated from the University of Washington with a Bachelor of Interior Design and Arts History.

She then went on to earn a degree in Arts Managements from the Cornish Art Institute. After graduating, Cynthia traveled extensively, living in Switzerland for five years. She later ventured to England, France and Italy to further her studies of art, architecture and the decorative arts, which she continues to reference on projects.

A Seattle native and 25-year veteran of the design industry, Cynthia started her design career with Weston Hotels, studied with two architectural firms, became Design Director for the national firm of HNTB, and Interior Design Director for a private Northwest client, before launching her full time residential practice in 1995.

Cynthia doesn't have a signature look, but rather tries to determine a client's lifestyle and taste and lets those design elements guide the outcome. She has the ability to produce distinct design environments in a variety of styles to meet each client's personal expectations and visions.

Cynthia creates interiors that work within the parameters of the space's architectural integrity and a client's tastes, dreams and expectations. "Each design is unexpected for me, because each one is tailored for the client," she says. "I don't ever go into a project with one set style. My goal is to facilitate collaboration between the owner, the architect and the builder."

If there's anything that divulges a design as Cynthia's, it's her use of custom furnishings, upholstery, lighting and cabinetry. "I design all my cabinetry and select all the architectural elements to include custom-specialized carpets," she says. "I believe in sumptuous color, using patterns and rich textiles to create an environment. The objective is to develop environments that affirm how my clients, live, work and entertain."

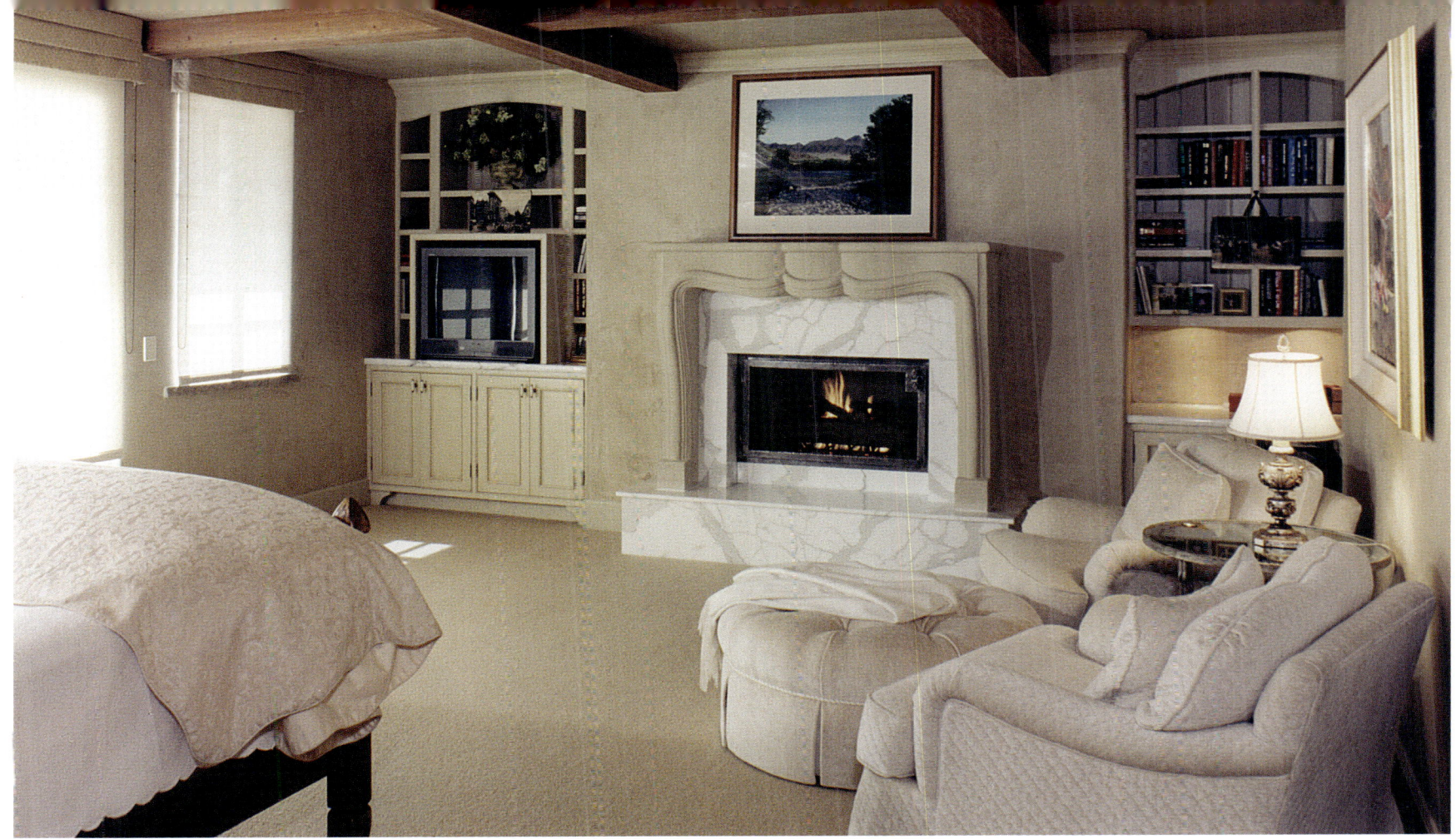

ABOVE
One is drawn to the master bedroom of wonderful light, great proportions and a mixture of textures, styles and glamour. The furnishings and bedding are a soft color palette incorporating fabrics of luminescent moirés, delicate silks, and chenilles. Hand-etched beam ceilings and a hand-carved marble fireplace of Carerra marble and limestone focus to the library wall of the room.

FACING PAGE LEFT
The owners are long term residents of Sun Valley. She is a talented gourmand, dreamed of creating a warm environment within which they could entertain family and friends. This high personality kitchen is reminiscent of Southern French kitchens, complete with a La Corneau Stone.

More about Cynthia…

DESCRIBE YOUR STYLE AND DESIGN PREFERENCES.

I am trained in all aspects of design. I have versatility and can design a multitude of styles that range from traditional to contemporary, rustic mountain lodges to beach retreats. I'm always looking to punctuate rooms with elements from different countries and cultures, creating a distinctive environment and unique look for each individual client.

WHAT SEPARATES YOU FROM YOUR COMPETITION?

I am known and respected among fellow designers for my unique approach to each project and attention to detail. I am also more deeply involved with the entire construction process, acting as the owner's representative from the initial design conception to the final move-in process.

WHAT EXCITES YOU MOST ABOUT BEING A PART OF THE SPECTACULAR HOMES OF THE PACIFIC NORTHWEST?

I am pleased to be included within a great group of designers, and to present significant work being completed within the Pacific Northwest.

Cynthia Mennella Design
Cynthia Mennella
1900 East Blaine Street
Seattle, WA 98112
206.329.0329
Fax 206.329.5288

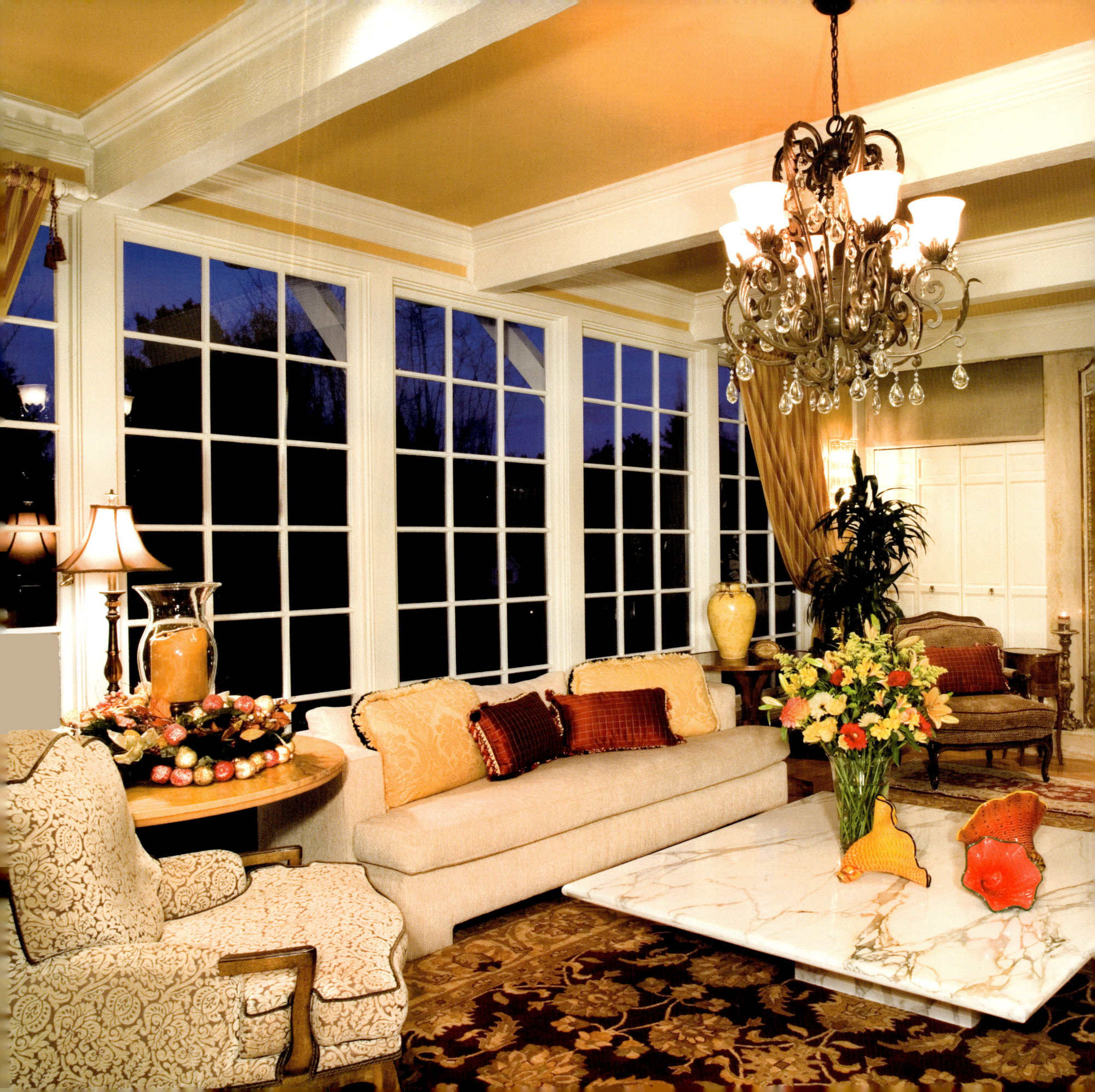

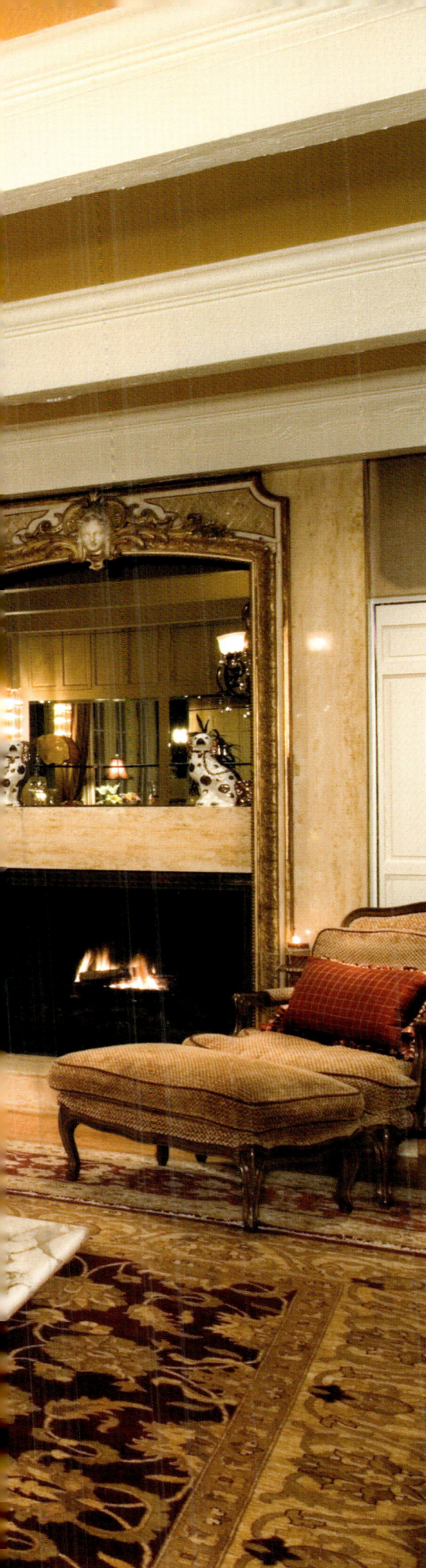

CHERYL K. MONROE
Monroe Design & Development Co.

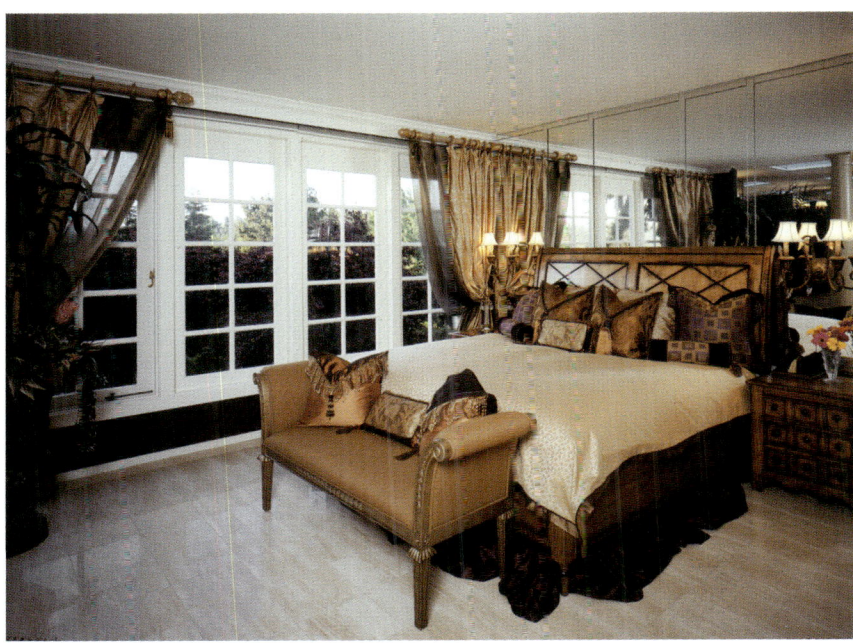

Cheryl K. Monroe might be considered a modern day Midas-everything this designer touches turns to gold. Whether she's giving a facelift to the historical Mayfair Hotel or fashioning women's fine jewelry for Saks Fifth Avenue, Cheryl's precise, creative touch makes every project sparkle.

Cheryl, a self-proclaimed workaholic, has based her design business in Washington for 37 years. About 80 percent of her workload is residential clients; the rest includes banks, hotels and stores.

Not surprisingly, Cheryl entered the design world with just as much passion and conviction as she has for the industry now. After graduating from the University of Washington, she received her M.F.A. from Fontainebleau Academy of Fine Arts in Paris. Her first project was for Wells Fargo Bank in San Francisco. It wasn't long, however, before she realized that she wanted to do her own thing. She returned to Washington and in 1967, started her own business.

RIGHT
The master suite is overlooking the French gardens below. Travertine marble floors give a villa expansive look. The furnishings of custom fabric pillows trims, and jewel beading provide detail and color.

LEFT
Antique fireplace mantle from Fountainebleau, France. The furniture is by Kreiss. Five oversized window panels allow view to the expansive gardens below.

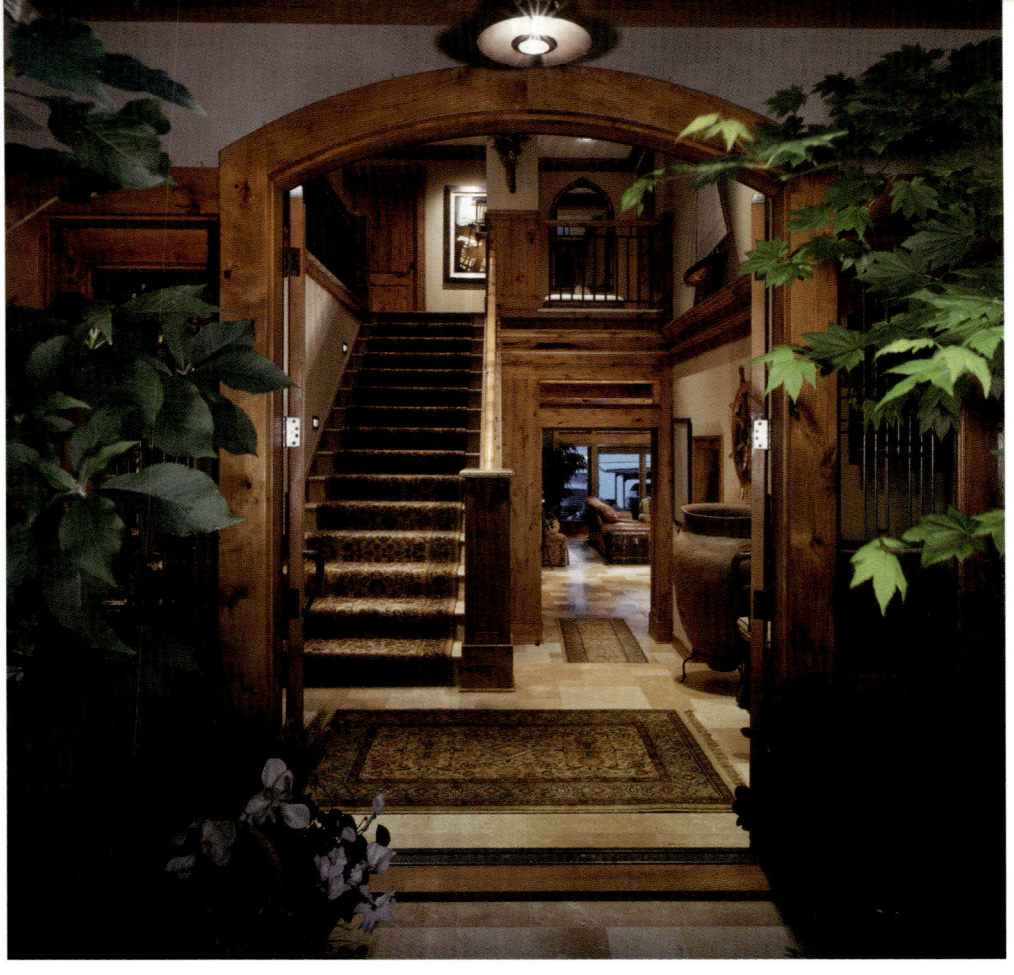

In the almost 40 years since she started, Cheryl's work has earned high praise and awards from organizations and publications. To name just a few: She received the MAME award for residential design by Seattle Master Builders Association and the Best Store of the Year award by the International Council of Shopping Centers. Her work has also appeared in publications such as *Great Designers of the World* and *100 Designer Rooms*.

But the accolades that matter most to Cheryl are the ones from her clients. She saves their letters–she loves knowing that she's helped them solve their creative challenges. "Our clients often say that we make the job enjoyable, that we take the pressure off of them," she says. "I listen to my clients, to what their requirements are, because I want to bring a solution that they'll be very happy with."

Never one to sit still for very long, Cheryl continues to travel, and loves to return to Europe, where she derives much of her inspiration. "So much of our architecture and design started in Europe," she says. "Traveling allows me to get an overall world input of what's happening in design."

Being on the road also allows Cheryl to keep in touch with her contacts around the world. Sometimes that means visiting a fabric mill to pick out something for a client. Other times, it means a trip to the Orient to choose semi-precious stones for the newest style in her 18K gold jewelry line.

For Cheryl, there is a huge parallel between jewelry design and interior design. "It's all the same design principles and the attention to details," she says.

Cheryl is proud of her business, especially because it's family owned and she has her three children, Jon, Kim and Scott Monroe, on board with her. "We already have two generations," she says.

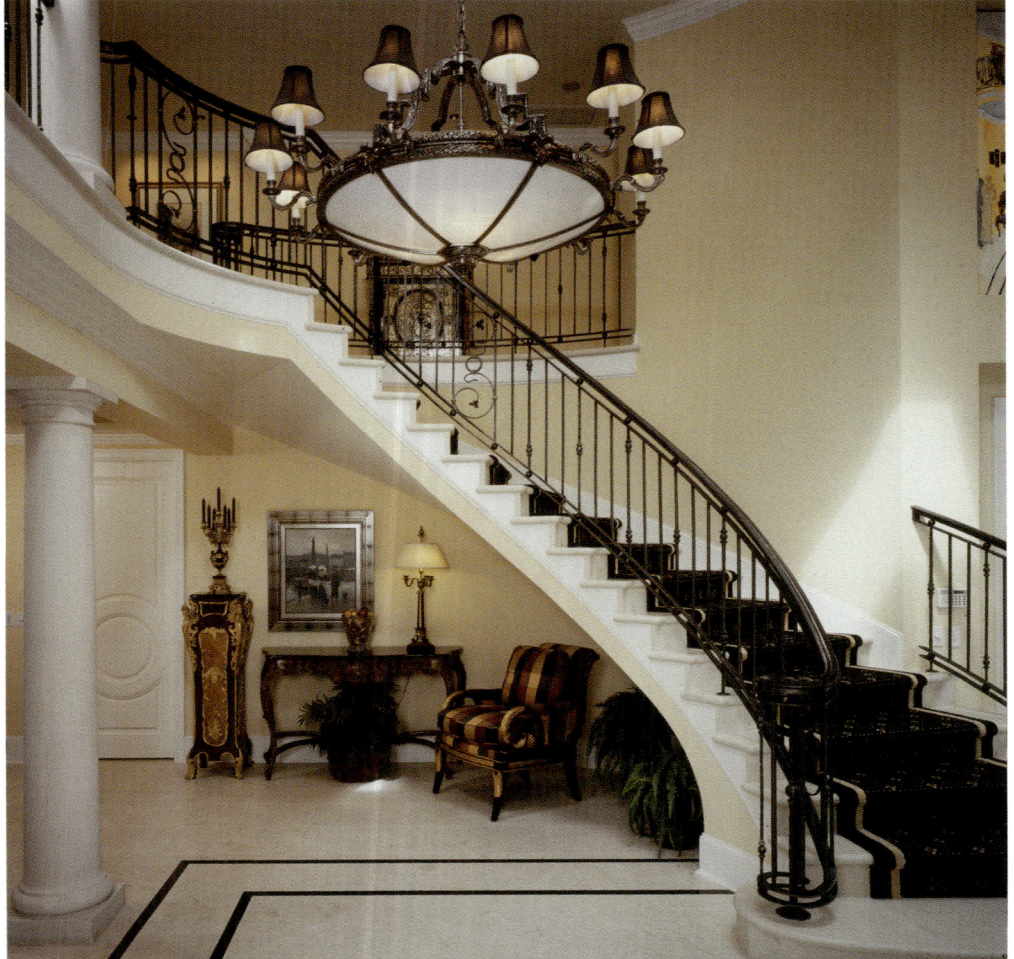

TOP
Entry foyer built with pecky cypress wood, rich wood details in beams and trims create an impression of a railroad baron's lodge.

LEFT
A residence with classic Italian character. Bulgari limestone floor with black absolute granite bands of stone. The steel staircase has limestone threads and a custom Wilton black carpet.

FACING PAGE RIGHT
Family kitchen dining with a view of formal dining room. Limestone fireplace lends warmth for family dining. The millwork is detailed with compound crown. Cove uplight in the lower beams. Cypress wood coffers.

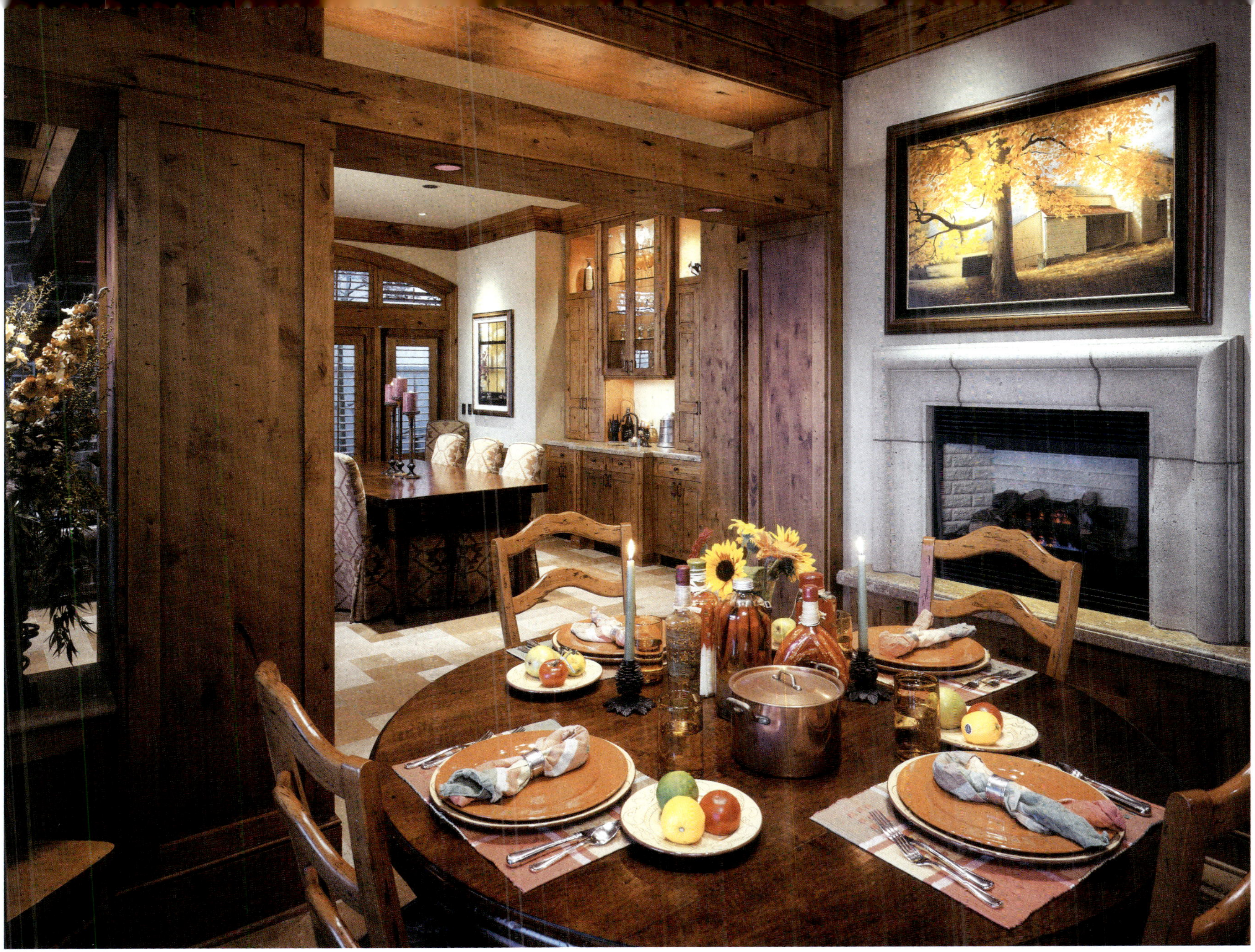

More about Cheryl...

ONE THING MOST PEOPLE DON'T KNOW ABOUT CHERYL IS ...

I was Rodeo Queen in Othello, Washington in 1956.

WHAT IS THE BEST PART OF BEING A DESIGNER/ARCHITECT?

The people we work with, they appreciate the design and uniqueness of each project.

YOU WOULDN'T KNOW IT, BUT CHERYL'S FRIENDS WOULD TELL YOU SHE...

Adores natural materials; wood, stone and outdoor living in the northwest.

WHAT COLOR BEST DESCRIBES CHERYL, AND WHY?

Yellow. It's a sunshine color, happy and expandable.

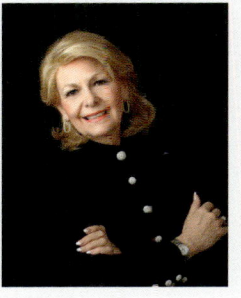

Cheryl K. Monroe
Monroe Design & Development Co.
8420 NE 10th Street
Medina, WA 98039
425.455.3227
Fax 425.455.4098

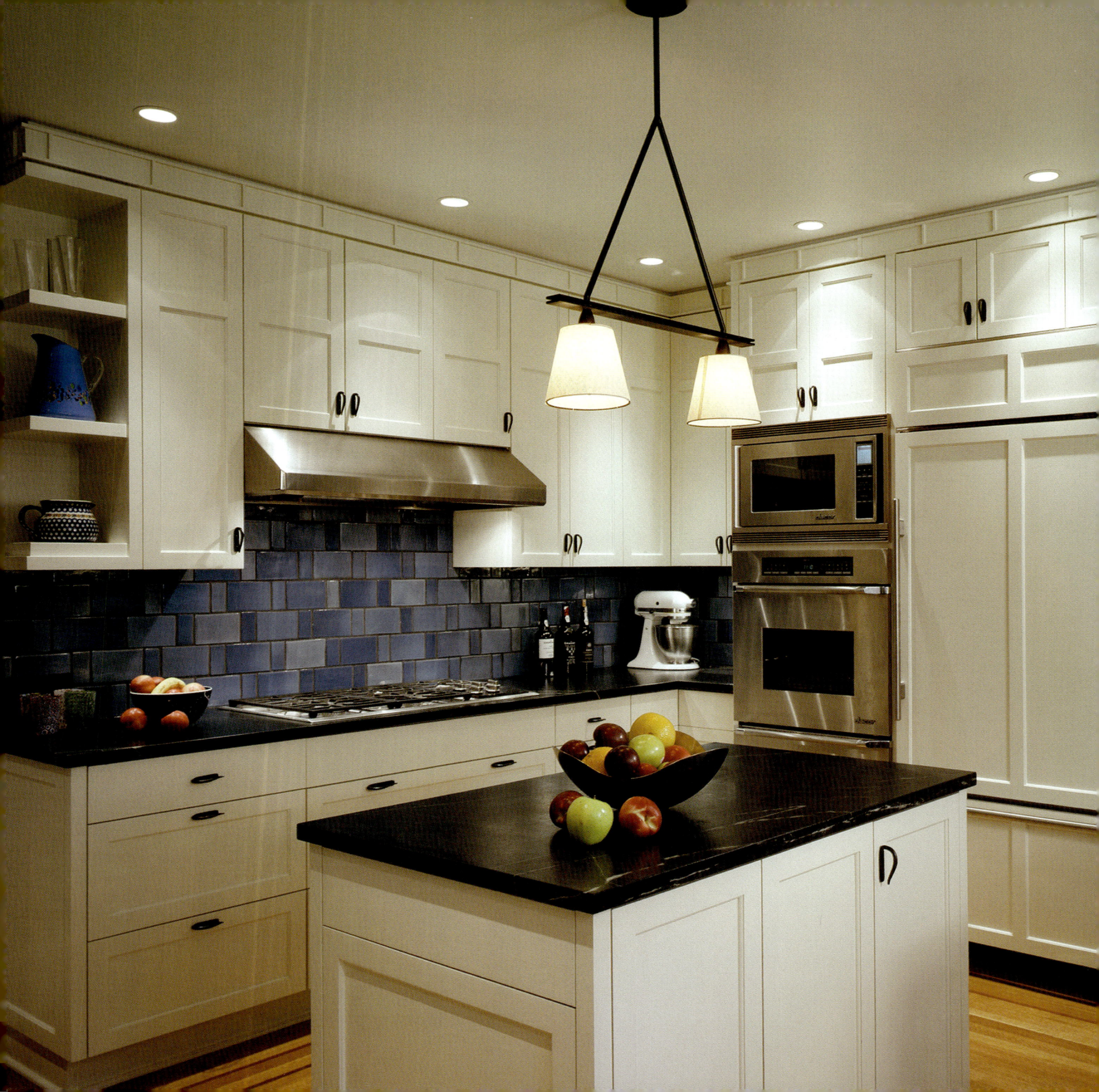

D. CRAIG NORBERG

Norberry Tile

Craig Norberg is a designer for designers. Meaning he's part designer, part designing coach and part design advocate. It's a lot of hats to wear, but Craig is proud to be able to say that he's made an impact on the design world at so many different levels.

Whether he's designing or teaching design, Craig's work gets noticed. He has received press in top design publications such as *Architectural Digest*, *Metropolitan Home*, *This Old Home* and *Old House Journal*, and even the *Puget Sound Business Journal*.

Craig creates and coaches on a variety of design styles, but his specialty—and his passion—is period design. "I love to design with respect to the past and then tweak the colors and materials to make the home more contemporary," he says.

About seventeen years ago, Craig noticed that many of his favorite historical design materials were no longer available. "Materials were disappearing," he says. "And materials are a big part of my passion, they're such an important part of getting really great designs out there."

Out of his desire to bring hard surface materials back in the forefront of design, Craig opened Norberry Tile, a specialty tile showroom, eight years ago. The showroom sells custom ceramic and mosaic, glass, recycled products and offers a variety of services, such as design assistance for designers. "My hope is to encourage quality design and inspire designers to work with these materials in the right way," he says. "If you design with handmade products, there's already an inherent beauty in it."

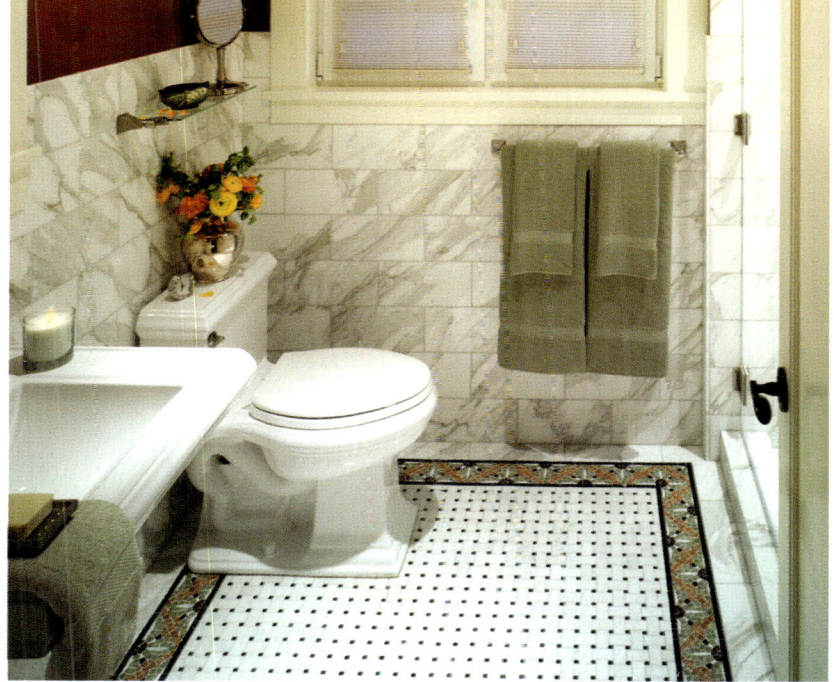

ABOVE
A colorful mosaic border in this small guest bathroom complements classic Calcutta marble wainscoting and basket weave flooring. The sense of space is expanded by the use of contemporary bath fixtures, lighting, glass shower enclosure and sleek window treatment. Tiffany Biggs, designer.

LEFT
Overlooking Lake Washington, this kitchen backsplash captures the blue reflection of the water. Various tile sizes add to the variation in the color. Most remarkable is how the kitchen appears changes with the light throughout the day, always different. Nils Finne, architect.

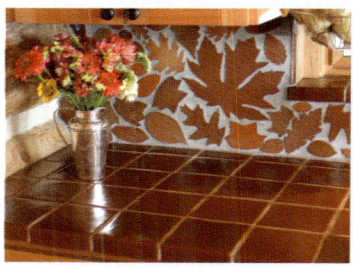

Norberry Tile
D. Craig Norberg
5701 Sixth Ave. South Suite 221
Seattle, WA 98108
206.343.9916
Fax 206.343.9917
www.norberrytile.com

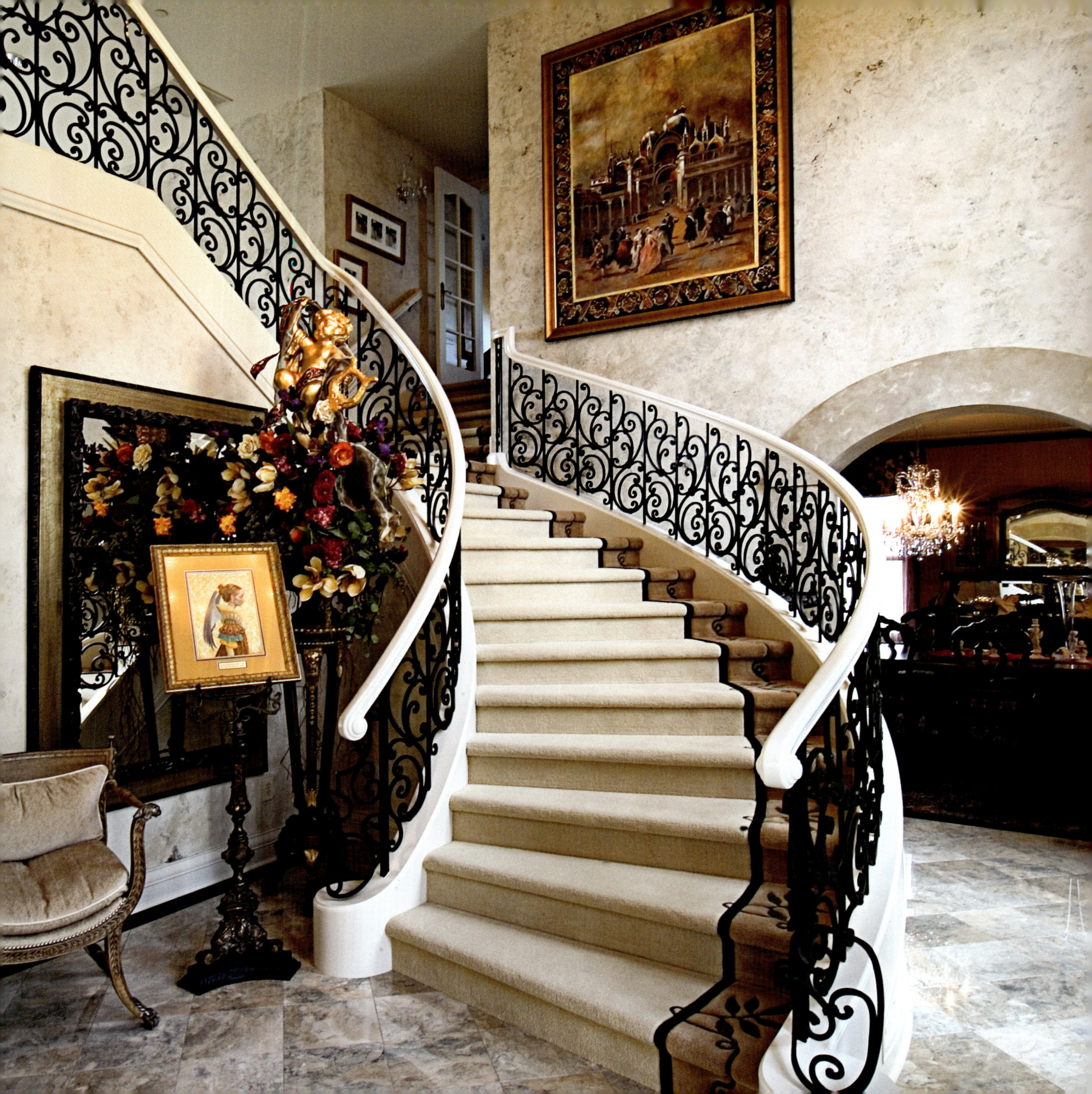

LINDA SCHOENER
Schoener's Interiors

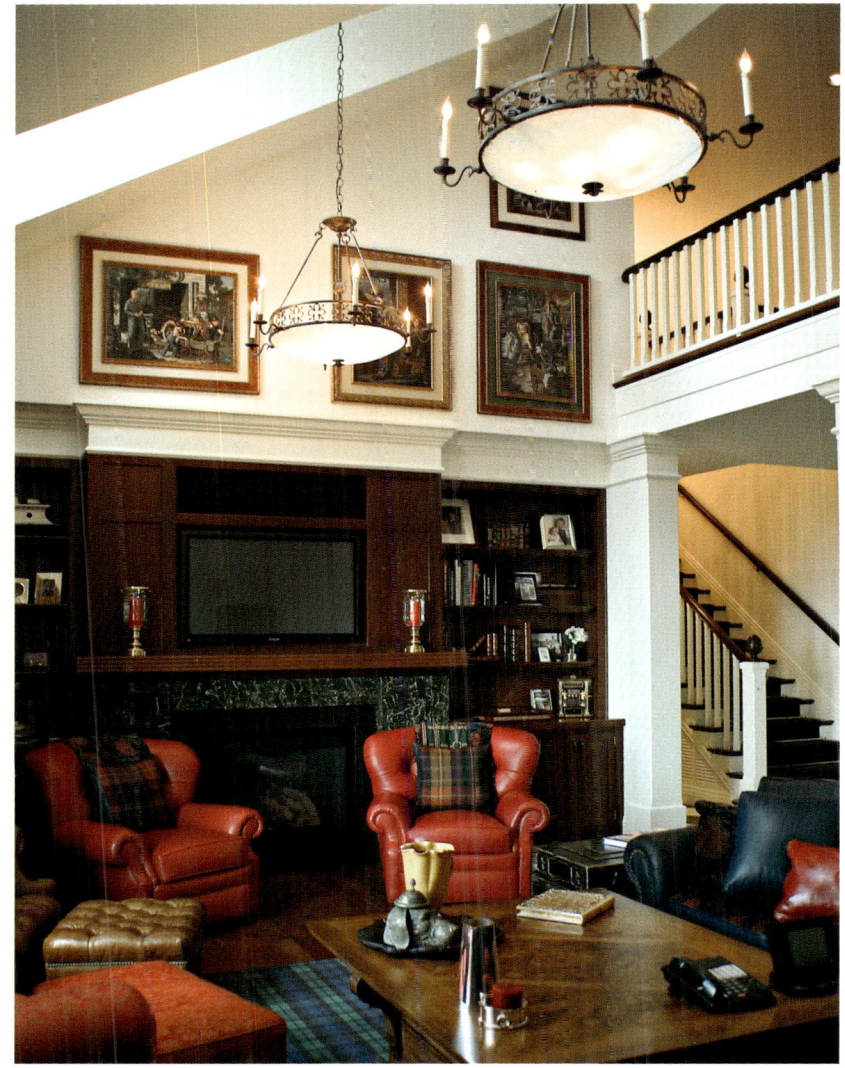

Working with an interior designer can be an intimidating experience. Linda Schoener of Schoener's Interiors not only enjoys changing this misconception, but guides her clients through the diverse and often challenging world of home design.

It's something she loves to do. Prior to her move into interior design, Linda acquired a mastery of fabrics and color as a fashion designer. After her first child was born, Linda made the bold leap from fashion to interiors by opening an upholstery shop in her garage. 29 years later, Linda's labor of love has grown from a small home-based company into the eight-person design powerhouse it is today. The loyalty of her satisfied clients, coupled with her keen eye for detail and color, has earned Linda a reputation as one of the top residential and commercial designers in the Pacific Northwest.

Today, Schoener's Interiors is a full-service retail store offering new construction and remodeling services, as well as space planning, upholstery and design accessories and window treatments. Linda and her team often design entire residential and commercial spaces. Currently the team is designing a new-style Herendon furniture store in Bellevue, that will become

LEFT
This European-influenced entrance hall with an ornate metal rail, marble floors, Venetian plaster walls and oil painting of Venice, will give any visitor a sense of elegance and glamour. A James Christensen's "Angel" painting certainly adds a feel of whimsey to this classic setting.

RIGHT Isabella
Vaulted ceilings add more interest as well as height to this spacious family room. The combination of a walnut bookcase and Byerly art gallery above, the elegant marble fireplace which is flanked with two red Ralph Lauren leather chairs, is an invitation to sit and read by the fire.

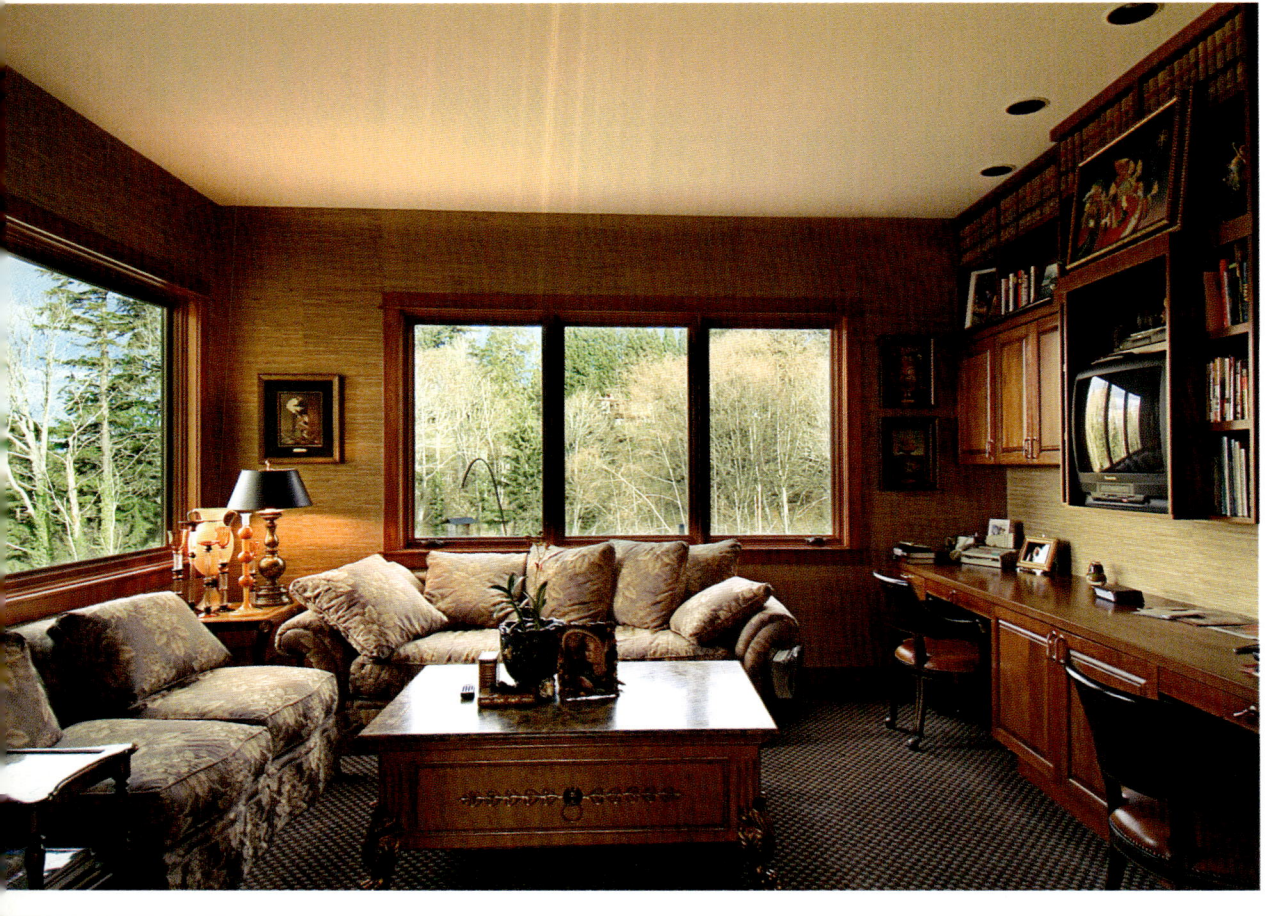

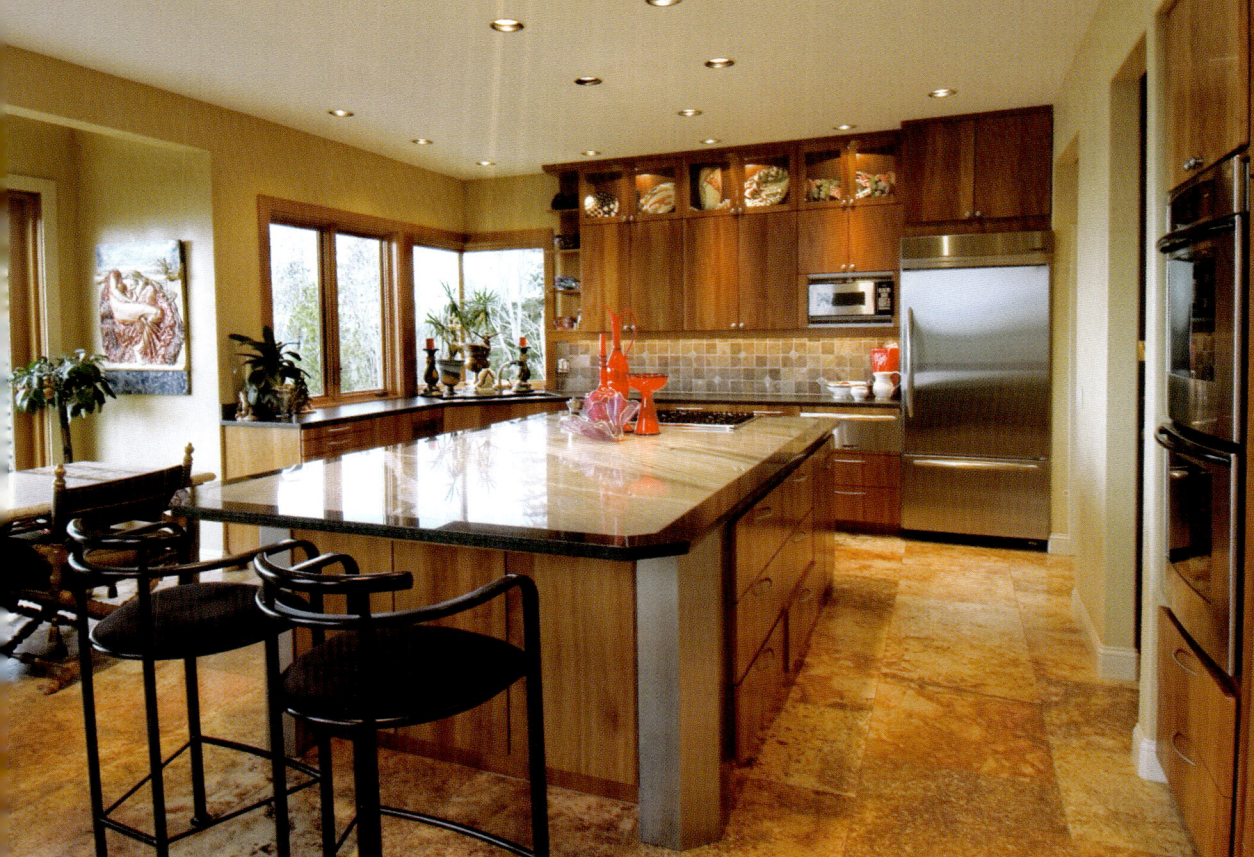

Schoener's Interiors' new home. "We do houses from blueprints all the way through," Linda says. "The store is a collection showing different furniture lines, with lots of accessories and gift items."

The expertise of Linda and her team appeals to clients on all levels and stages of design. Whether building a house from the ground up, reviving an existing space, or feeling the desire to "just add something," Linda assists her clients throughout the process.

A firm believer that every client is different, and thus, every design should be different, Linda's works are never formulaic. Instead, she uses color, fabrics, glass and other design elements to create the setting and mood that best fits each client. "I would hope you couldn't look at a design and pick it out as mine," Linda says, "I strive to come up with something unique for each person."

In her practice, Linda values the dialogue that happens between designer and client, especially when she can enlighten her clients about the creative process. Helping her clients discover their own design style to complement their lifestyle is her ultimate goal.

It is one thing for a designer with a well-trained eye to know what would be perfect for a client's space. That would be easy ... and a vast disservice to her clients. Linda expertly navigates that fine line between offering her clients suggestions and making sure they have a say in every step of the process. "It's such a fine line. I do suggest things, but I always keep it open so the client can feel comfortable having an open dialogue and discover their own design desires in the process."

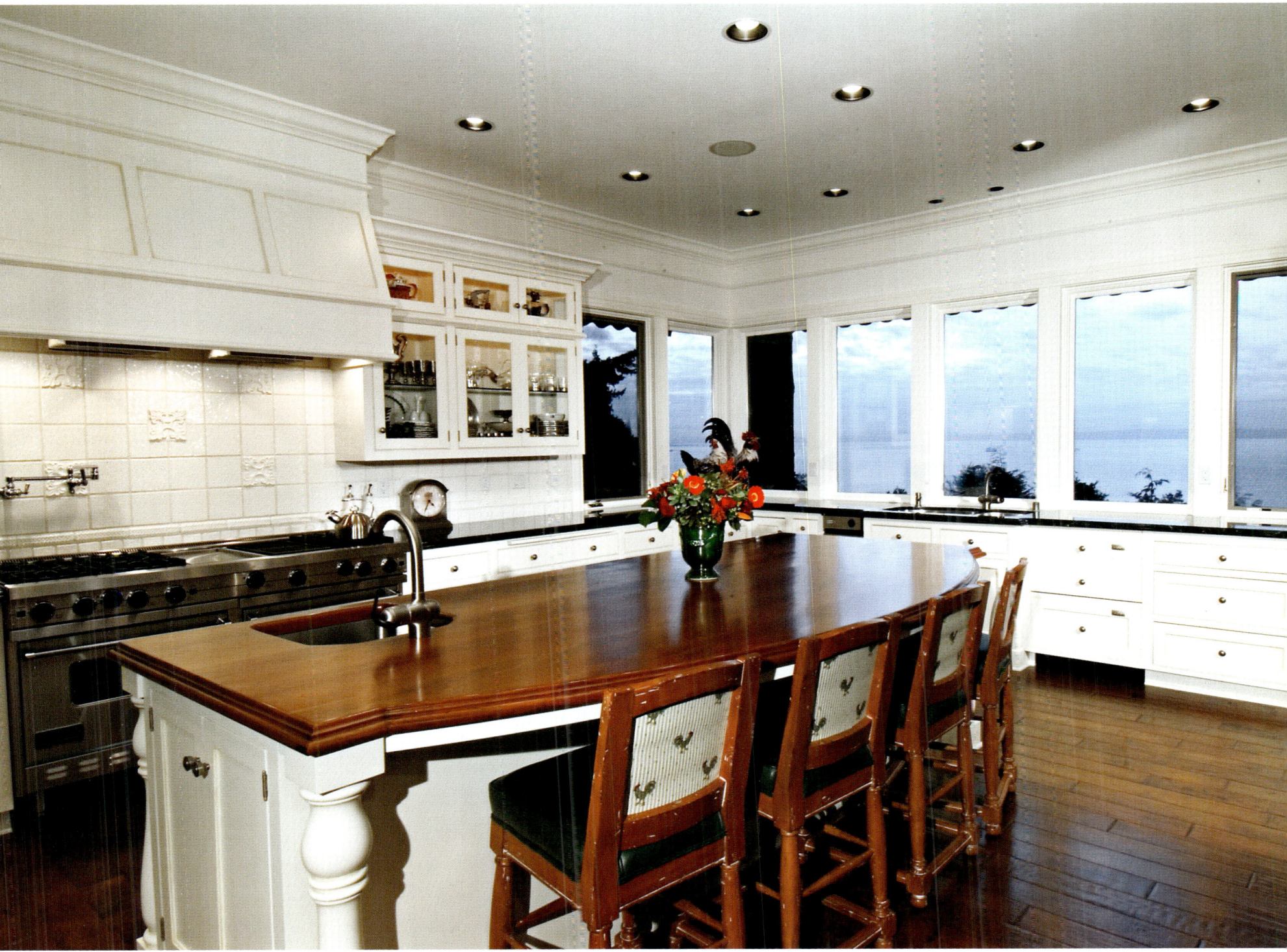

ABOVE
Sweeping kitchen overlooking the Puget Sound features antiqued white cabinets with black/green marble counter tops, a handcrafted tile back splash and a custom island topped with 4" solid Cherry wood.

FACING PAGE TOP
Home office created for him and her with built-in desks and wrap around bookcases, featuring a rolling ladder to access the loft. Grass cloth wall covering and textured Bentley carpet make this an office to sit back and enjoy.

FACING PAGE BOTTOM
This magnificent island with an exotic granite top, is the gathering spot for friends and family in Linda's home.

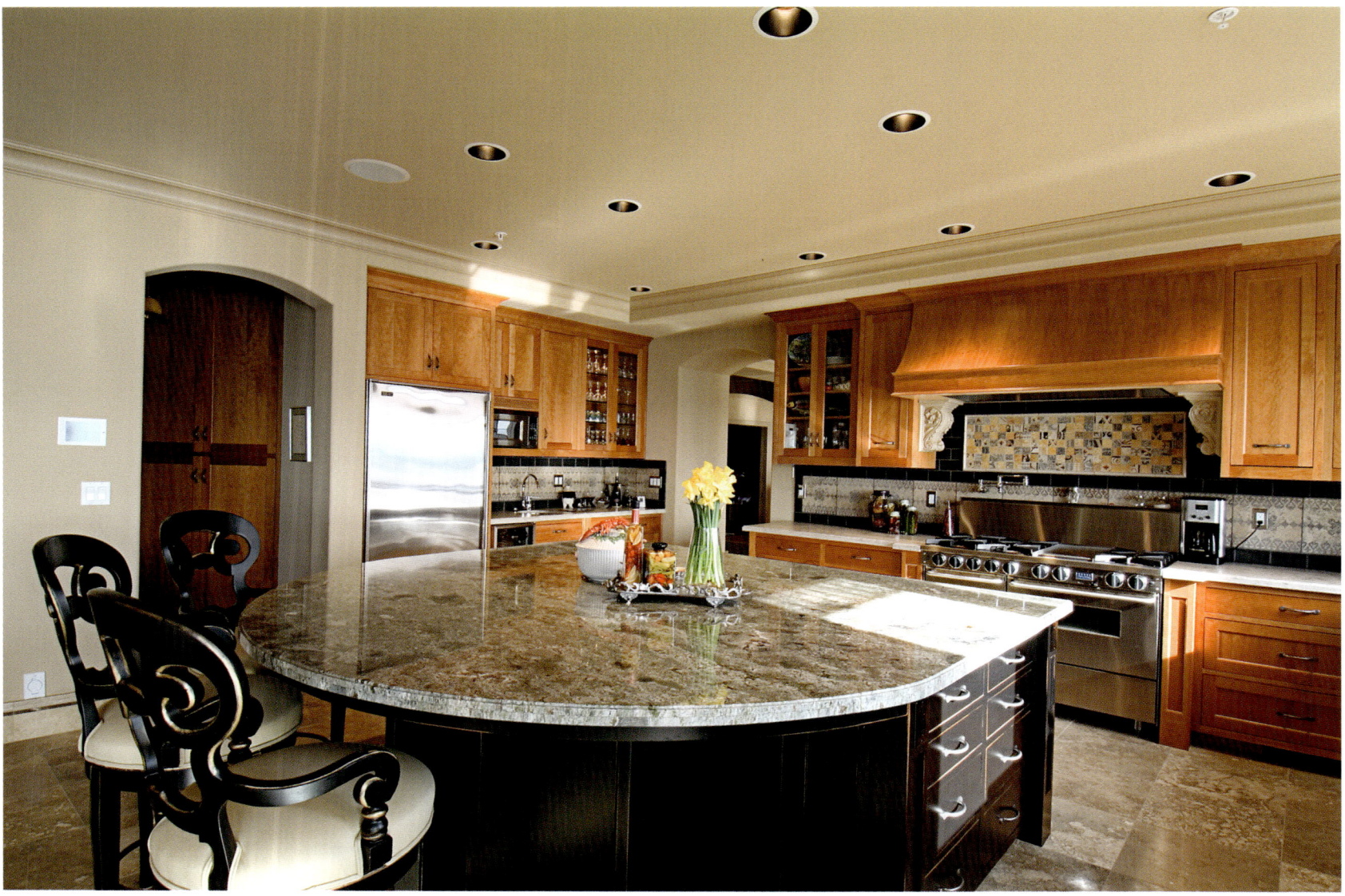

ABOVE
Modern kitchen with an Old World charm. The 7 X 11 foot island in Brazillian granite with rubbed black cabinets below set the stage for this magnificent natural cherry kitchen. Travertine floors and base molding and hand-carved/etched granite back splash gives this remodel a spectacular look.

As an avid art glass collector, Linda combines her love of that color and splash on a smaller scale with the culture of Seattle, which is famous for that element. Whether a major component of the design or placed as a finishing accessory, it's these touches which make a home uniquely personalized.

Linda's own home personifies her design philosophy. As a woman with a full business and personal life, Linda designed her own home to offer a restorative and calming space in contrast to her busy life. "Everything I normally deal with is crowded," she says, "So when I go home, I need a space where everything is all cleaned up and put away."

True serenity for Linda is the knowledge that she makes a difference in the quality of life her clients enjoy. "I'm so fortunate to have a job that I enjoy," says Linda, "A job that's so demanding, so rewarding. I am one of those people who spends my life feeling very fortunate for what I get to do." And Linda isn't the only one who feels fortunate so, too, do her many clients.

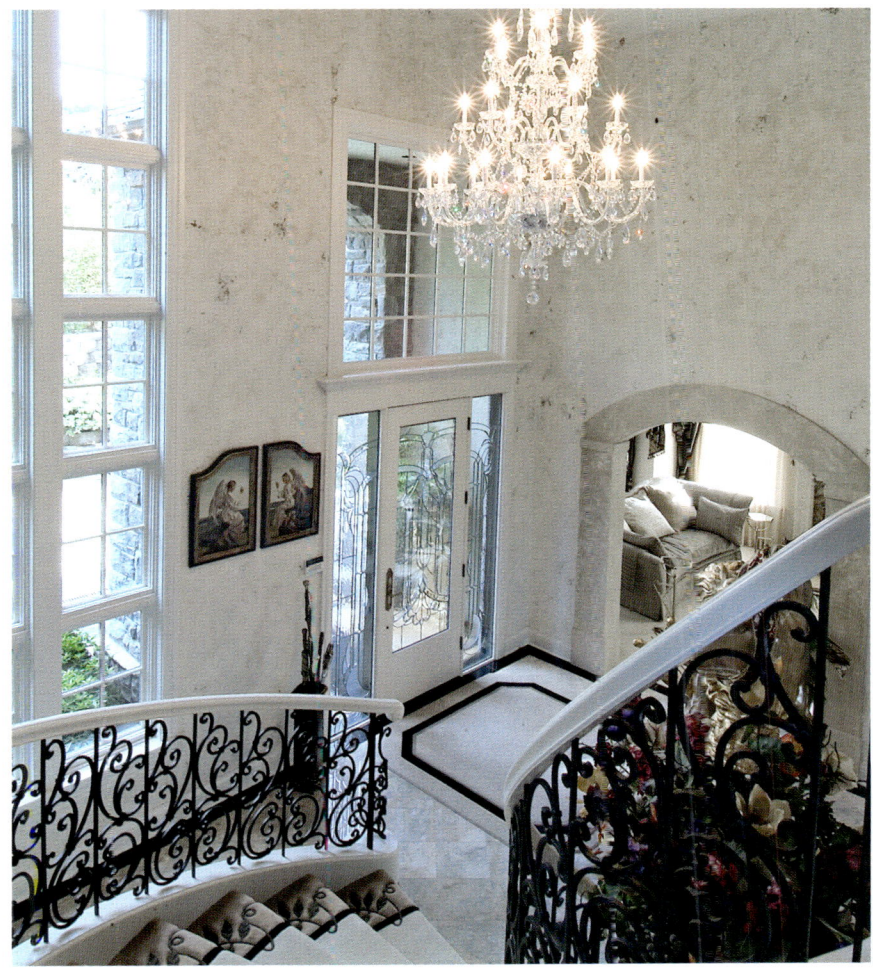
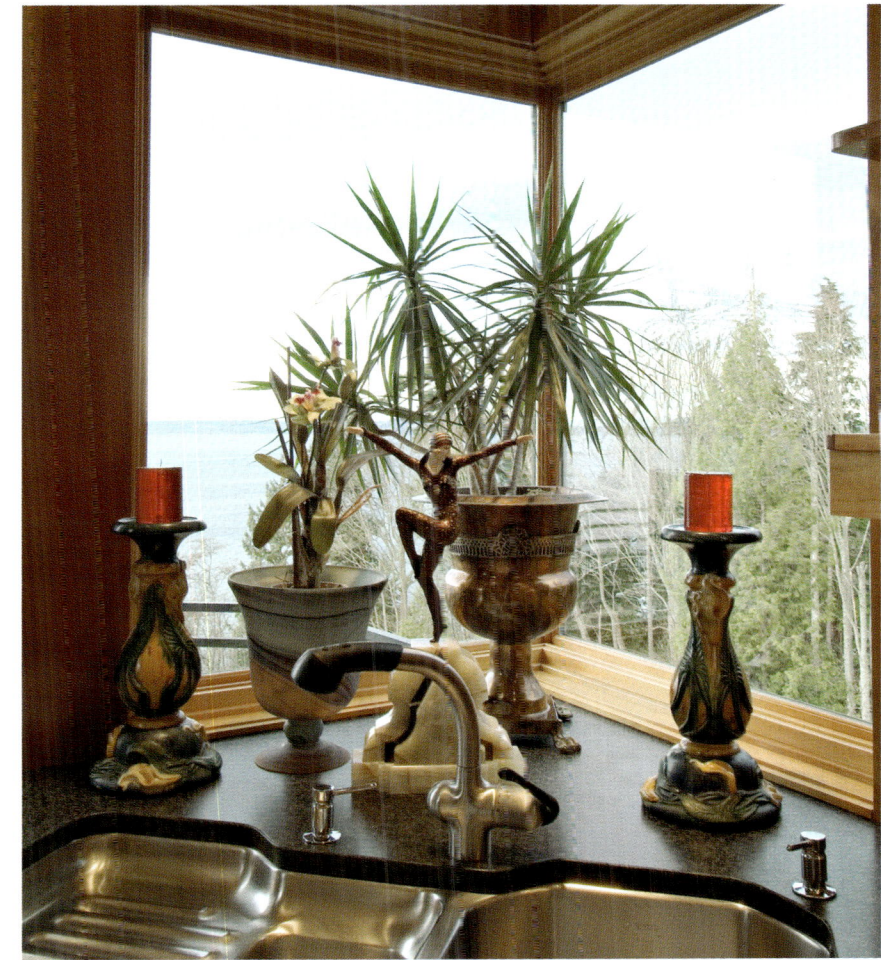

LEFT
A second look at the staircase from the upper bridge hallway to the entry. A Swarovski crystal chandelier adds more flair to this European charm. Custom-designed doors and side lights have beveled and inlayed glass.

RIGHT
Presenting an Art Deco look in the kitchen window of the designer's own home. A Chiparus Ivory, bronze and marble statue dancing in the spectacular view of the Puget Sound.

More about Linda…

WHAT PERSONAL INDULGENCE DO YOU SPEND THE MOST MONEY ON?

Glass art.

IF YOU COULD ELIMINATE ONE ARCHITECTURAL TECHNIQUE FROM THE WORLD, WHAT WOULD IT BE?

Knock down furniture.

WHAT IS THE ONE THING THAT YOU WOULD DO TO BRING A DULL HOUSE TO LIFE?

Accessorize.

WHO HAS HAD THE BIGGEST INFLUENCE ON YOUR CAREER?

Marlowe Goldsby-one of the owners of the Burton James.

YOU CAN TELL I LIVE IN THE NORTHWEST BECAUSE I…

We are able to go to the San Juan islands on our boat. Garden in the rain-a perfect time to weed.

WHAT IS THE MOST UNIQUE/IMPRESSIVE/BEAUTIFUL HOME YOU'VE SEEN IN THE NORTHWEST? WHY?

My friends Diana and Michael-a reflection of them.

Schoener's Interiors
Linda Schoener, Allied Member ASID, NWSID
Henredon
Lincoln Square
700 Bellevue Way NW, Suite 220
Bellevue, Washington 98004
425.454.9000
www.schoenersinteriors.com

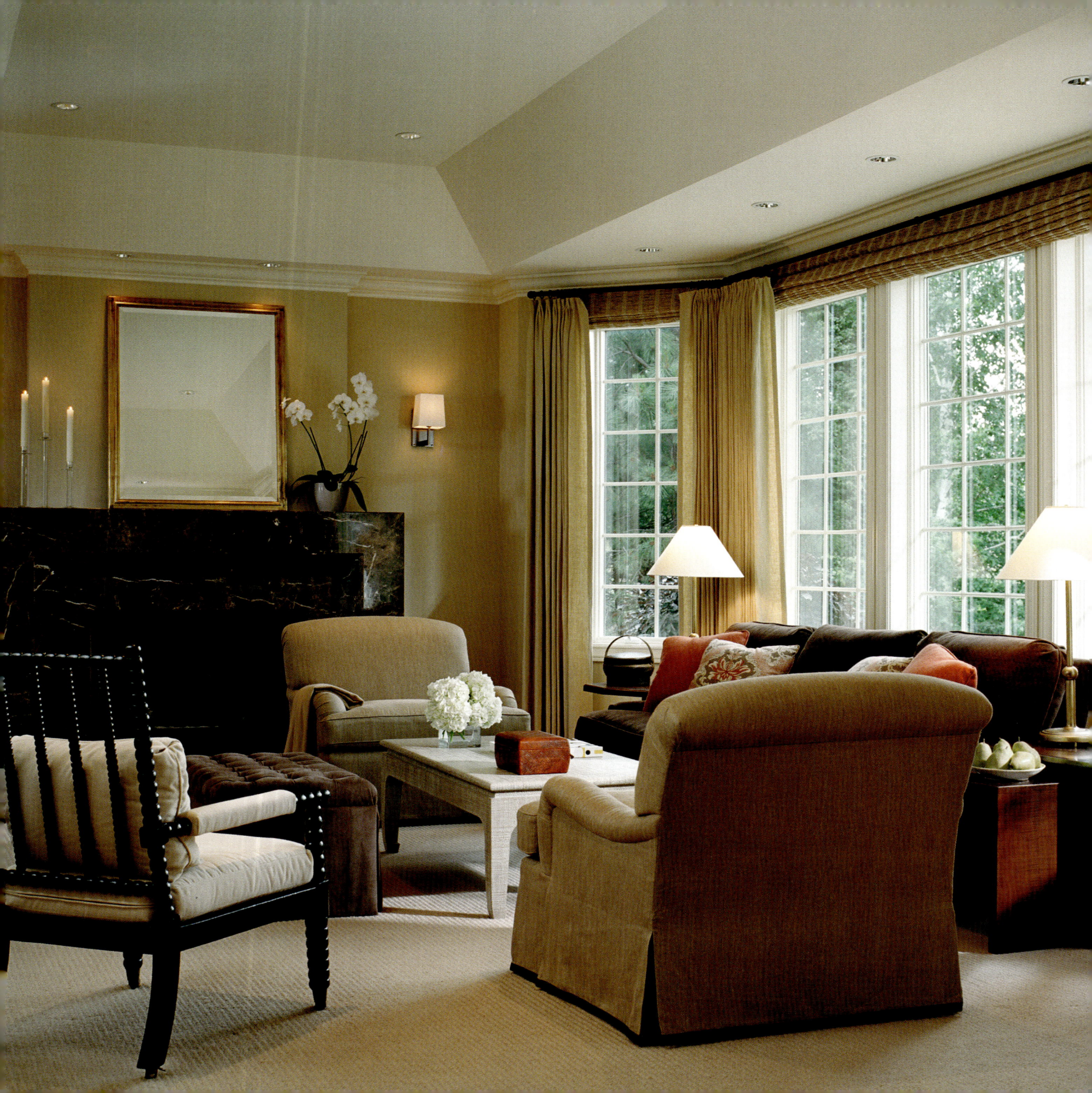

KYLEE SHINTAFFER

Kylee Shintaffer Design

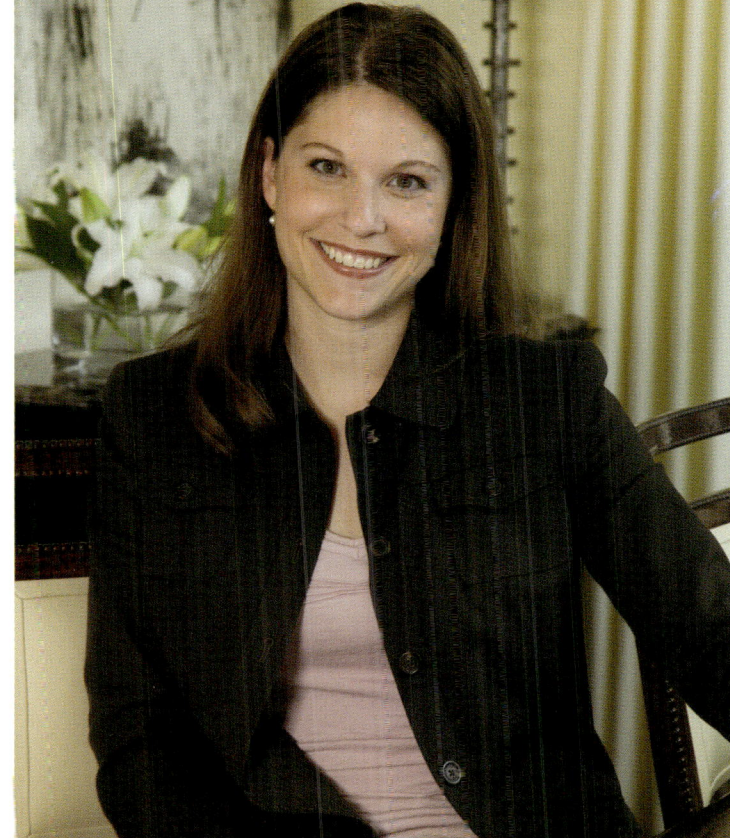

Kylee Shintaffer may be new to the design world—she's only been in business for a few years—but she's already making waves, in more ways than one. She was included in *House Beautiful's* 2005 article, "The Next Wave," which features 25 top U.S. designers who own their own firms and are under the age of 40. "I'm flattered by the honor and am pleased to be in the company of so many wonderful designers," Kylee admits.

Her passion for design started at an early age. As a child, Kylee was "the girl who thought art supplies were so much better than dolls." She even created a pretend art gallery where she displayed her art for her friends. As an adult still drawn to art, she went on to work as the creative director for a card and gift company before opening her own design firm.

Now, Kylee works on projects ranging from from in-city homes to lakeside retreats to desert getaways. No matter what style she's working in, Kylee believes that every interior should be a reflection of a client's personality, lifestyle and dreams.

LEFT
A marble fireplace makes a bold focal point mixed with the casual elegance of the room. Antique bobbin chair c. 1830 from Ann Morris Antiques, custom-designed upholstery, lacquered raffia coffee table.

RIGHT
Kylee Shintaffer.

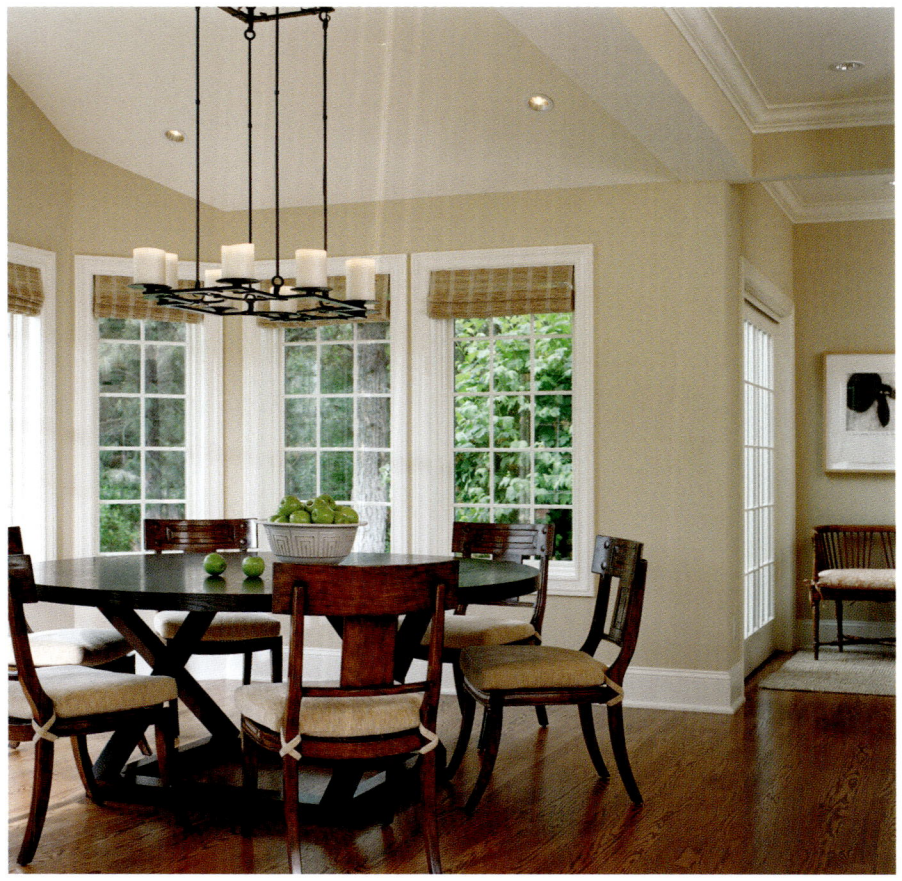

One of Kylee's trademarks is her practice of custom designing much of the furniture and lighting pieces that she uses in her projects. She has worked hard to develop a network of art and antique dealers across the country that offer her clients access to one-of-a-kind pieces.

Shape, texture, line and form are important elements of Kylee's designs. She strives for well-edited rooms that combine both modern and traditional pieces to create truly timeless, elegant interiors. The anchors of Kylee's work are neutral fabrics, layered textures and simple contrasts.

Kylee is driven by the desire to create a better environment, and thus a better life, for her clients. A firm believer that home is a place where one can escape from life's daily requirements, Kylee's interiors offer comfort, livability and beauty. For her, there is "nothing more satisfying than positively impacting my clients' quality of life by bringing beauty, warmth and comfort into their homes."

TOP
Informal dining room off of the kitchen is conducive to the clients' casual entertaining style and their family. Kevin Reiley chandelier, Michael Taylor dining chairs. Antique French Baguette bench covered in Fortuny fabric in back hall.

BOTTOM
Kitchen includes a custom steel hood with grooved details. Steel complements bronze detail inset into cream tile from Waterworks. Custom mahogany island adds punch to kitchen. Shaw's original farmhouse sink.

FACING PAGE RIGHT
Elegant yet bold, room has reading area with wonderful light pouring in from the windows. Custom bedding. Antique sunburst mirror. Lacquered bedside tables with antique hardware.

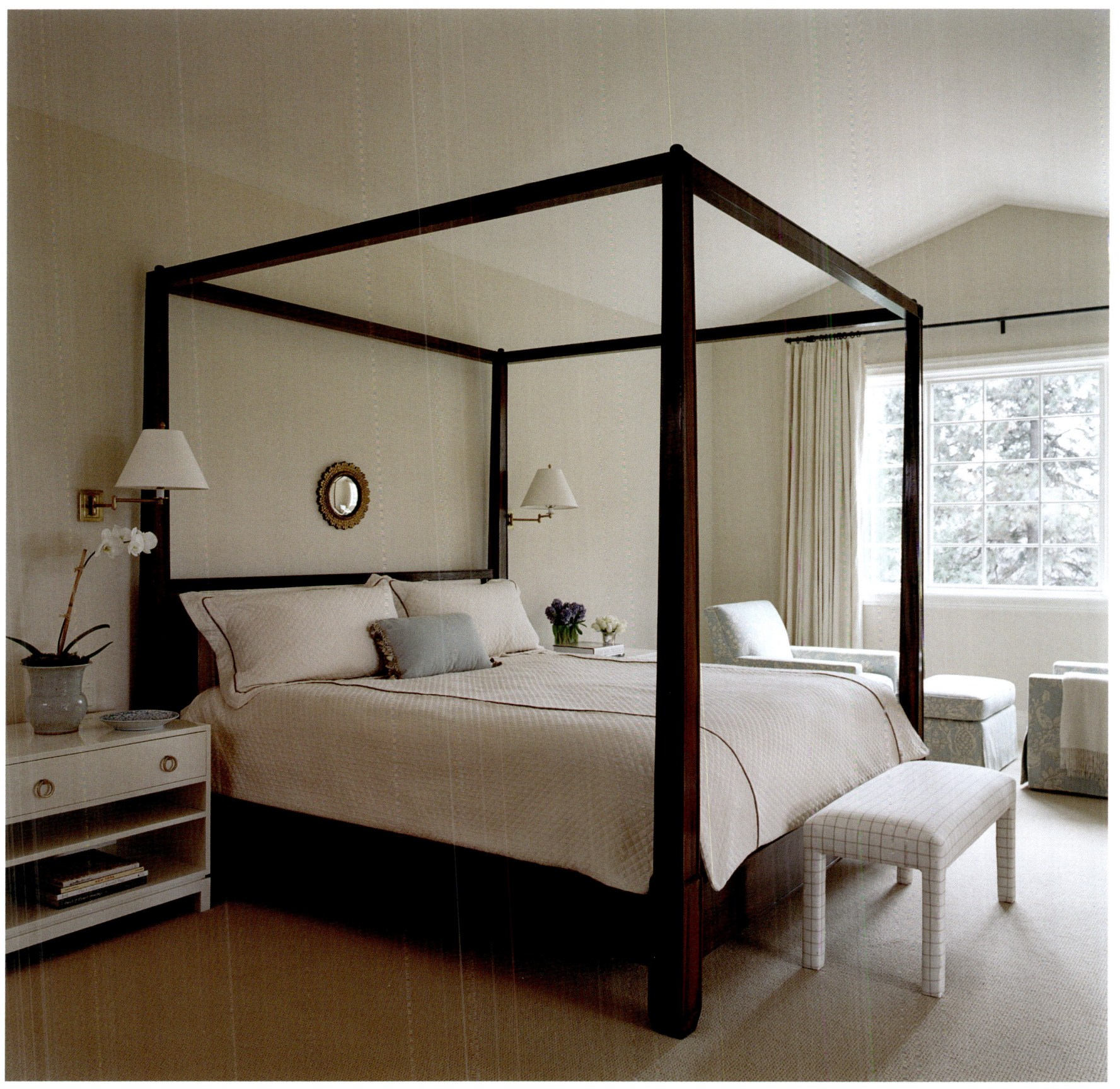

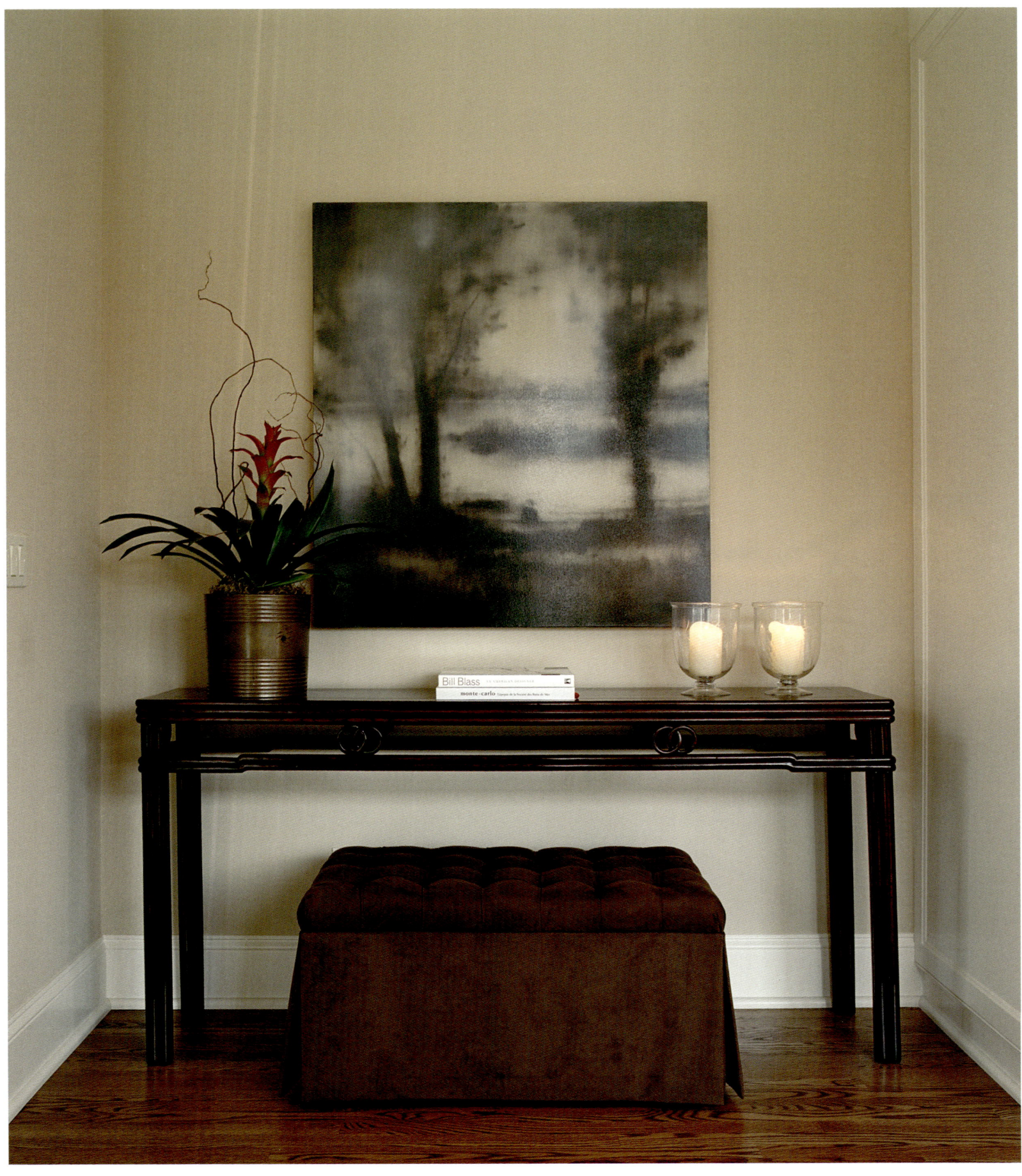

More about Kylee...

WHAT PERSONAL INDULGENCE DO YOU SPEND THE MOST MONEY ON?

Art, food and travel.

YOU CAN TELL I LIVE IN THE PACIFIC NORTHWEST BECAUSE I...

Love using subtle colors and natural materials that reflect the surroundings in the Northwest.

WHAT BOOK ARE YOU READING RIGHT NOW?

I'm always reading several books. I just started reading the out-of-print book on Parish-Hadley and am also reading a spy thriller series by Vince Flynn.

WHO HAS HAD THE BIGGEST INFLUENCE ON YOUR CAREER?

With regards to furniture, French designers Andre Arbus and Jean Michel Frank for their amazing ability to create pieces with beautiful lines that are both modern and timeless, something I strive for in my design. From an interiors standpoint, I am also inspired by Albert Hadley and Billy Baldwin, whose designs are innovative and bold, but maintain an elegant, well-edited aesthetic that has withstood the test of time.

WHAT ONE ELEMENT OF STYLE OR PHILOSOPHY HAVE YOU STUCK WITH FOR YEARS THAT STILL WORKS FOR YOU TODAY?

Listen to my clients and follow my instincts.

Kylee Shintaffer Design
Kylee Shintaffer
1938 Boyer Avenue East
Seattle, WA 98112
206.856.7920
www.kyleeshintaffer.com

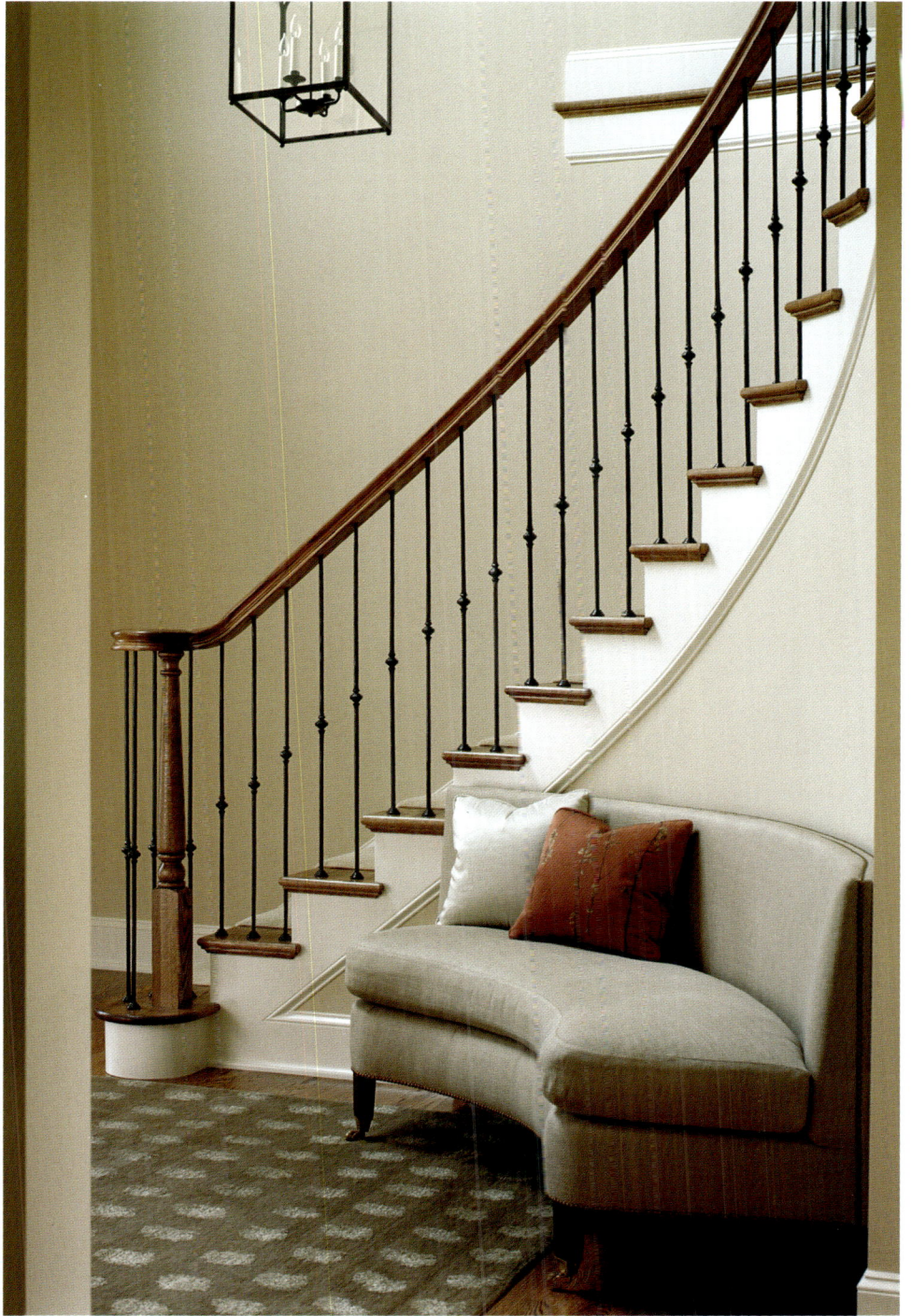

ABOVE
Graceful curving staircase welcomes guests into home. Custom curved sofa sits atop rug from Odegaard.

FACING PAGE LEFT
Niche off of living room provides a visual retreat. Brad Durham painting hangs above Chinese console c. 1800. Copper vessel is from Blackman Cruz. Tufted bench is on casters to create flexible seating in living room.

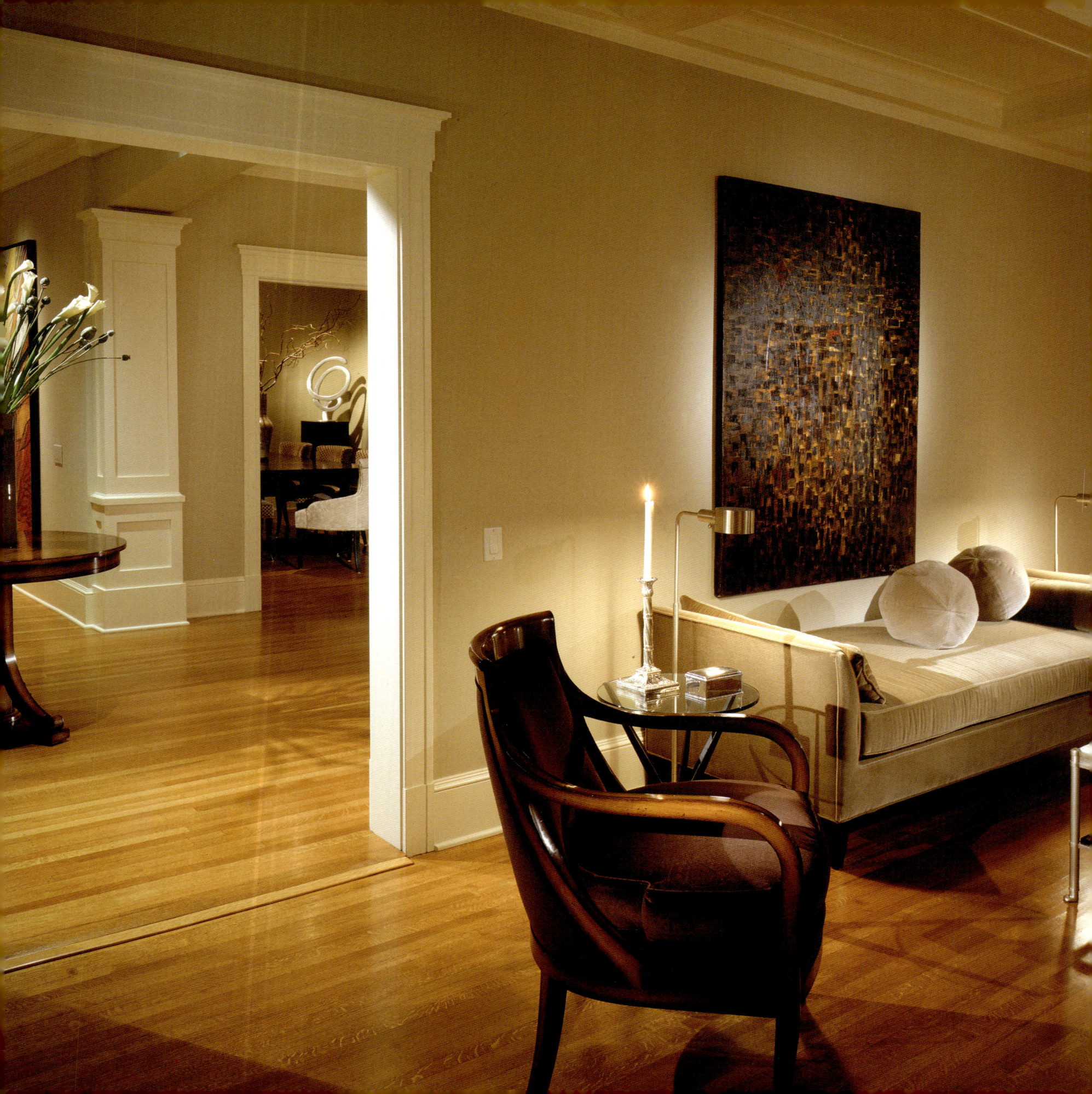

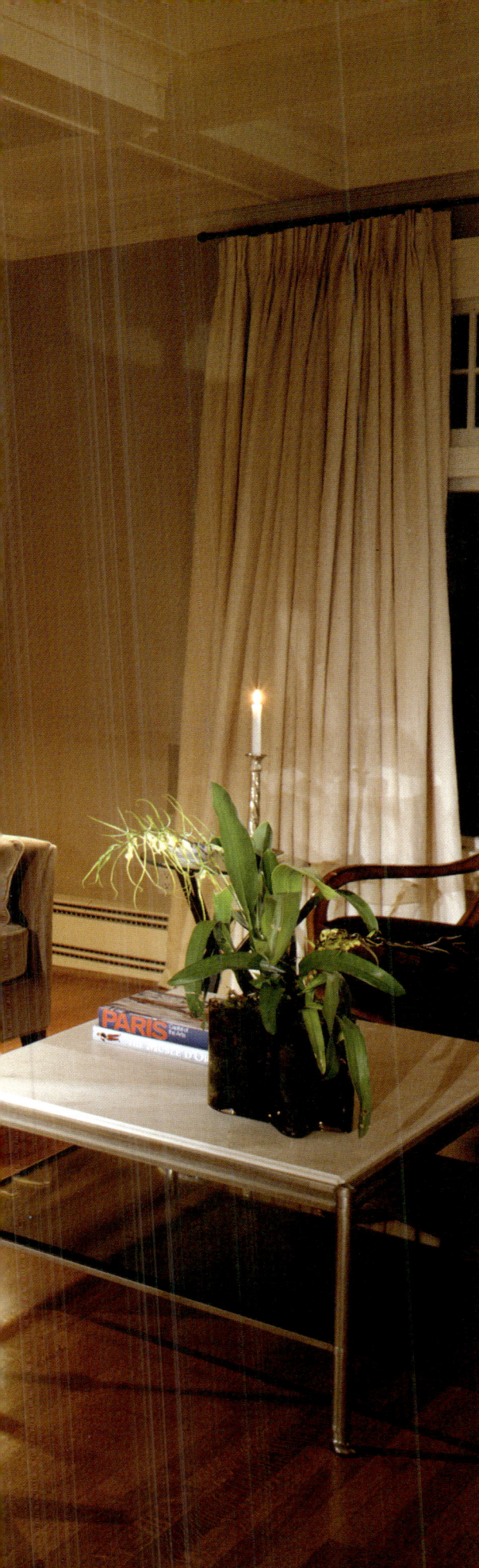

TED TUTTLE
Ted Tuttle Interior Design

For Ted Tuttle, design entails two important elements: matching and mixing. To him, matching means creating a unique interior, perfectly suited for each individual client. Mixing means adding something special to every project, whether he's combining an ultra-modern interior with a few incredible antiques, or creating a neutral color palette accented by bold art.

A Northwest native, Ted got his start designing interiors for dozens of Nordstrom stores, placing a strong focus on furniture and artwork. A natural transition evolved through assisting Nordstrom executives with the creation of their own homes. Now, with 27 years experience, this Seattle-based designer produces tailor-made residences around the country, including recent projects in New York, Arkansas and California.

LEFT
The living room of neutrals in chocolate and mink has a Todd Haas settee with a mixed media painting by Alfonso Pena. A Holly Hunt coffee table and Nancy Corzine chair complete the clean look. In the background, a stainless sculpture by Steve Jensen.

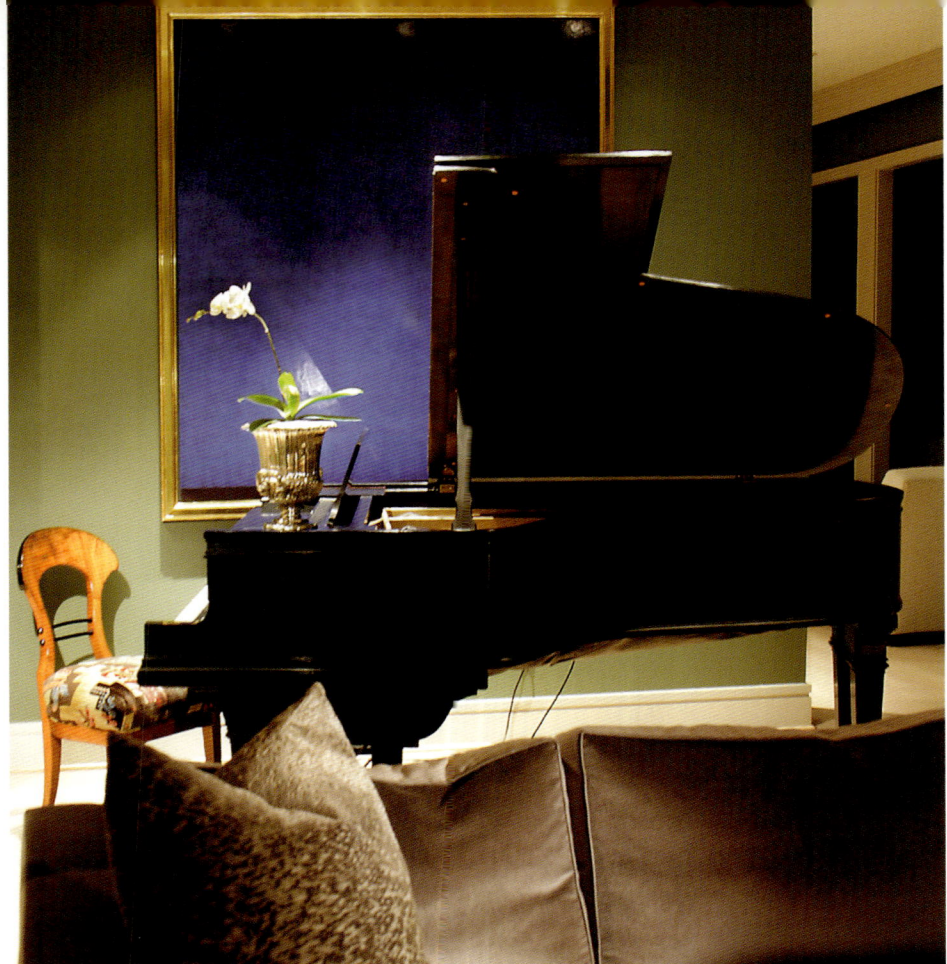

Ted's interiors tend to be neutral, using beiges, taupes, and subtle greens. Using a monochromatic color format allows unique pieces of art and one-of-a-kind antiques to become a dramatic focus—an important part of the mix.

During his career, Ted has been influenced by the late Jean Jongeward, a renowned interior designer in Seattle, as well as Jim Olson, a Seattle architect.

Ted believes that the client-designer relationship is not only one of the most important parts of his job, it is also the most rewarding. After working with clients for a year or two, such a bond is often created that he is asked to design additional projects.

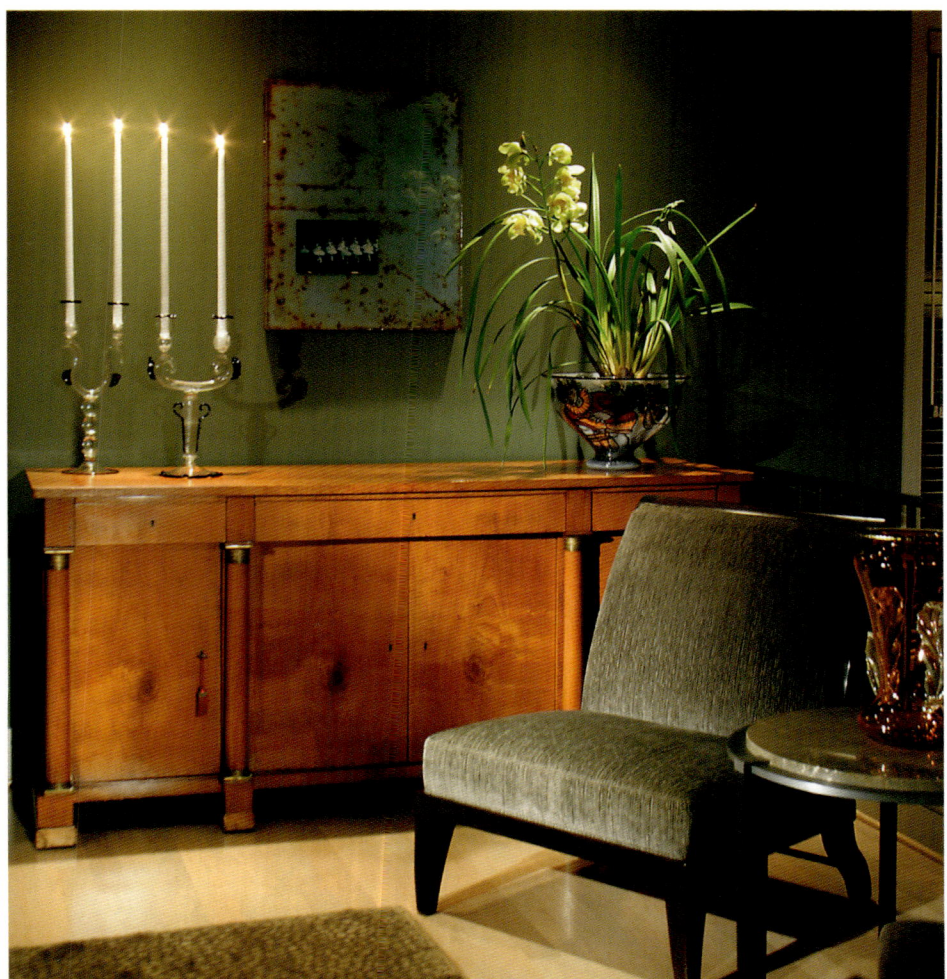

TOP
Bold blue artwork by Tom Bolles of San Francisco is the back-drop for the early 20th century Steinway player piano. The Holly Hunt sofa in the foreground is covered in Great Plains mohair.

BOTTOM
A wonderful antique sideboard displays part of the clients' Pilchuck art glass collection. "Blue Ballerinas" by Gordon Huether hangs above.

FACING PAGE RIGHT
Matching Todd Haas sofas ground the seating area in the living room. Both are covered in Glant mohair. A striking bronze statue by Tom Corbin dominates one corner.

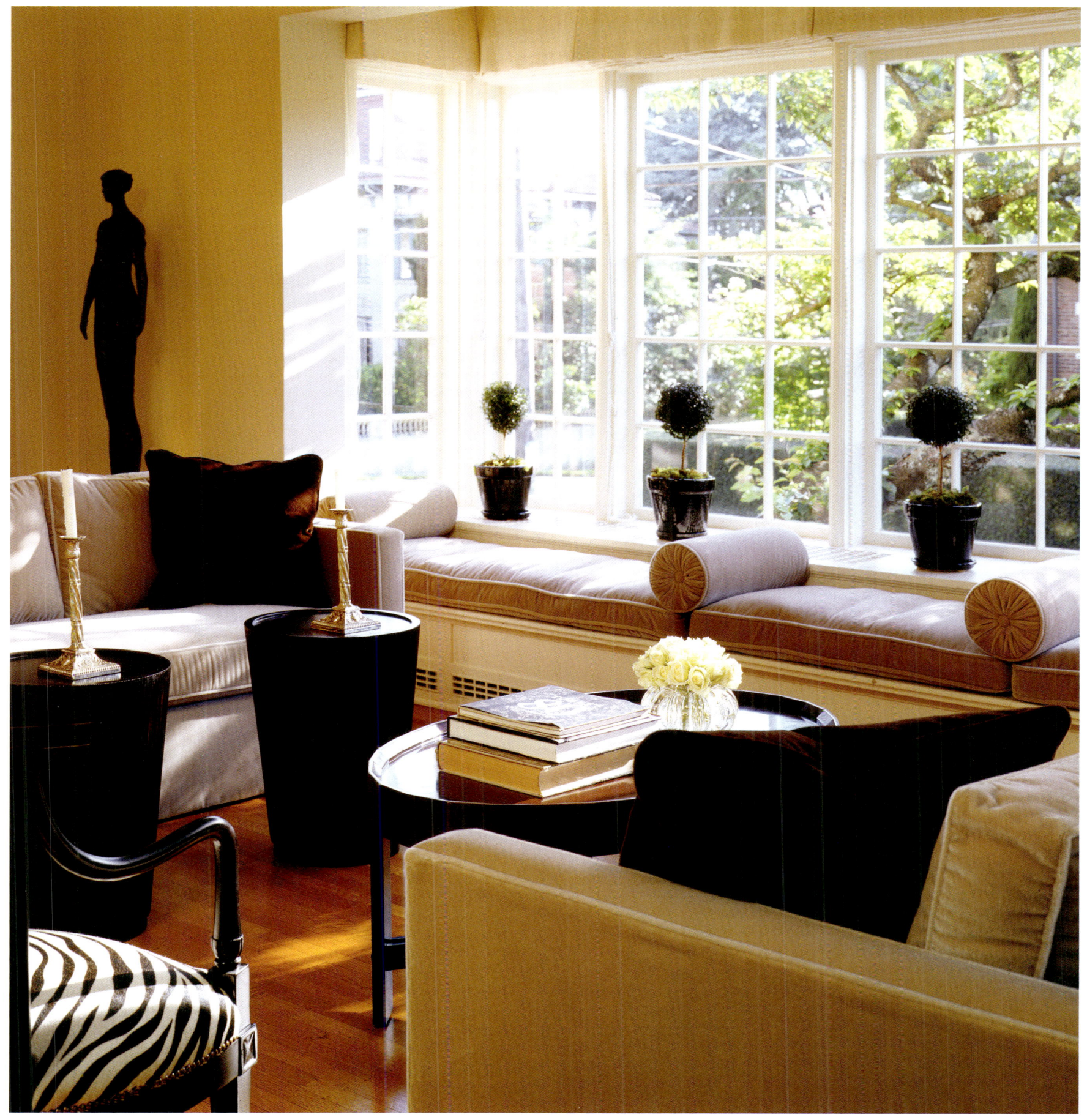

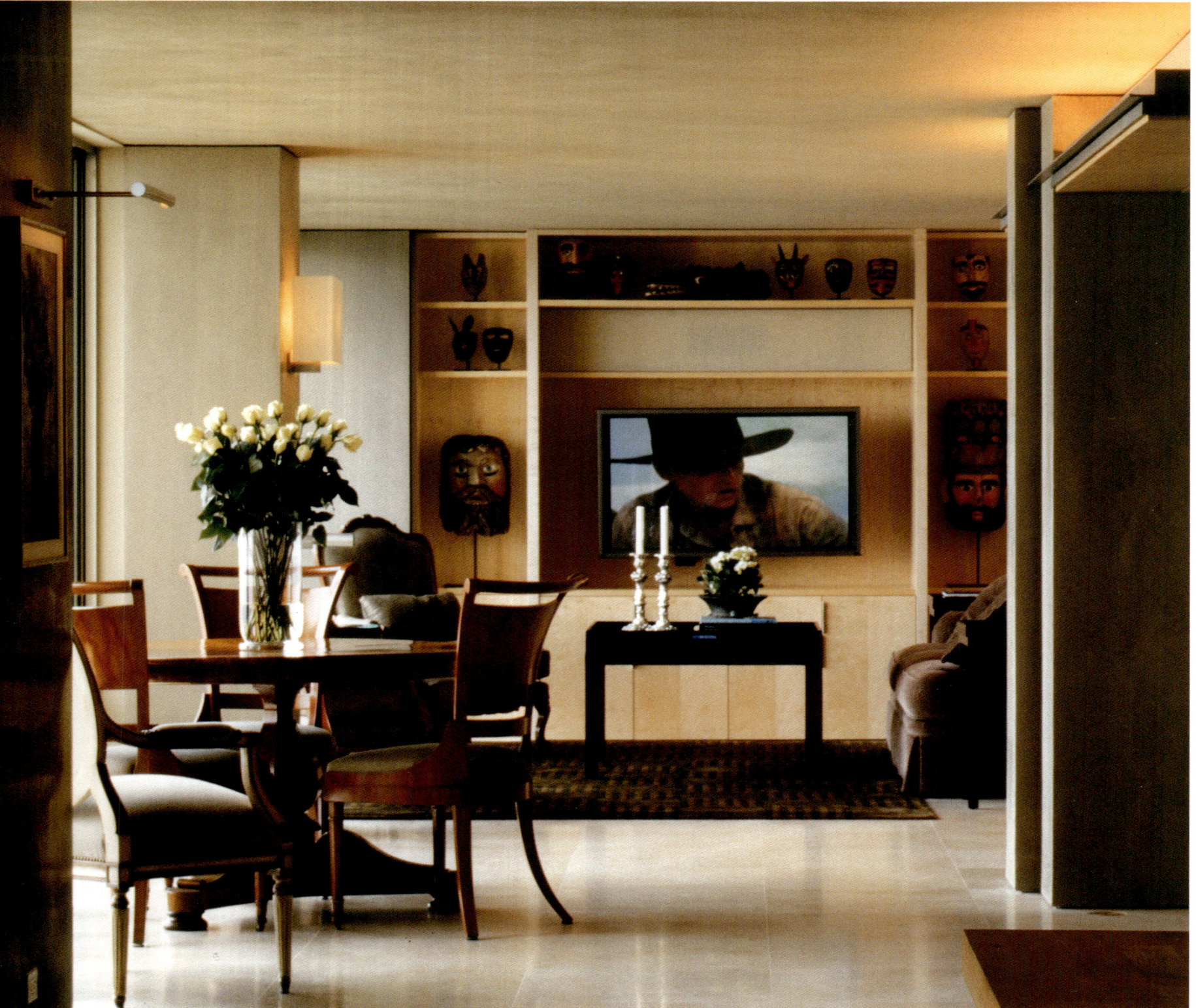

ABOVE
The clients' collection of African masks is displayed in the den. Carpet is by Edward Fields. An antique table is surrounded by chairs from James Jennings.

FACING PAGE RIGHT
A checkerboard carpet by Edward Fields grounds the living room. Chairs by Rose Tarlow and Michael Taylor warm the room. In the background, "The Wake" by Tony Sherman.

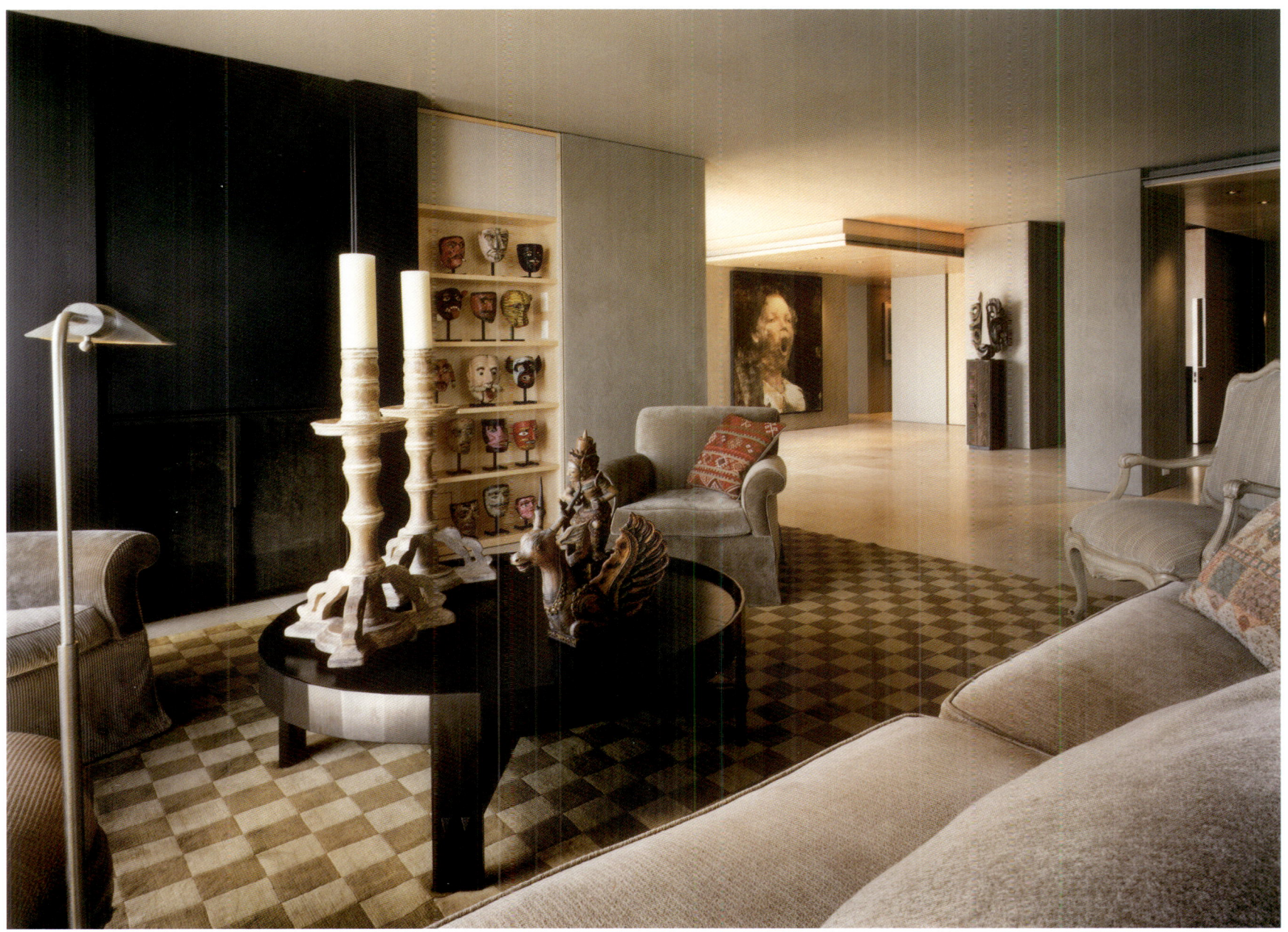

More about Ted…

WHAT PERSONAL INDULGENCE DO YOU SPEND THE MOST MONEY ON?

Artwork.

WHAT SEPARATES YOU FROM YOUR COMPETITION?

The ability to listen and give each client a unique space.

WHAT IS THE BEST PART OF BEING AN INTERIOR DESIGNER?

Working with wonderful clients that give me the freedom to create great spaces.

WHAT DO YOU LIKE ABOUT DOING BUSINESS IN THE PACIFIC NORTHWEST?

The abundance of terrific resources.

Ted Tuttle Interior Design
Ted Tuttle
511 East Roy, Suite 102
Seattle, WA 98102
206.329.2373

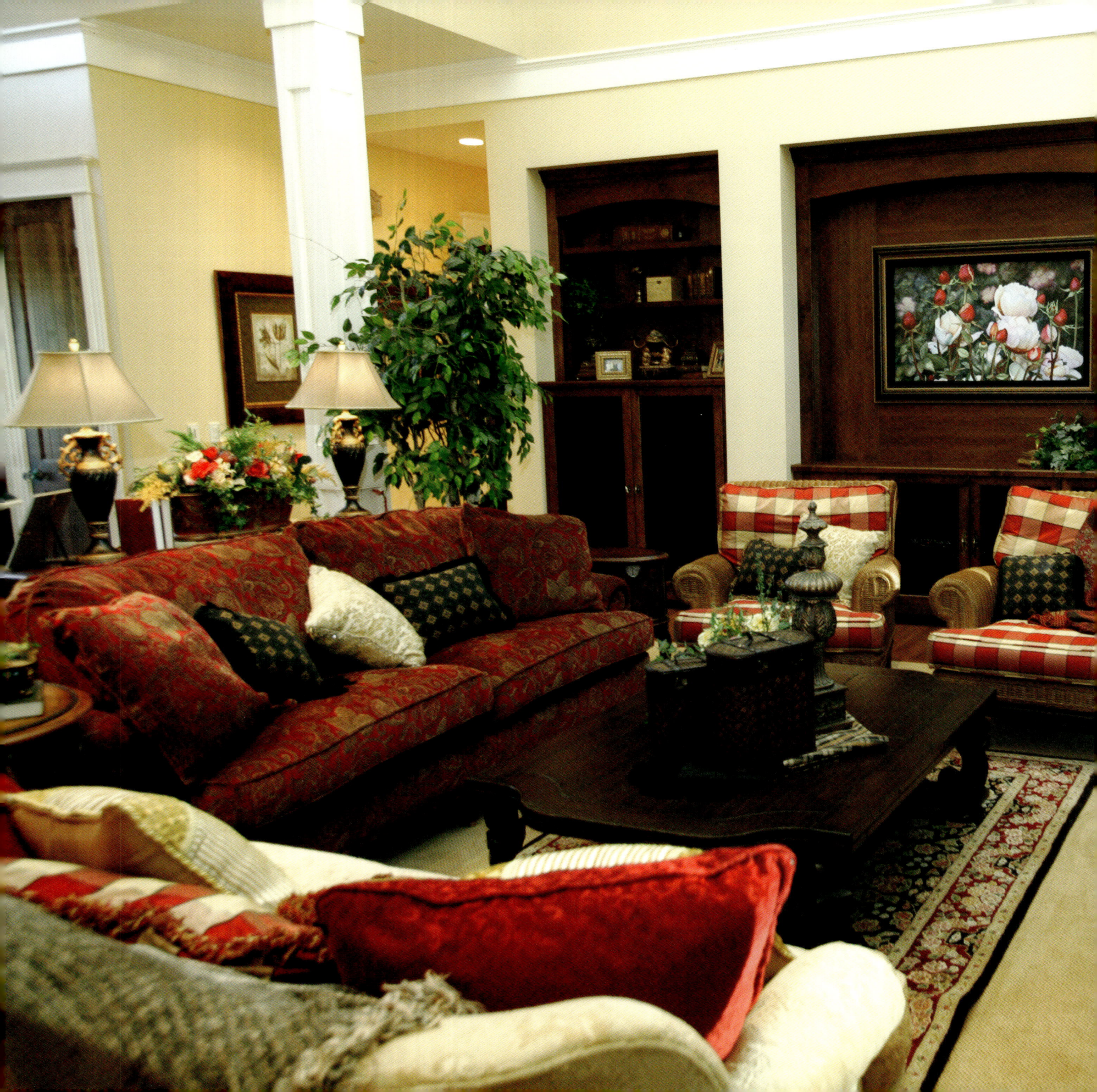

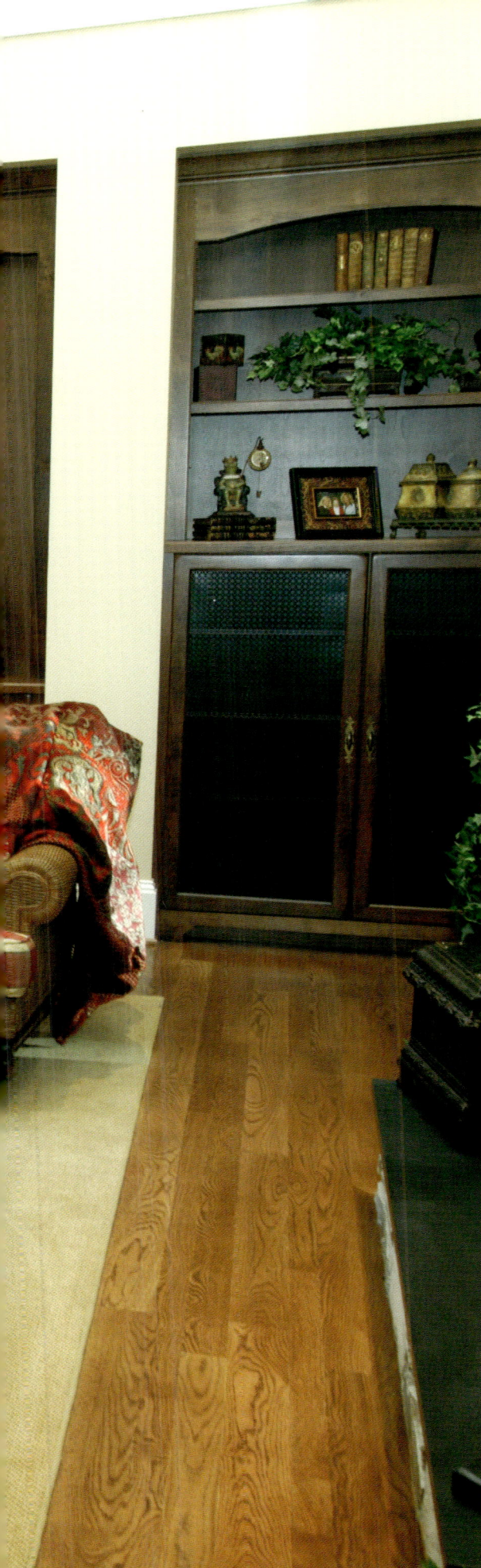

Diane Wainhouse & Val Scalzo

Heartland Interiors, Inc.

Nearly 20 years ago, when Val Scalzo and Diane Wainhouse opened a small wholesale gift company, they never dreamed they would become the owners of a successful furniture store as well as Interior Designers, but that is exactly what happened to these Northwest Natives.

They started their company with $75.00 each, creating and manufacturing a gift line in their homes that they sold to specialty gift shops in the area as well as Nordstrom's. Soon outgrowing their homes, they moved into a small manufacturing space, and then into their first retail store where they incorporated their own gift line with other merchandise from local artists and suppliers. From the very beginning, the store took on its own personality and offered the public a fresh new look in home furnishings.

Since that humble beginning, Val and Diane have grown their company into Heartland Interiors, a 7,000 square-foot retail store that offers artwork, lighting, furniture and accessories. It's filled with everything you'd need to furnish a house from the ground up. The company also offers a design service, consulting their clients on both small and large tasks, from choosing paint colors to furnishing an entire home.

"Our goal is to help our clients blend the elements and principles of design with their own personality and lifestyle," Val says. "We believe your home should be your refuge, a place where you can relax, spend time with loved ones and restore your spirit. For the comfort and beauty of our surroundings are indeed connected to our enjoyment of life."

LEFT
"Buy what you love" is the basic philosophy of Heartland Interiors. We like to introduce a variety of patterns and furnishings that reflect your personal lifestyle.

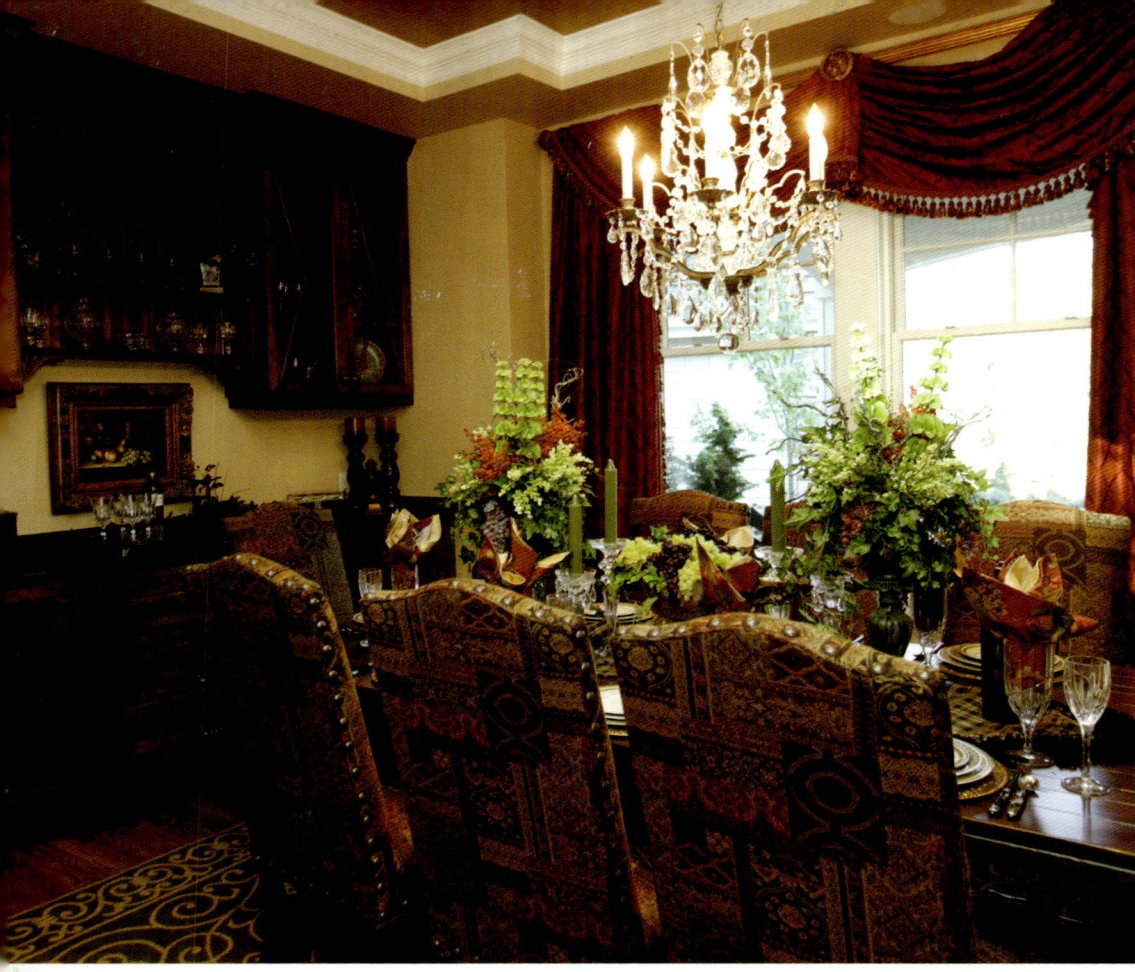

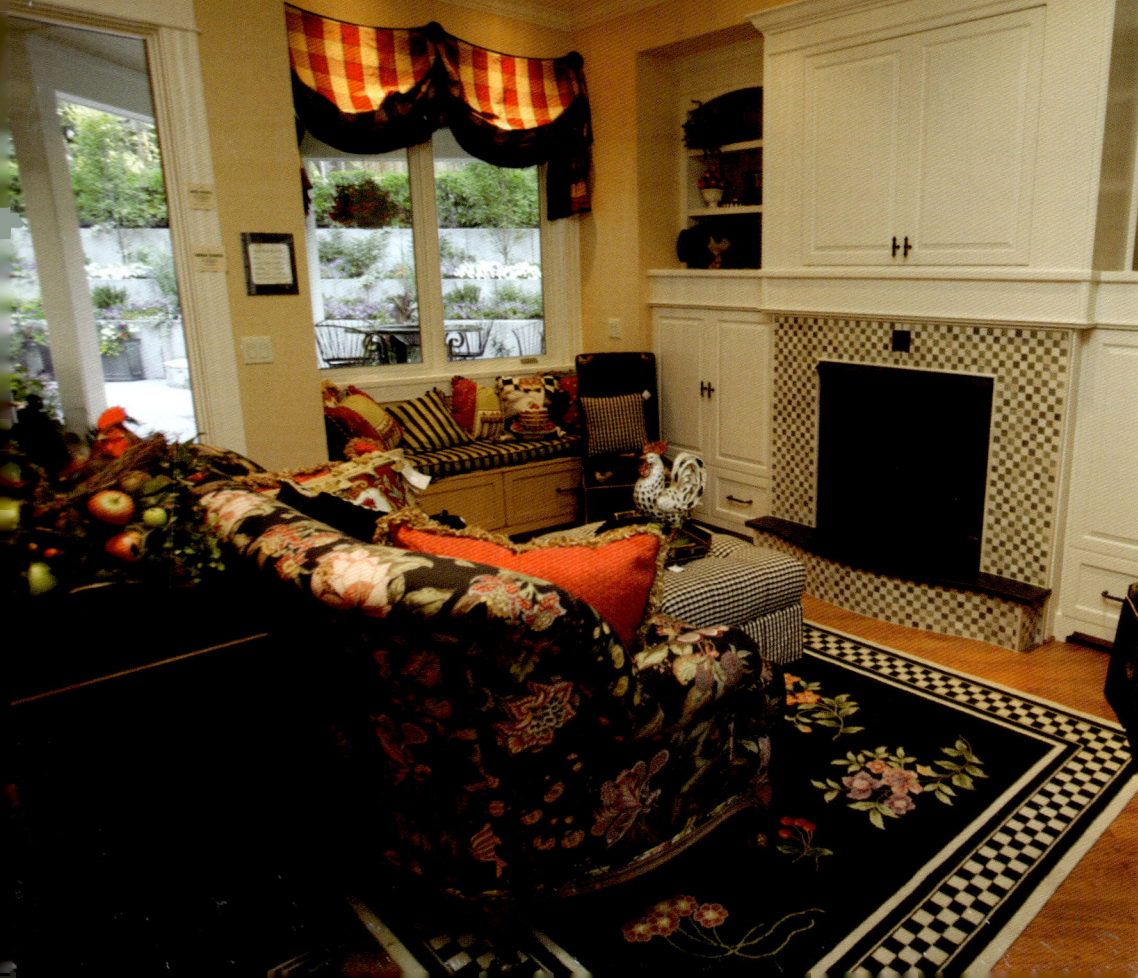

Heartland Interiors offers clients a style that is a unique fusion of elegant French country chic and the natural, relaxed design of the Pacific Northwest. "People ask what our style is and it's very hard to define," Diane says. "We are big into color, texture, ambiance and mixing things up so that the space is visually pleasing and reflects personality."

To contrast the often gray climate of the Pacific Northwest, Val and Diane stay away from using a lot of grays, taupes, and monochromatic settings. Heartland tends to be bold with color, using a palette rich in reds, golds, greens and browns, and of course black for added drama and interest.

Not surprisingly, the beautiful, eclectic and personal style has earned Heartland a place in publications such as *Better Homes and Gardens— Windows and Walls*, *The Seattle Times* and *Eastside Journal*. Heartland has also participated in the Seattle Street of Dreams home show numerous times and has won many awards for excellence in design including the Master Builders MAME Award for Best Interior Design for the Street of Dreams "Welcome Home" project.

Val and Diane attribute their success to their casual, professional and hometown approach to interior design, as well as their enjoyment of working together. They share very similar tastes and a passion for what they do. They both will tell you, "We are so fortunate to work in such a creative and energized field with a very talented and professional team. At Heartland we are like family and our clients become friends. To live the American dream of having a successful business that allows you creative freedom and the enjoyment of working with great people is a true blessing in our lives."

TOP
For an impressive statement, warm woods and rich fabrics were used to produce a grand yet warm comfortable feeling in this dining room.

BOTTOM
Incorporating a touch of black in fabric and accessories is an easy way to add drama and distinctive style to any room.

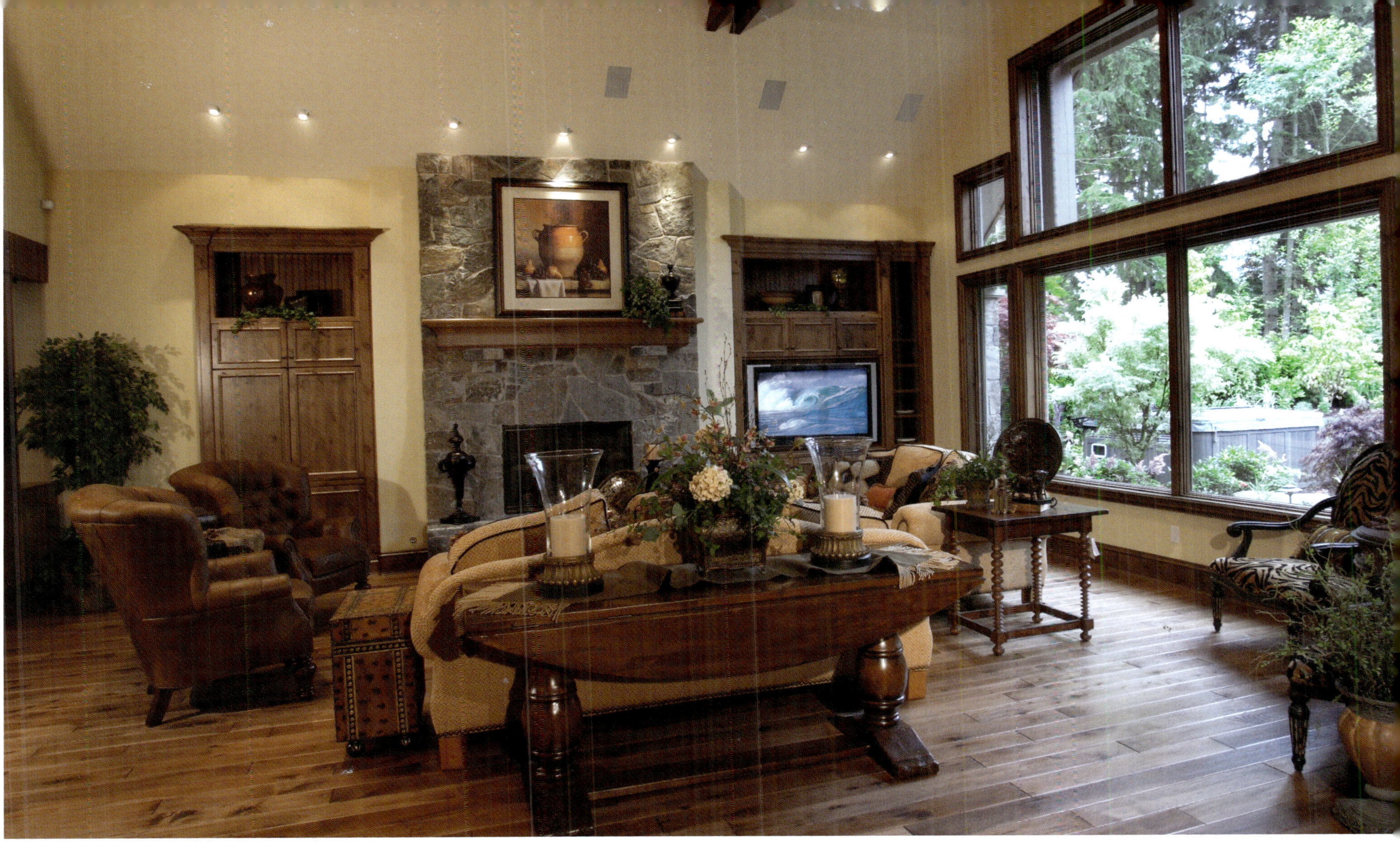

ABOVE
Allow yourself the freedom to experiment with various textures and natural elements to bring the outside in.

More about Diane & Val…

WHAT IS THE HIGHEST COMPLIMENT YOU'VE RECEIVED PROFESSIONALLY?

After completing our 2005 Seattle Street of Dreams home, The Breckenridge, the house was sold and the new owners purchased everything in it.

WHAT ONE ELEMENT OF STYLE OR PHILOSOPHY HAVE YOU STUCK WITH FOR YEARS THAT STILL WORKS FOR YOU TODAY?

"Buy what you love." Design is personal and whether it's a color you're painting, a piece of furniture you're purchasing or an entire home you're furnishing, the end result should bring both satisfaction and enjoyment.

WHAT IS THE BEST PART ABOUT BEING AN INTERIOR DESIGNER?

Two things getting to meet and work with people who start as clients and become very good friends and getting to walk into a project space and see what "is" while immediately getting a vision for how beautiful it will be when completed.

WHAT IS ONE SINGLE THING YOU WOULD DO TO BRING A DULL HOUSE TO LIFE?

Add color! Whether it's as simple as painting a wall, adding pillows and a piece of art, or changing the sofa, color has the power to uplift, inspire and influence any space.

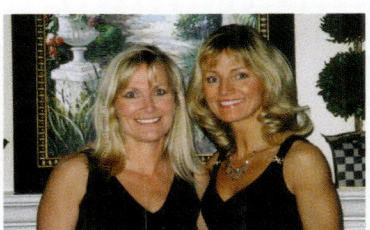

Heartland Interiors, Inc.
Diane Wainhouse & Val Scalzo
23716 8th Ave. SE
Bothell, WA 98021
425.485.1877
Fax 425.486.0828
www.heartlandinteriorsinc.com

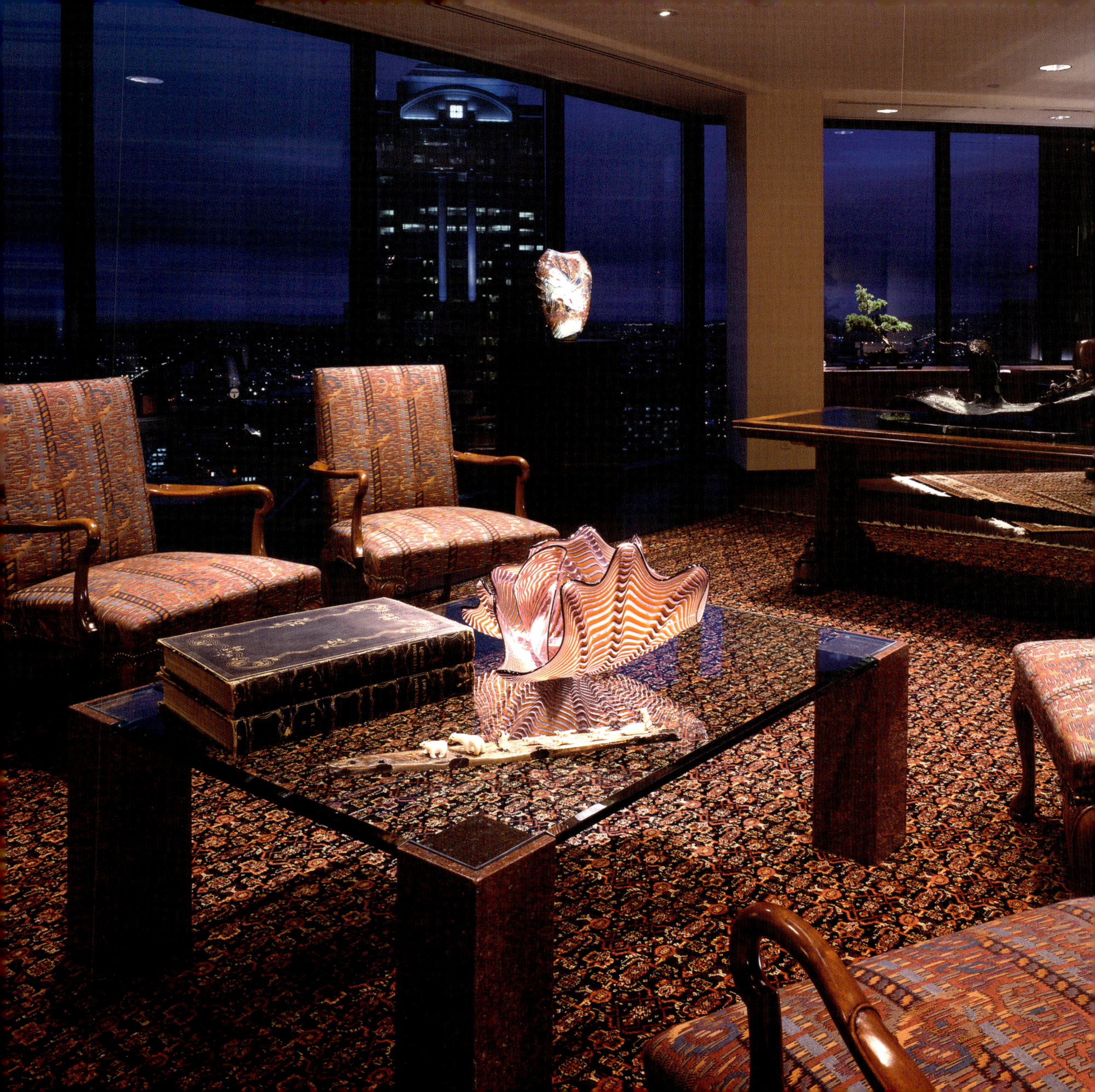

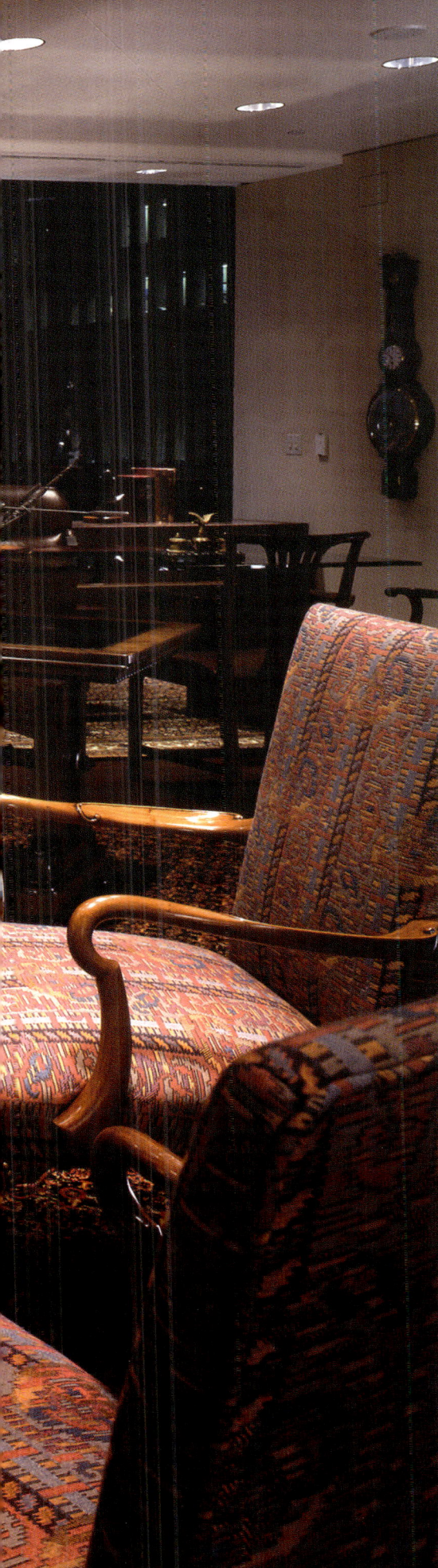

DAVID WEATHERFORD
Weatherford Antiques and Interiors

If you have a passion for antiques, then you've likely heard of David Weatherford. One of the most respected antique dealers and interior designers in the Puget Sound area, David is known for his livable, timeless designs.

Since his introduction into the antique world more than 50 years ago, David has immersed himself in what he calls the "foreign language" of antiques and design. Now, he's considered a master in the language of design by his clients, peers and design organizations.

His expertise has been recognized through dozens of awards and publications, including *Traditional Home Magazine*, *Architectural Digest*, *The Seattle Times* and the *Seattle Post-Intelligencer*. David's work has garnered dozens of awards, including the American Society of Interior Design's prestigious lifetime achievement award.

Gaining the level of talent and knowledge that David possesses is a life-long journey. David began his antiques and design education at the tender age of 18. A college student at the University of Washington, David spent his summer working at one of the premier antique and interior design studios in Seattle. "I was mainly polishing silver and delivering furniture, but I really liked it," he says. "I liked it so much, I went back to school and changed my major to interior design and architecture."

LEFT
Office space designed for the President of a Multinational Corporation.

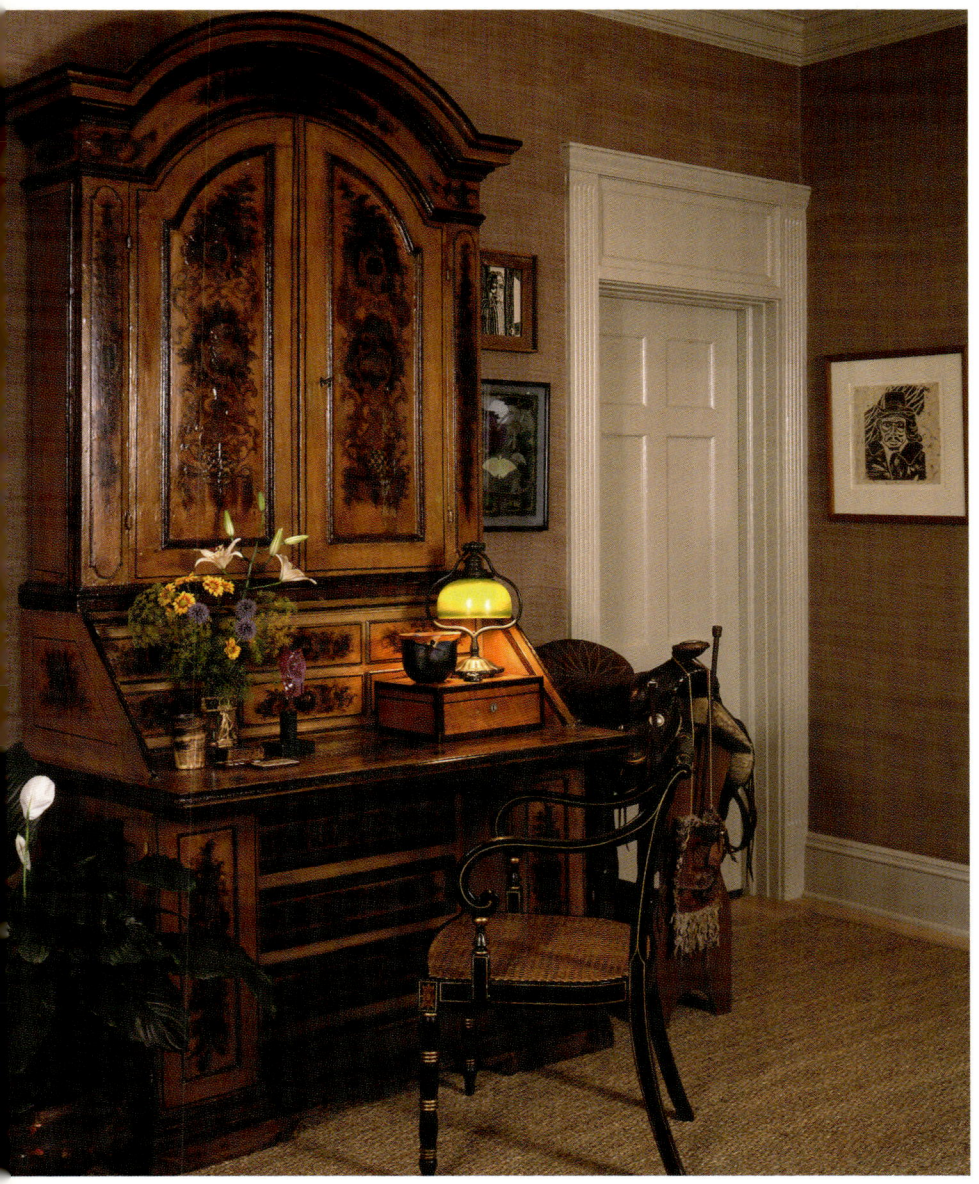
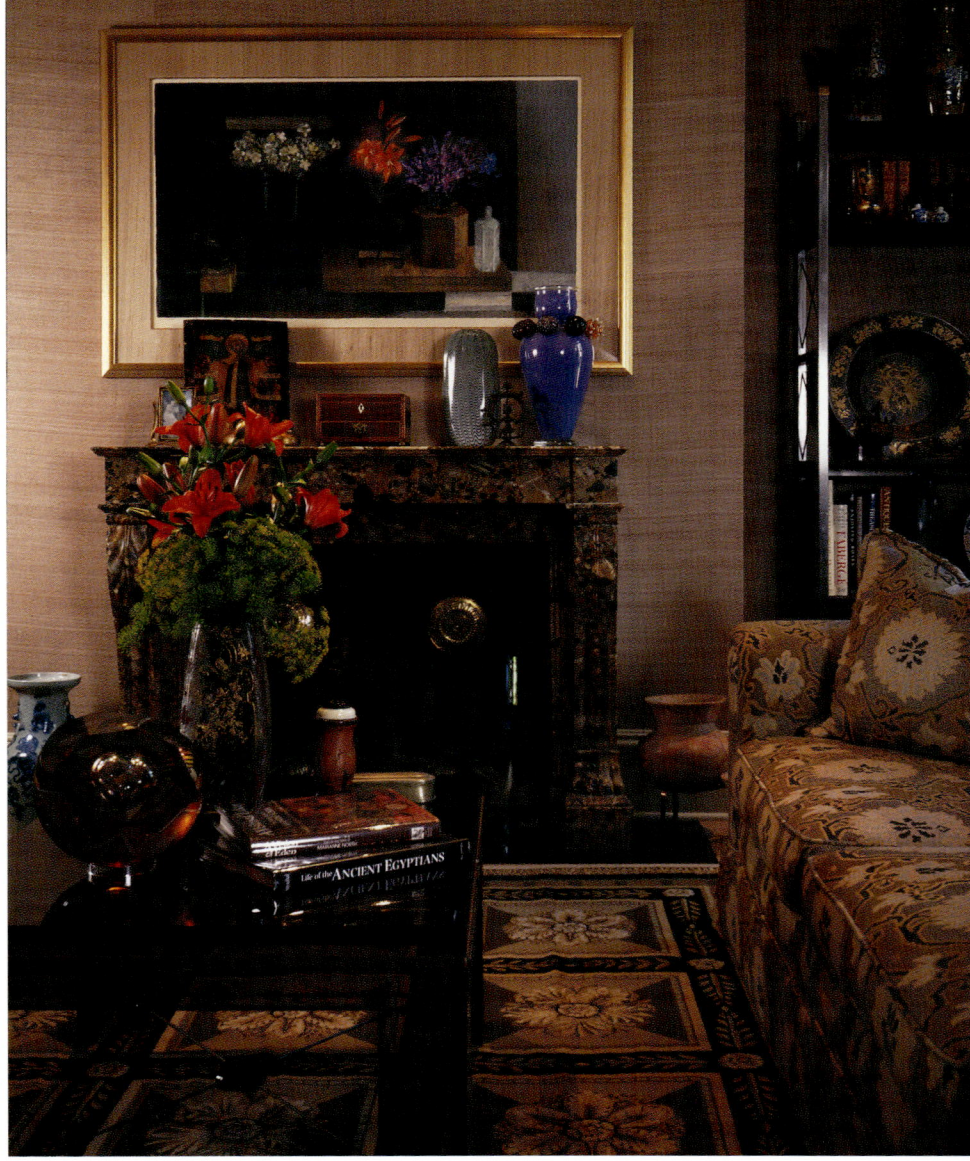

After spending years honing his knowledge and skills, David opened his own business, David Weatherford Antiques and Interiors, in Seattle in 1969. Akin to an old-fashioned design studio combined with an antique showcase, David Weatherford Antiques and Interiors offers more than 4,000 square feet of fine art and authentic antiques, as well as full design services. Not surprisingly, David surrounds himself with others who are just as dedicated and talented as he is. His senior designer, Jonathan O'Brien, has a BA in fine arts from New York University. He has also completed design programs at New York School of Design and Harvard Graduate School of Design.

When it comes to design, David believes that no two clients—and, thus, no two houses—are the same. In fact, David prides himself on making each space different from anything he has done in the past. "Every house is a painting for the person who lives there," he says. "It is a blank canvas, and you and the client have the chance to fill it. You are setting the stage for their lives."

In some cases, David has set the stage for his clients more than once. "I started with some clients when they were twenty, and now I've done their houses four or five times over," he says. "You become a part of the family. You know their kids and grandkids and the names of their pets."

Clients get the benefit of David's wide experience, both within the design world and in the world at large. David often travels the world to choose the best fabrics and furniture. "My design is influenced by every place I go," he says. "You take with you all of that knowledge and all of those experiences."

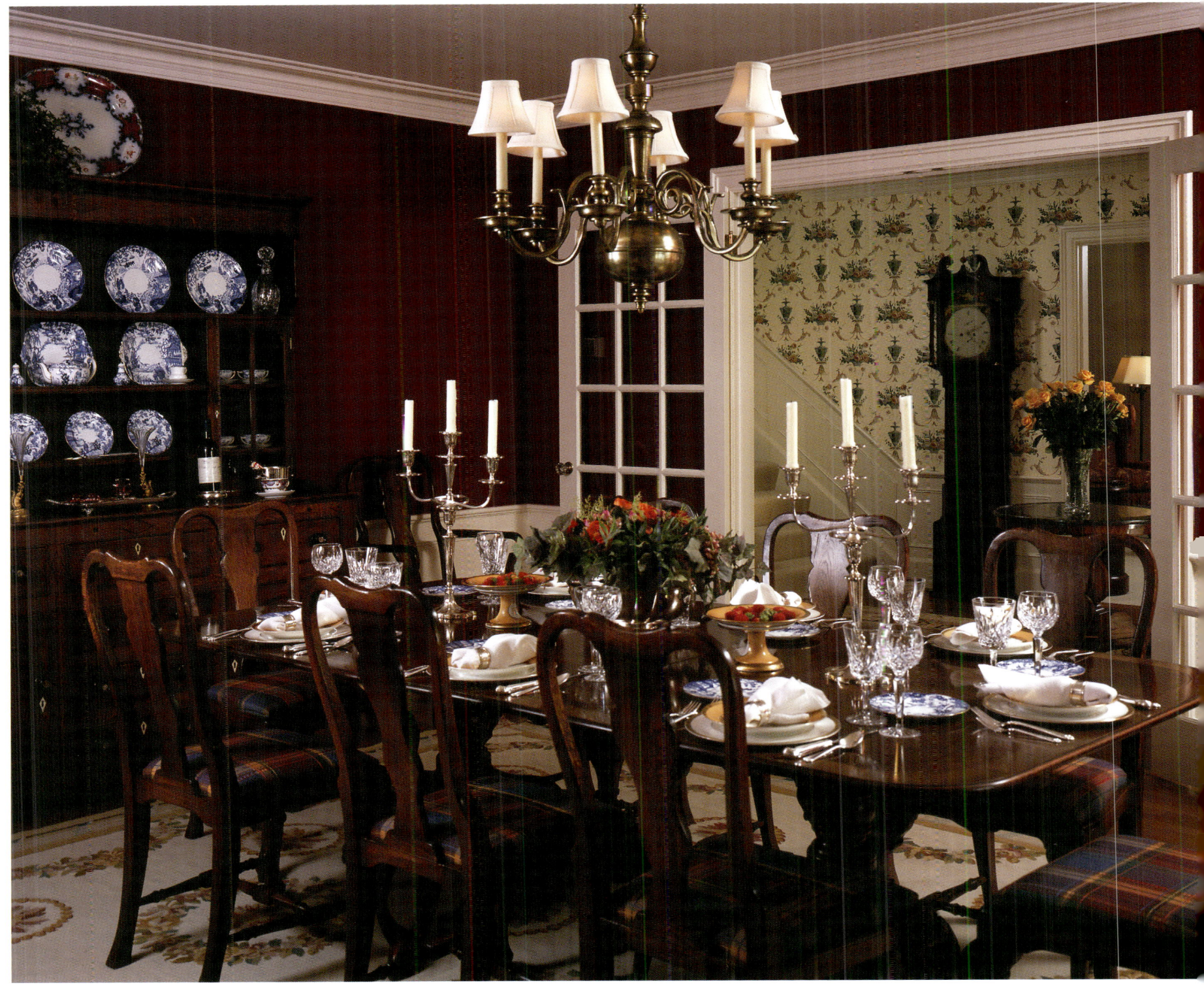

ABOVE
Informal dining room in a traditional country house on Lake Washington.

FACING PAGE LEFT & RIGHT
A mix of contemporary and antique pieces in a small in-city cottage.

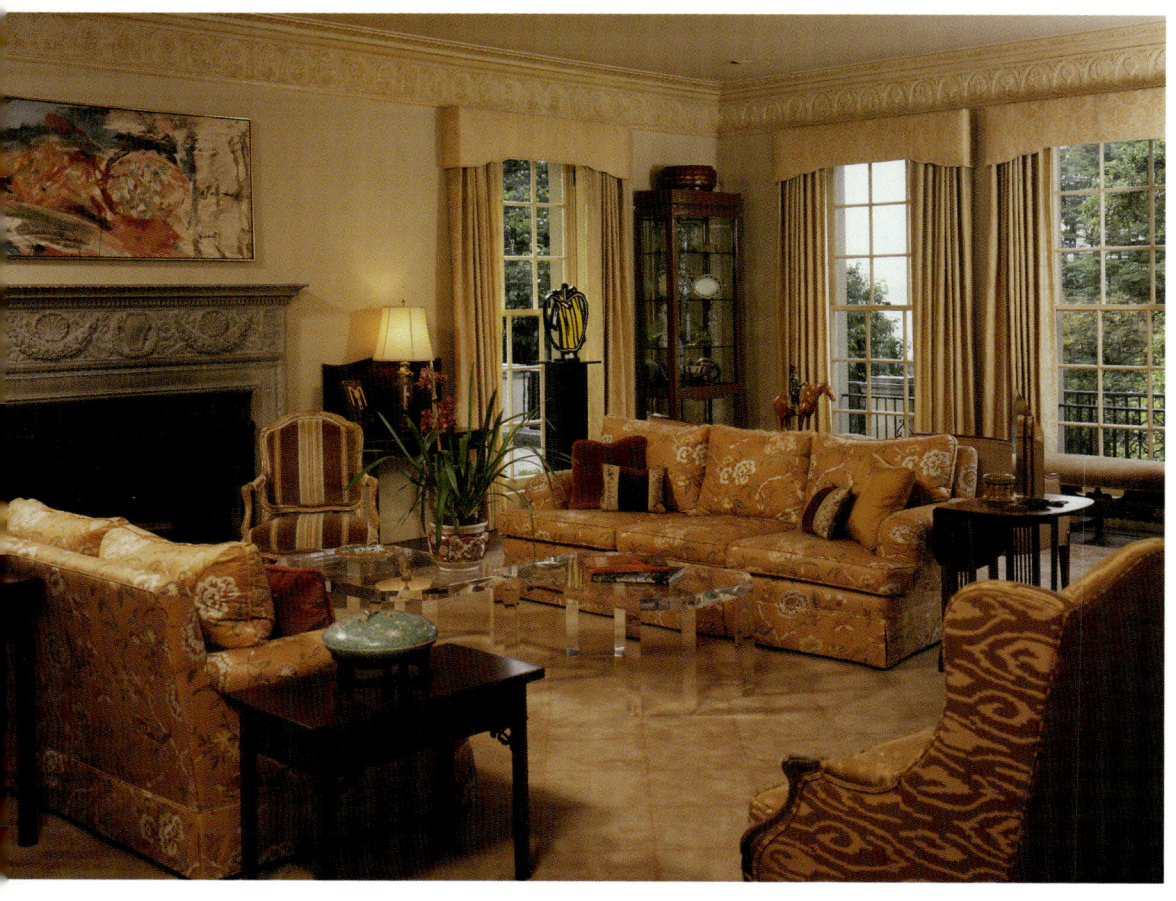

David is a firm believer in being part of the design community. Currently, he is a member of ASID, Better Business Bureau of Washington and is the only business in Washington State that is a member of the Art & Antique Dealers League of America. Over the years, David has sat on several boards related to the arts community, including The King County Arts Commission, The Seattle Art Museum, The Henry Art Gallery, and The Museum of History and Industry.

In addition to his work as a designer, David makes a valuable contribution to his community through donations and charity work. "I think as a designer, it's very important to not only take from the community, but to give back," David says. "You're part of the lifeblood of the community."

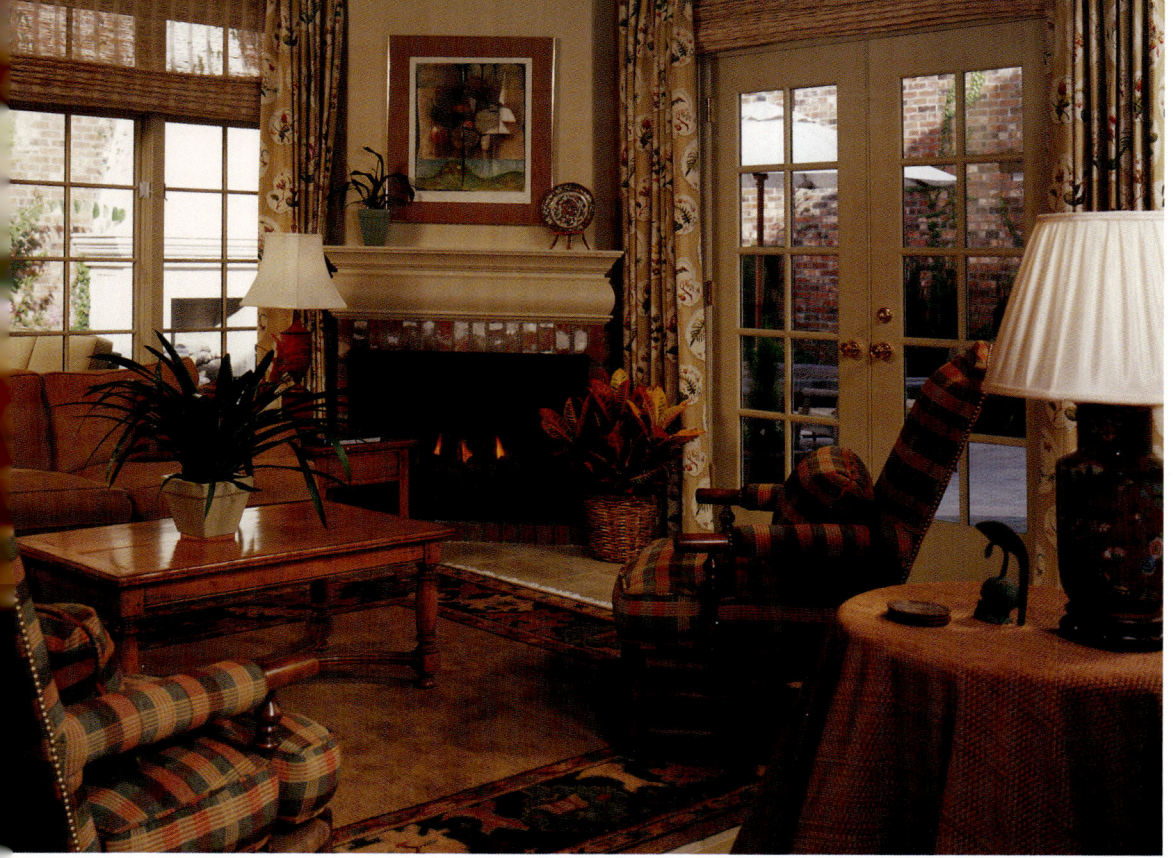

TOP
A gracious formal living room in a grand estate.

BOTTOM
An inviting family room in a Northwest contemporary home.

FACING PAGE LEFT
A striking vignette in a renovated classic home.

FACING PAGE RIGHT
Window treatments and fabrics bring color and life to any room.

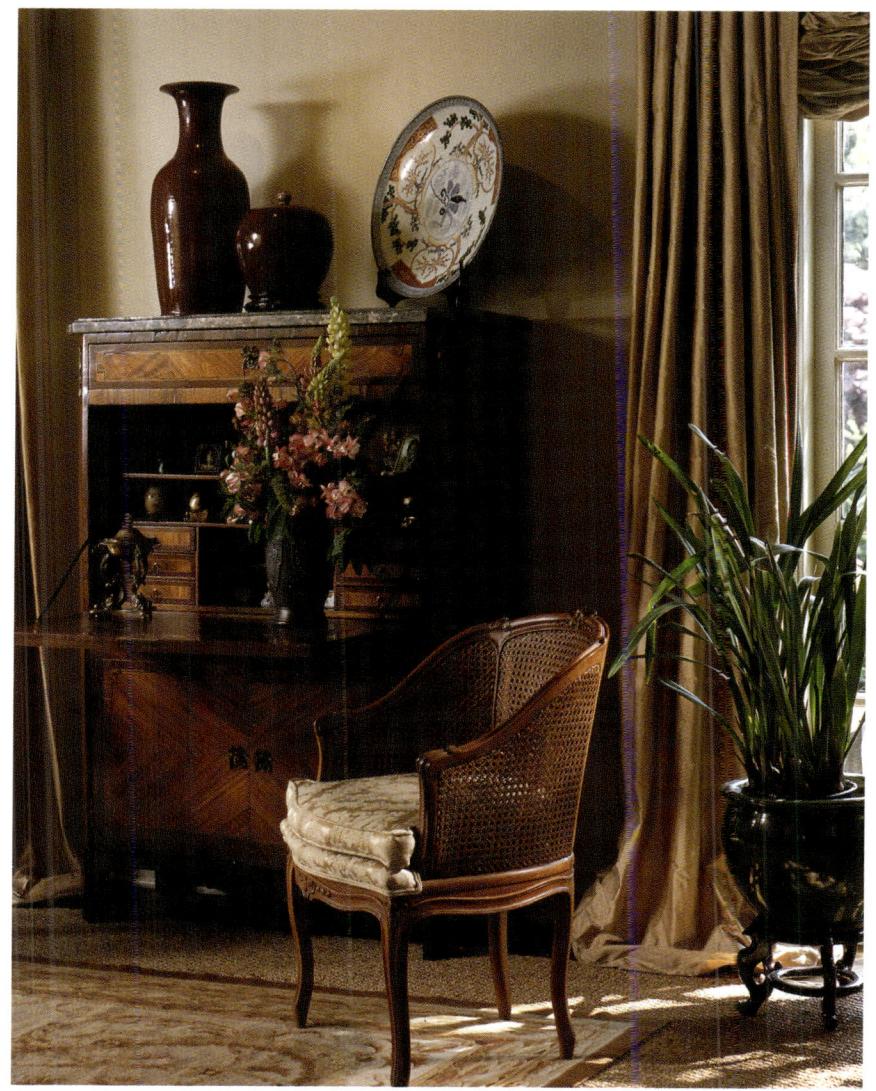
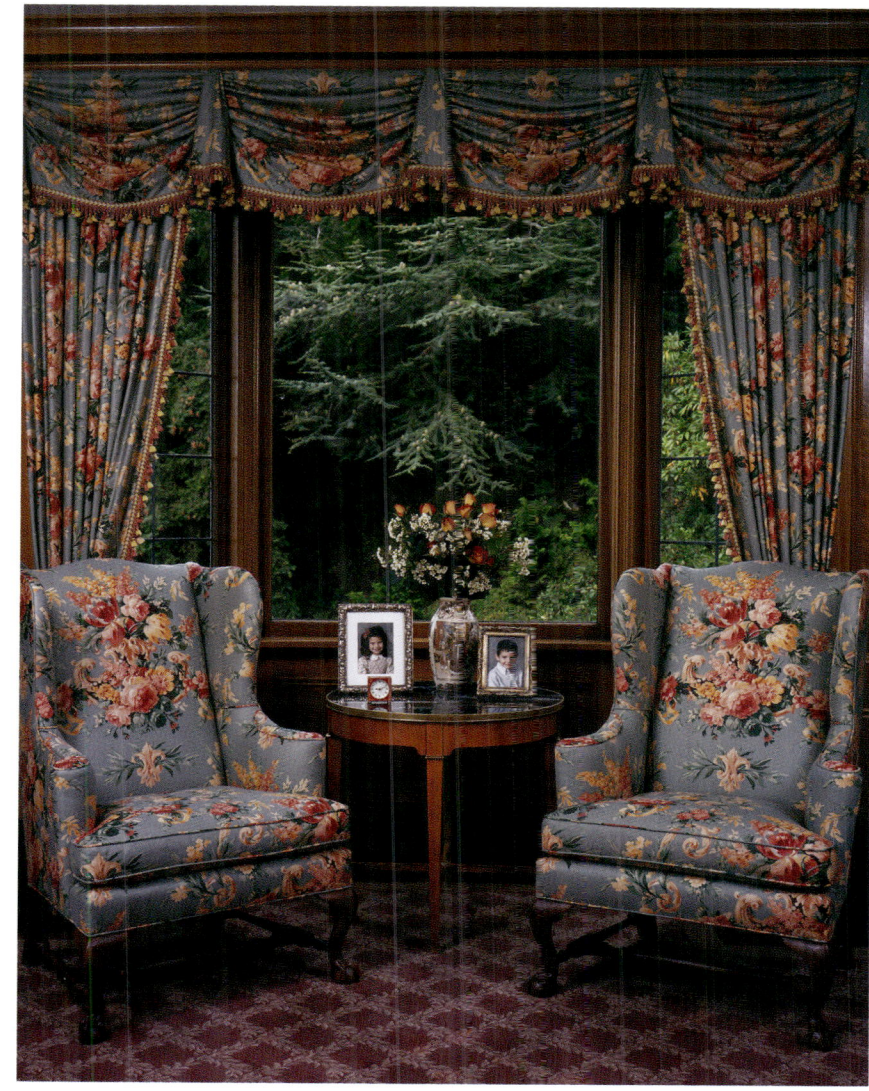

More about David...

WHAT PERSONAL INDULGENCE DO YOU SPEND THE MOST MONEY ON?

Buying art and antiques, travel.

WHAT IS THE BEST PART OF BEING AN INTERIOR DESIGNER?

Meeting new people and giving them the kind of home they always wanted.

WHAT IS THE HIGHEST COMPLIMENT YOU'VE RECEIVED PROFESSIONALLY?

That my designs are timeless.

DESCRIBE YOUR DESIGN STYLE...

Classic, timeless, livable design.

WHO HAS HAD THE BIGGEST INFLUENCES ON YOUR CAREER?

Fredrick E. Davis, Sr. Partner WMC Davis and Hope Foote Dean of Design at the University of Washington.

WHAT DO YOU LIKE ABOUT DOING BUSINESS IN THE NORTHWEST?

People are very approachable and open to new ideas..

Weatherford Antiques and Interiors
David Weatherford
133 Fourteenth Ave.
East Seattle, WA 98112
206-329-6533
Fax 206-329-9348
www.davidweatherford.com

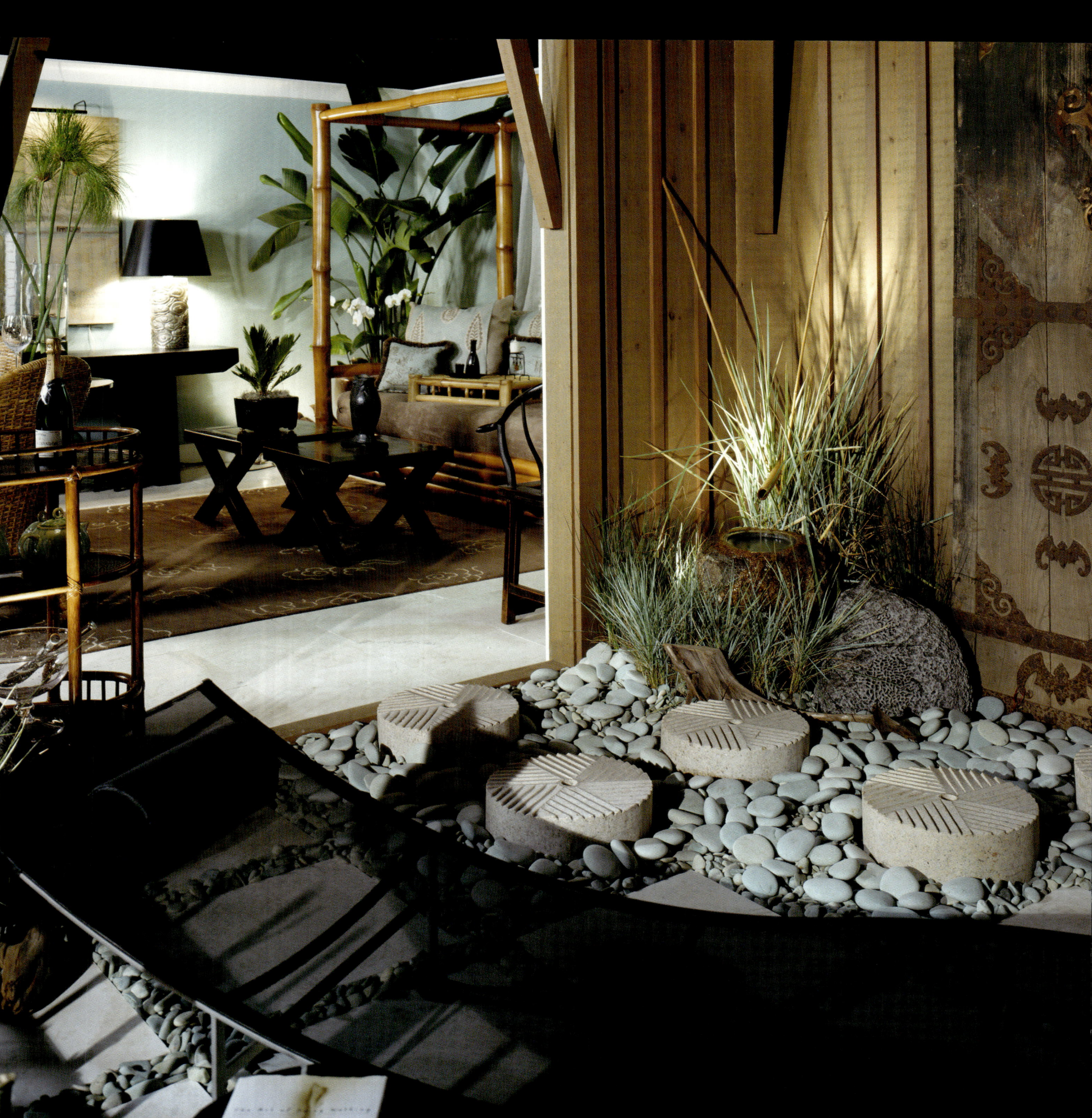

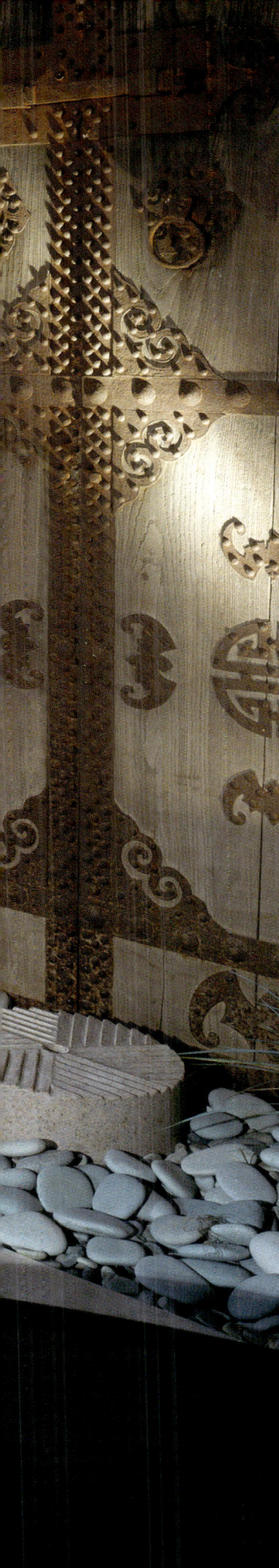

KATHLEEN WILLIAMS

Design by Kathleen Williams, Inc.

Kathleen Williams brings unparalleled expertise and a worldly, sophisticated vision to the design process. From luxurious urban penthouses to classic family homes, from yachts to coastal and mountain retreats, Kathleen has designed interiors for them all.

An interior designer in the Seattle area since 1983 and the owner of her company since 1993, Kathleen thrives on her hectic schedule. She is at her best when balancing a diverse range of jobs, from assisting clients with selections for new construction and remodeling projects to tracking down the perfect accessory to complete a home. "To see a project that you have worked on with a team of highly talented architects, contractors, craftsmen and artisans completed is very rewarding. To know your clients are happy with their home and to know that you have enhanced their quality of life with your design is the best part for me," she says.

Kathleen often enlists the assistance of a team of qualified and talented professionals-architects, contractors, craftsmen and artisans-to best enhance her clients' quality of life with her designs.

LEFT
Asian inspired "Coastal Retreat" shows a pair of antique Chinese doors in a "Zen garden." Budji bamboo opium bed, McGuire cloud lamp.

RIGHT
An antique Chinese cabinet holds a custom glass sink. Kohler falling water faucet. Aqua pebbles are inset in Florentine limestone floor.

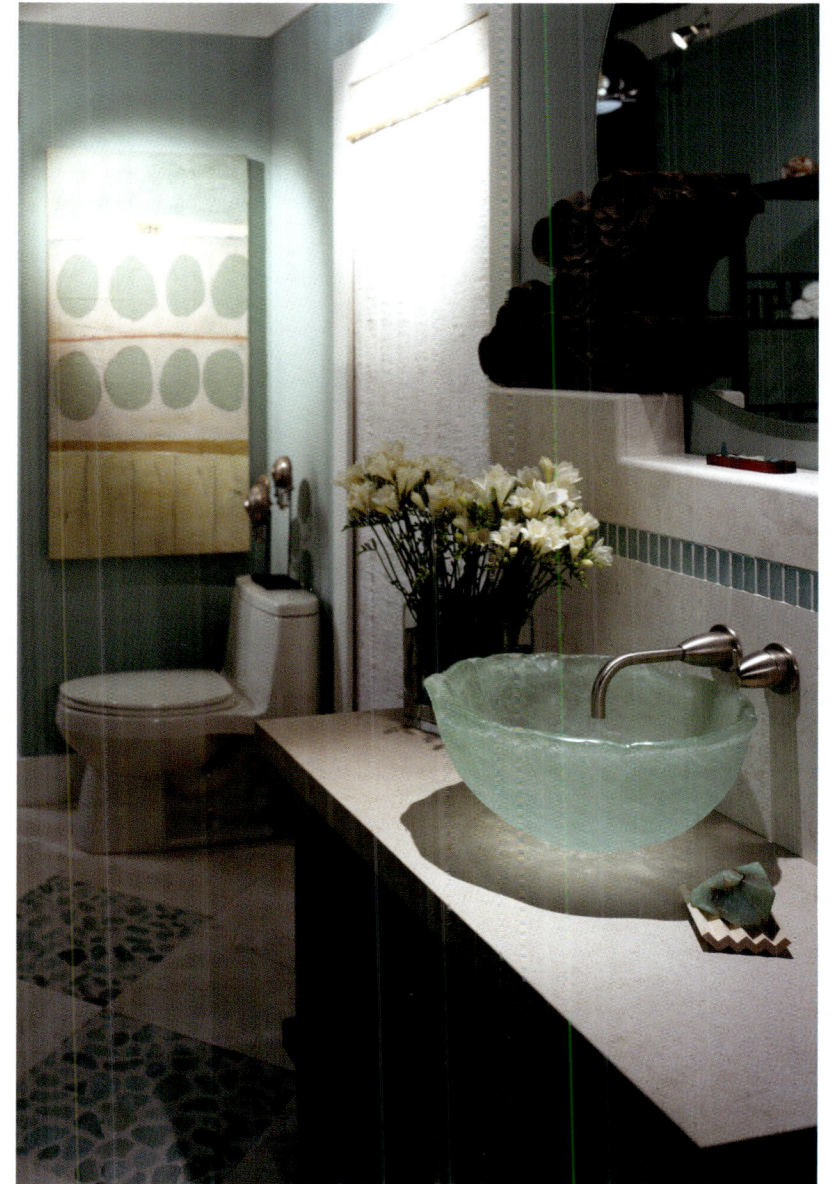

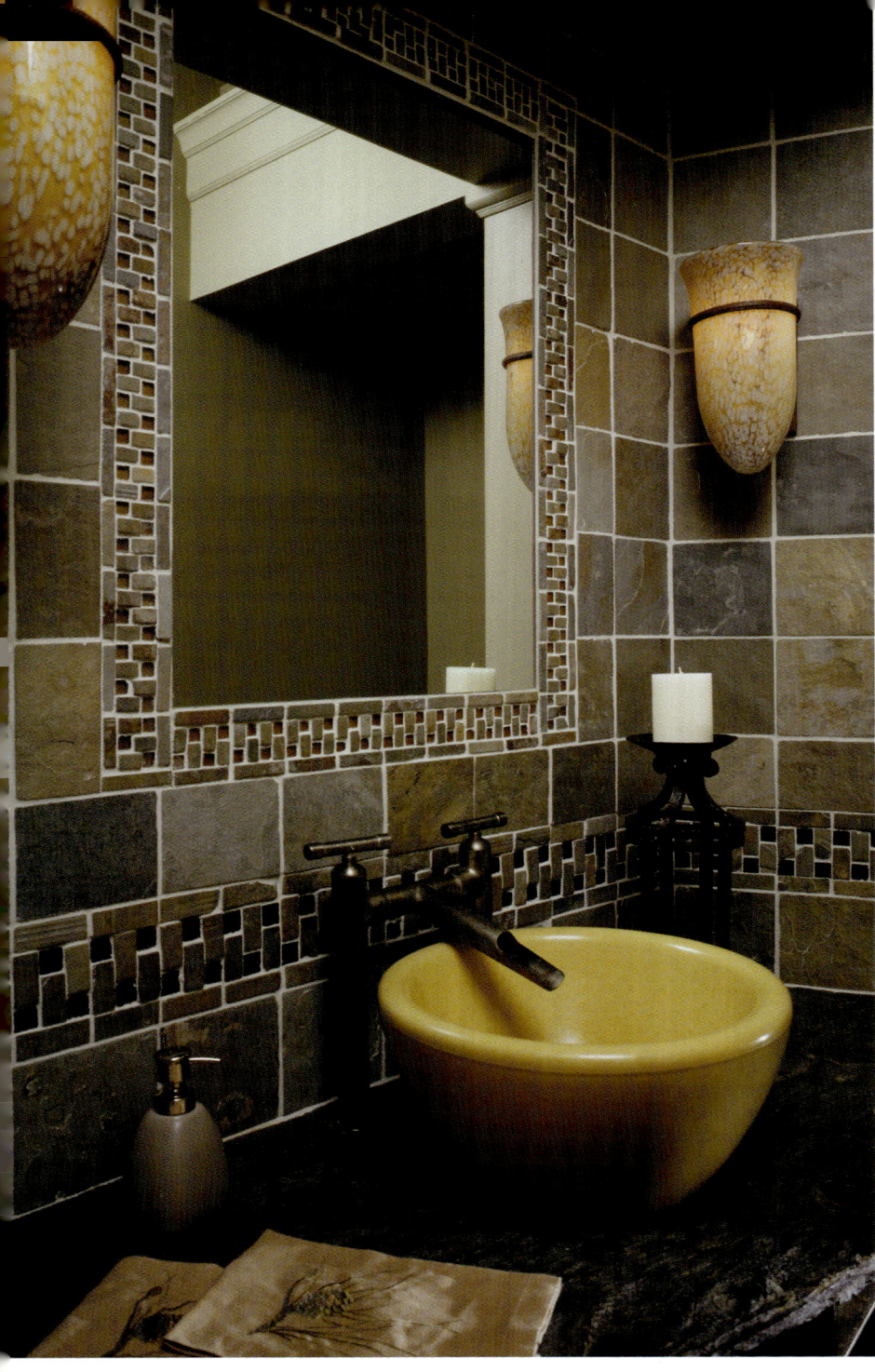

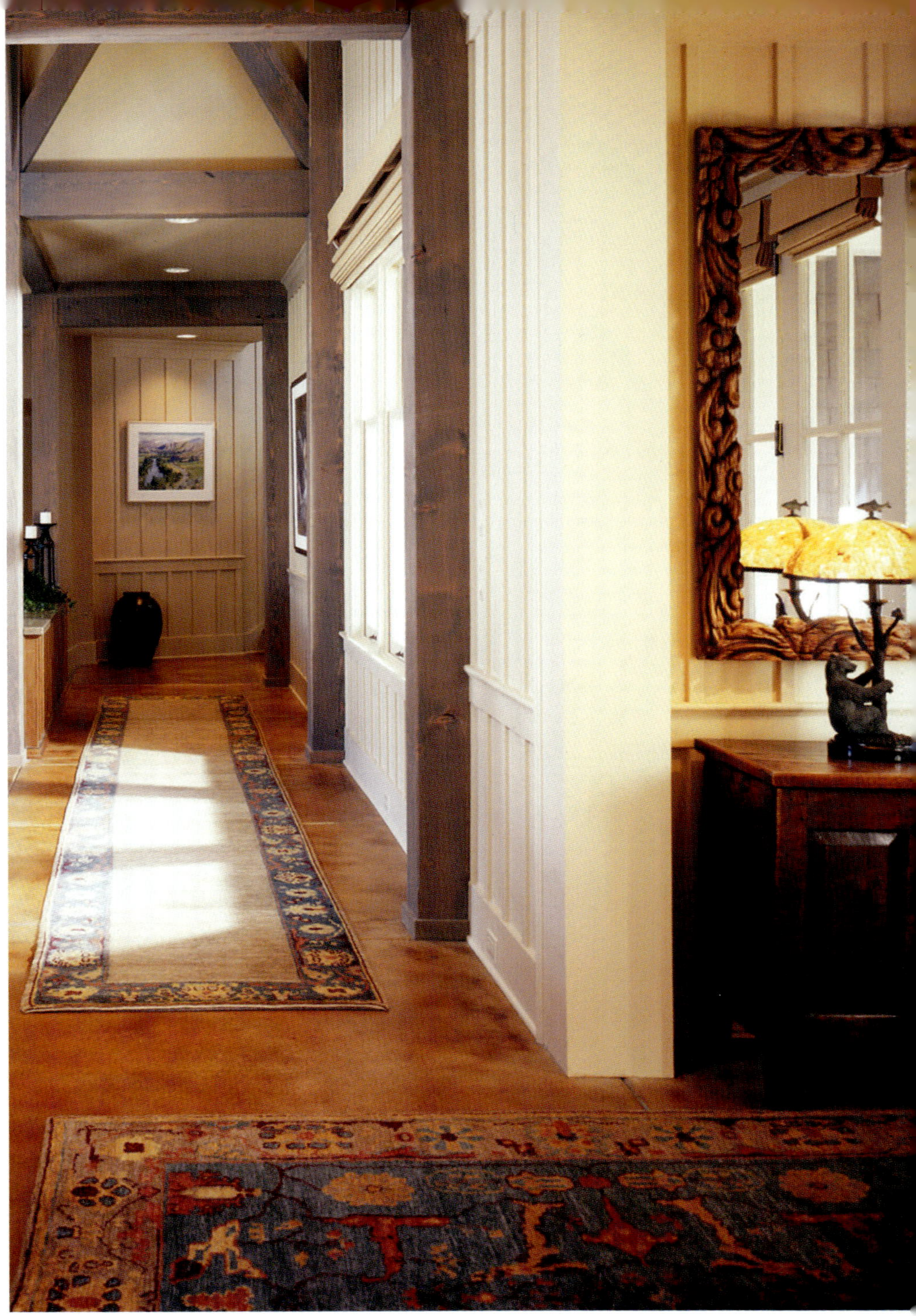

LEFT
Slate and glass mosaic borders provide accents in slate-tiled wall. Concrete sink and rustic faucet top natural edged slate top. Custom lighting designed by Kathleen Williams.

RIGHT
Custom Tibetan carpets top acid-stained concrete floors. Antique Asian mirror hangs above antique English coffer in entry.

FACING PAGE RIGHT
Kitchen cabinets are distressed and contrast with artisan tile backspash. Hanging pendant lights were handblown by artist in Pioneer Square.

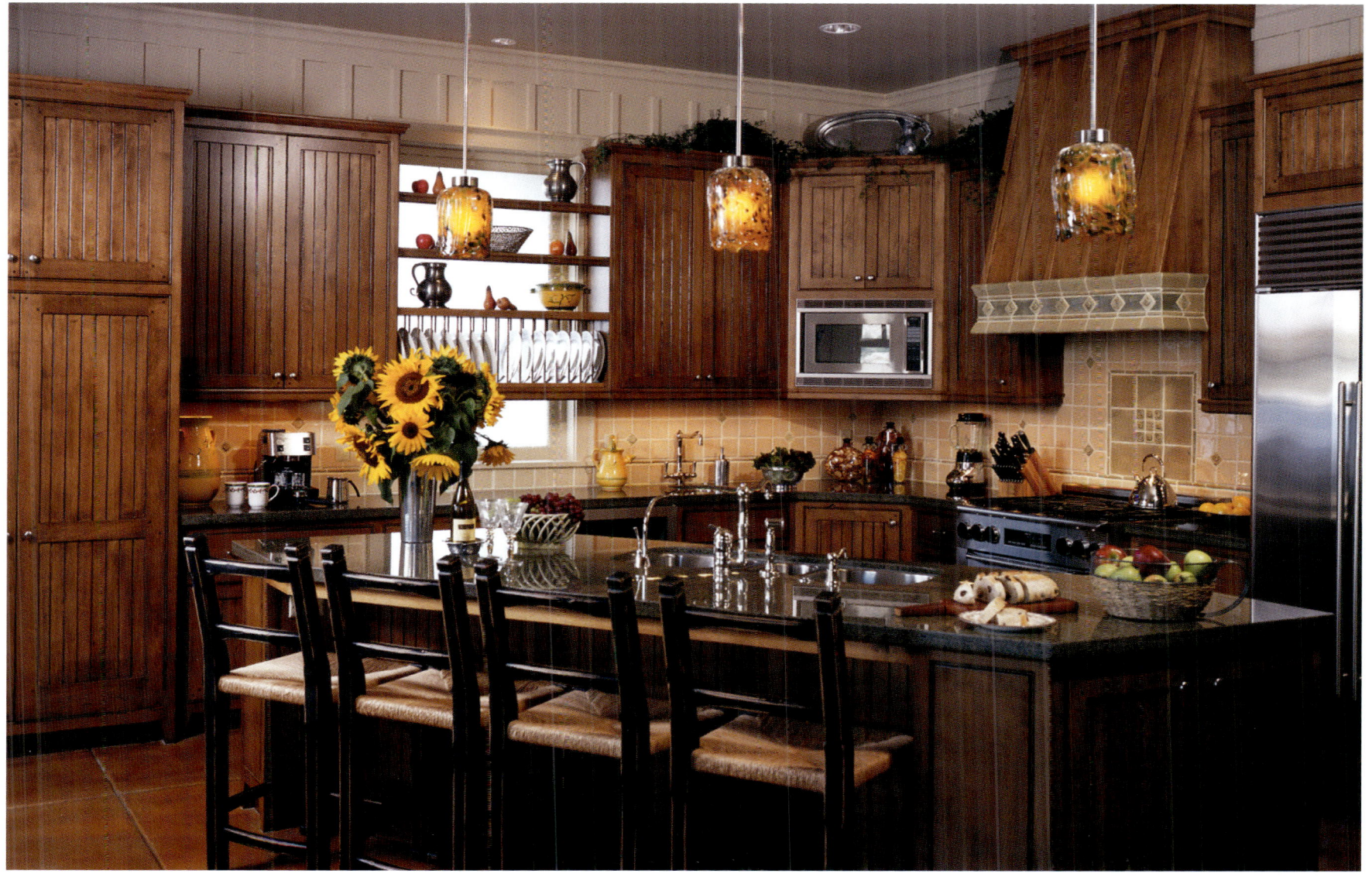

Numerous awards attest to the quality of Kathleen's work. She is a two-time recipient of the ASID Awards of Excellence Silver Award for a complete residence, the ASID Awards of Excellence Gold Award for Outdoor Space and the ASID Design for Life Award for Weekend Retreat. In the 2003 Seattle Interior Show, Kathleen received her most memorable awards, including Judges Choice, Designers Choice and a gold award for her room called "A Coastal Retreat." She has also been published in *Seattle Homes & Lifestyles* magazine several times.

A long-time resident of the Pacific Northwest, Kathleen's design style is strongly influenced by the world around her. She loves unfussy, clean lines and the sumptuous textures and subtle colors found in nature. Inspired by the Pacific Rim, she enjoys the simplicity and practicality of Asian antiques paired with soft Tibetan carpets and furniture that you can be comfortable in. She is equally at home using European influences to create a home that reflects her clients' personality.

Kathleen's clients appreciate her ability to listen and to help them make the best design choices for their lifestyle. She does not believe in the "cookie cutter approach," insisting instead that every project reflect her clients unique taste and lifestyle. Many of her clients' become lifelong friends. Working in multiple homes for the same client simultaneously can be very challenging, especially if one of the projects is long distance. I keep them on track and focused, helping them to envision the "whole picture."

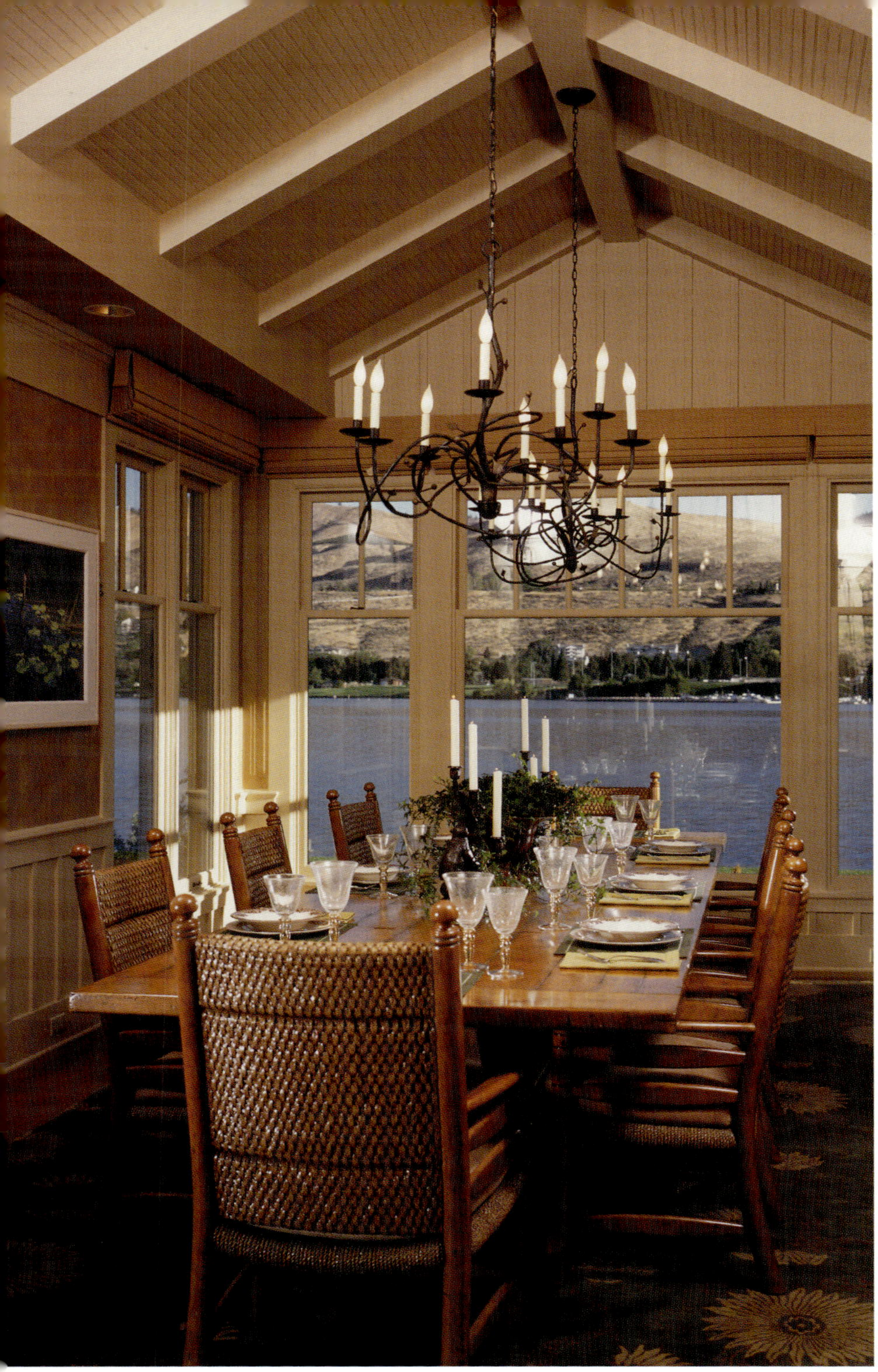

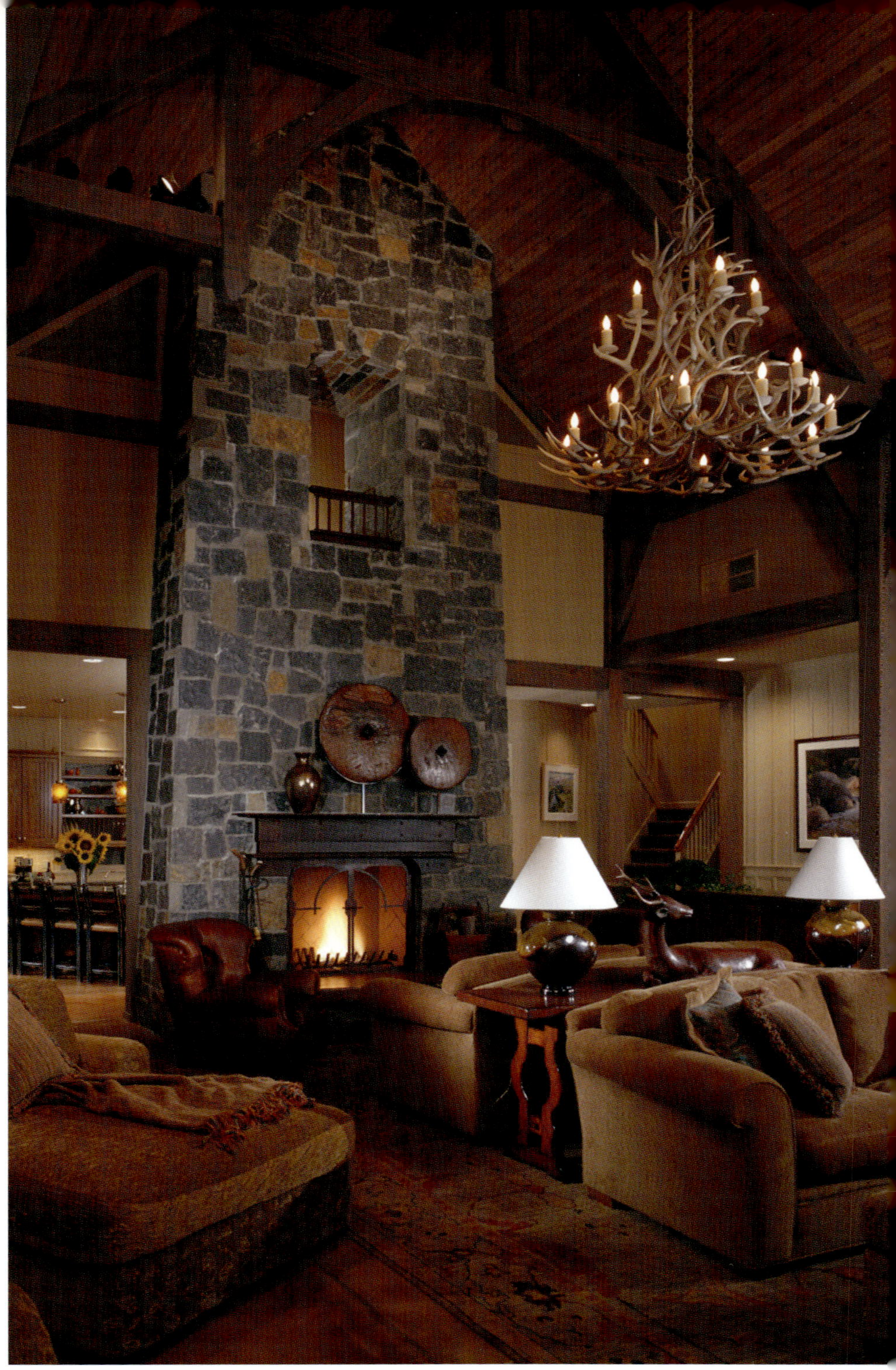

LEFT
A rustic Guy Chaddock table is surrounded by water hycinth and wood chairs. Whimsical chandeliers are from France.

RIGHT
The great room has two seating areas, one that faces the cozy fireplace and the other facing the entertainment center. Glant fabric on sofas.

FACING PAGE RIGHT
A canoe suspended from the ceiling and a naturally shed antler chandelier reinforce the lodge feeling these clients were looking for.

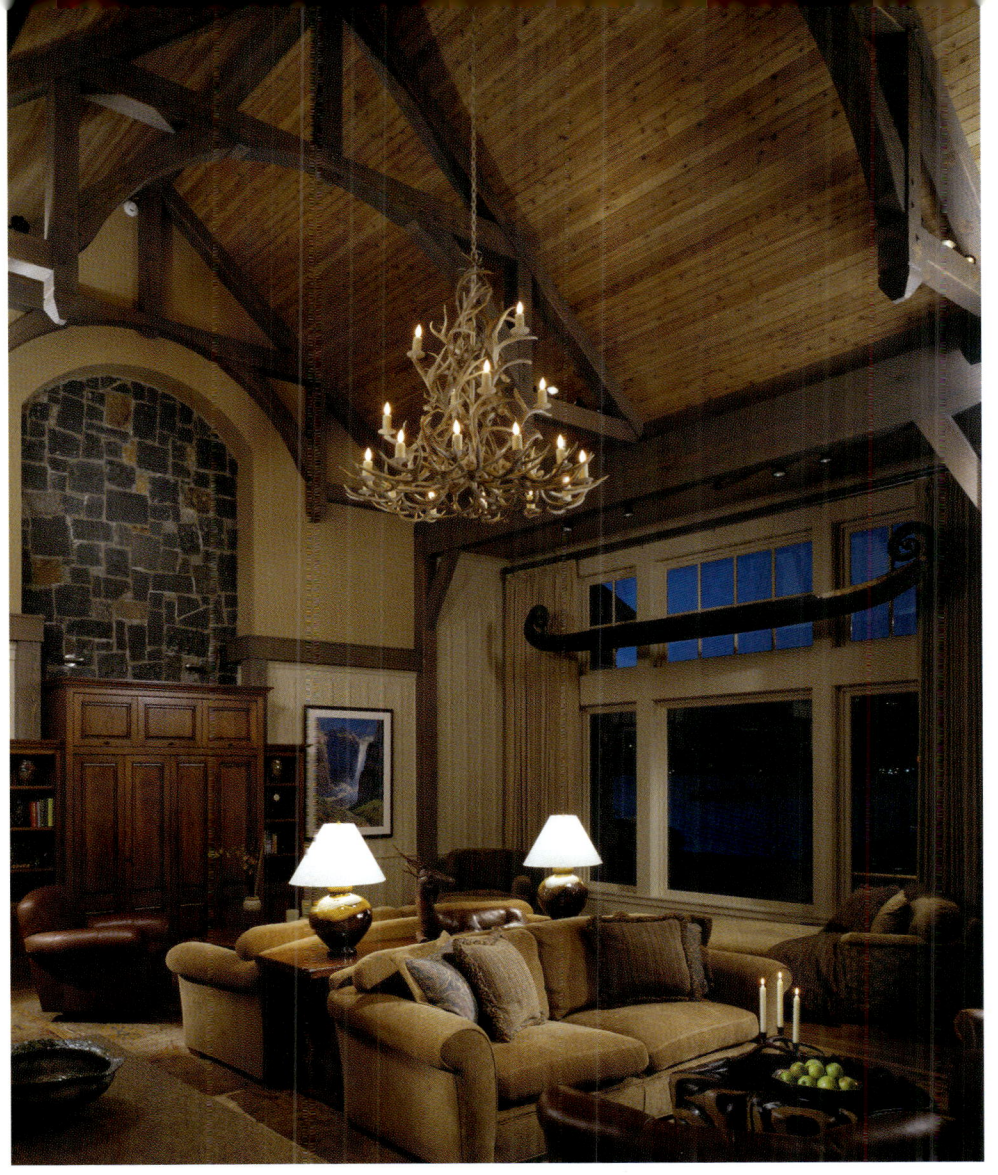

More about Kathleen...

WHAT PERSONAL INDULGENCE DO YOU SPEND MONEY ON?

Asian antiques and travel. She loves the simplicity of Asian design and the serenity it creates in her home. She and her husband, Tom, also love to travel to just about anyplace with crystal clear turquoise water and palm trees.

WHAT COLOR BEST DESCRIBES YOU?

She absolutely loves the color beach glass aqua, that lovely soft color that is so diffused and calming. Growing up near the ocean instilled a love of the water that has stayed with her all of her life.

YOU CAN TELL SHE LIVES IN THE PACIFIC NORTHWEST BECAUSE.....

She never carries an umbrella. And she can always spot the transplants by their bumbershoots.

WHAT IS THE SINGLE THING YOU WOULD DO TO BRING A DULL HOUSE TO LIFE?

Buy fresh flowers–an orchid will last for months and give you a sophisticated, exotic element that tells people "an interesting person lives here."

Design by Kathleen Williams, Inc.
Kathleen Williams, Allied Member ASID
2000 124th Avenue NE
Suite B-102
Bellevue, WA 98005
425.455.1818
www.kathleenwilliams.com

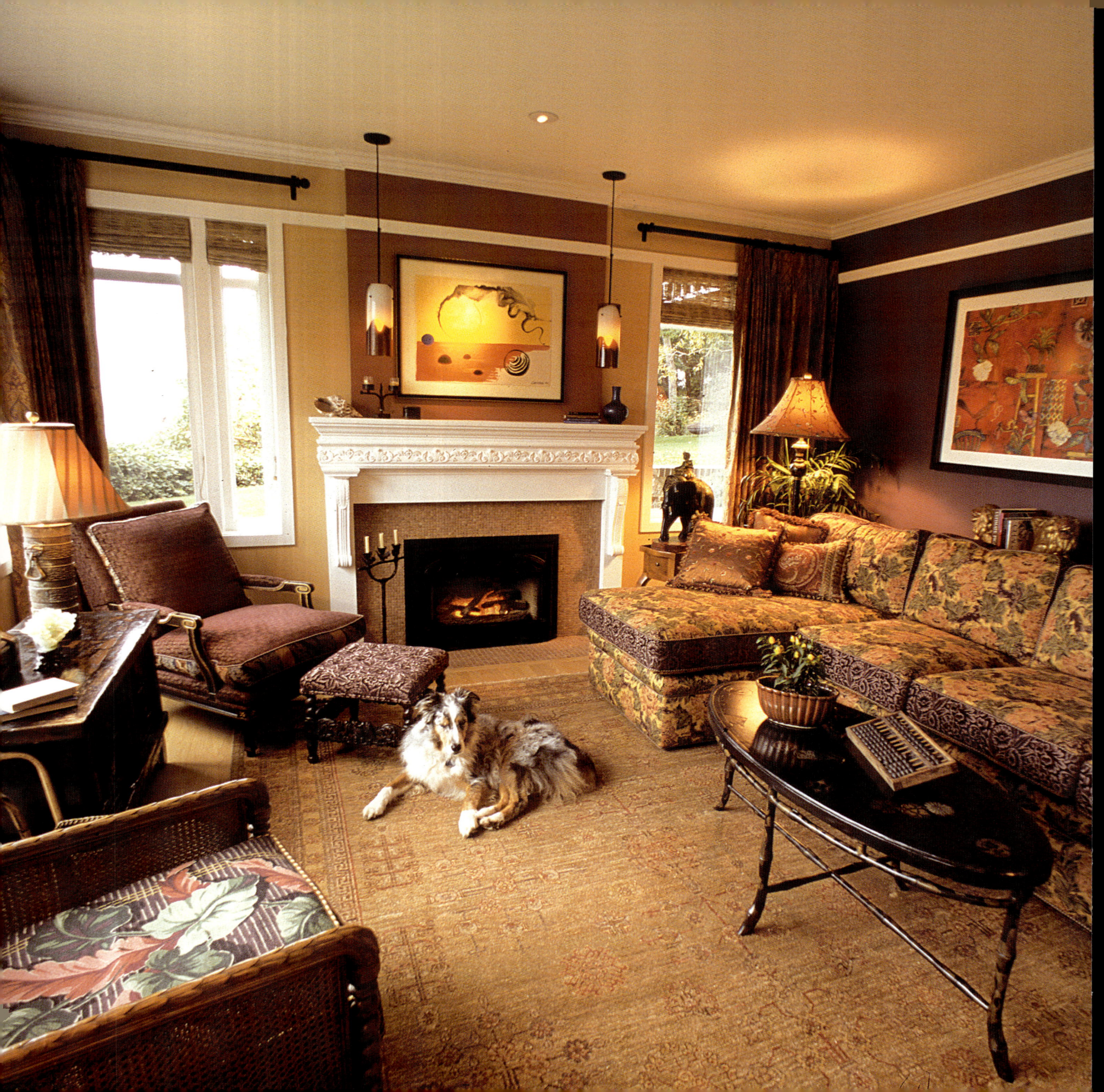

ANN JONES WILSON
Jones-Wilson Designs

"Comfort and beauty, cheerful and nurturing," Ann Jones-Wilson's energy and enthusiasm is focused. "I love what I do…it's understanding Life. People's stories. I listen and look—clients send messages with words, with body language, with their environment. Clients seldom realize how much they already know about design. I had a client say,'I hate green, I can't live with green' and I looked in the closets and they had all this green. I'm excited when I help them discover what they already know."

Jones-Wilson works with clients, as well as client/architect and client/contractor combinations, from detail consultant to total project involvement. She excels at big jobs, little jobs, working solo or bringing together a team for the timely, nourishing, mostly-cheerful process, backed by Karen Perlot's Design Support Services.

Asking about Jones-Wilson's bold juxtapositions of unusual elements: "I was 12 years old when my mother had a friend who noticed my design skills. She took me down to a furniture store and I picked out her furniture and some art. Growing up, I assumed anyone could visualize space the way I could. And

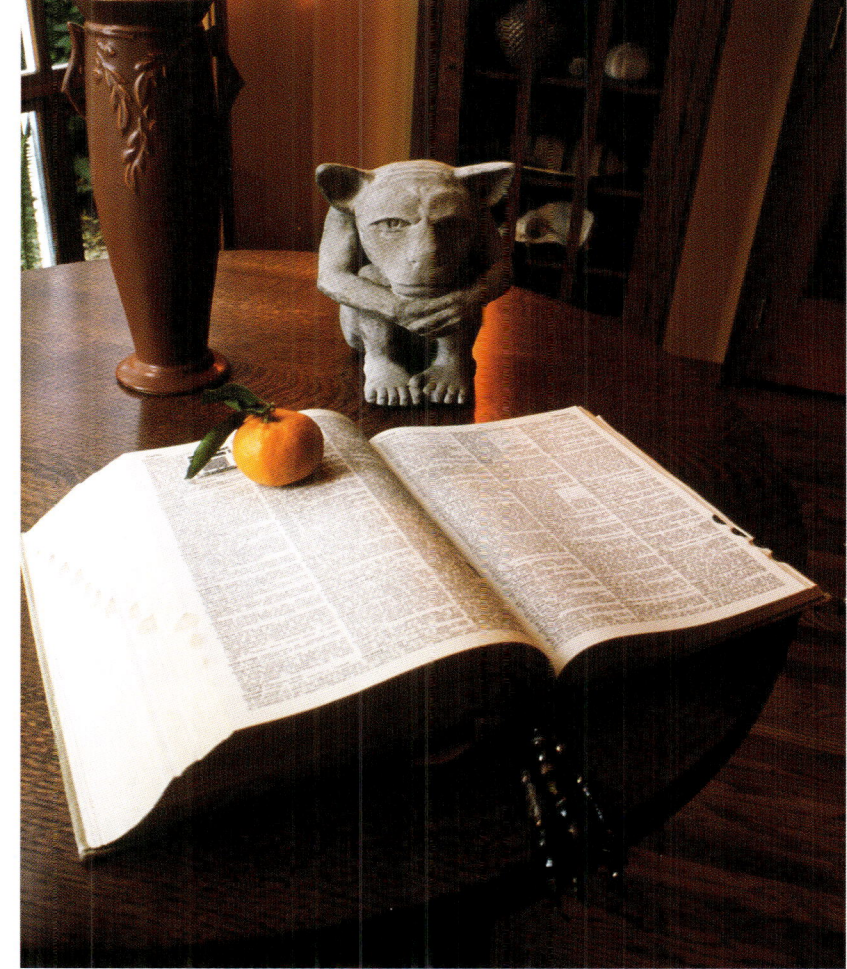

LEFT
An antique English foot stool, an Ironies table, Kim Osgood's monotype "Pleasure," elephants and Asian statuary: Bold juxtapositions of unusual elements each newly acquired to create a collection expressing the owner's personal history, anchored by Alexander Calder's 1966 watercolor

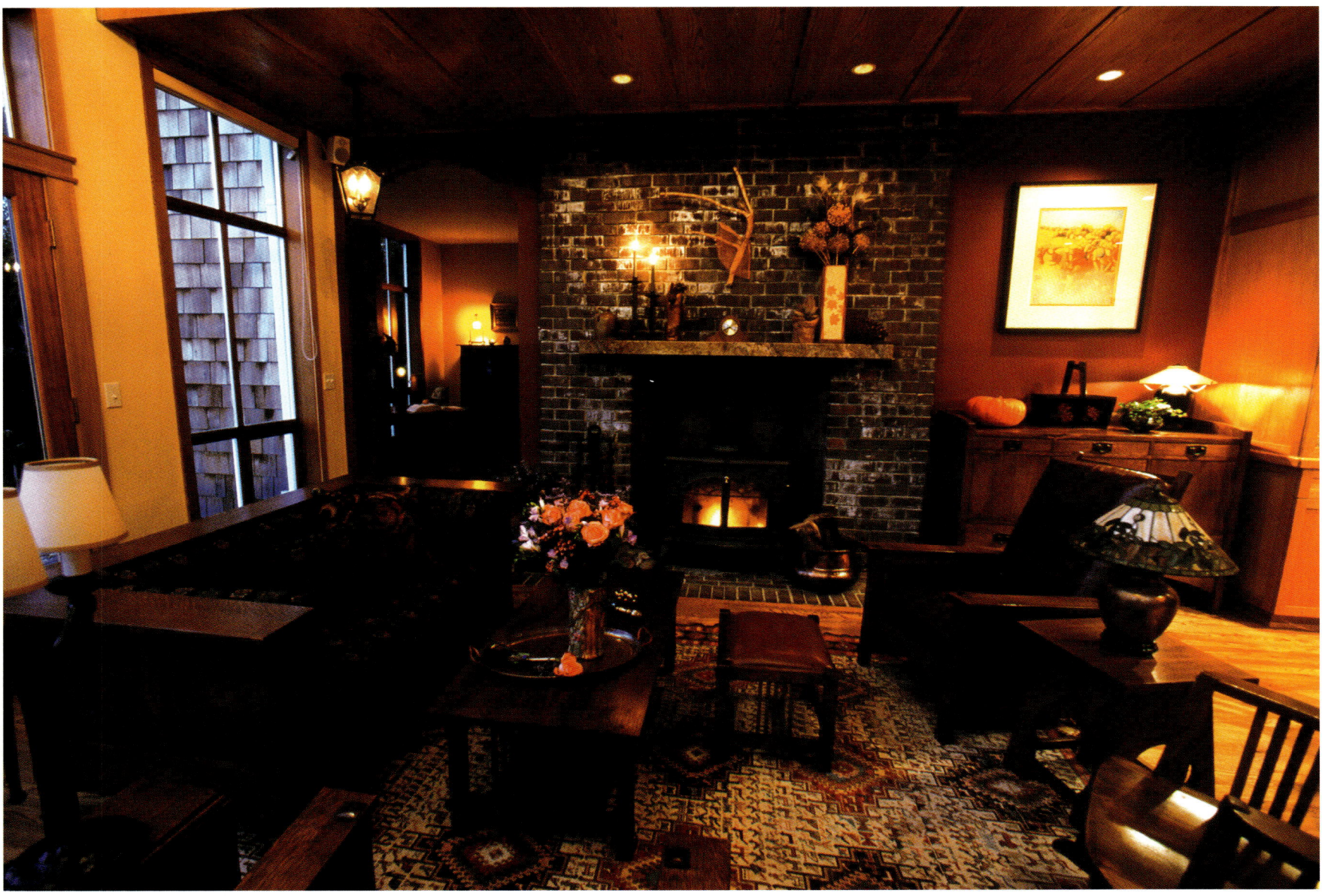

then I realized it was a gift I had: being able to walk into a space and 'fit' it to the people's dynamics, their activities, their treasures. Good design really does change family dynamics. 'Create a space and they will come'."

Jones-Wilson continues, "Invite beauty. Looking and listening encourages clients to share with me their self-discovery of what beauty, what intimacy, what playfulness they want to invite—what can inspire."

Materializing the guiding vision of designer-client interactions come the materials and tools Jones-Wilson orchestrates: Furniture, wall paper, paint, fabrics, art, window treatments, light, space, the building's structural 'bones.' Aware and knowledgeable about daily and seasonal sky intensities, color temperatures, directions and qualities of natural light—with all its mysterious dances with the soul—she overlays the quantity and quality of artificial light. This all couples with memories, imaginings to conspire to create homes and public spaces beautiful, comfortable, efficient and regenerative for mind, body and spirit.

But it wasn't always this way. Jones-Wilson talked about her extensive experience. She used the phrase, "the generosity of the universe." The details from further questioning were fascinating and insightful.

"When I moved to Bainbridge Island and had two children, commuting to Seattle wasn't an option. I spent time in the trades. In the '70s few Island people sought out designers so I used my background in design and sculpture creating stained glass windows and doors and designing and installing custom tile. My last fling was installing the hand-made Totten Tile in cartoonist Gary Larson's home. It was beautiful, a whole room of pattern, color and texture.

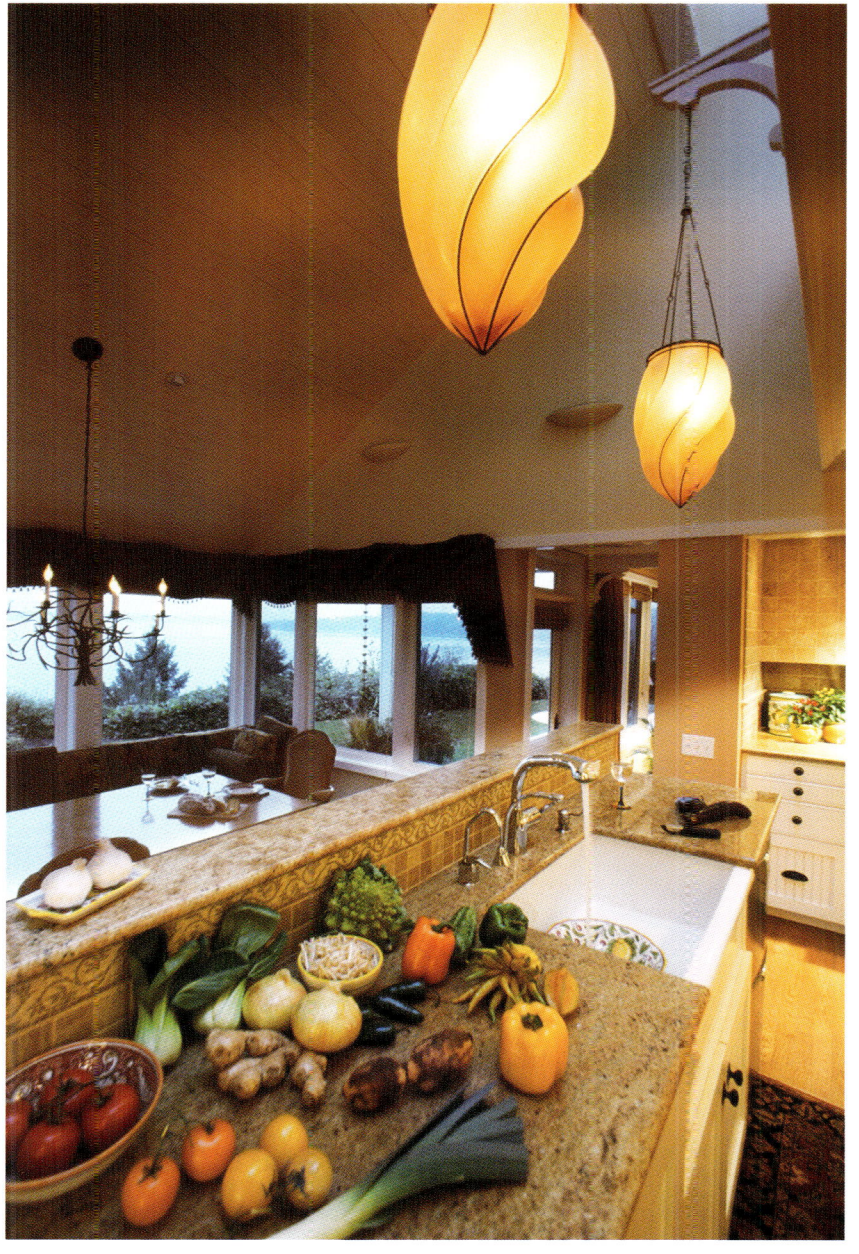

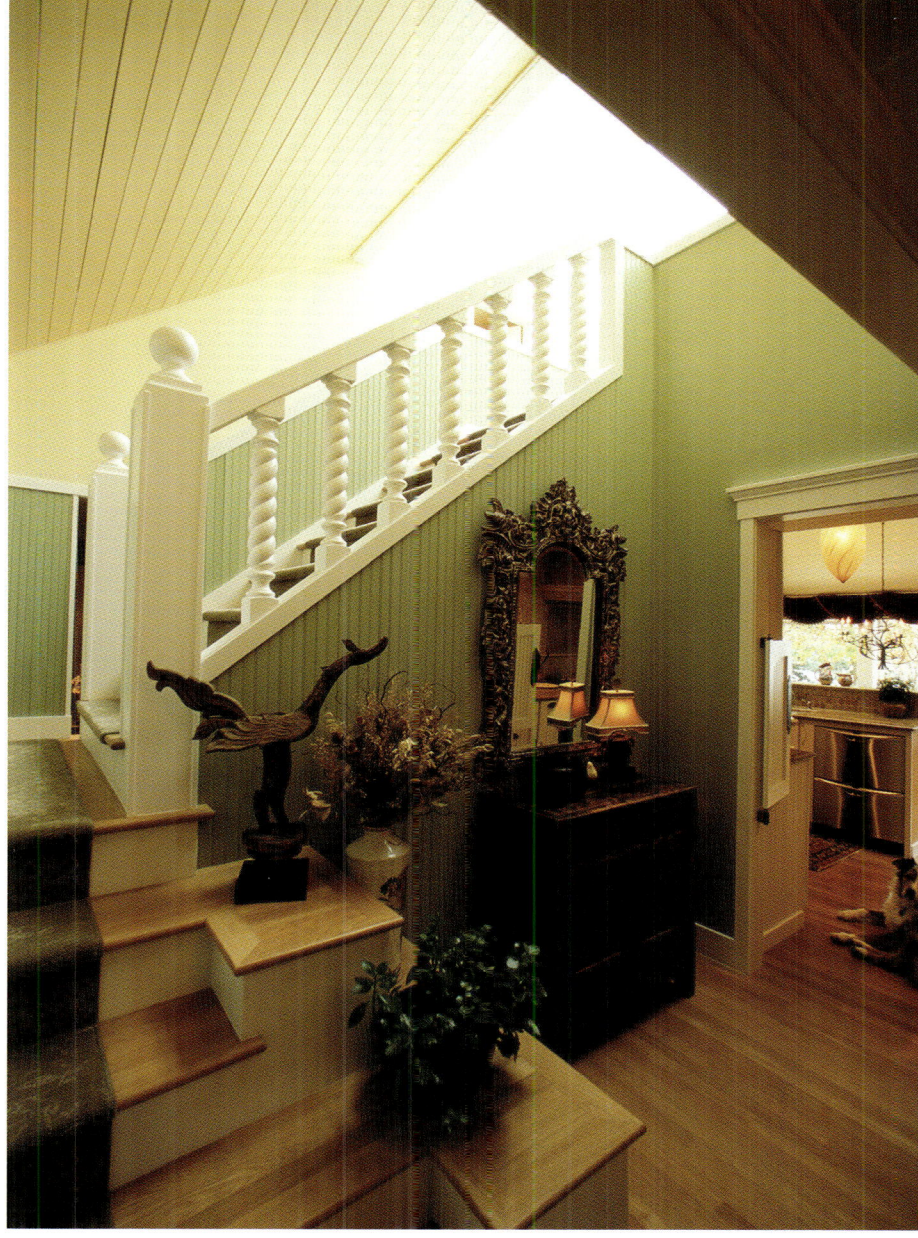

The times changed on Bainbridge. "Both kids finished graduate school," she says. "I began designing and overseeing entire house projects. Now I was hiring the trades to materialize my visions. I understand in perfectionist detail what I ask them to do. How far we can stretch. What the challenges are. My tradesmen and women are artisans. We are cooperators in a timely, on-budget process and I think, designers' clients reap benefits when designers have spent time in the trades."

"From drawings to reality takes more time than clients expect. They just see torn up board-and-mortar! Client-designer trust carries these days. I'm on the job site often. Also for input on the expected unexpecteds: Perhaps it's helping find the best solution for a junction where tile and wood come together, or suggesting an upright's slight shift to strength a design repetition. Experience is invaluable for

LEFT
"Even after removing the wall, kitchen space will be small." Sumptuous lighting and beauty-enhanced utility will unify kitchen to dining area.

RIGHT
Walls came down; geometry humanized. Interior views opened up creating a home to invite and inspire—and accommodate the family dog! An Indonesian Phoenix memorializes the extensive remodel.

FACING PAGE LEFT
Stickley furniture, a Noah's Ark heirloom carpet, wood-burning stove and the owner's passion, expressed by her driftwood sculpture: Good design changes family dynamics. "Create a space and they will come."

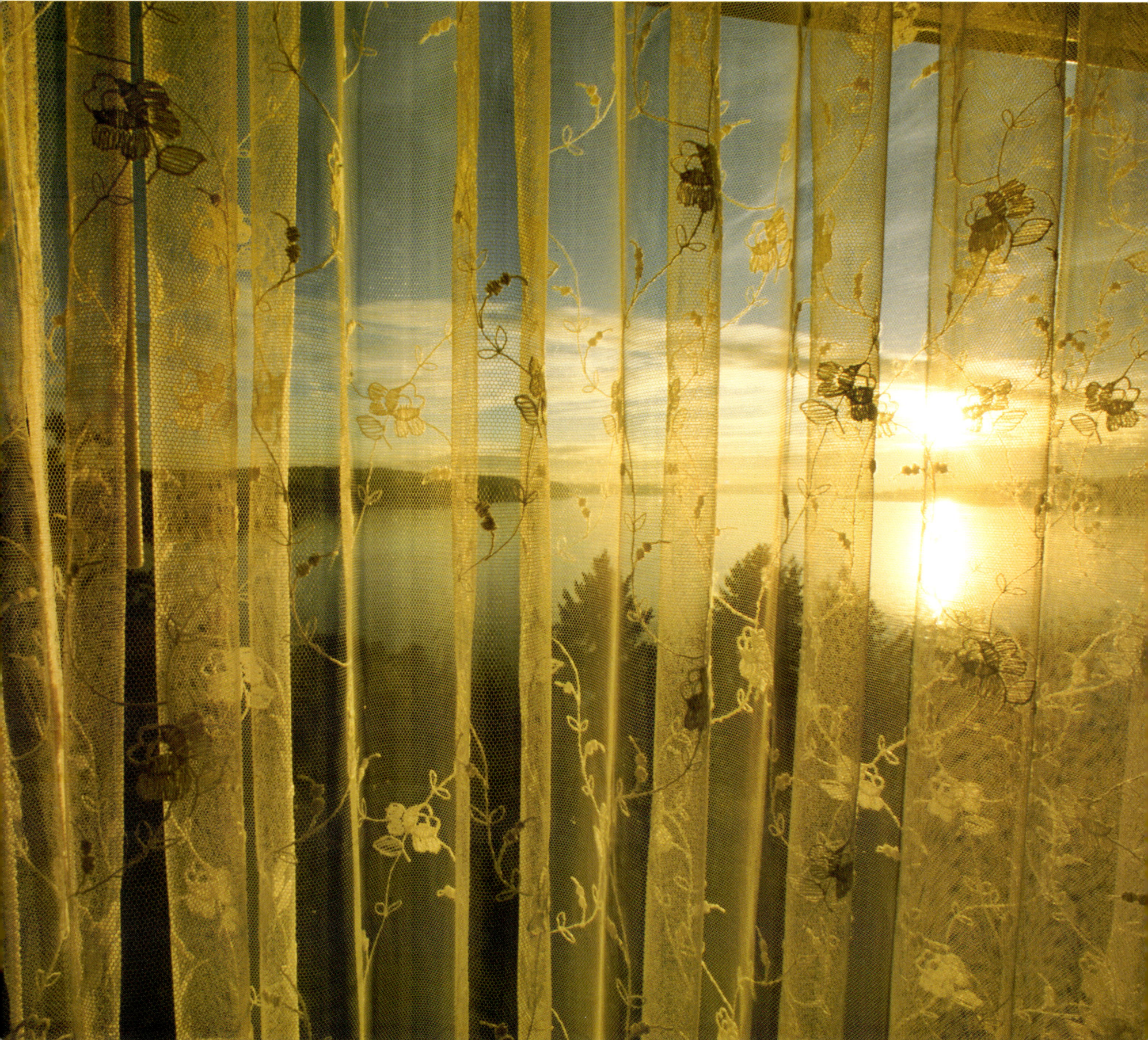

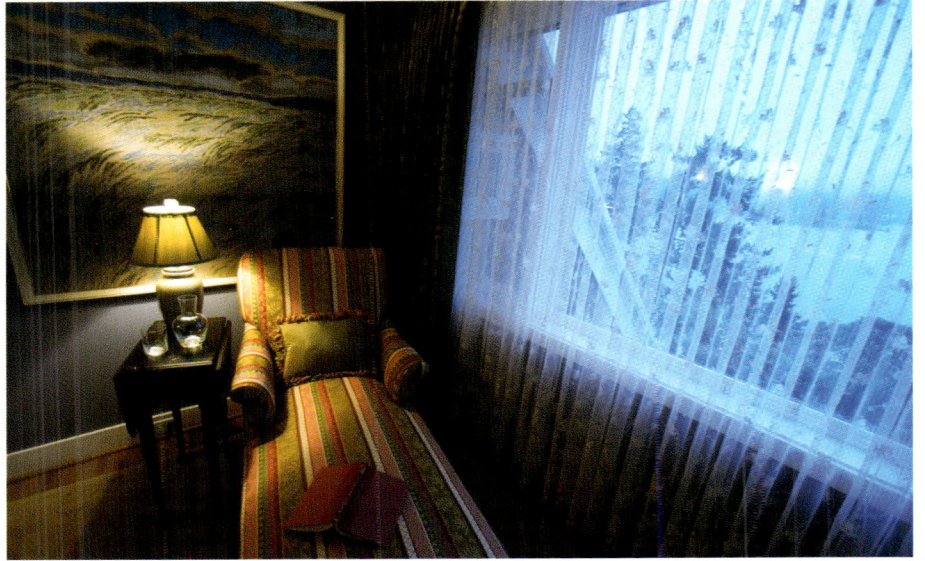

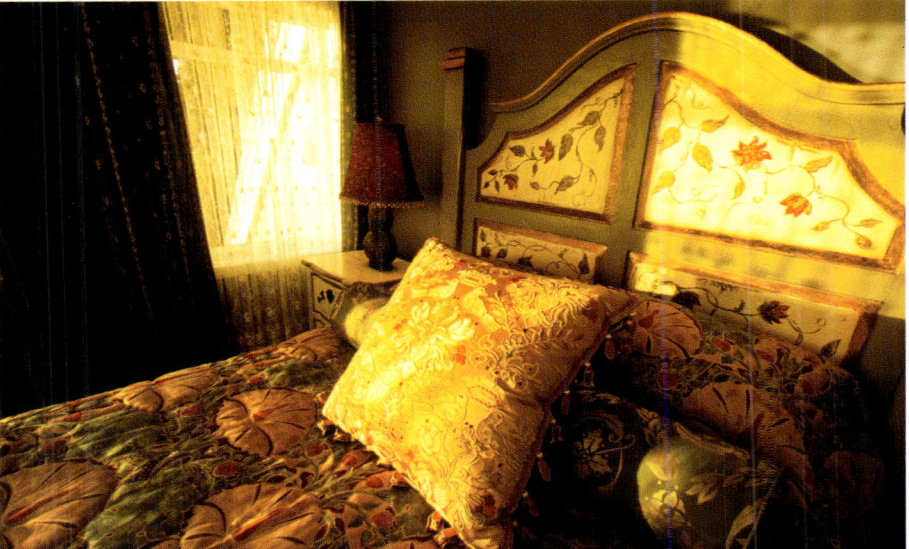

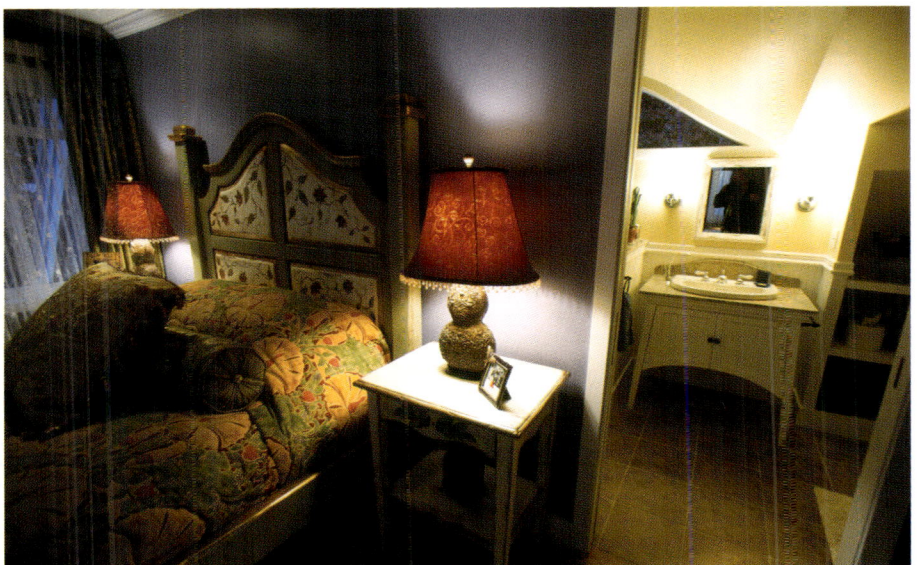

turning these challenges into serendipitous opportunities ... with just a touch of finesse."

Jones-Wilson Designs' phone rings. Her energy refocuses: "A 24' x 14' basement room into a walking meditation room? ... and feel like you walk up into the light though you've actually walked downstairs? ... Exterior drainage concerns ... A cork floor. Feng shui."

"We could create the illusion of natural light with backlit shoji screens. Should visit some grass cloth. Walls of sky ... hmm, a splash of blue... perhaps globe light fixtures for roundness and surprise. I could meet with you ..."

More about Ann...

YOU CAN TELL I LIVE IN THE PACIFIC NORTHWEST BECAUSE I...
Use colors and patterns that balance and are enriched by our gray weather, and which stay cheerful and comforting year-round.

WHO HAS HAD THE BIGGEST INFLUENCE ON YOUR CAREER?
My clients, especially the world-traveling clients who say, "Why go anywhere—my home is the most wonderful place I know." Also my college professor, who really drove home the ideas that "form follows function" and "always question."

WHAT BOOK ARE YOU READING RIGHT NOW?
It Can't Happen Here, by Sinclair Lewis

WHAT PERSONAL INDULGENCE DO YOU SPEND THE MOST MONEY ON?
Original art and gardening.

WHAT DO YOU LIKE BEST ABOUT DOING BUSINESS IN THE PACIFIC NORTHWEST?
I live in a small community where word-of-mouth means everything. People are active outdoors, love their gardens, and appreciate nature and casual elegance.

Jones-Wilson Designs
Ann Jones-Wilson
P.O. Box 10433
Bainbridge Island, WA 98110
206.842.5422
Fax 206.842.3275

FACING PAGE LEFT, TOP, CENTER & BOTTOM
Light defines the feeling. Sublime window treatments coax Impressionistic magic from sunsets, storms, night skies—and tomorrow, the dawn. An exquisitely proportioned chaise, opulent pillows on sumptuous fabrics, the headboard's encore of master bath's eyebrow window nourish this master bedroom. Safe and cozy. Lovingly sheltered in beauty. Welcoming. Need a home be more?

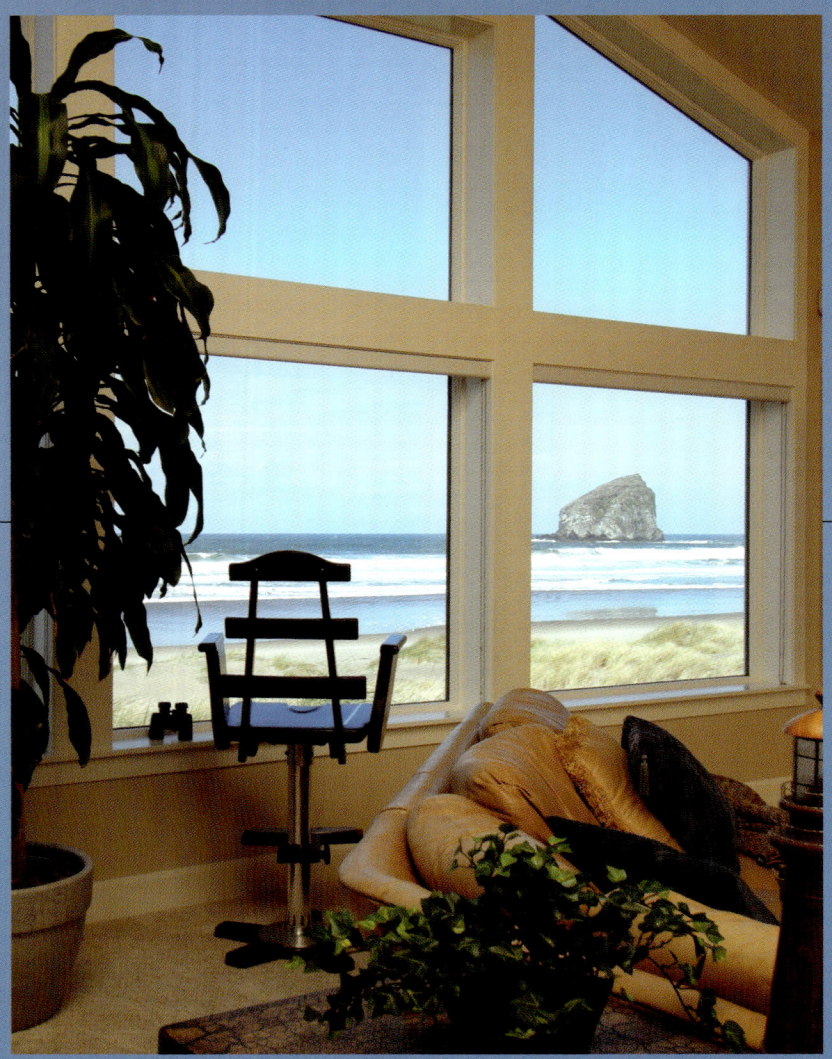

DESIGNER LORI BROCK, BROCK DESIGNS, page 125

OREGON
AN EXCLUSIVE SHOWCASE OF THE PACIFIC NORTHWEST'S FINEST DESIGNERS

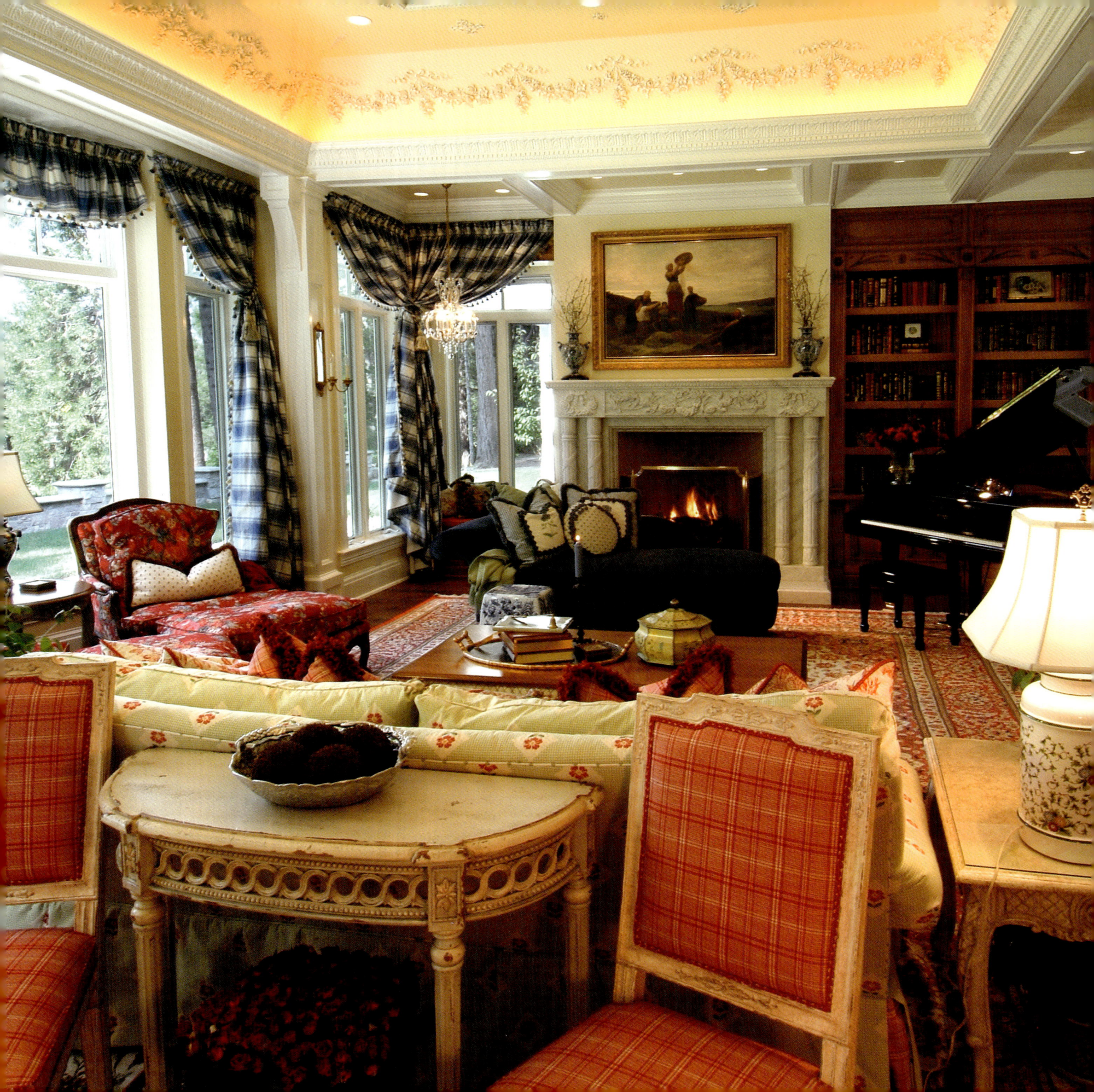

CAROLYN ALLMAN
C. Allman Design Group

For Carolyn Allman, great design is all about making connections–to spaces, to styles and especially to her clients. She loves when her clients get as excited as she is about a design direction, and believes the highest compliment a designer can receive is repeat business. Many of Carolyn's clients have hired her to work on various projects for more than a decade. There's a reason for that: Carolyn has a background in design and space planning that makes her clients feel confident that she will get the job done.

Carolyn isn't new to the design world. She grew up in a family of builders–as a child, she watched her mother execute any project as well as the men in her family–but it wasn't until her own kids were in school that she decided to turn her passion for design into a career. After attending a lecture given by an interior and architectural design team, she was committed to becoming a professional. She even tackled the two-hour commute each way, from Bakersfield for four years to get her bachelor's degree in Interior Design from California State University, Fresno. As soon as she graduated, she scouted out the best architectural firm in town and offered to work in exchange for the experience. Learning the connection of education and practical application was a very valuable lesson.

LEFT
P.H.B. Construction brought architect Mike Casella's design to life ... with intricate details, a coved ceiling mural and a view of Southern Oregon's Rouge River.

RIGHT
This intricate vanity, built by Grantwood and hand-finished by Cindy Strickland & Tom Stevens is a tranquil beginning for this energetic homeowner's day.

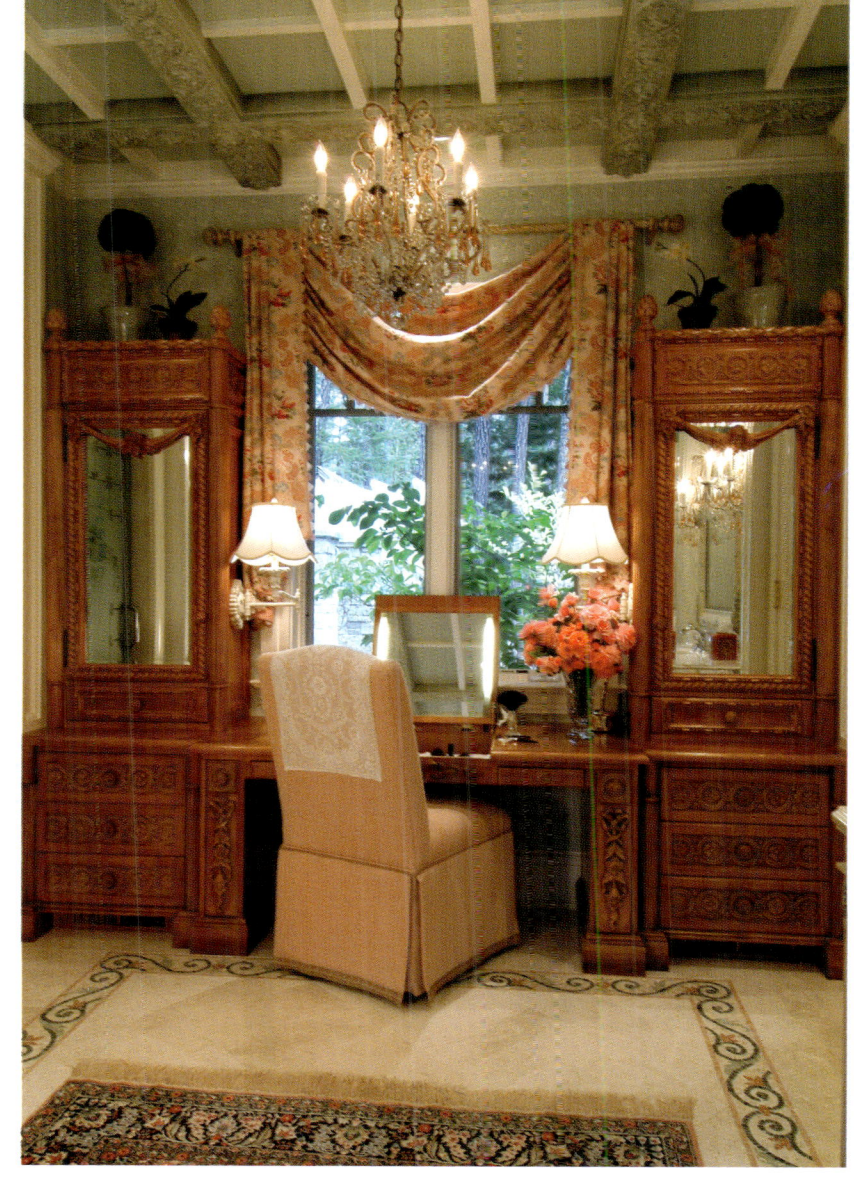

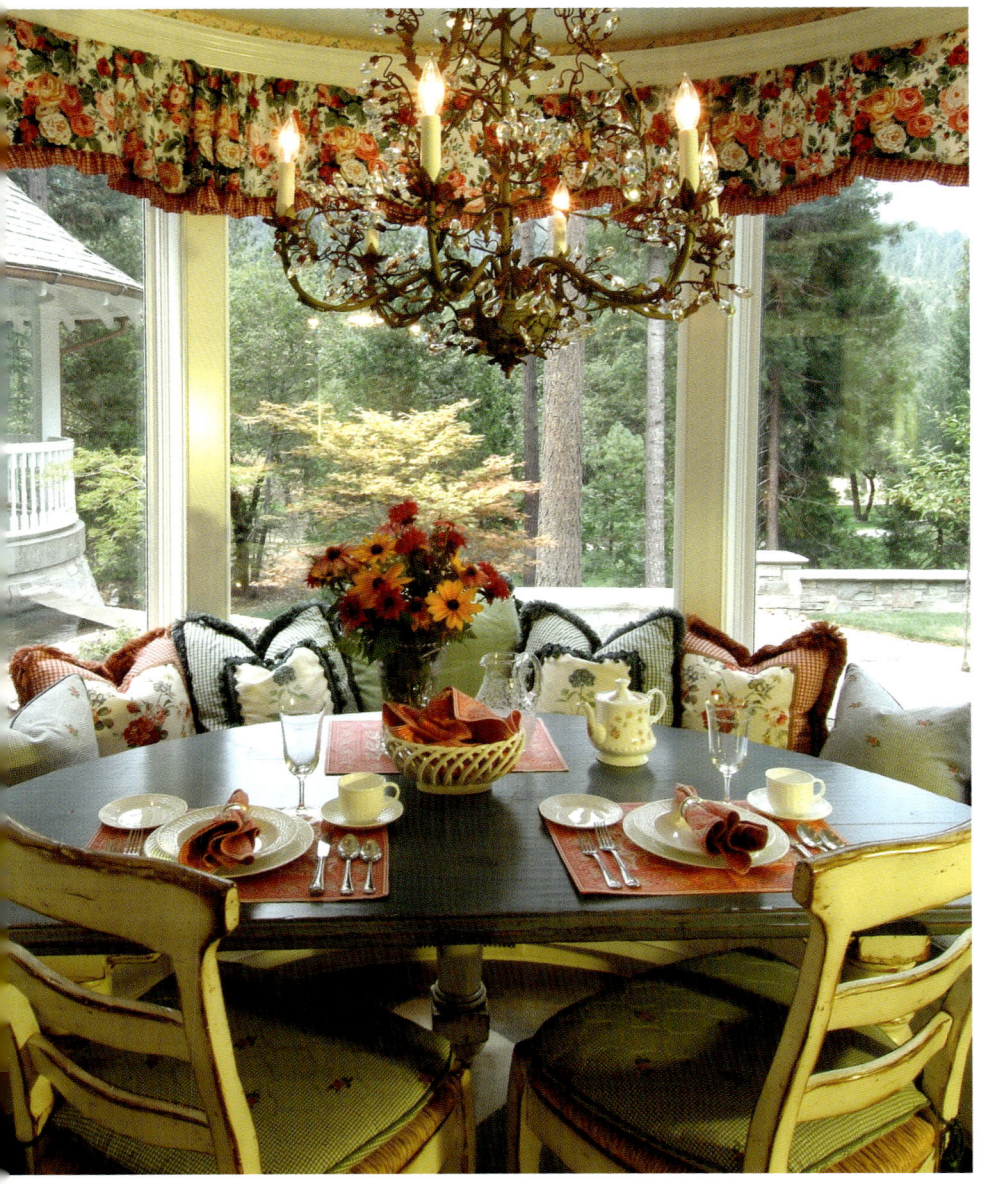
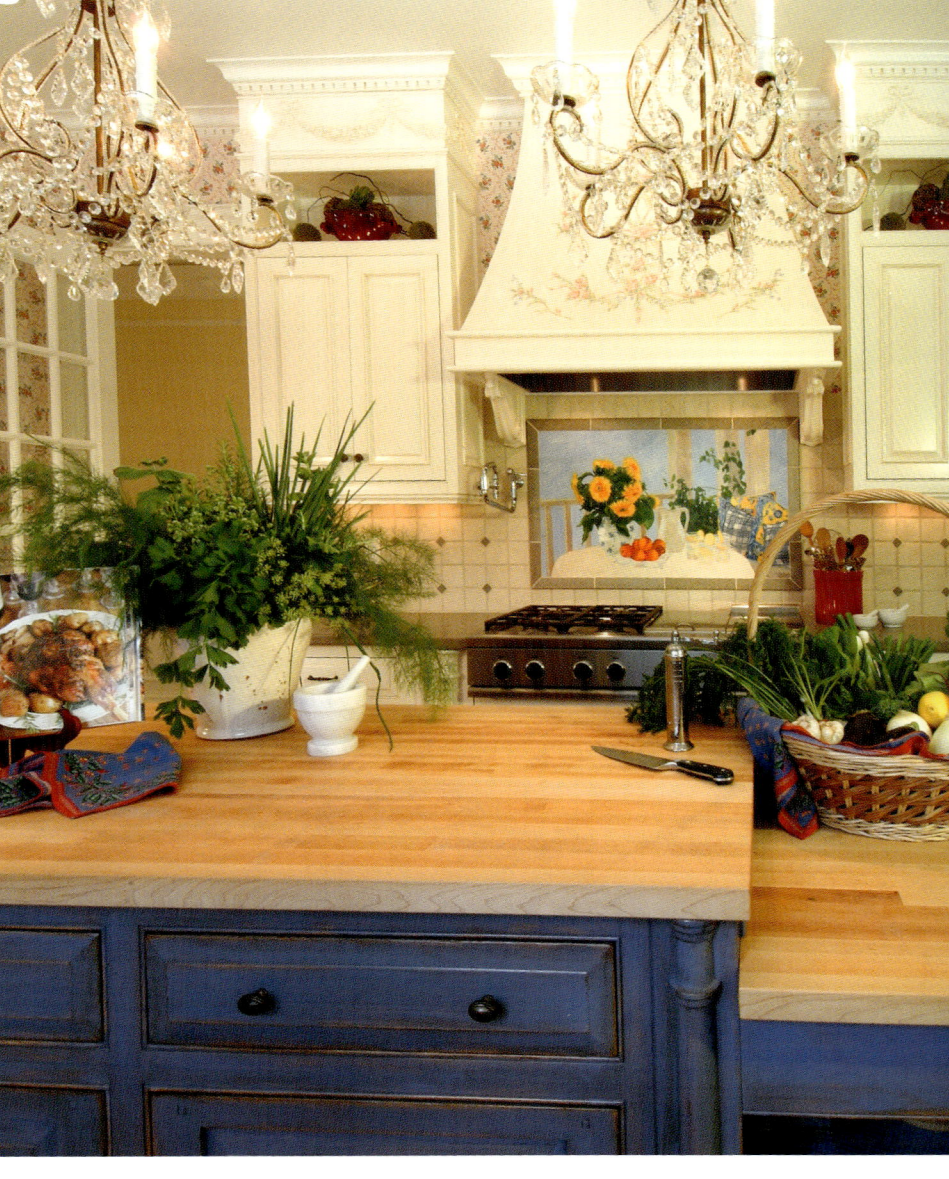

Carolyn has had her own business since 1993–but still appreciates the value of learning everything she can about the ever-changing world of design. Although she lives in a small town, Carolyn stays current and inspired by attending design events, markets and conferences regularly. She has passed the National Council for Interior Design Qualification, and is an active professional member of the American Society of Interior Designers.

Carolyn and her team–designers Diane Shenk, ASID and Maria See, Allied ASID, and office manager Theresa Gann–bring the perfect balance of knowledge, styles, skills and personal attention to every project. In 2004, she and her husband purchased the 5,000-square foot building that she had been renting a space in for the past 11 years. Together, they created a "trade only" studio and showroom on its main floor for all of the designers in Southern Oregon. Carolyn believes that providing the opportunity for clients to sit on upsholstered pieces and to view the furniture accessories and finishes is a real asset.

When it comes to personal style, Carolyn admits that she's a bit of a romantic and that antique, one-of-a-kind pieces are at the top of her design list. She believes you should never buy anything just because it is a good deal; instead you should surround yourself with things you love to create your style. Her favorites are Northwest-inspired elements like fireplaces, warm wall colors, and large windows with views of the trees, water, mountains and sky.

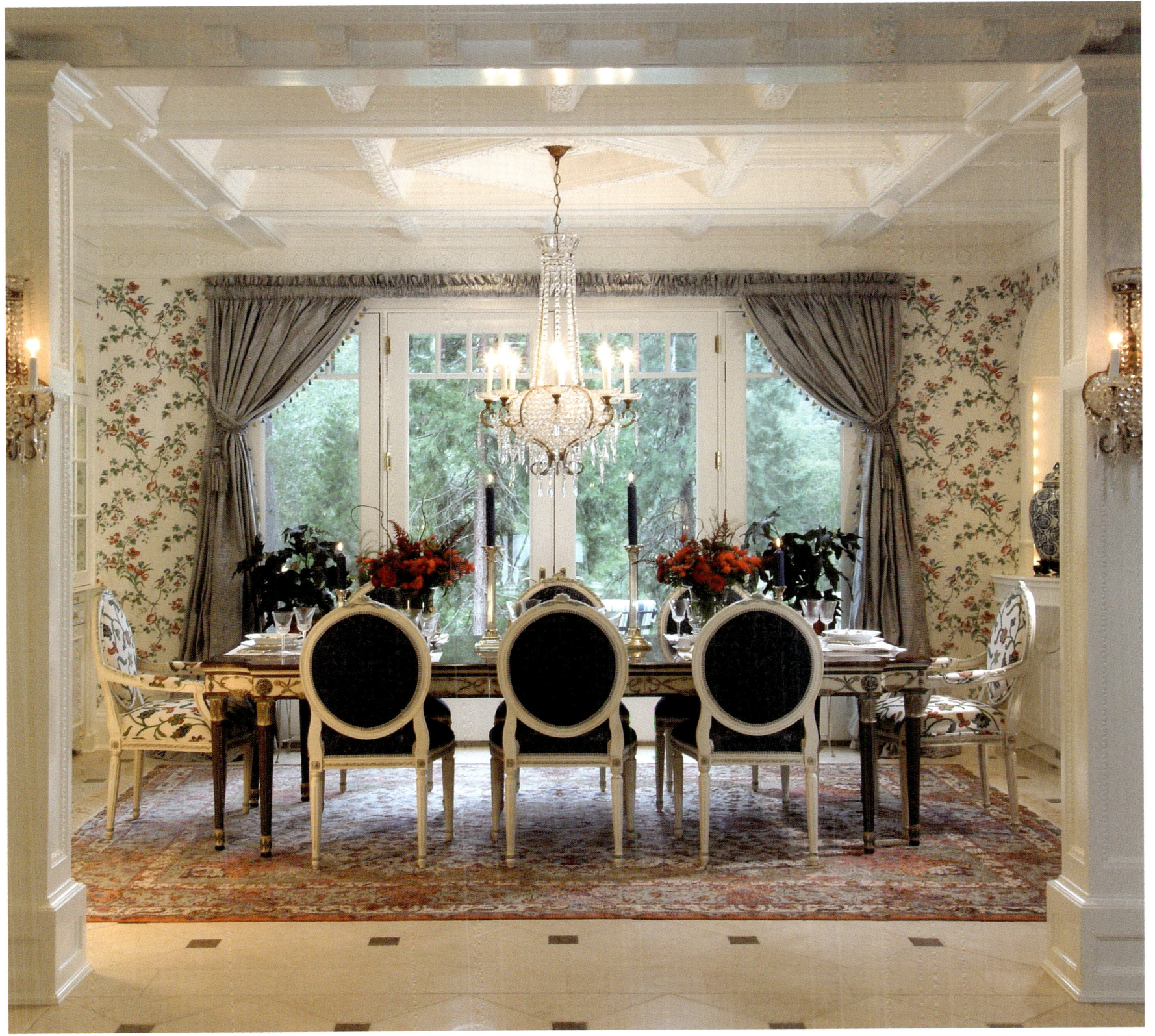

ABOVE
EJ Victor Furniture, Highland Court and Schumacher fabrics, Brunswig & Fils wallpaper and Bradburn Lighting. Rezek lighting design installed by Helco Electric.

FACING PAGE LEFT
Views of the river, grounds and reflecting pond, provide panoramic art in this cozy breakfast nook. Upholstery by Brumley Upholstery.

FACING PAGE RIGHT
An organic garden provides abundance for this functioning kitchen. Mural by artist Nicole Marcelle. Handpainting by Cindy Strick and. Cabinet design by CADG.

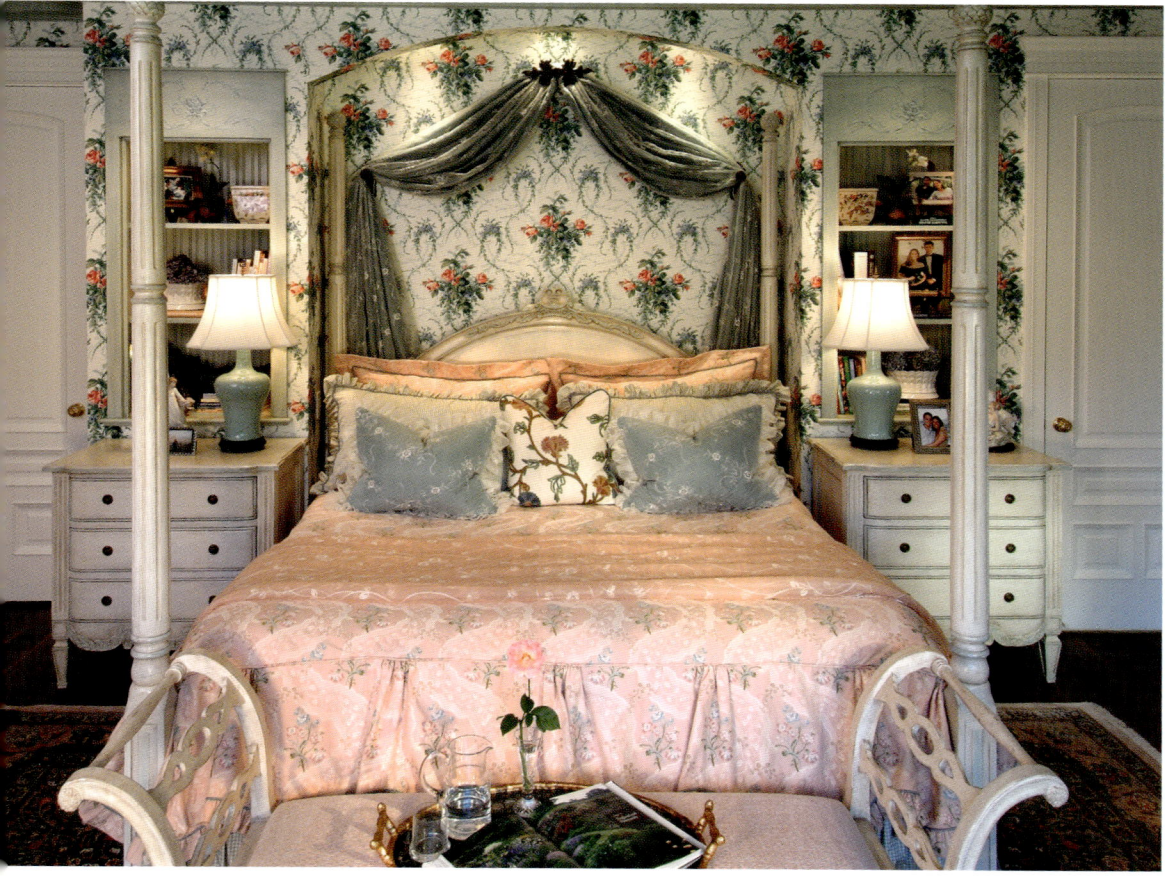

Carolyn is passionate about many aspects of design, but she always begins with function. Spaces that don't feel balanced are uncomfortable to live in. While furniture placement and the proper accessories are sometimes enough, there are times when a space needs to be physically changed to achieve the right feel. Although Allman Design Group often works with new construction, remodeling existing homes to create a family gathering kitchen or a serene master suite are two of her favorite projects. Ah, the power of the after!

Carolyn's ideal design opportunity: to partner with the client to achieve their vision and interject an eclectic blend of materials, furniture and art that tells the story about the person who lives there.

With her positive design attitude, her experience and diverse team, and her passion for connecting with clients and their homes, Carolyn creates spaces with vision, creativity and comfort.

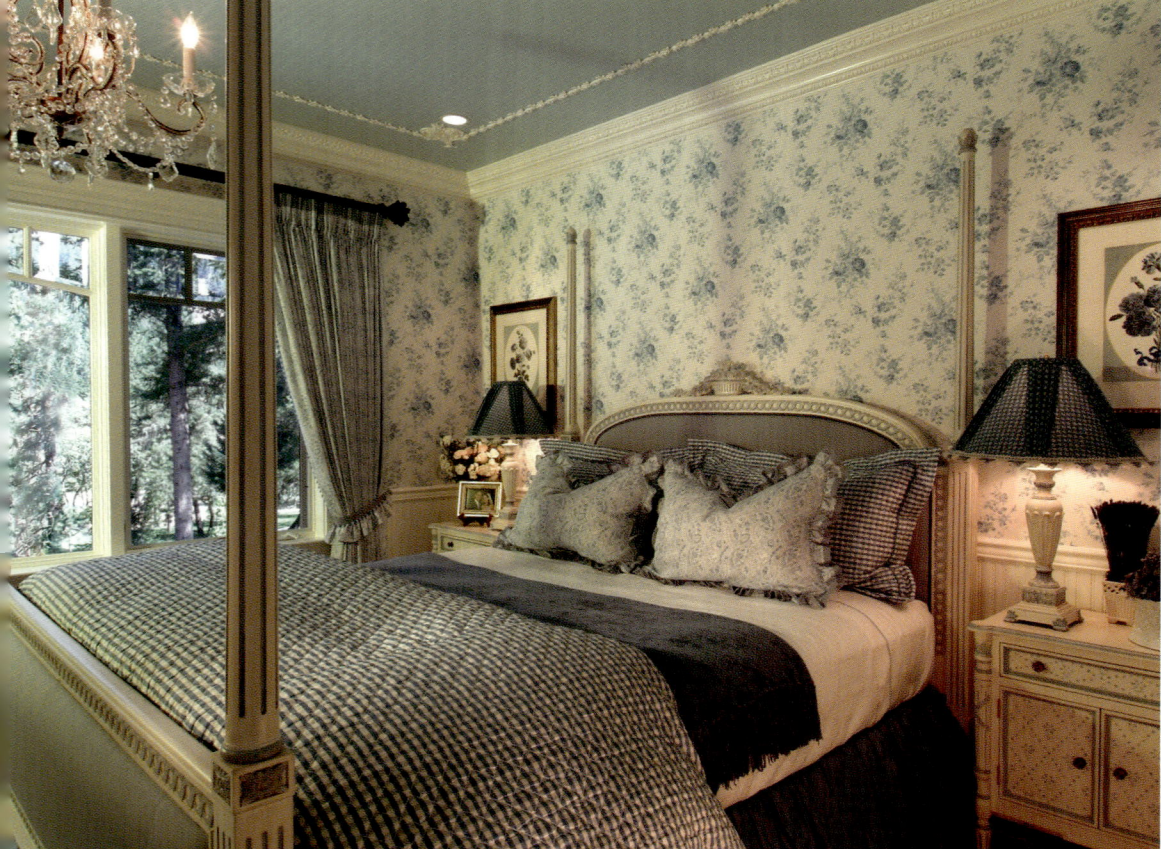

TOP
A relaxing master bedroom feels like a retreat. Bedding by SilverThreads, wallcovering by Creative Paperhanging and handpainting by Cindy and arched niche wall covered by Creative Paperhanging.

BOTTOM
This guest bedroom uses a serene blend of materials: Julia Gray furniture, Kravet Fabrics, custom bedding and drapes by Silver Threads.

FACING PAGE TOP
The upstairs bath is crisp, clean and inviting. Mural by artist Nicole Marcelle. Waterworks tile installed by Bill Siemon.

FACING PAGE BOTTOM
Adjacent to the cutting garden and large conservatory, flowers and vegetables are cleaned and prepped daily in this charming work area.

More about Carolyn...

WHAT IS THE BEST PART OF BEING AN INTERIOR DESIGNER?

Being a part of creating an interior that enables an individual or family to enjoy their lives more completely. Putting together a well-planned and executed interior allows such freedom for daily lives, entertaining, relaxation and pride.

WHAT ONE ELEMENT OF STYLE OR PHILOSOPHY HAVE YOU STUCK WITH FOR YEARS THAT STILL WORK FOR YOU TODAY?

The connection of the interior of the home with the exterior. Usually when a home owner has a contemporary exterior and an English cottage interior, one of those elements is true and one is for the neighbors. There is a pressure some clients feel to create a home that will impress others. When a home owner succumbs to that pressure they almost always are unhappy or move in a few years. Once they decide, discover or admit their real style preferences then a designer can take that style in a more formal or relaxed direction as needed for the home.

WHO HAS HAD THE BIGGEST INFLUENCE ON YOUR CAREER?

My husband: I wouldn't have a career without him. When I decided as an adult mother of three to go back to school, he took up the slack by helping with laundry, cooking and shopping, all while having a very busy career of his own. In the middle of the night when I would be trying to finish a project that was due the next day he would get up and ask, "What can I do to help"?

WHAT IS THE MOST UNUSUAL TECHNIQUE YOU'VE USED IN ONE OF YOUR PROJECTS?

One technique that always works for me, whether on a contract or residential project, is to photograph the space "before" and show those photographs to the client. The power of a single photo is amazing. They can live in the space for years and not really see it anymore. I photograph the room, then use that photograph with a flimsy overlay for sketches and notes out to the side. It is a very powerful tool in allowing you to see not only the problems with a room but the possibilities.

WHAT EXCITES YOU MOST ABOUT BEING PART OF SPECTACULAR HOMES OF THE PACIFIC NORTHWEST?

So many times on a project the main individuals-the designers and the builder-get all of the credit. We all know nothing that we design or oversee is possible without a dedicated group of talented individuals who do the work. What excites me most is that those individuals will have a copy of this book and be able to share with their families the part that each of them played in bringing this home to life.

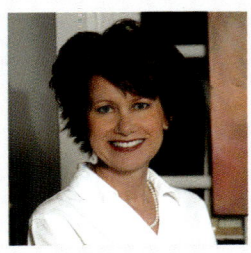

C. Allman Design Group
Carolyn Allman, ASID
29 South Grape Street
Medford, OR 97501
541.772.9296
www.allmandesign.com

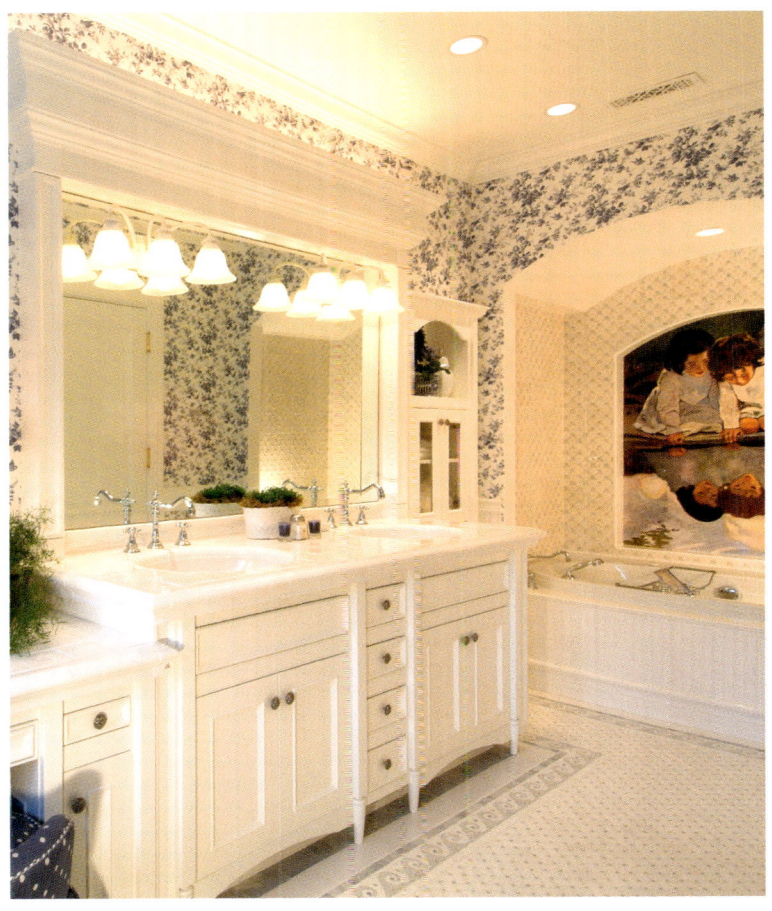

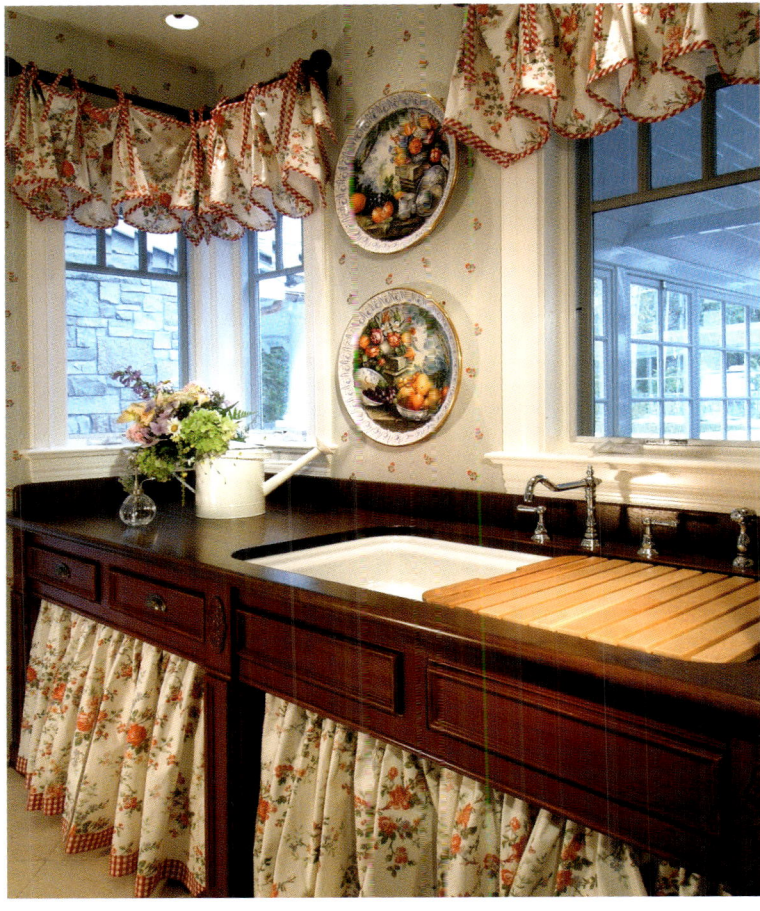

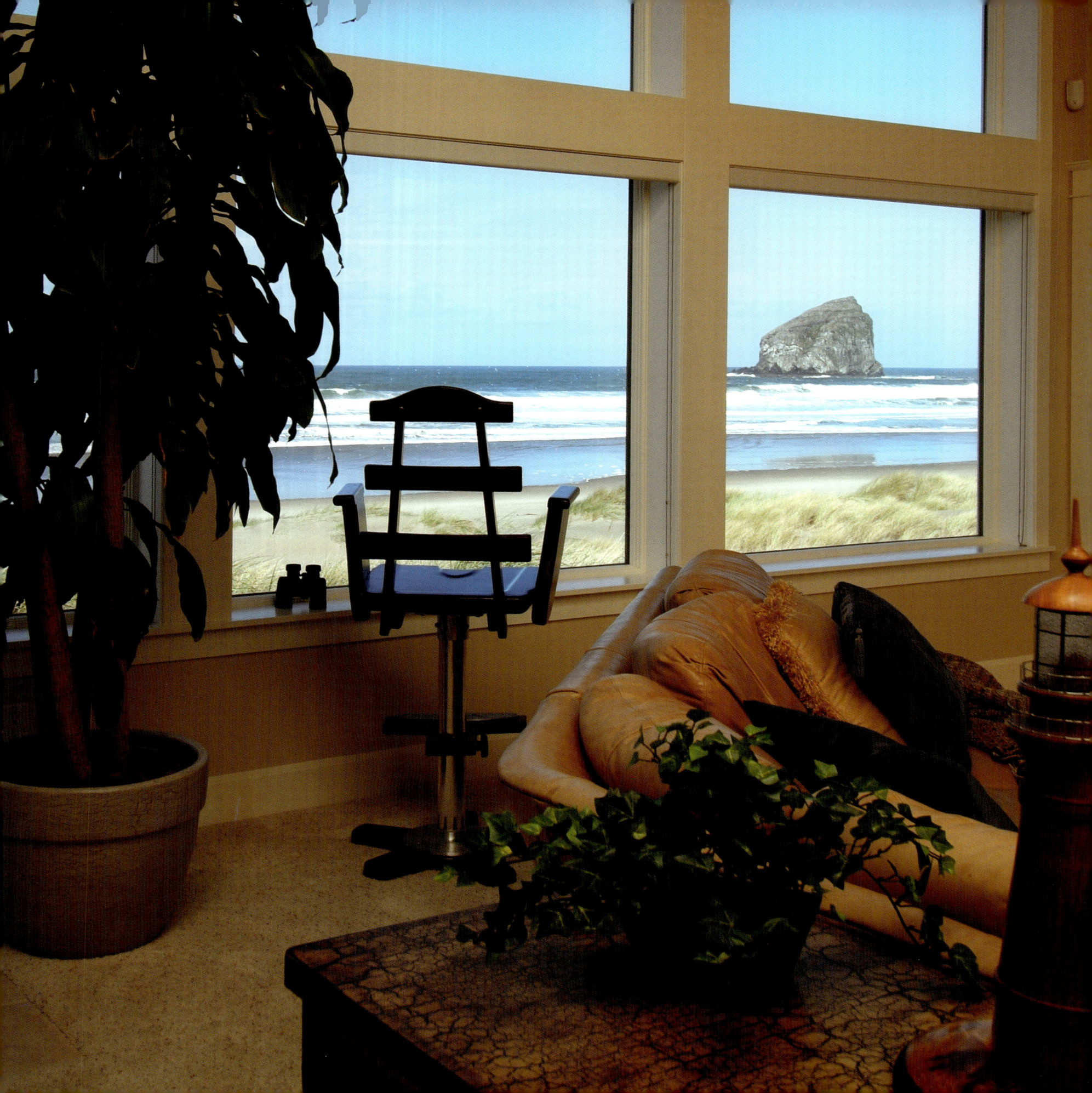

LORI BROCK
Brock Designs

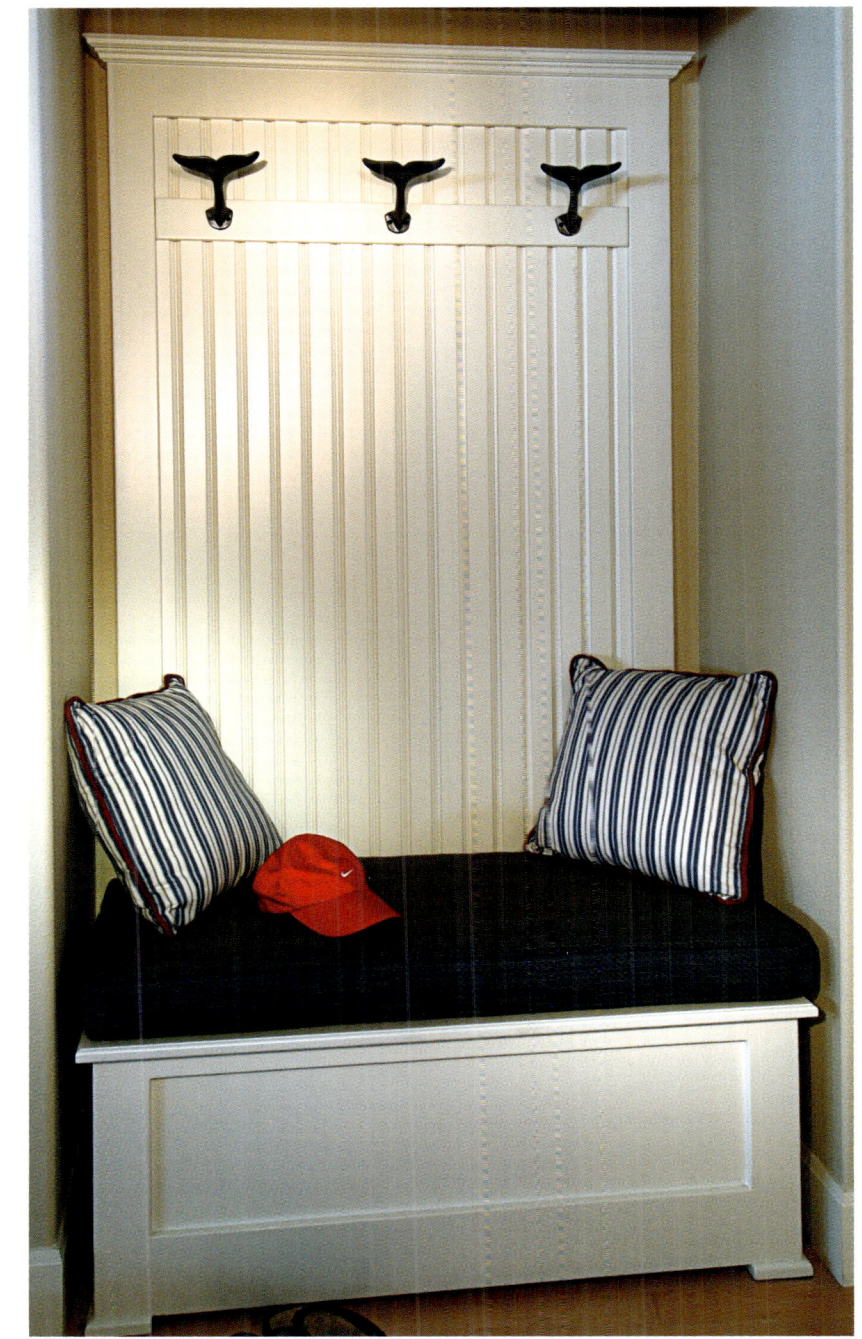

Lori Brock has both design and the Pacific Northwest in her blood. Growing up in the house her parents built in Beaverton, Oregon, 56 years ago, Lori often spent time looking over her father's shoulder while he sketched plans for local remodeling jobs. Lori and her father aren't the only ones in her family who are design inclined. Among her seven siblings, she counts two general contractors, an engineer, a commercial designer, a furniture showroom designer and a landscape designer. Thus, it is no surprise that she runs a thriving full-service design business in Portland, Oregon that specializes in kitchen and bath design.

Being Northwest-born brings advantages to Lori. Her long-term relationships with subcontractors and vendors, an understanding of the area, and a comprehensive knowledge of the resources that are available all make it easy for her to offer outstanding service and design. She is adept at maximizing the Pacific Northwest's rare light and beautiful outdoor views and finds great joy in tackling the challenge of the area's grey days to showcase the "spectacular, unrivaled beauty the sunshine brings."

LEFT
The view from this stunning ocean front room serves as a backdrop for the ultimate "front row seating" of the playful Captain's chair.

RIGHT
A nautical styled bench sets the tone for the entry of this beautiful Pacific City, Oregon home. Careful attention to detail is apparent in the striped fabric and whale coat hooks.

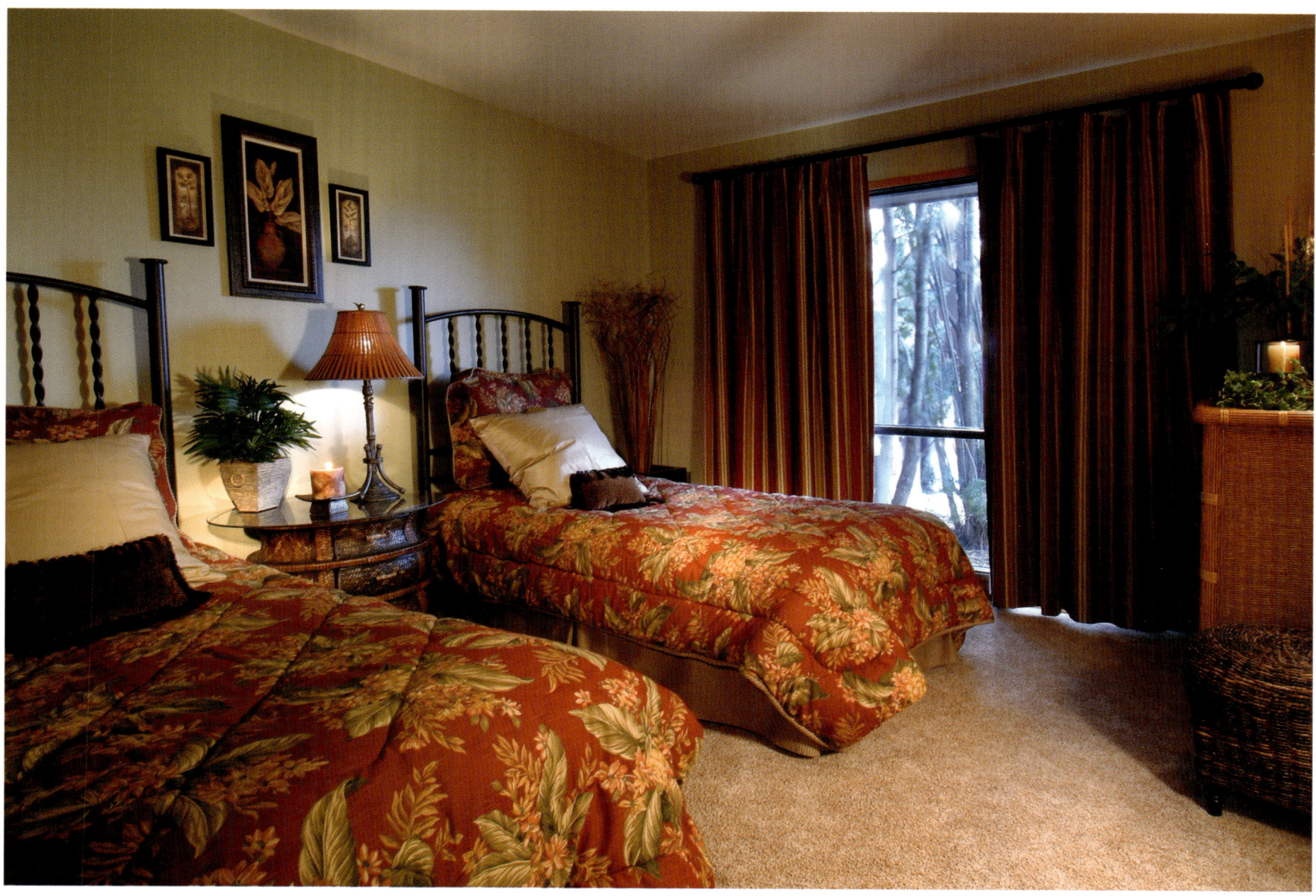

Although her husband's football career took the couple around the country for 16 years, Lori and her husband returned to her hometown in 1994, when her business name and address was changed to the current Brock Designs. In 2004, Army football was in need of an offensive line coach; instead of moving the business, Lori decided to keep Brock Designs open in the Pacific Northwest. The passion for her work keeps Lori commuting from New York to Portland to assist her long list of new and returning clients.

Lori, who defines design as "collaboration between the design team and the client" relies heavily on her design associates, Ivette Newport and Christina Alderman. Another important part of her team is her older brother, Dave (Joshua Construction) along with their well-respected lineup of subcontractors. Lori organizes a coordination meeting on projects where the designers, subcontractors and clients can come together and discuss the different aspects of the job. Together, they plan the details of the work before it begins, giving each party a sense of ownership to their particular role in bringing the design to fruition.

As a kitchen and bath specialist, Lori's work has garnered a variety of accolades. Recently she was honored by being named in *NW Home and Garden* magazine as one of the "Hot 25 Designers" in the NW. She has had cover features in *Design/Build Business* as well as *Impressions* magazine, and has written numerous articles in trade publications and on appliance manufacturers' websites as an expert in her trade.

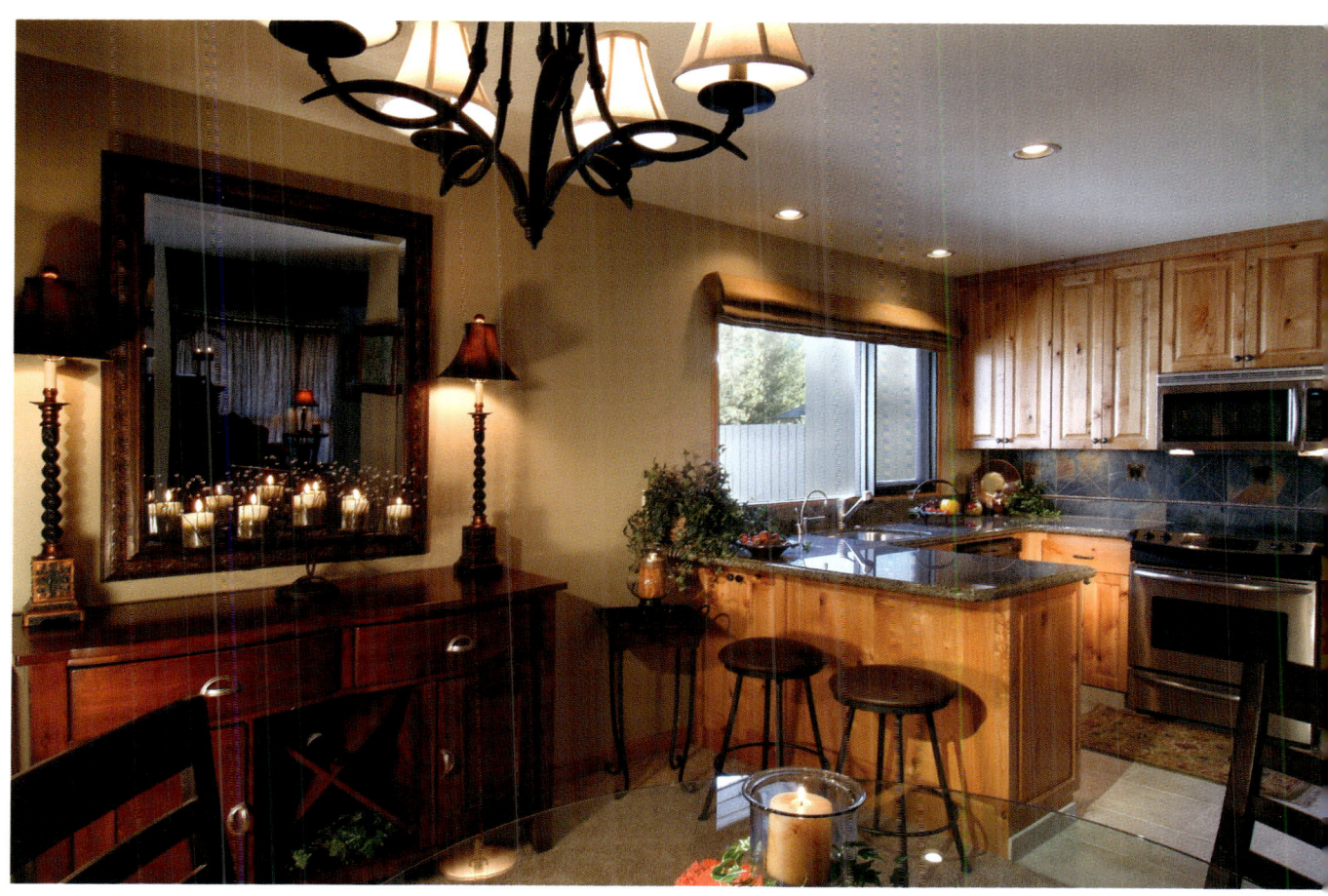

FACING PAGE LEFT
Natural surroundings called out for wrought iron and cane furniture in this cozy bedroom suite in Central Oregon.

TOP
This small space has exceptionally big style. The combination kitchen / dining room of this Sunriver, Oregon cottage includes knotty Alder cabinetry and hand-cast bronze pinecone accent tiles.

BOTTOM
The rustic feel of the adjoining living room is accentuated by the strong textures and rich colors of fabrics and accessories such as the reclaimed door—from a nearby vendor-hung over the sofa.

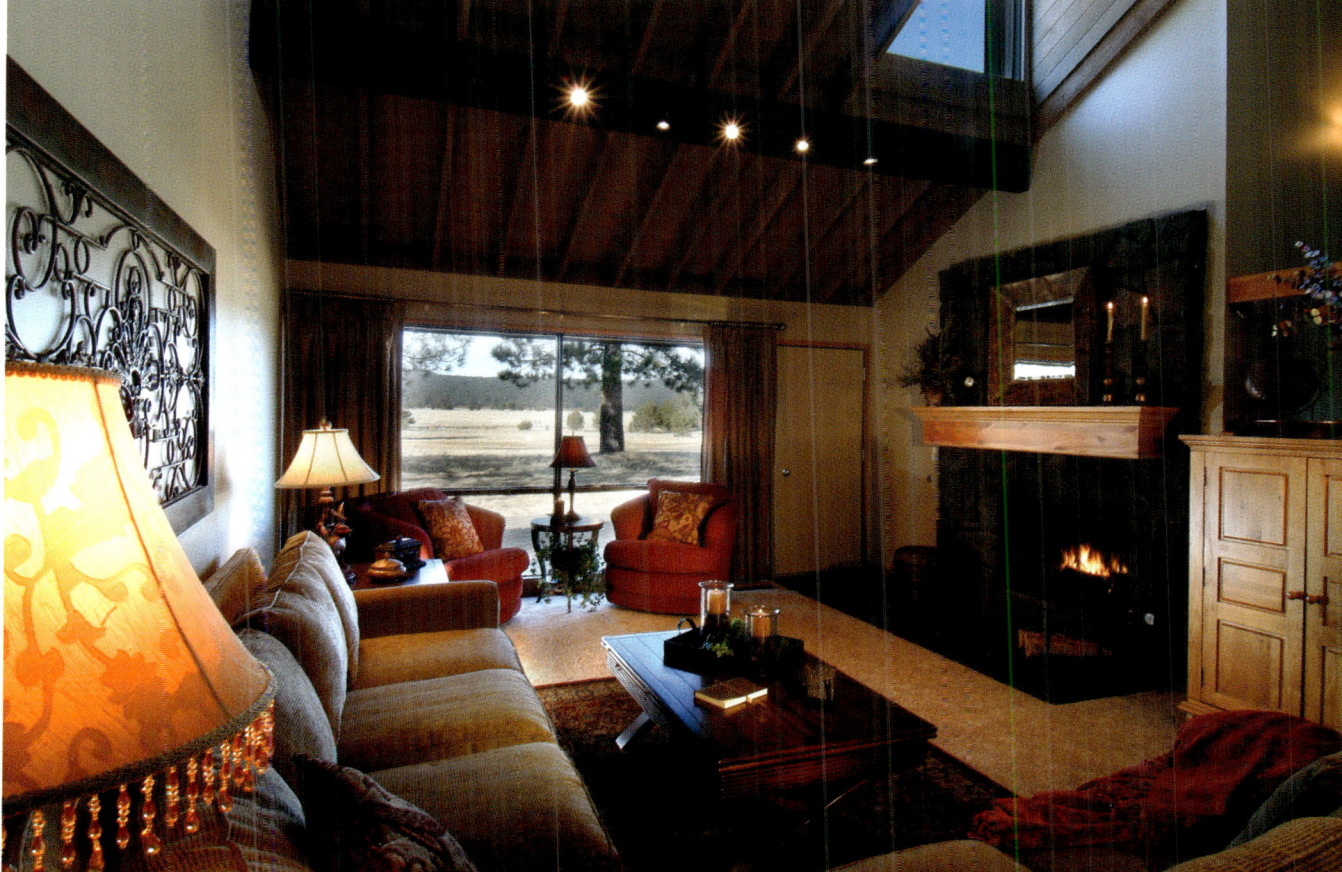

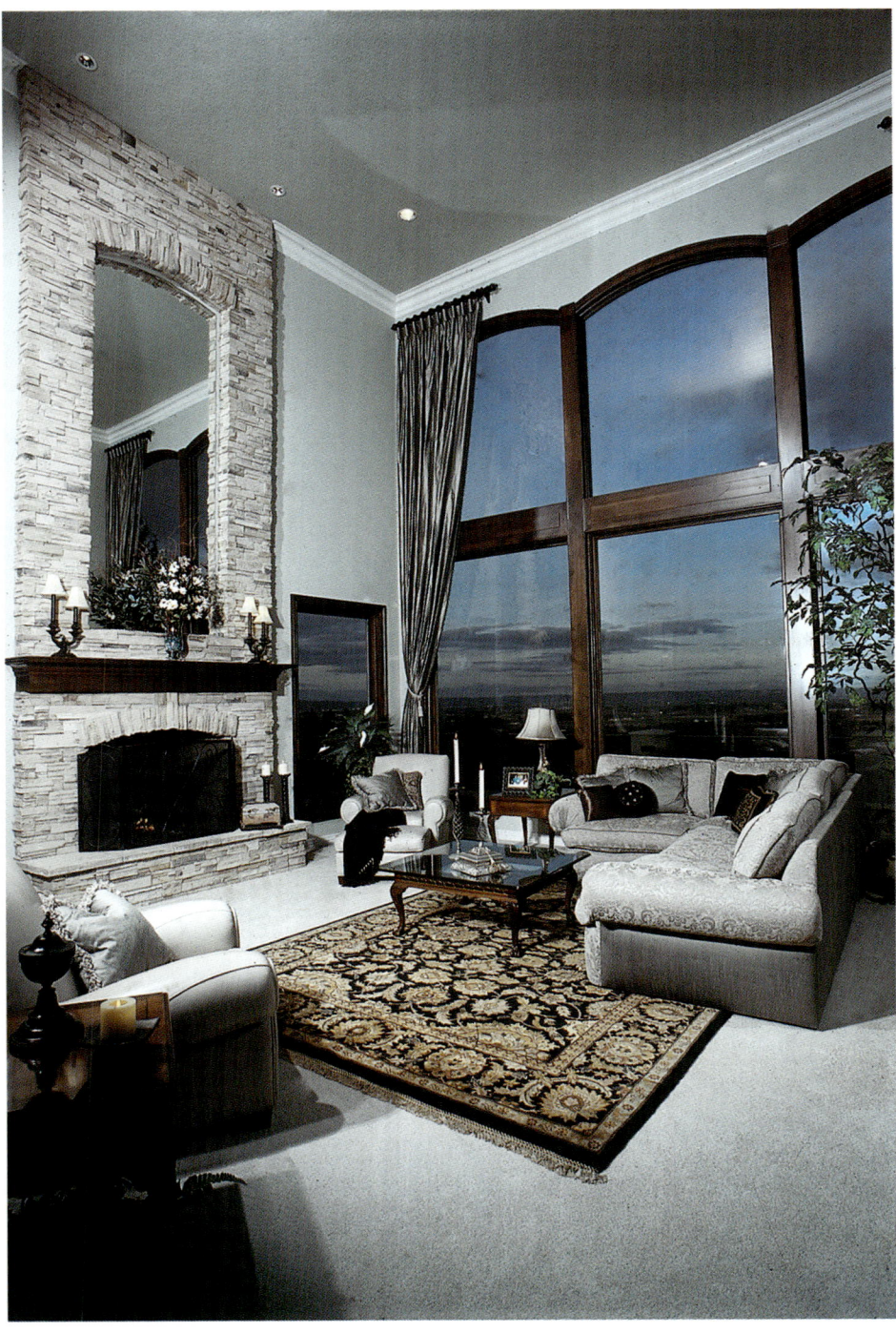

In addition to being a spectacular designer, Lori is involved with a number of industry organizations. She is a board member of the National Kitchen and Bath Association, an associate member of the Northwest Society of Interior Designers, a member of the Construction Contractors Board as a licensed general contractor, and is a member of both the National Association of the Remodeling Industry, and the Oregon Remodeling Association.

Lori's signature style has just as much to do with listening as it does with designing. Every client who comes to her has a specific personality, style and preference–the goal is to inspire each client in new and imaginative ways. Then, she creates a design that is sensitive to each client's lifestyle, budget, and schedule. Often, it is important to incorporate sentimental pieces of artwork or furniture into the designs for clients. Lori believes that each client needs to feel they can take something special that they love and incorporate it into the new design. Some of the most unusual pieces have found their way into a design where they didn't originally seem to fit. The key is to find a way to make it work-both for the design and the client.

As a do-it-all designer, Lori is proud to offer on-site consultations and project management from start to finish. The multiple facets of Brock Designs gives Lori great pride in being able to "stay with the client from conception of a design plan to having the last piece of artwork hung in place.

ABOVE
Overlooking the beautiful Tualatin River Valley and four mountain peaks in Oregon and Washington, one can see the level of detail achieved in this spectacular space.

FACING PAGE LEFT
The ultimate indulgence–watching stormy, crashing waves while being warmed by a fireplace and soothing tired muscles in the air-jetted tub.

FACING PAGE RIGHT
This spa inspired bath blends natural materials for a classic look with a Zen feel. Rice paper glass overlay and hand-cast bronze accent tiles add an Asian influence.

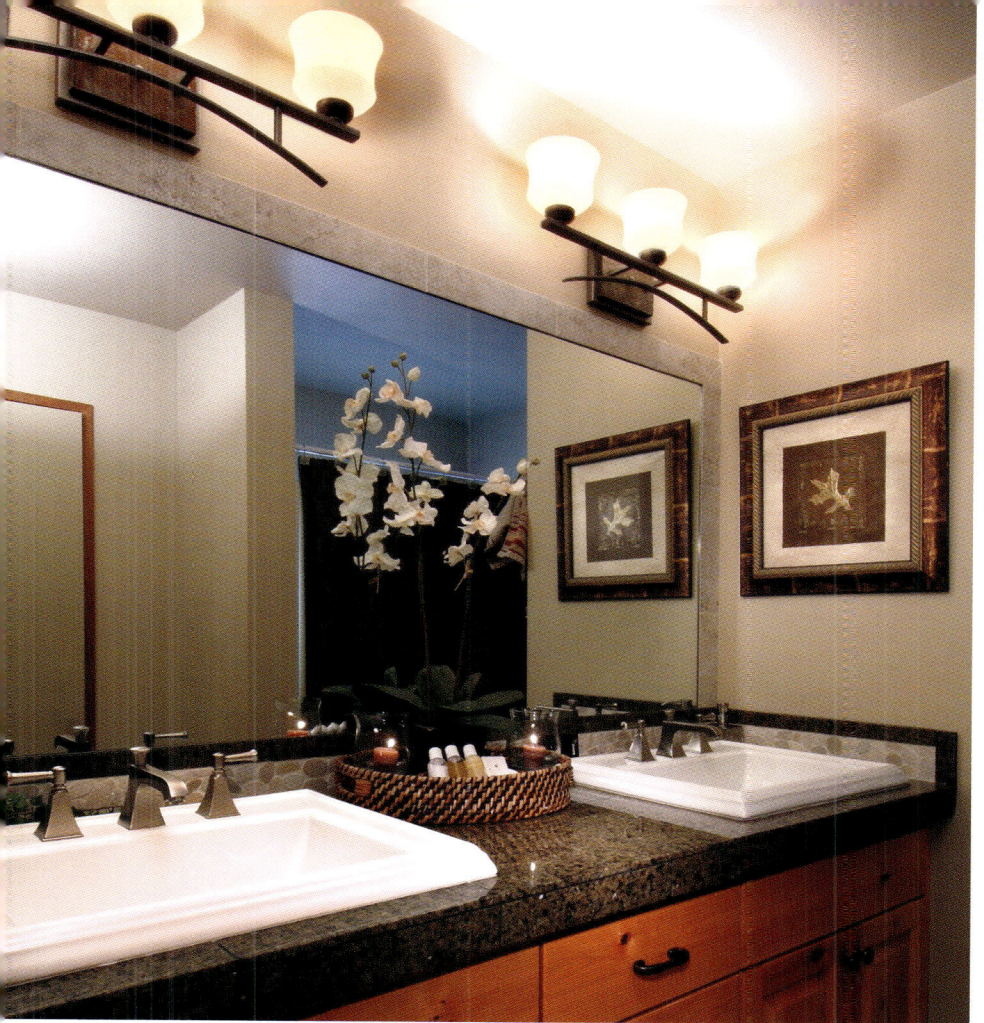
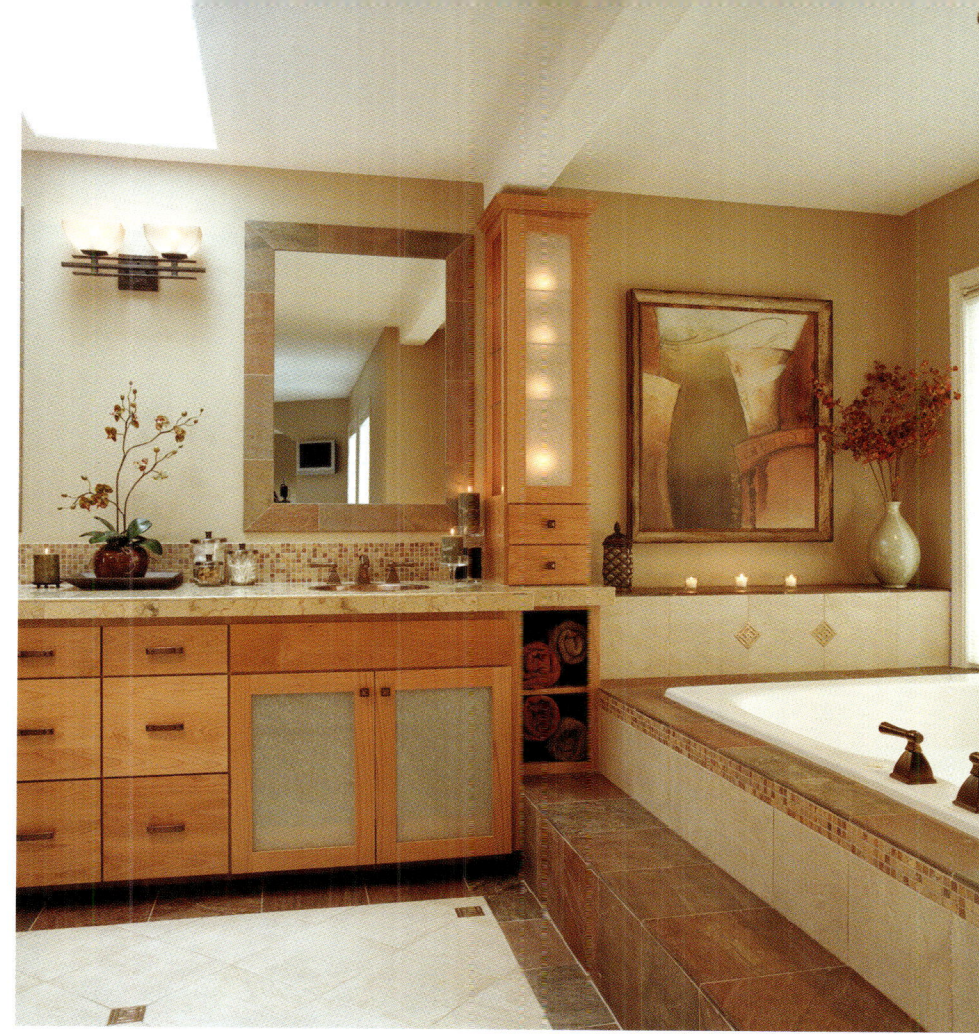

More about Lori...

WHO HAS HAD THE BIGGEST INFLUENCE ON YOUR CAREER?

The initial influence would have to be my parents. My mother and my father, who was an accomplished finish carpenter and remodeling contractor, allowed me the freedom to experiment with design ideas at an early age; my siblings who are always there to help with solutions to design challenges; and my colleagues at NKBA and NWSID who have helped my business thrive. Though many of them are independent designers, they never failed to give me the support I needed to grow my business. I am most proud of the members of these two groups-they know that by helping each other it makes everyone's business better in the long run.

WHAT ARE THE MOST IMPORTANT THINGS TO REMEMBER WHEN WORKING WITH CLIENTS?

I believe in teamwork, trust and listening. From the very first meeting with the clients, there needs to be an open communication and sense of trust that the team will work together to realize the client's vision of their dream space.

WHAT DESIGN PHILOSOPHY HAVE YOU STUCK WITH FOR YEARS THAT STILL WORKS FOR YOU TODAY?

A home is a reflection of my clients and their particular lifestyle. It is my passion to help my clients create an ambiance and functionality they can feel comfortable in on a daily basis. When my clients walk in their front door, I want them to be happy to be home.

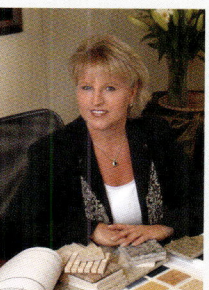

Brock Designs
Lori Brock, NKBA Board Member/NWSID
Associate/Nat'l Assoc. Remodeling Industry/
Oregon Remodelers Assoc./Construction
Contractors Board Licensed General
Contractor #145794
8835 Canyon Lane Suite 408
Portland, OR 97225
503.291.1515
Fax 503.291.1517
New York Office 503.348.3701
www.brockdesigns.com

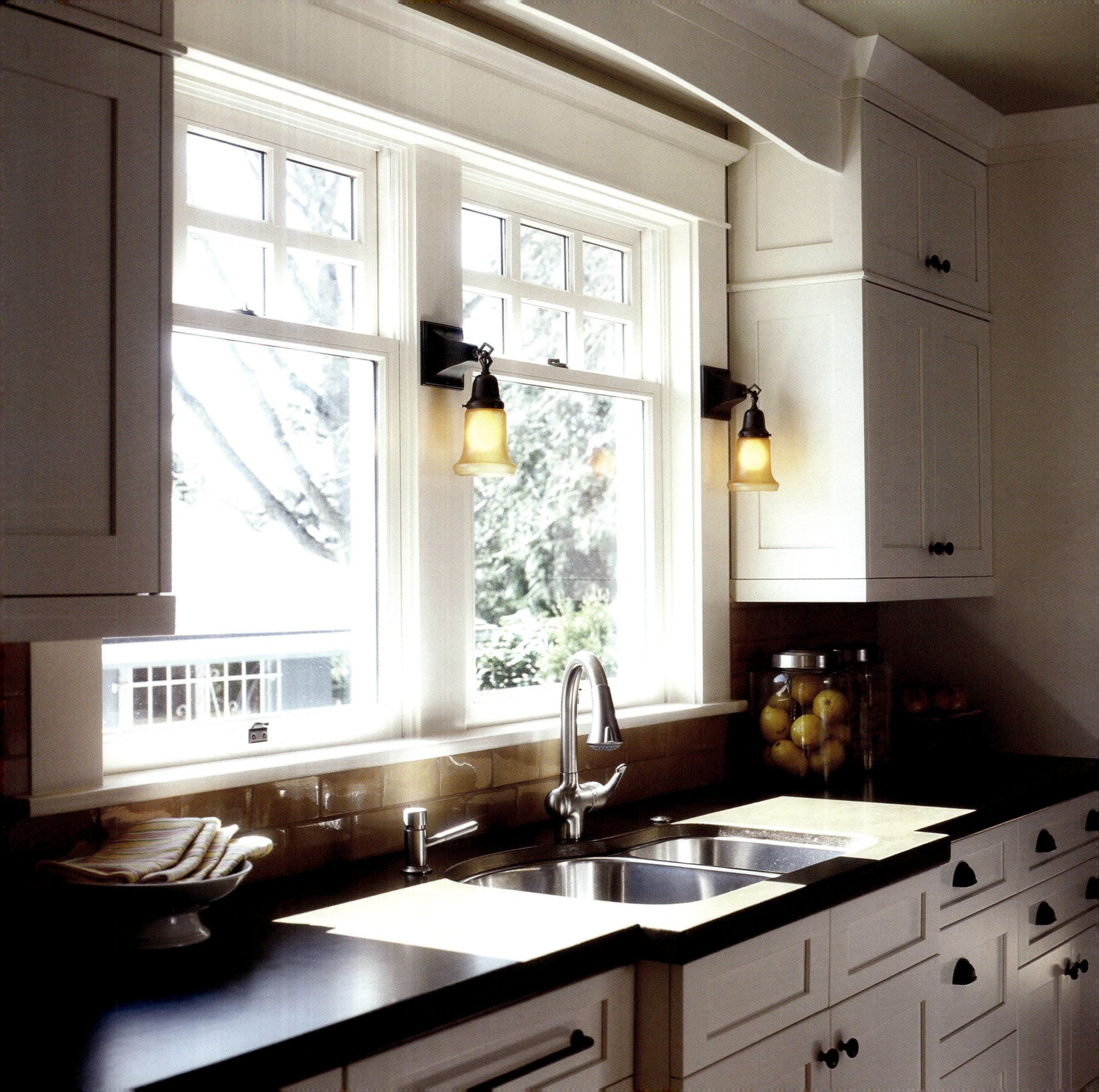

Erin Davis, Arlene Lord & Stephanie Ness

Mosaik Design

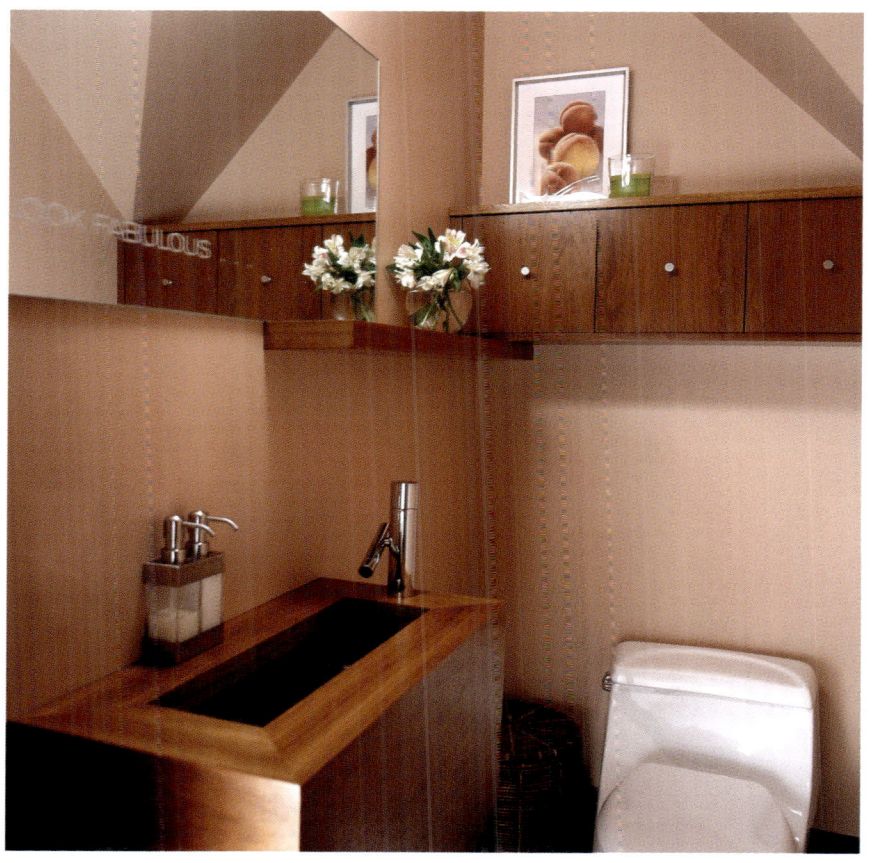

Erin Davis, Arlene Lord and Stephanie Ness know the meaning of teamwork. Not only do these design experts collaborate with each other to come up with unique, out-of-the-box designs, they also work closely with clients to give them the homes of their dreams.

Embracing what they've termed a "wholistic approach," this trio loves to tackle an entire project—from design-and space-planning to remodeling and project managing. Along the way, they work closely with in-house project manager, Scott Jaworski, to integrate each remodel and design seamlessly with the existing architecture, as well as with the client's tastes.

Because these designers are so in tune to their clients' needs and wishes, they can work in a variety of styles, from French Country to Asian Contemporary. Their versatile designs have even garnered them cover spots and features in a handful of publications, such as *Better Home and Gardens*, *Kitchen and Bath Design News* and *Renovation Style*.

The primary goal of this design team, no matter what style they're working with, is to create clean, simple lines, a rich color palette, and to provide clients with an elegant, yet approachable living space.

ABOVE
This space was once a closet, then a scary powder bath and now, well, it's fabulous.

LEFT
A once dark, cramped bungalow was transformed into a light-filled ecologically minded, richly textured, inviting family space.

Mosaik Design
Erin Davis, Arlene Lord &
Stephanie Ness
0112 SW Hamilton St.
Portland, OR 97239
503.726.2222
www.mosaikdesign.com

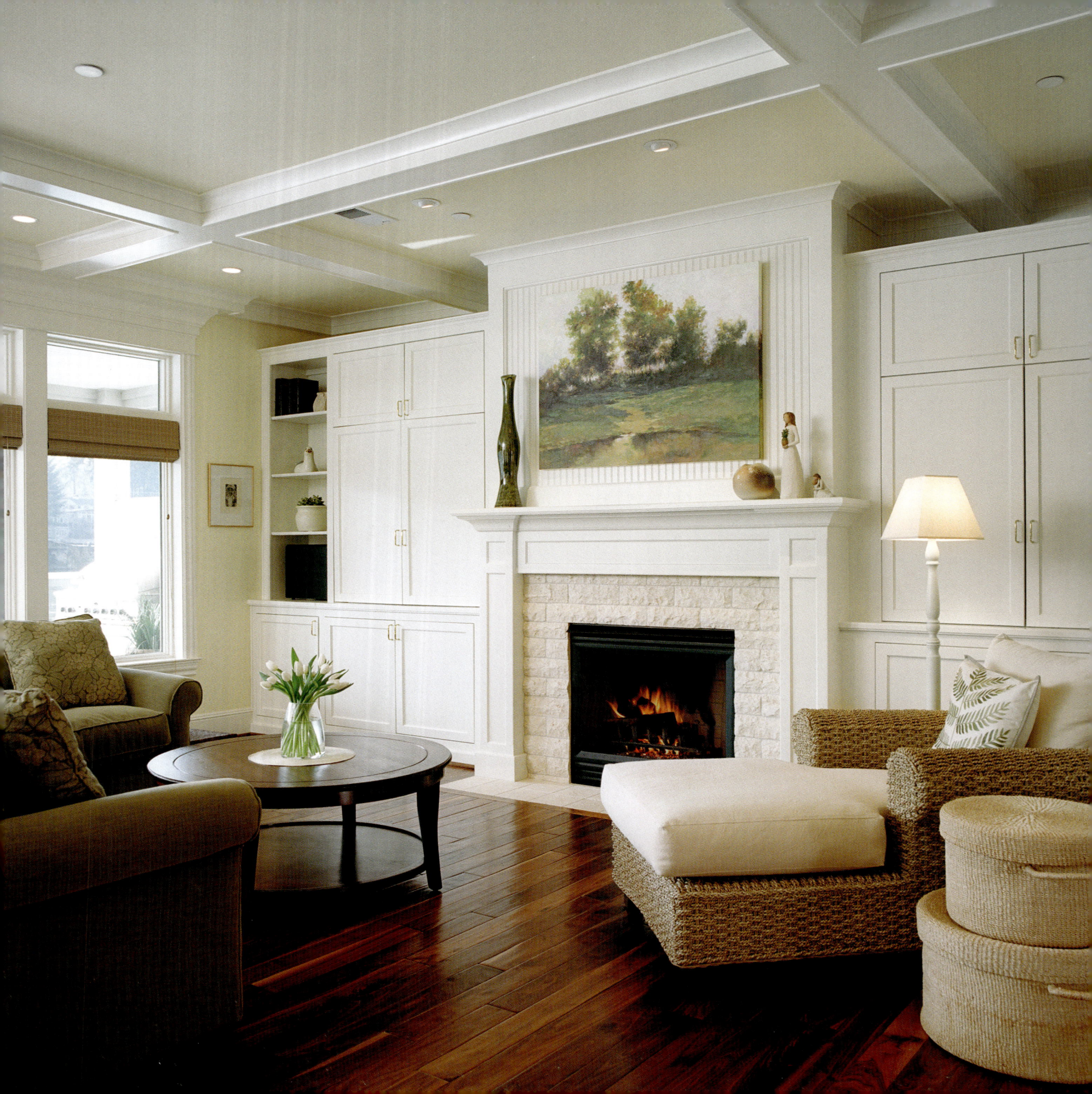

Keri Davis

Keri Davis Design

Keri Davis has never been one to play it safe. This talented and boundary-breaking designer is always ready to seize new opportunities, whether it's covering kitchen walls in stone or gently pushing her clients beyond their design comfort zone.

Keri's design vision has been developing for a long time. As a child Keri dreamed of being an interior designer and says that she spent more time decorating her doll houses than playing with the dolls themselves.

Already sure of her calling, Keri earned her bachelor's degree in interior design at Western Washington University in 1993. Keri then spent more than nine years with Neil Kelly, focusing on two of her loves: kitchens and bathrooms.

Since she started her own company in 2004, Keri has gently helped clients of all walks of life stretch beyond their comfort zone in order to find the long-term living space that's right for them. Keri believes this growth is an all-important step in design—not only do clients get a bigger bang for their buck, but they will also "love their space for a longer period of time than if they take the safe route."

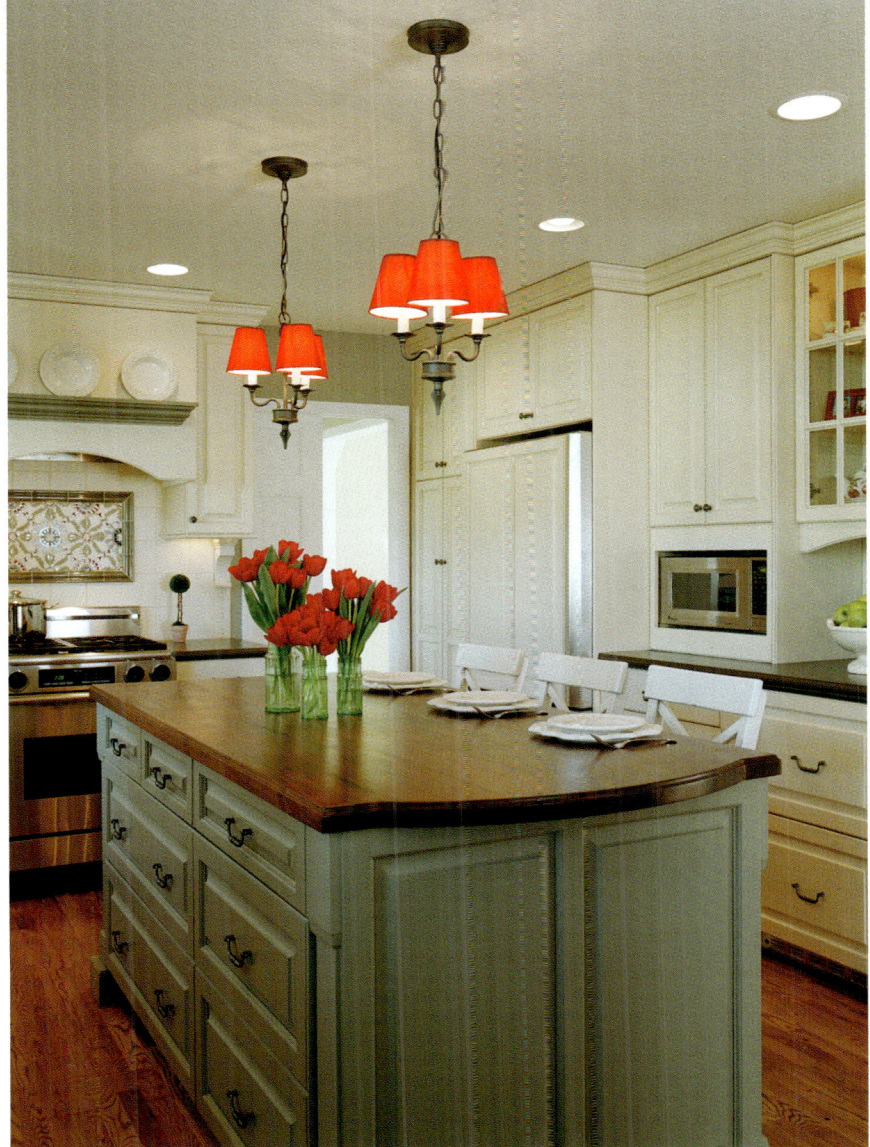

LEFT
A crisp, clean feeling was the theme for this room. Architectural details were important such as the built-in cabinetry and boxed-beam ceiling. The flooring is distressed walnut.

RIGHT
The multicolored tile started the inspiration for this kitchen. The perimeter counters are concrete and the island counter is walnut. A splash of red in the light fixtures creates a little punch of color.

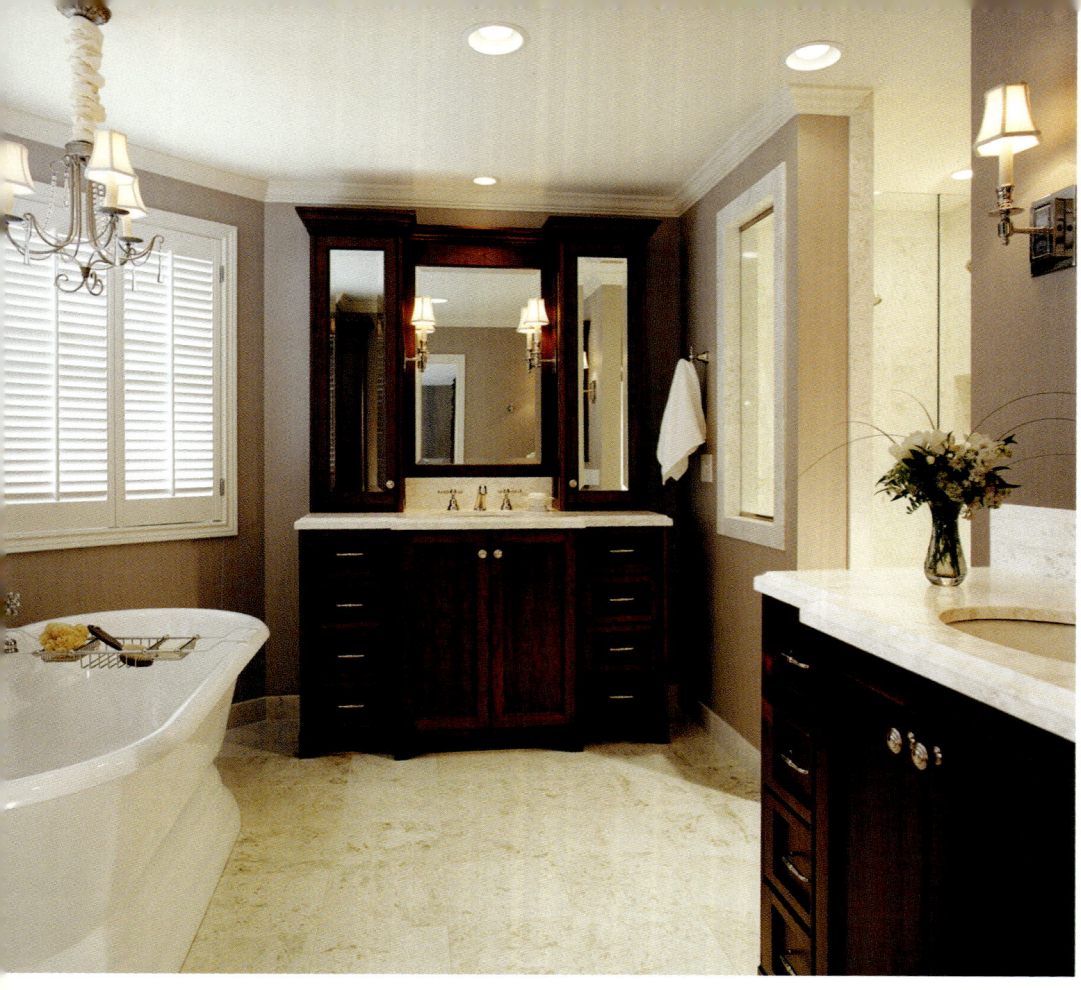

In order to guide her clients comfortably towards new design heights, Keri listens carefully to the client's needs and then offers a variety of solutions. A perfect example is a client who wanted to create heavy textures on her kitchen walls using straw. Instead, Keri suggested covering all the walls in a cream-colored, very textured stone for a more elegant, refined feel. The client loved the idea—and her new kitchen.

From a design standpoint, Keri is known for her versatility, although she favors a traditional feel. With her high level of attention to detail and her strong space-planning skills, Keri creates efficient interiors that flow. She is known for walking into a space and pointing out which walls need to be moved where and what pieces of furniture or art need to be added in order to create the proper feel.

When a designer is as talented and passionate as Keri, it doesn't take long before the rest of the world stands up and takes notice. Keri has won two awards through the Oregon Remodelers Association for her kitchen and bath remodels, and she won a national award for bathroom design through the National Kitchen and Bath Association. Her work has also been featured in publications such as *Oregon Home, Sunset, Woman's Day* magazine and *American Homestyle & Gardening* magazine.

Ask this cutting-edge designer what she likes best about her work, and she'll be quick to respond. "I never get tired of my job. There is always something new to try, there is always a new client to get to know and the reward of seeing a finished project is unbelievably satisfying."

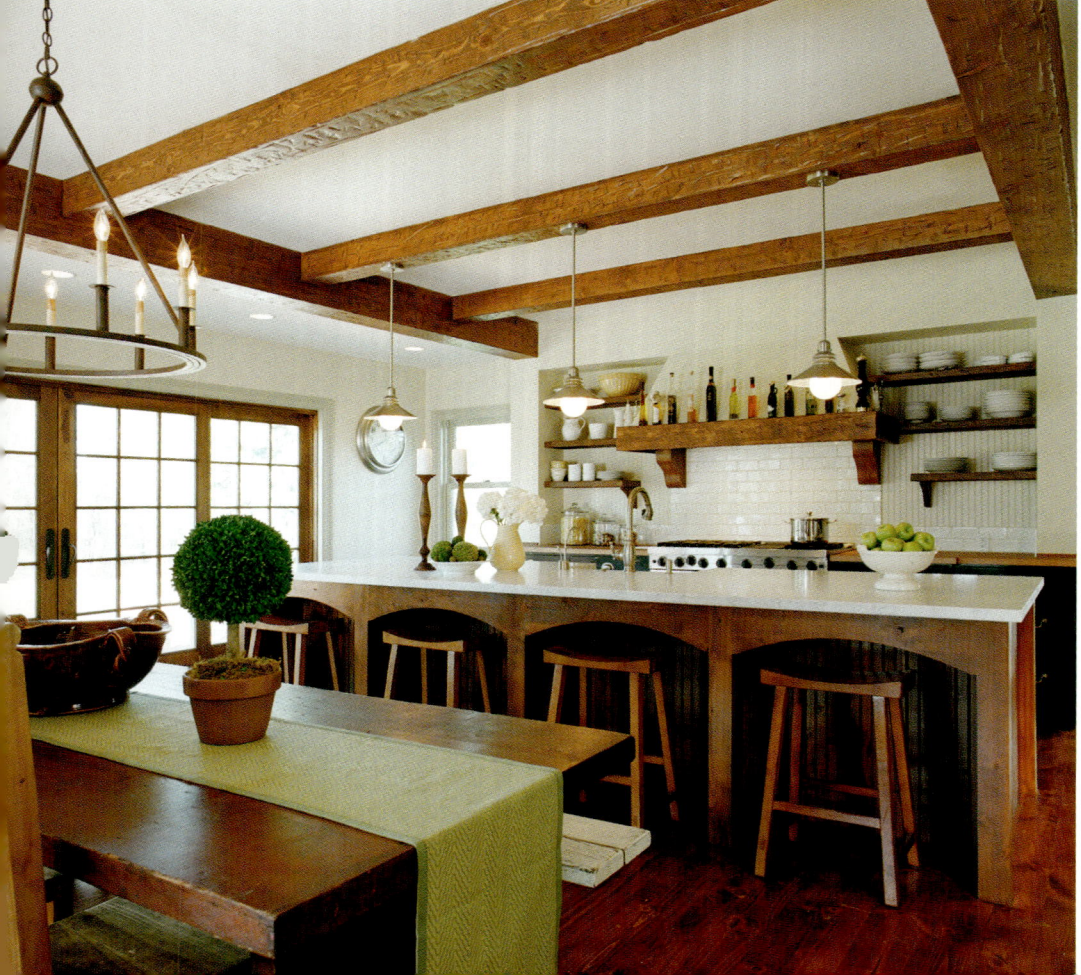

TOP
A traditional feel was the goal for this bathroom, achieved by the dark wood cabinetry, marble counters, floors and shower. The chandelier added some sparkle.

BOTTOM
East Coast Nantucket is the style here. Rustic yet refined. Knotty alder cabinetry, distressed and stained, and a Carrera marble countertop were the materials used.

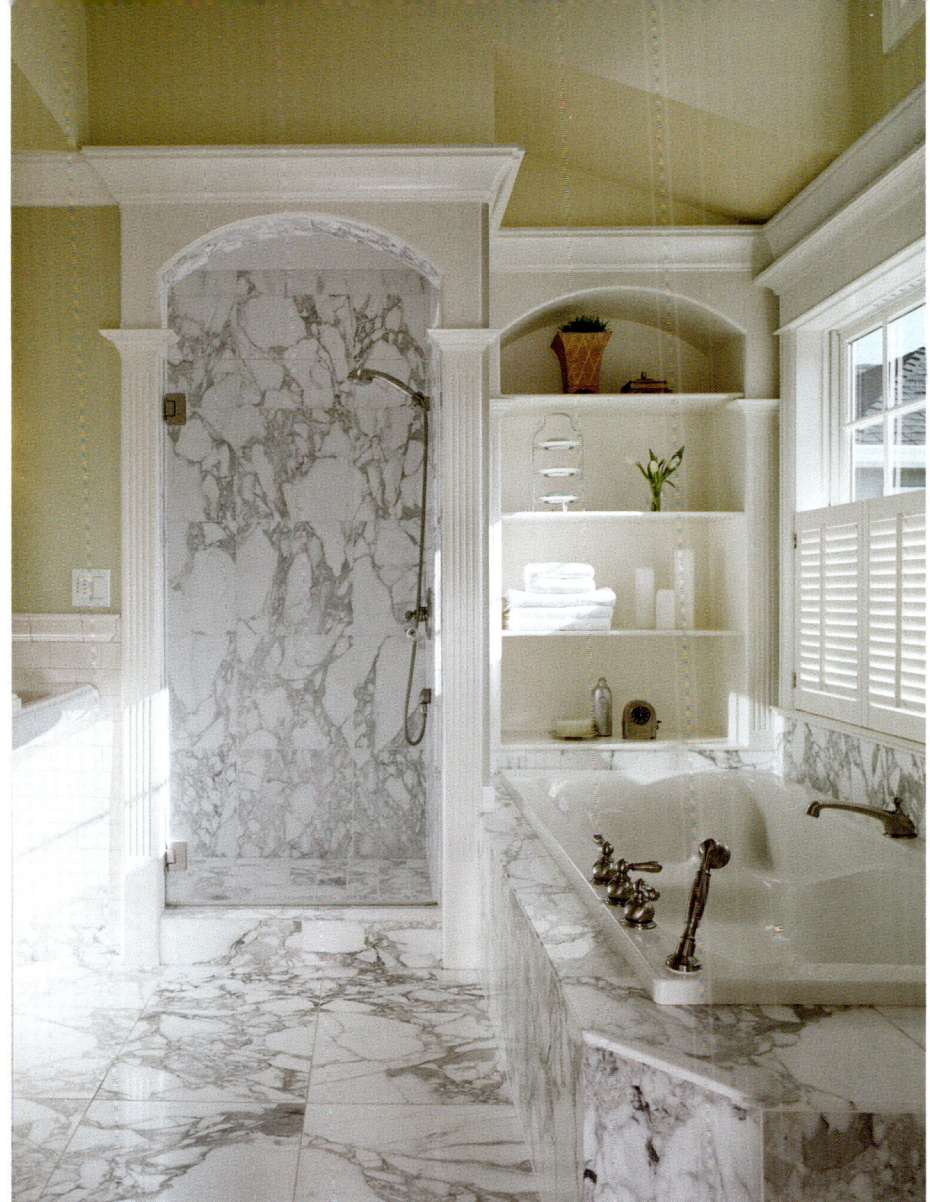
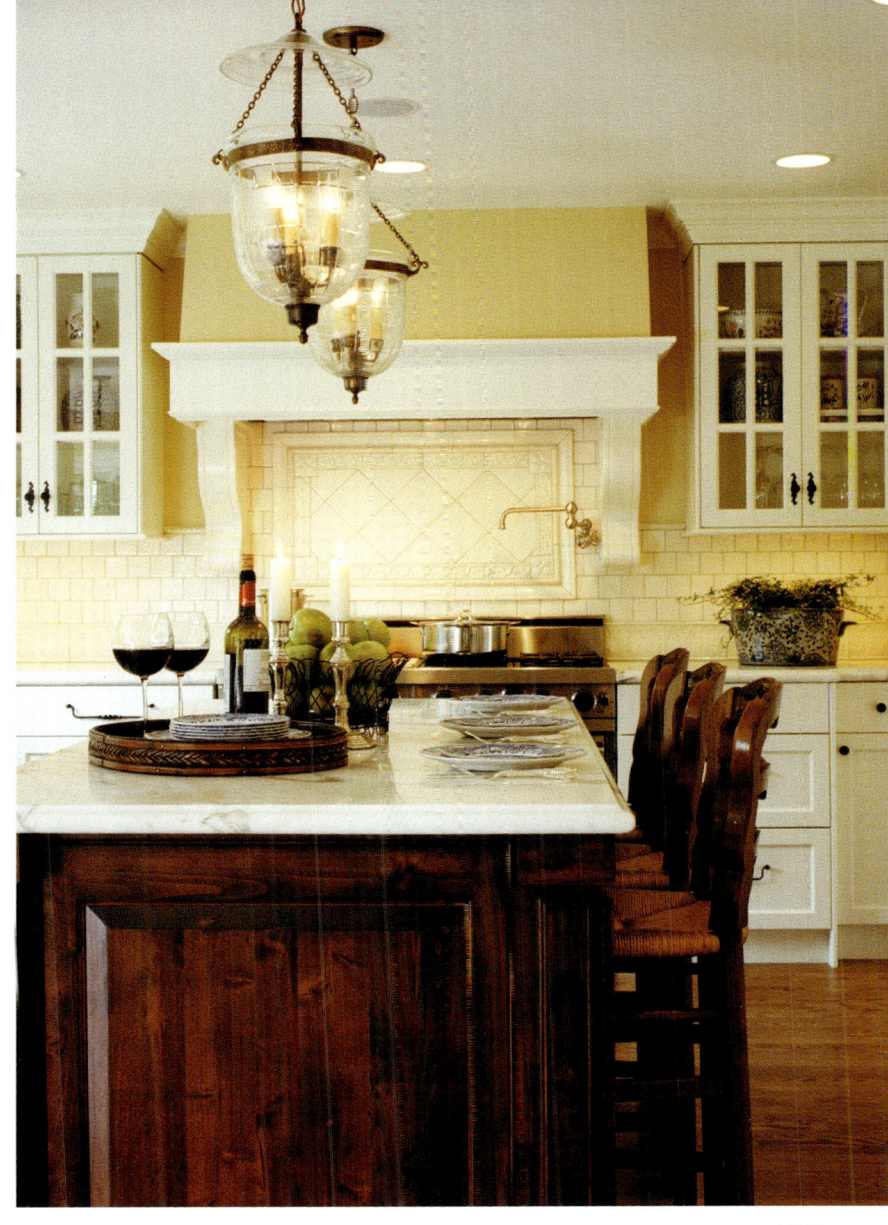

LEFT
This bathroom is refined and elegant. Marble was used on the floors, shower and tub deck. Special attention to detail was paid creating the arches and the fluted columns.

RIGHT
The hood and tile behind the stove created the focal point and were the inspiration. The island is Knotty Alder and the counters are Calcutta Luna marble.

More about Keri…

WHAT COLOR BEST DESCRIBES YOU?
Green, because it is a calming, even-keeled color and, like green, Keri stays calm and collected, even in this sometimes high-stress business.

YOU CAN TELL KERI LIVES IN THE PACIFIC NORTHWEST BECAUSE…
She needs light therapy!

WHAT BOOK ARE YOU READING RIGHT NOW?
Rich Dad, Poor Dad, by Robert Kiyosaki.

Keri Davis Design
Keri Davis
616 Cabana Lane
Lake Oswego, OR 97034
503.475.5883
Fax 503.699.0966

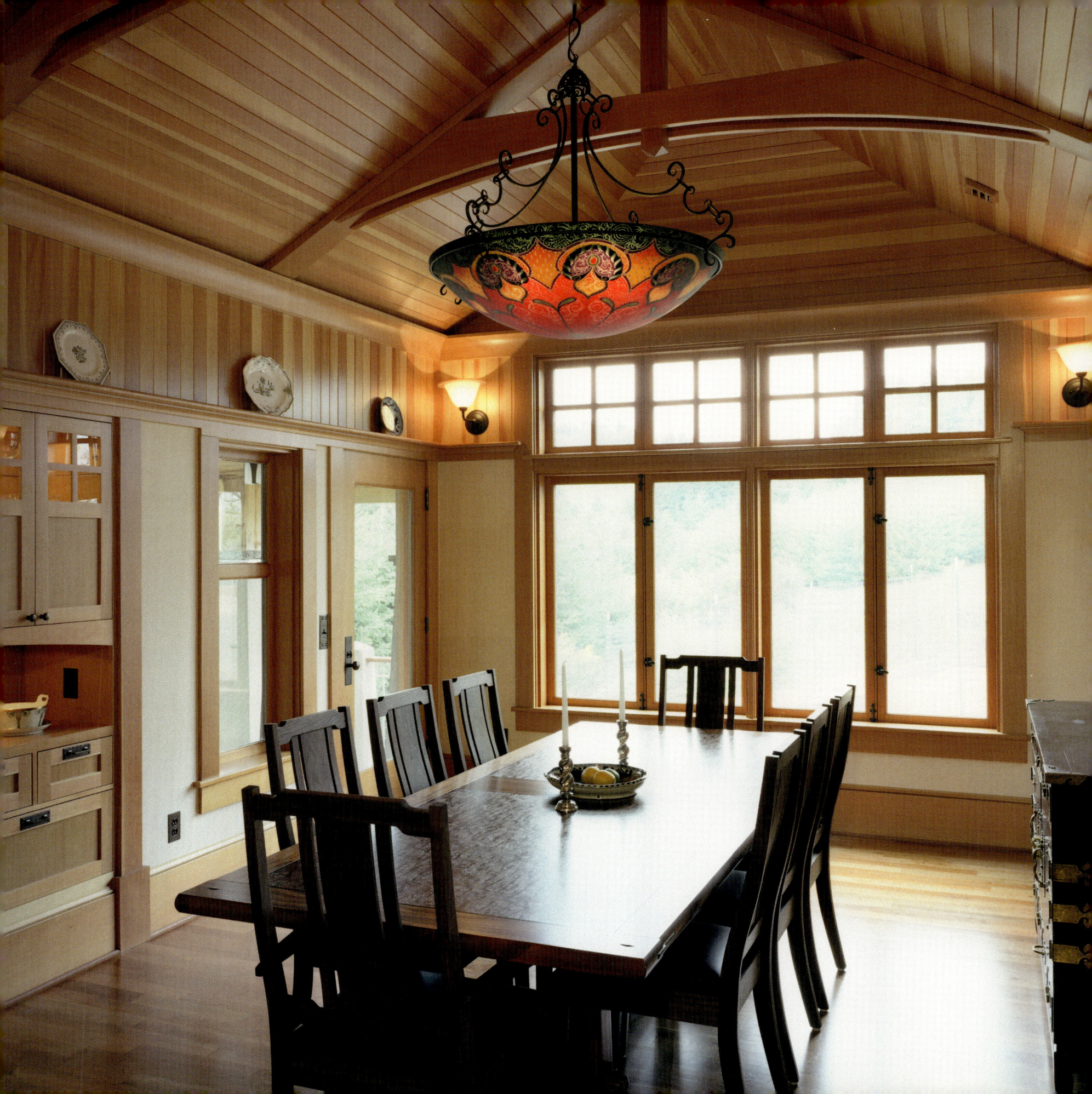

MELODY EMERICK

Emerick Architects P.C.

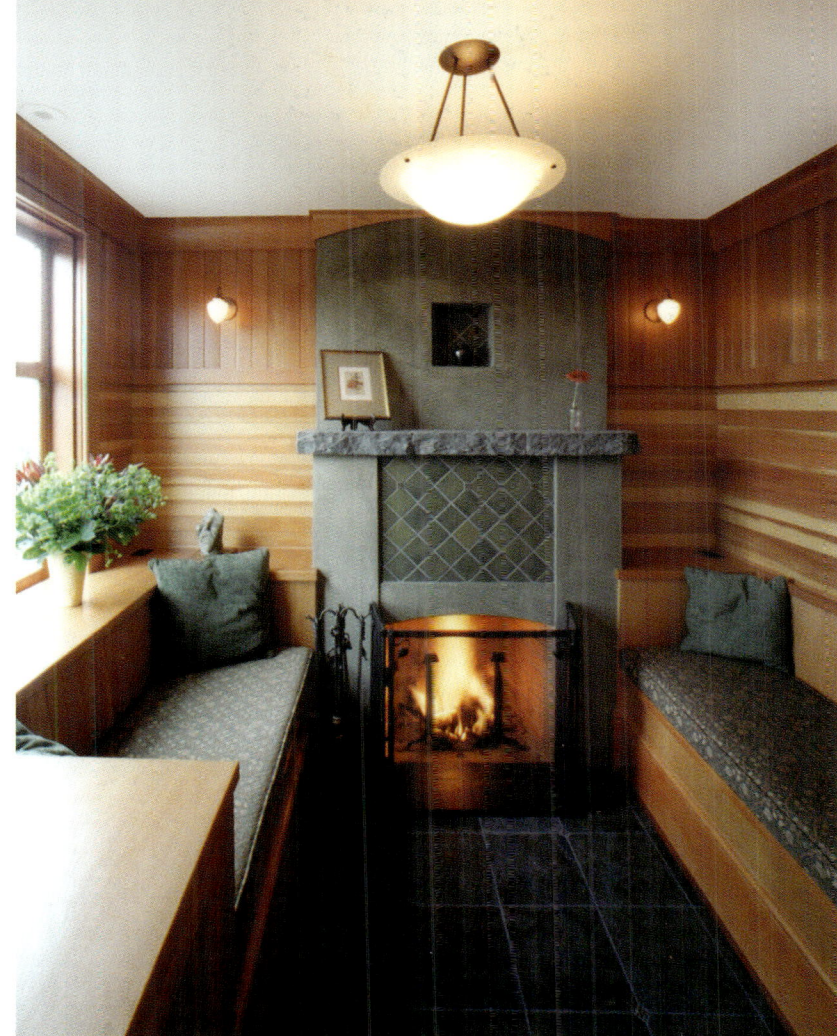

In everything she does, Melody Emerick believes in quality over quantity. This is especially true in her work as an architect and designer whether she's choosing sustainable wood for a home or working with clients on a design that will meet their needs for the next 50 years. Long lasting, sustainable and breathtaking are Melody's main goals for every space—and she and her husband, architect Brian Emerick, have succeeded in meeting these goals for her clients for more than 13 years.

The Emericks' philosophy is a perfect fit for the Northwest, where long lasting, sustainable and breathtaking are often synonymous. Whenever possible, Melody chooses natural, recycled and reused products in her designs to capture—and pay homage to—the true spirit of the Northwest.

"We are big on creating spaces that feel a part of the Northwest," Melody says. "This comes from the materials as well as quality of spaces. We refer to this as humble elegance—very livable, and made to endure beyond trends.'

LEFT
Gently curving trusses accent the vaulted fir ceiling giving the dining room a rich wood feel. The art glass pendant centers the room and augments the general sconce lighting of the room.

RIGHT
A fireplace is built into a cozy inglenook adjoining the living room. The stone and tile work was carried through.

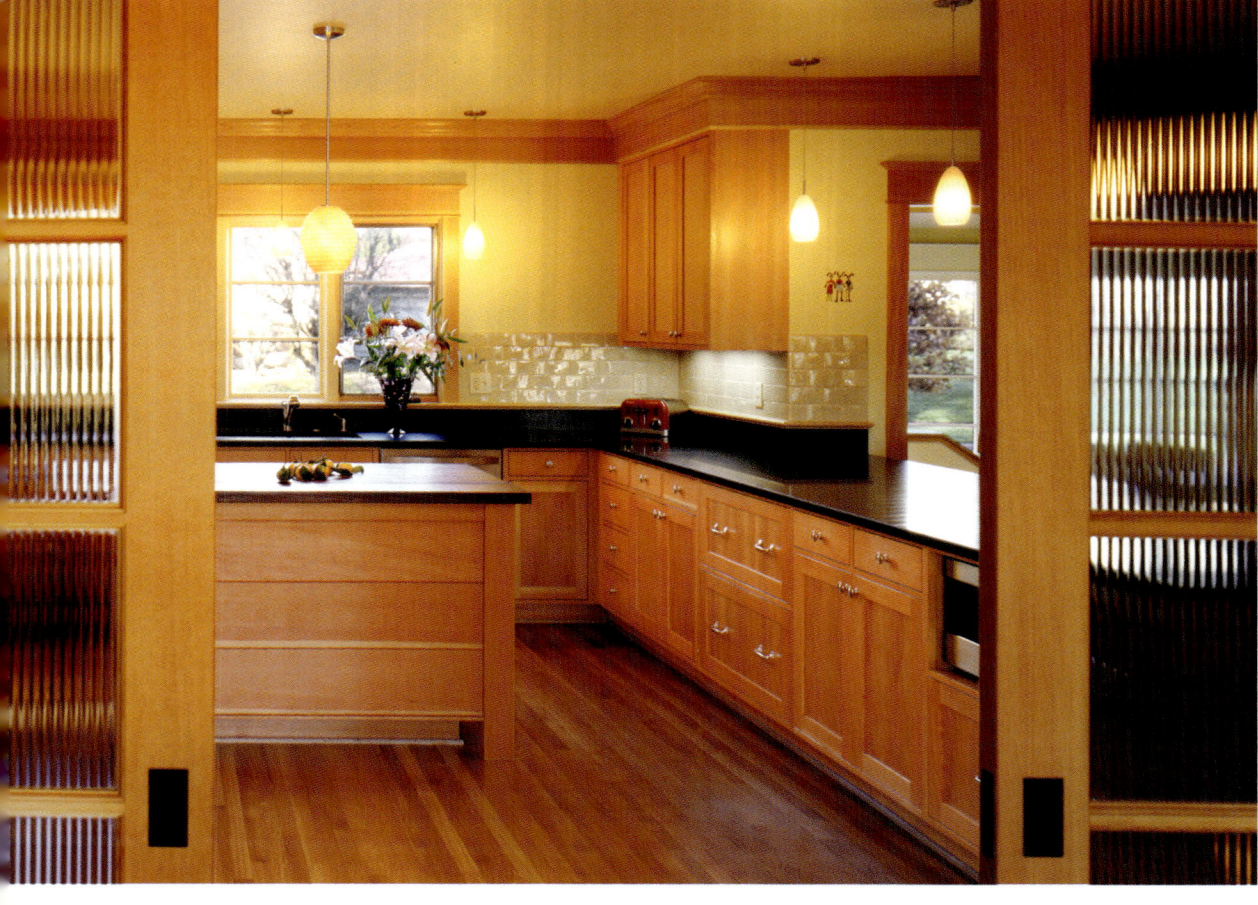

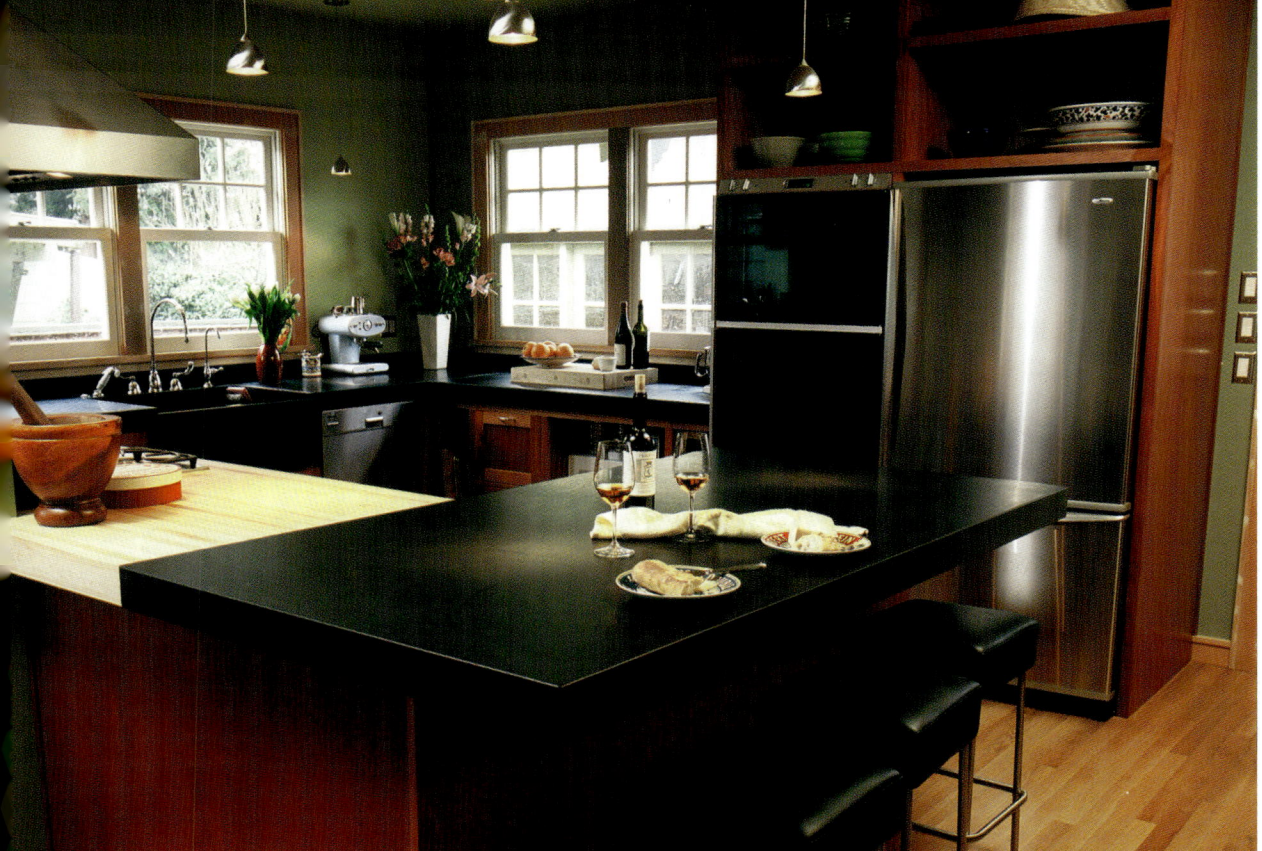

A Northwest native, Melody earned her degree in architecture from the University of Oregon, which is also where she met her husband. Nearly eight years ago, the two created Emerick Architects, a firm that specializes in approaching spaces in a holistic way. Since then, the Emericks have developed a reputation for timeless designs among both clients and top-rated publications in the industry, including *Sunset* magazine, *Oregon Home*, *Portraits of Portland* and *Better Homes and Garden*.

The Emerick's architectural design skills allow them to complete every aspect of a space, from scouting the best land and location for a home to custom designing lights and everything in between. Sometimes that means creating a water runoff system and a radiant-heat floor. Other times, it means doing research into roof gardens and creating rooms that flow from inside to out.

Melody's style rarely learns toward trend-based interiors. Instead, she aims to create classic spaces that will meet her clients' aesthetic and practical needs for as long as possible. "Our process is always rooted in understanding how the client lives, being sensitive to site and structure and then tailoring the project to eloquently meet those needs," she says.

TOP
This updated kitchen echoes back to its roots with natural wood cabinetry and a vintage tile backsplash.

BOTTOM
Open, light filled and fresh, this kitchen puts the chef right in the middle of it all.

FACING PAGE RIGHT
Naturalistic elements of stone, tile and wood, as well as the vignette window, give this bathroom a distinctive feel.

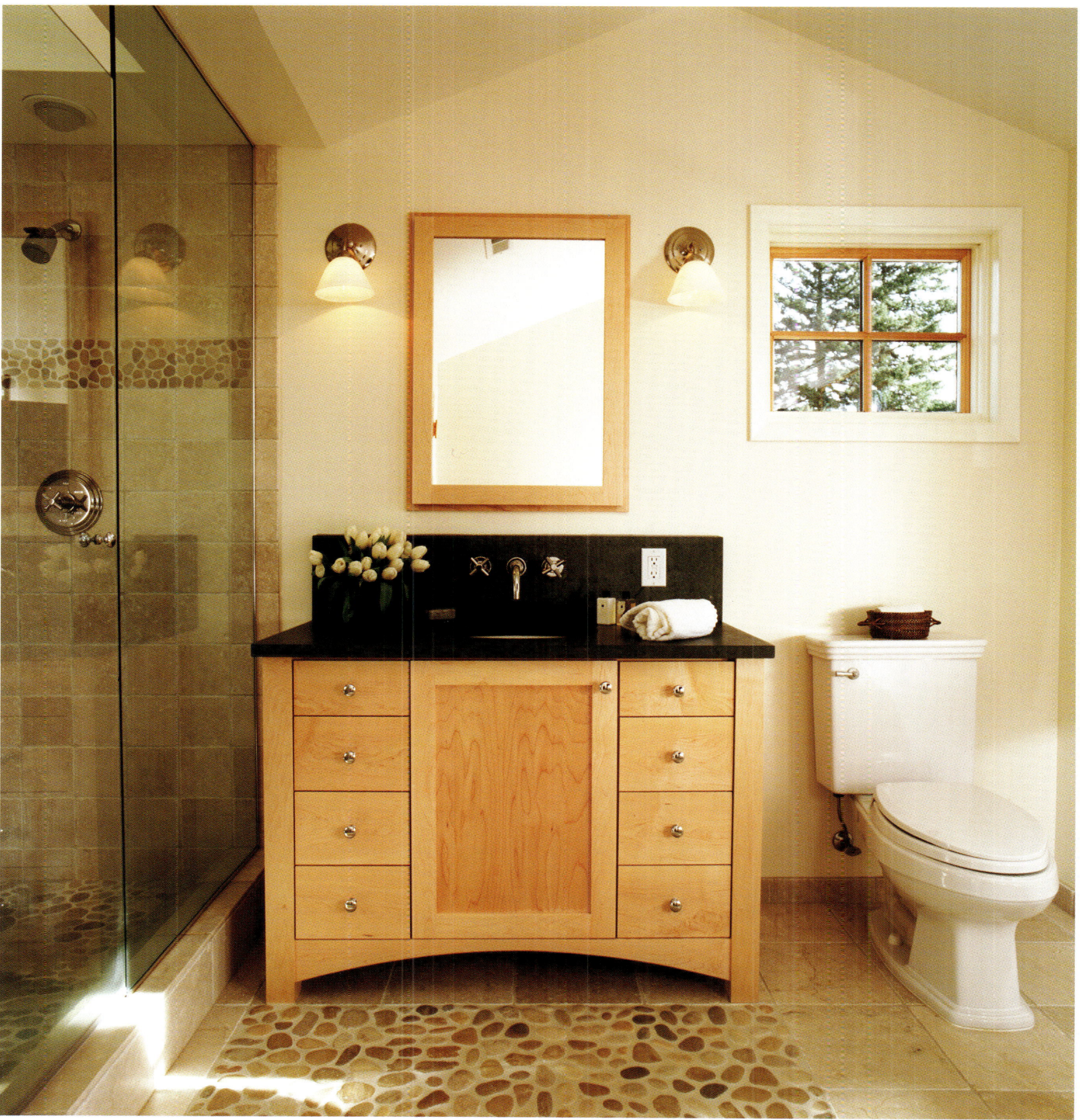

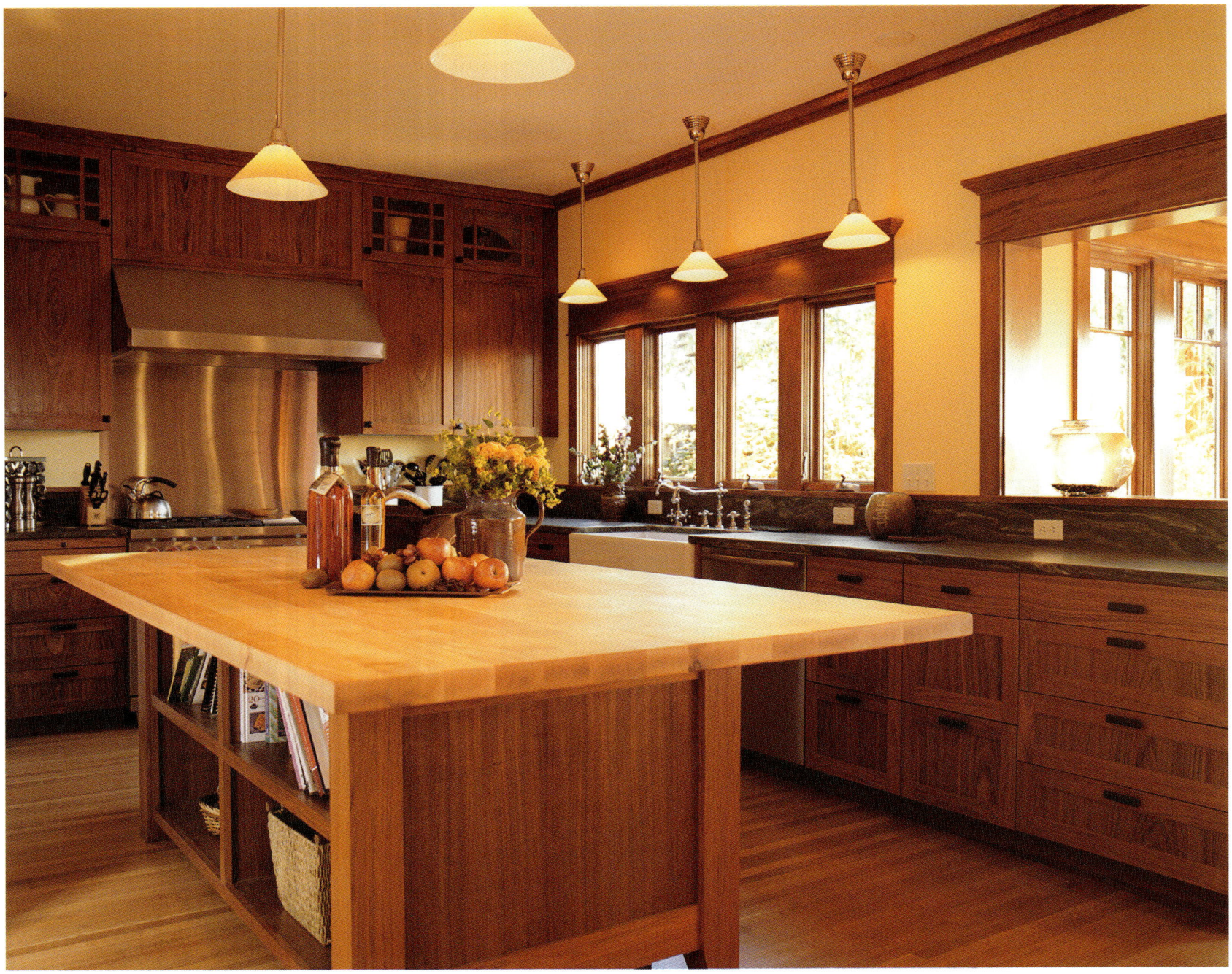

Feeling blessed to live and work in an area with such raw, natural beauty and a strong-forward-thinking community, Melody draws inspiration from these qualities and is especially interested old barns, which she loves for their simple structures, quality building materials and fine bones. "When I was growing up, I lived out in the country," she says. "What I love about it is that the buildings are simple and functional, and that's what makes them so beautiful. Often, design is about editing a space down to the most simple, beautiful things."

Melody likes to take advantage of the Northwest's beautiful weather whenever possible, both in her design work and in her personal life. "We live in a mild climate, so we work hard to connect rooms to the outside through folding doors, oversized windows and porches," she says. When not at work, she spends time camping, hiking and biking the Northwest with her husband and daughters, Lily and Iris.

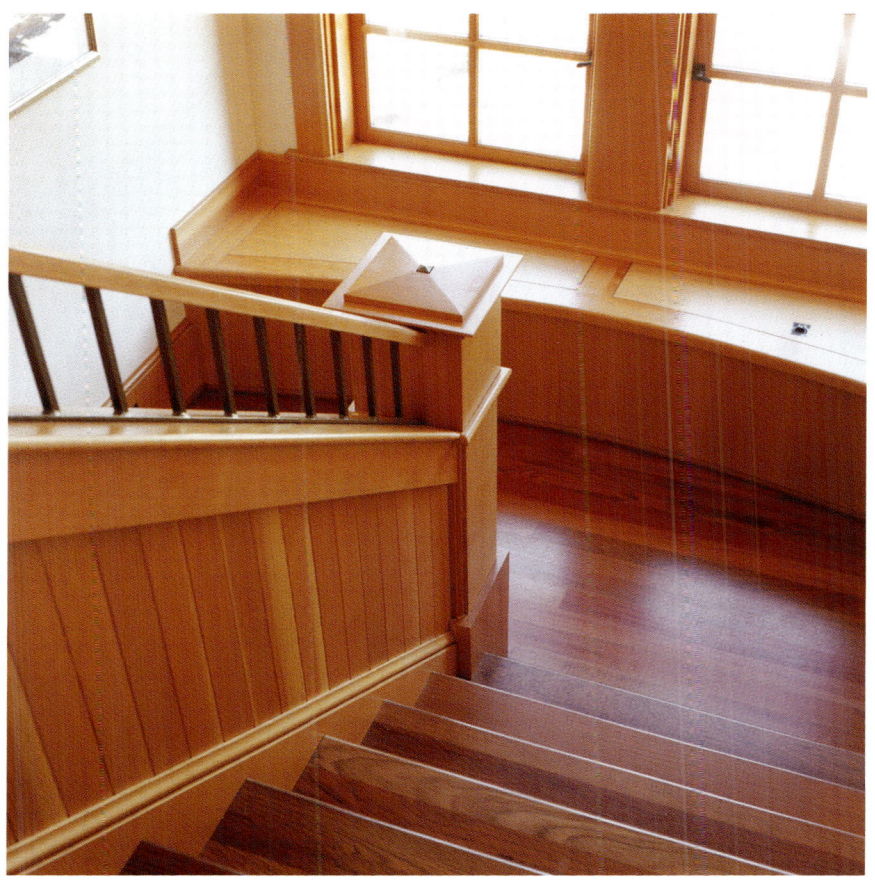
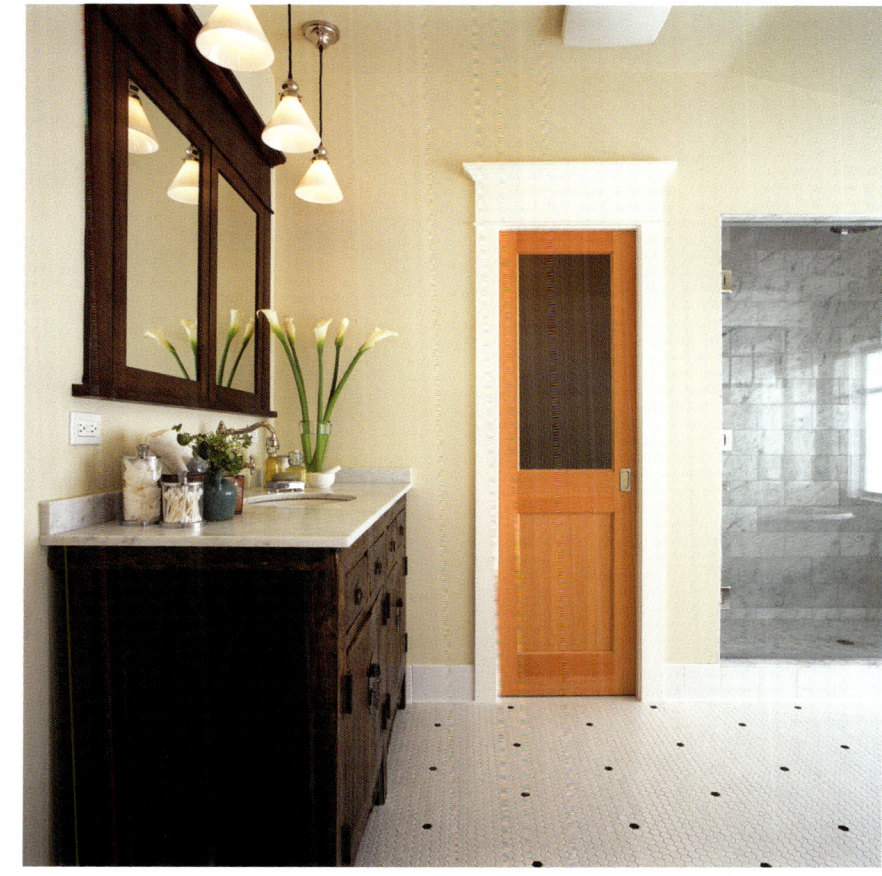

LEFT
A window seat on the landing with built-in storage and 12' high windows provide a place to pause.

RIGHT
The bathroom vanity cabinet was a found object restored and installed as a built-in to add a rustic quality to this modern bathroom.

FACING PAGE LEFT
This extra large island creates a great center to this kitchen with plenty of open workspaces highlighted with pendant lighting.

More about Melody…

WHAT PERSONAL INDULGENCE DO YOU SPEND THE MOST MONEY ON?

CD's. The musicians I like best are singer/songwriters who inspire me because their sound evolves but always stays true to their voice: Lucinda Williams, Gillian Welch, Bruce Springsteen, Junior Wells. Classical music or a good Billie Holiday CD are my favorites while working late at night.

IF YOU COULD ELIMINATE ONE ARCHITECTURAL TECHNIQUE FROM THE WORLD, WHAT WOULD IT BE?

The trendy, throw-away mentality. Construction uses a lot of resources, and buildings can last longer than people think. I believe in getting it right the first time.

WHAT IS THE ONE THING THAT YOU WOULD DO TO BRING A DULL HOUSE TO LIFE?

Invest in the bones. Great windows and natural light always transform a room.

YOU WOULDN'T KNOW IT, BUT MY FRIENDS WOULD TELL YOU I WAS…

Intense, persistent and focused.

WHAT BOOKS ARE YOU READING RIGHT NOW?

Poetry books for inspiration. My favorites are e.e. cummings, William Stafford and Robert Frost.

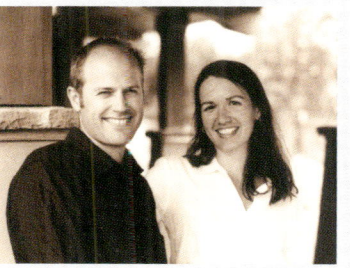

Emerick Architects P.C.
Melody Emerick
208 SW First Avenue
Suite 320
Portland, Oregon 97204
503.235.9400
Fax 503.235.9310

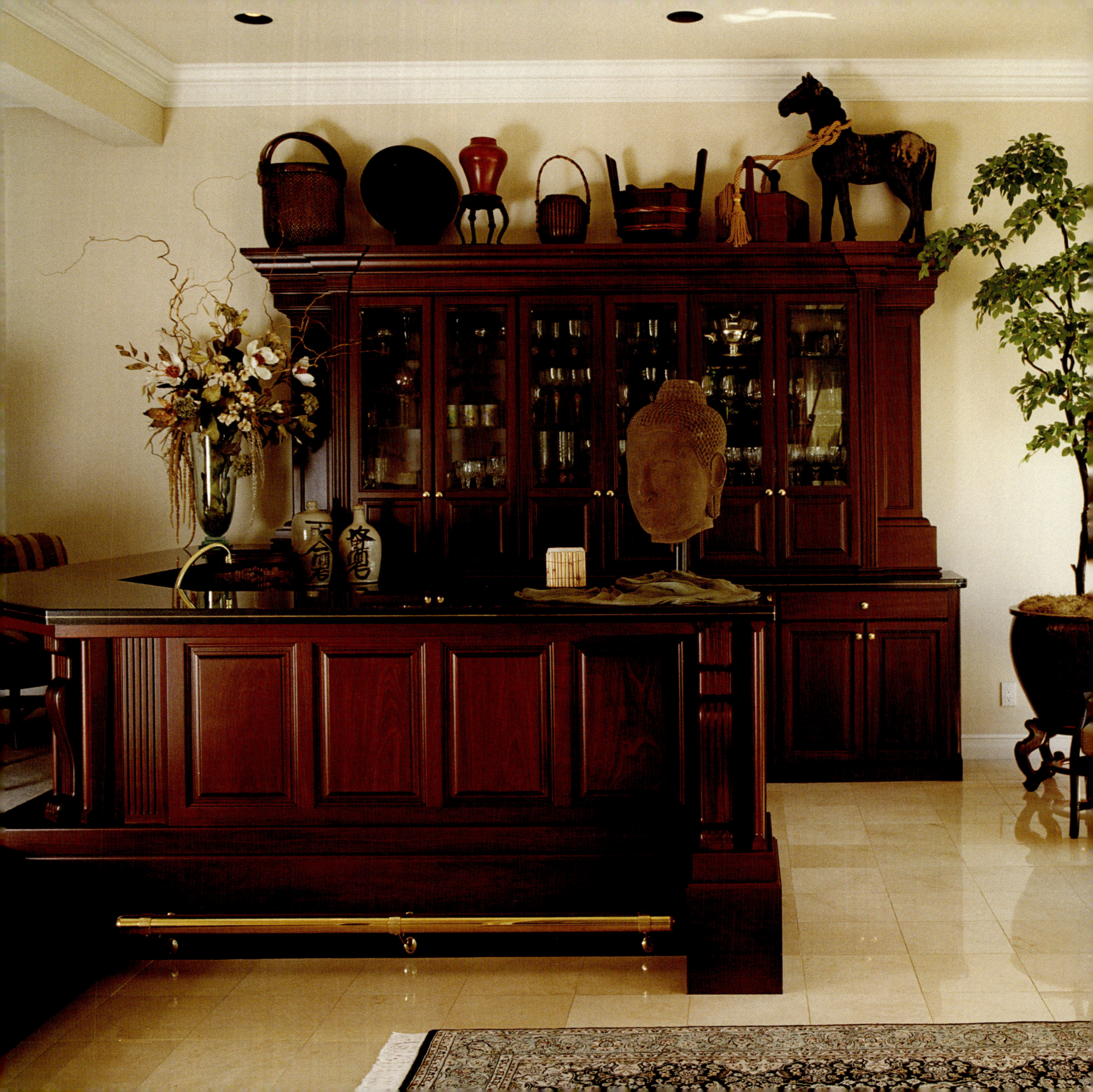

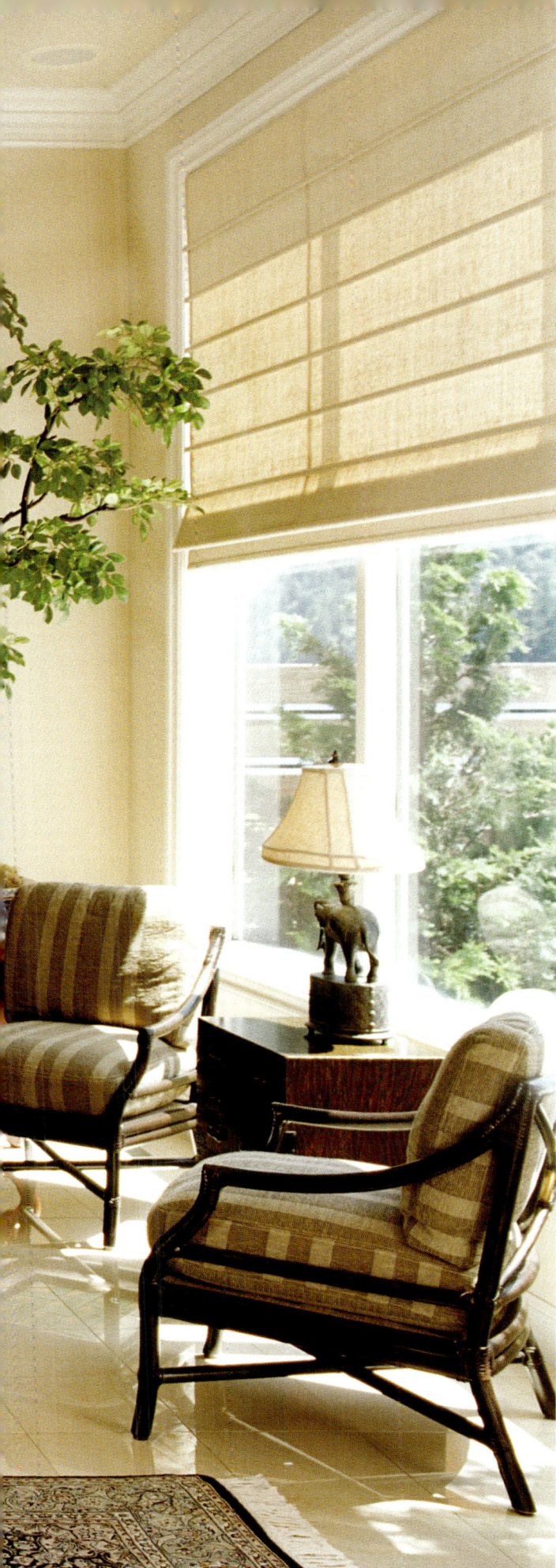

KATHIE POZARICH

KP Design Group

With 25 years of experience in interior design, Kathie Pozarich has built a reputation for being one of the Northwest's finest interior designers. Well-known and respected in the industry, Kathie has worked with clients across the Northwest, in Oregon and Washington as well as Southern California.

Kathie believes that design starts in the imagination, and she has a unique talent for shaping her clients' ideas with her own creativity and expertise to form spaces that are unique to each individual. Color, form and texture turn dreams into great designs.

The ability to interpret her clients' needs and desires is truly Kathie's gift; She gets to know her clients so well that they often let her loose in their home, office, retail establishment or restaurant with the words, "Just go ahead and do it—you know what I want."

Since founding her own business in 1980, Kathie has focused her energy on building long-term relationships with her clients. From these relationships come trust, understanding and excellence in design. Kathie believes her job as a designer is akin to a psychologist: listen carefully to the client's wants and needs, pay attention to their lifestyle, and then make sure that the entire process is as smooth and stress-free as possible. Her primary objective is to "to capture the essence of the environment my clients are imagining." Kathie finds that this philosophy creates not only repeat business from satisfied customers, but often leads to life-long friends. These relationships, some spanning more than 20 years, are "the biggest reward" in her career.

LEFT
Entertaining is a delight in this tasteful and simple bar with its mahogany cabinets and granite countertops. The antique Asian artifacts add interest and dimension, balancing the old with the new.

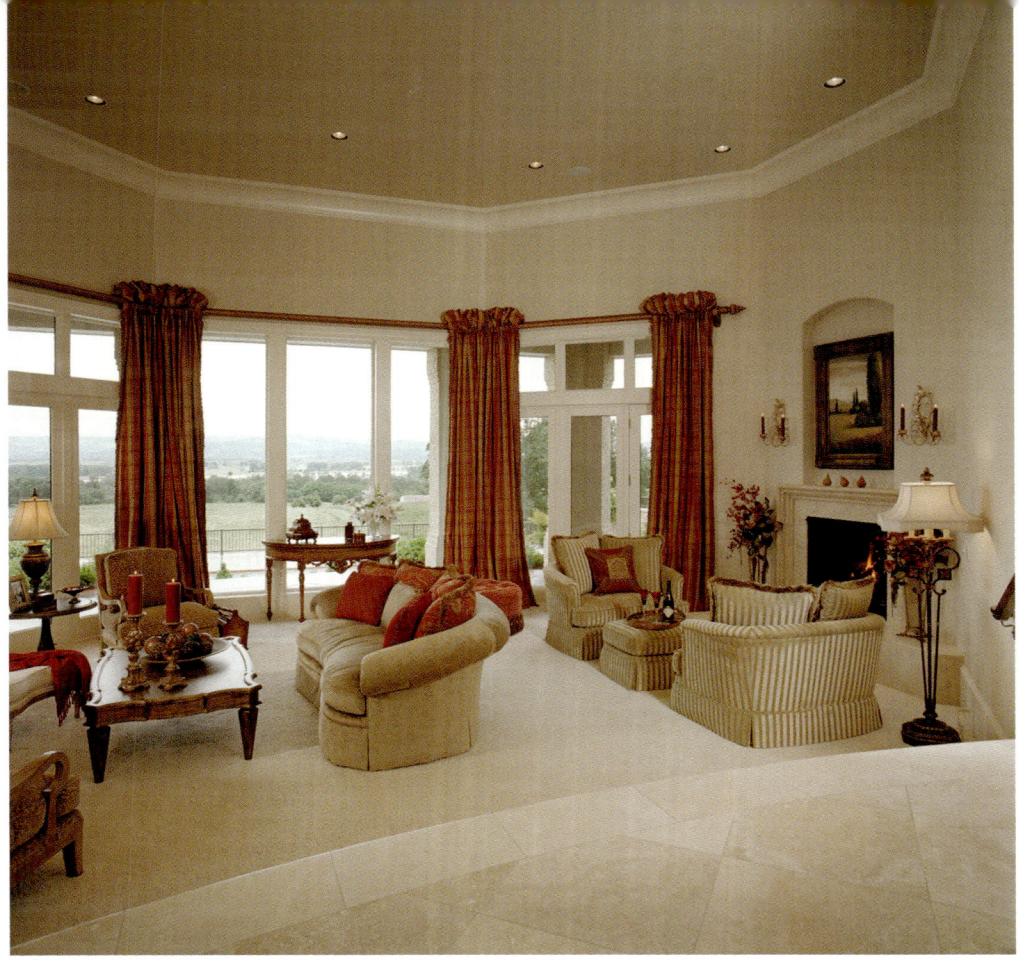

Believing that colleague relationships are just as important as client relationships, Kathie stays actively involved with industry organizations. She is a charter member, the past president and a professional member of the Northwest Society of Interior Designers and is an allied member of the American Society of Interior Designers.

As an award-winning designer for the NW Natural Street of Dreams in 1982, 1983, 1985 and 1986, Kathie also received a regional Northwest Society of Interior Designers award for Best Cabinet Design in 2000. Her homes have been featured in many publications, including *The Columbian*, *The Oregonian*, *Western Living* magazine, *Designers West* and *Home* magazine's "Best Ideas for Kitchen and Bath."

Kathie's philosophy is that "great design looks simple." For Kathie, that simplicity comes through space planning, research, foresight and insight into the individuals involved, all of which help her to achieve the most successful design for the client's individual environment. Creativity is another important element that Kathie uses to enhance and create an ambiance that allows people to relate more to their environments.

According to Kathie, the old adage, "the difference is in the details," really rings true. For her, perfecting the architectural details and choosing the right accessories are the "frosting on the cake," the necessary elements to finishing any space.

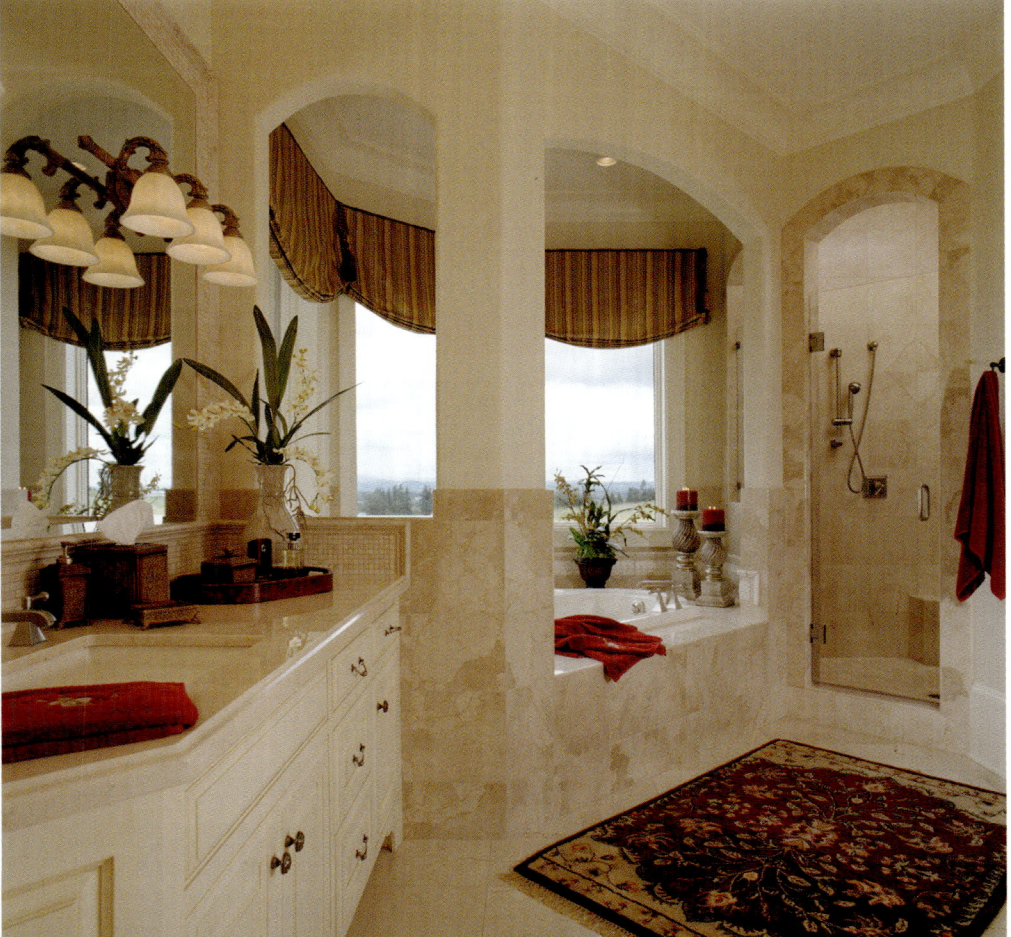

TOP
This living room allows for a formal seating area and a place to cozy up by the fire. Either way the endless views are not lost and add to the greatness of the space.

BOTTOM
The richness of red and gold enhance and warm this elegant master bath with its classic marble design and furniture-inspired cabinetry.

FACING PAGE RIGHT
Woven shades, silk drapes and glazed walls add texture and depth to this dramatic dining room.

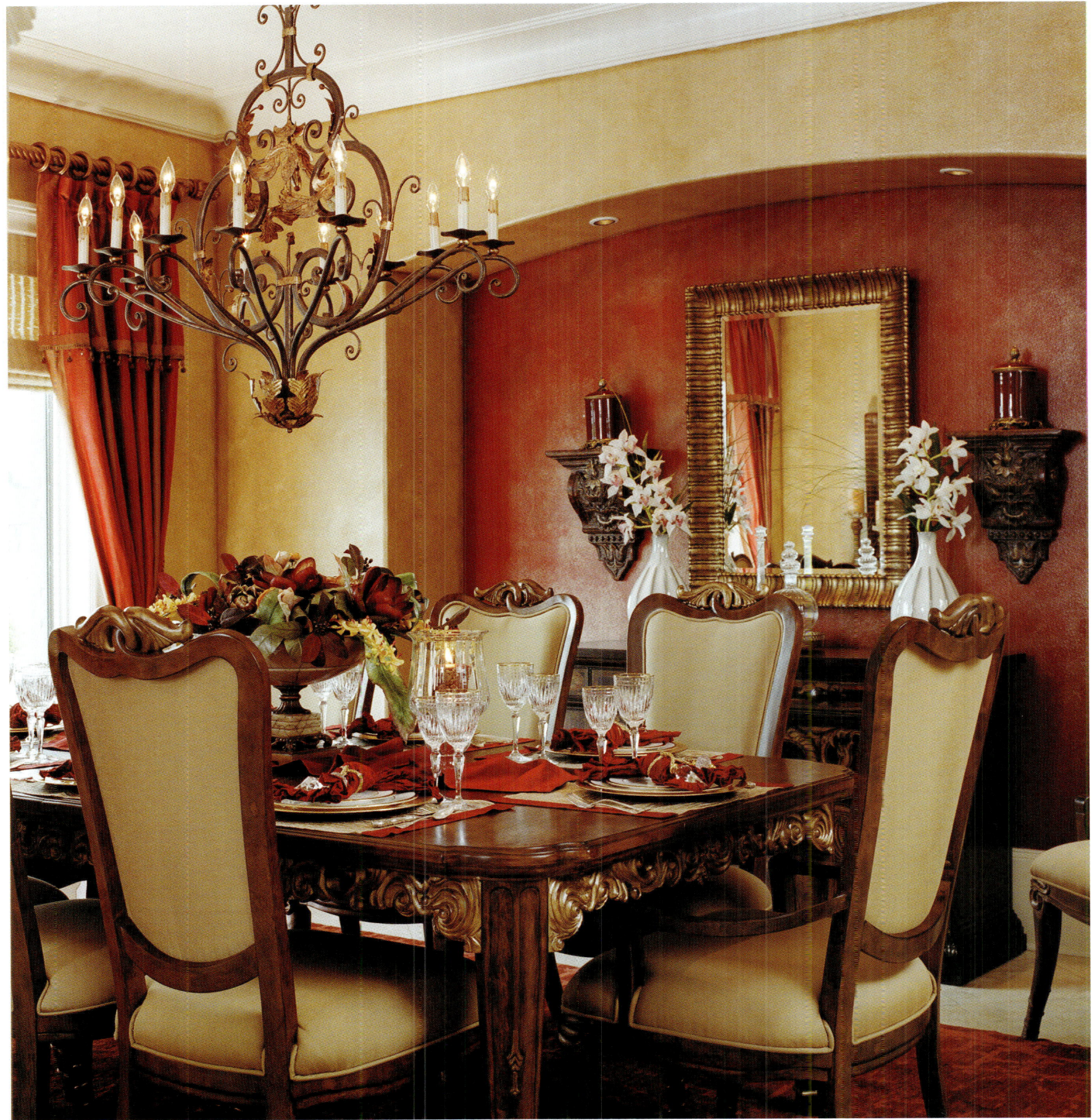

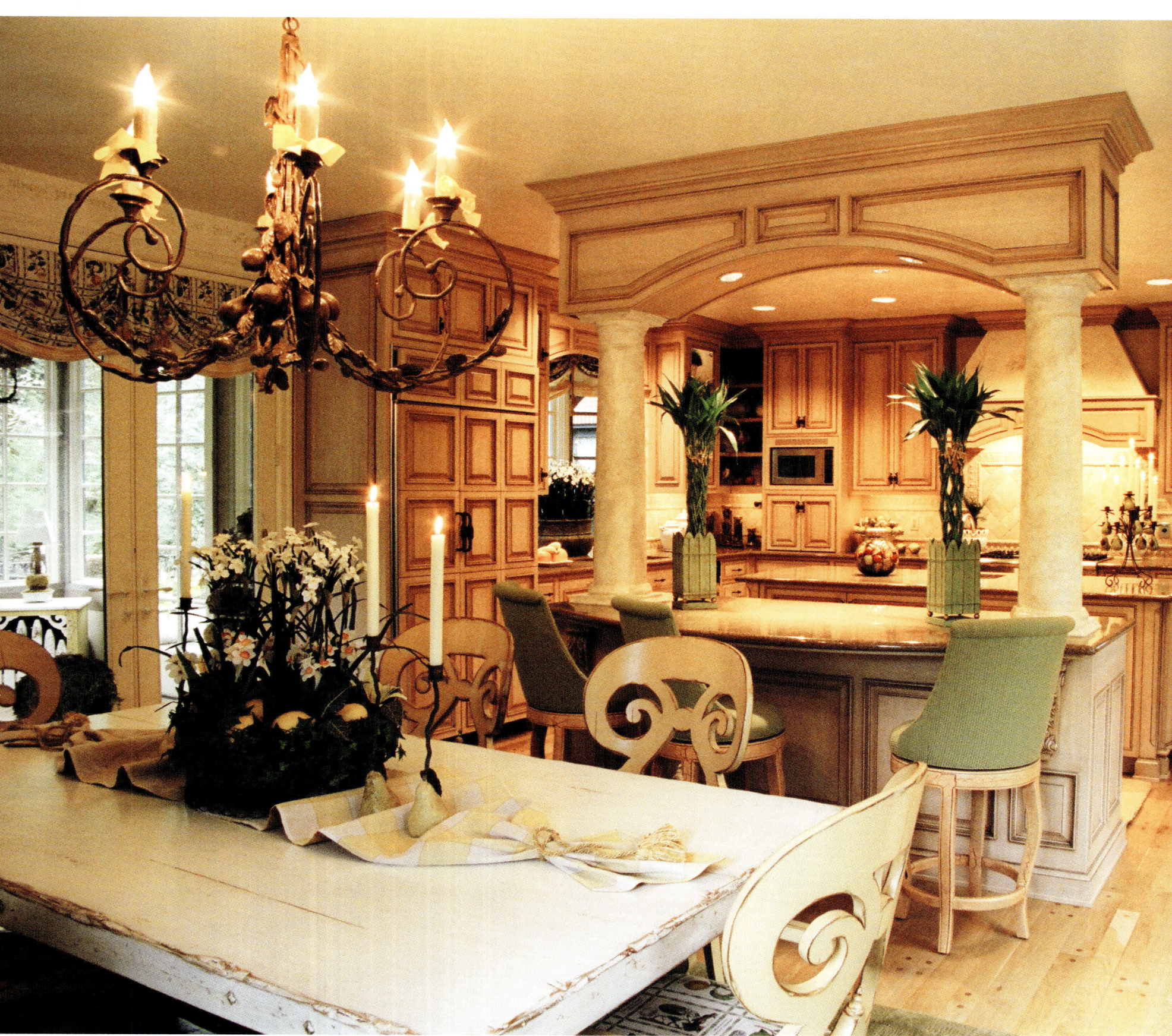

Kathie's portfolio is diverse and she sees every project as an opportunity to build something entirely new. Her interiors are personalized to each client's lifestyle due to her skills at meeting every individual's diverse backgrounds and tastes to create livable, yet highly polished detail interiors for luxury homes.

Kathie, whose sole employee is also her daughter, feels blessed to be surrounded by family in the Pacific Northwest. She also has a son in the real estate business, and spends as much time as possible with her two grandchildren.

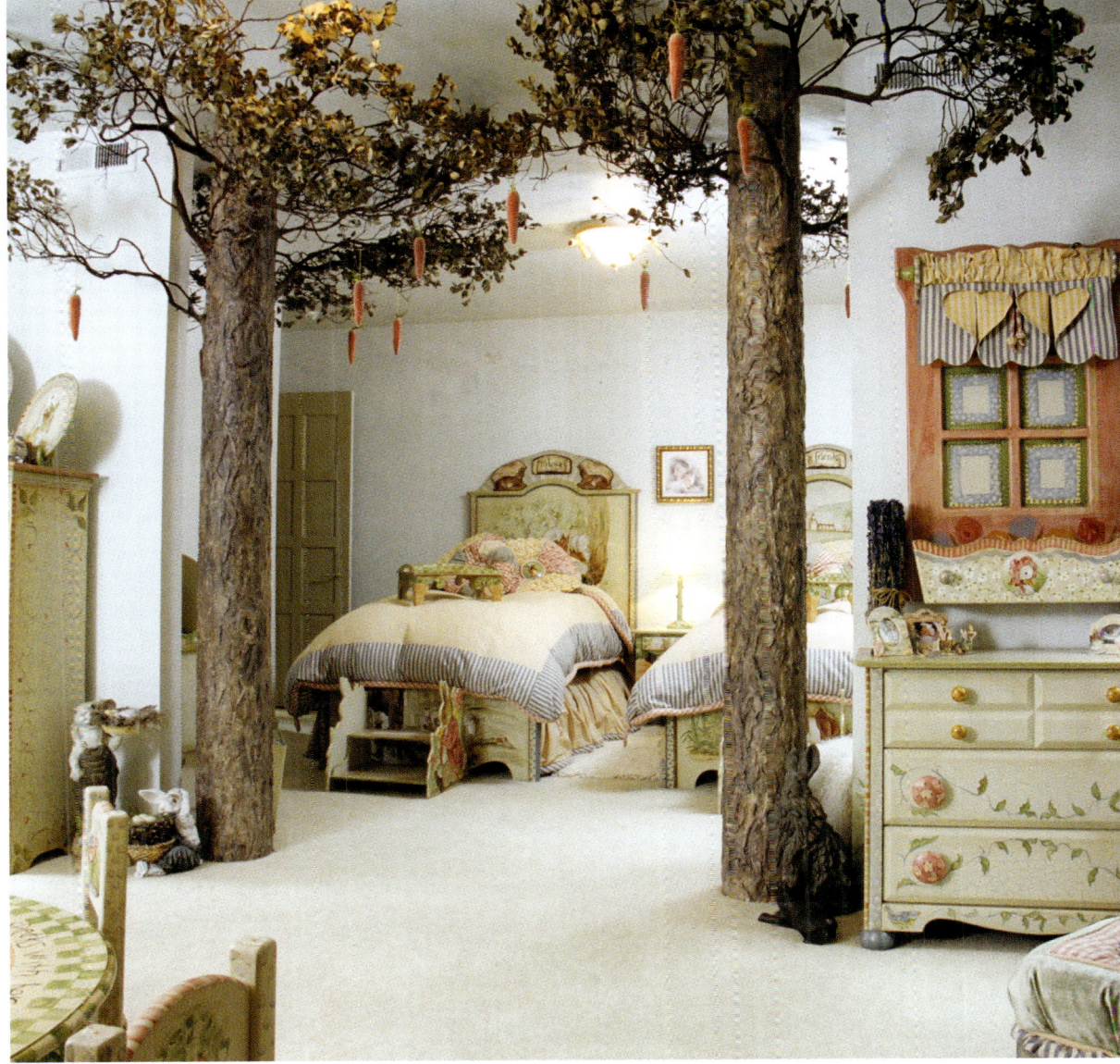

RIGHT
A child's fantasy comes to life with this Beatrix Potter inspired theme. Support columns turned trees umbrella this enchanting space.

FACING PAGE LEFT
The European inspired kitchen is comfortable and functional with its two-island design. Open and inviting with attached nook make this kitchen great for entertaining family or friends.

More about Kathie…

WHAT ONE ELEMENT OF STYLE OR PHILOSOPHY HAVE YOU STUCK WITH FOR YEARS THAT STILL WORKS FOR HER TODAY?

Keep it classical and functional.

IF YOU COULD ELIMINATE ONE DESIGN/ARCHITECTURAL/BUILDING TECHNIQUE OR STYLE FROM THE WORLD, WHAT WOULD IT BE?

She wouldn't! There is room for all creativity in the world.

WHO HAS HAD THE BIGGEST INFLUENCE ON YOUR CAREER?

Her children, especially her daughter and project manager, who inspires her every day to be the very best she can be.

WHAT IS THE MOST UNUSUAL TECHNIQUE YOU'VE USED IN ONE OF YOU PROJECTS?

She turned columns into tree trunks for a child's bedroom.

WHY DO YOU LIKE DOING BUSINESS IN THE PACIFIC NORTHWEST?

The people here are hard-working, down-to-earth and so appreciative of the lifestyle. It is like nowhere else in the country. She also feels blessed to be surrounded by her family and friends.

KP Design Group, Inc.
Kathie Pozarich, Allied Member
ASID, NWSID
4690 Auburn Lane
Lake Oswego, OR 97035
503.635.3400

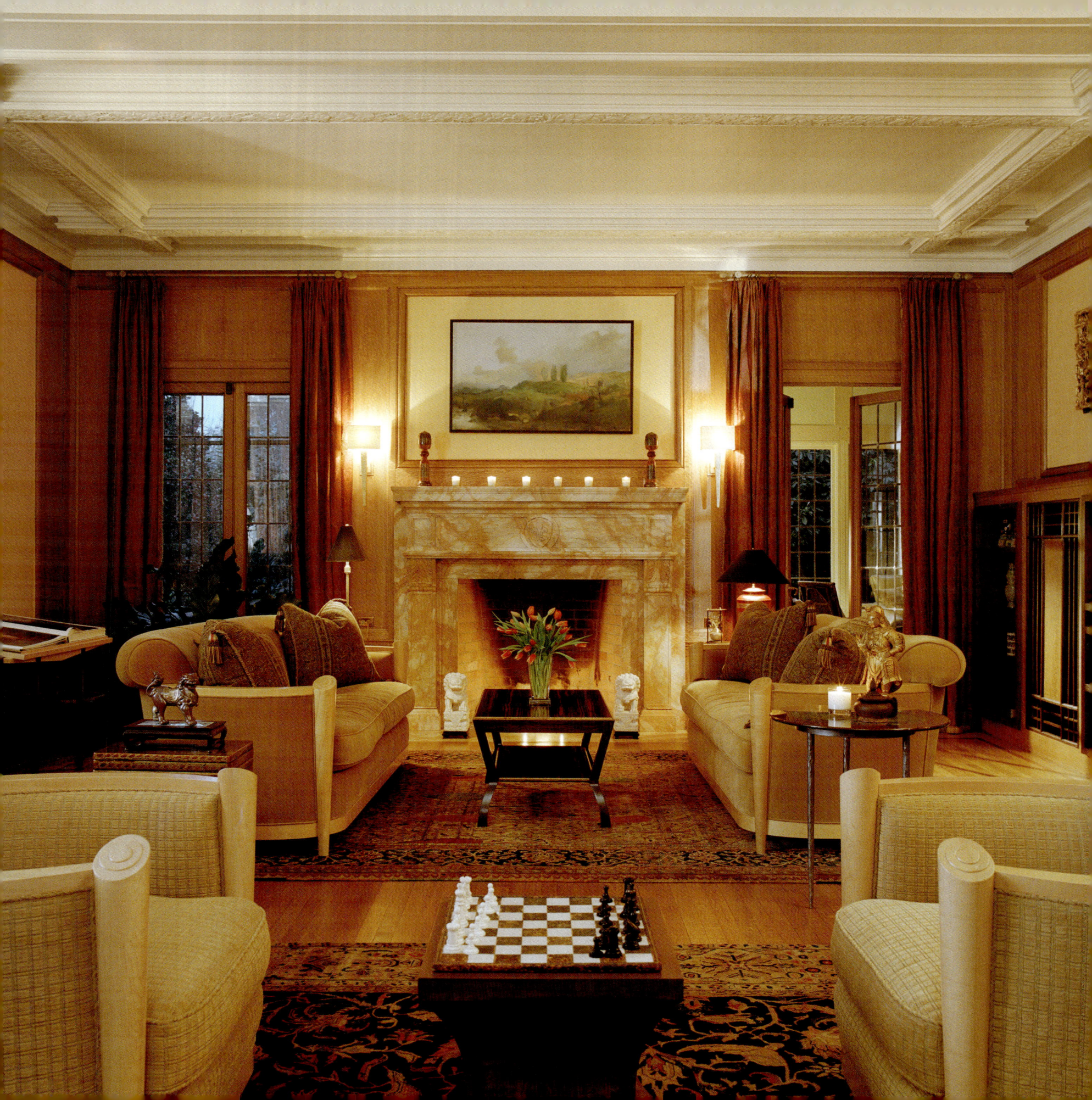

CAROL WILLIAMSON

Carol Williamson + Associates

If you'd told Carol Williamson 30 years ago that she'd be designing everything from the Nike World Campus Headquarters, the Abraham Lincoln Museum, high-end residential and luxury motor yachts, she would have been amazed by the idea. But this accomplished designer is doing just that.

A graduate of the University of Oregon, Carol has been making waves in the design industry for nearly 30 years. In 1984, she opened her own company, Carol Williamson + Associates Limited, a full-service interior design and space planning firm with four employees.

Carol's design career has included commercial interior design and space-planning projects such as the Nike World Headquarters North campus expansion, the Abraham Lincoln Museum in Fort Wayne, Indiana, and multiple projects connected with the Signature Project at Lewis and Clark College in Portland, Oregon, but her portfolio doesn't stop there.

Once Carol got her hands on residential design, she found that she had a talent for residential color palettes and fine fabrics and materials not

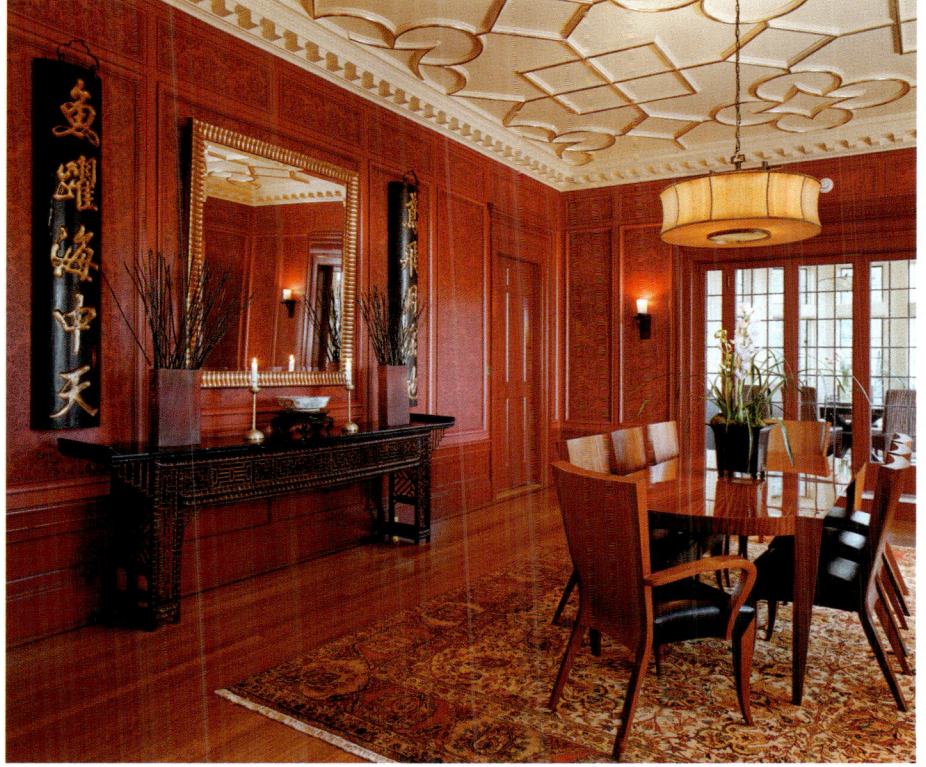

ABOVE
The area carpet was selected to incorporate the deep red damask painted walls into the floor plane and create a warmer feel to this spacious room. Antique ebony and gold figured bamboo panels were added to the room to incorporate the Asian influence the owner enjoys.

LEFT
The overall design for this room was developed around the owner's request that the formal living space be arranged in three distinct arrangements. Formal seating at the fireplace, lounge seating in front of the custom-designed wood and golden onyx topped freestanding bar (not shown) and the billards area highlighted by the antique Brunswick pool table that was custom restored for the owner.

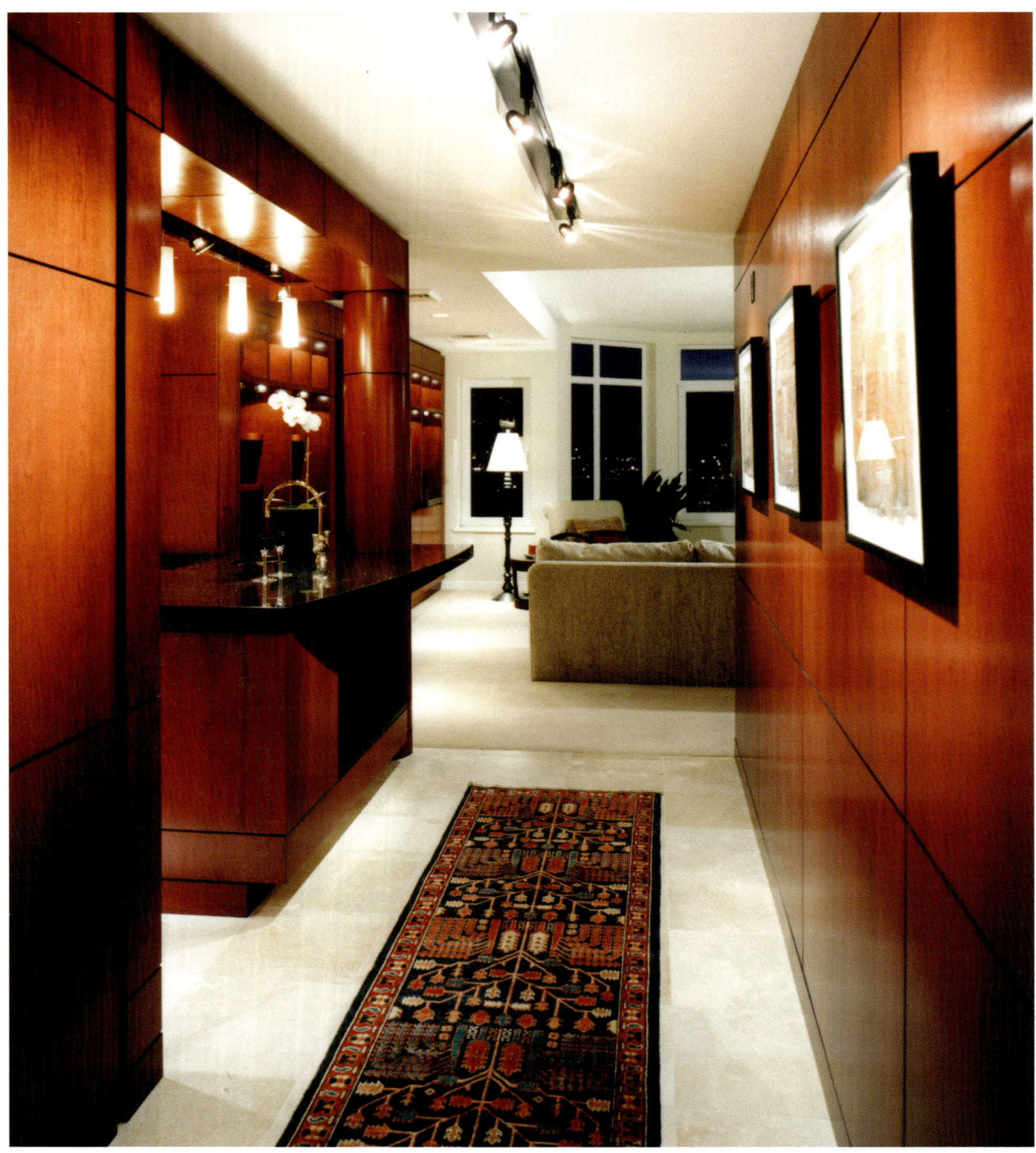

traditionally found in commercial work. When a residential client asked Carol to design his motor yacht, it didn't take her long to say yes, even though she'd never done anything like that before. Now, she regularly works on yachts at Christensen Shipyards in Vancouver, Washington.

Carol believes that the experience gained in one design discipline contributes to the success of all of her other projects. She often gleans ideas and materials she has utilized from one project type and applies them to another project design in ways that are unusual and unique. Residential planning, for example, has influenced her to bring a warmer and more textural environment into her commercial projects.

No matter what she's designing, Carol's philosophy is "keep the design simple, understated and classic." For her, this belief pertains not only to the design but to the process as well. Carol takes great pride in her ability to make the experience an enjoyable one for her clients.

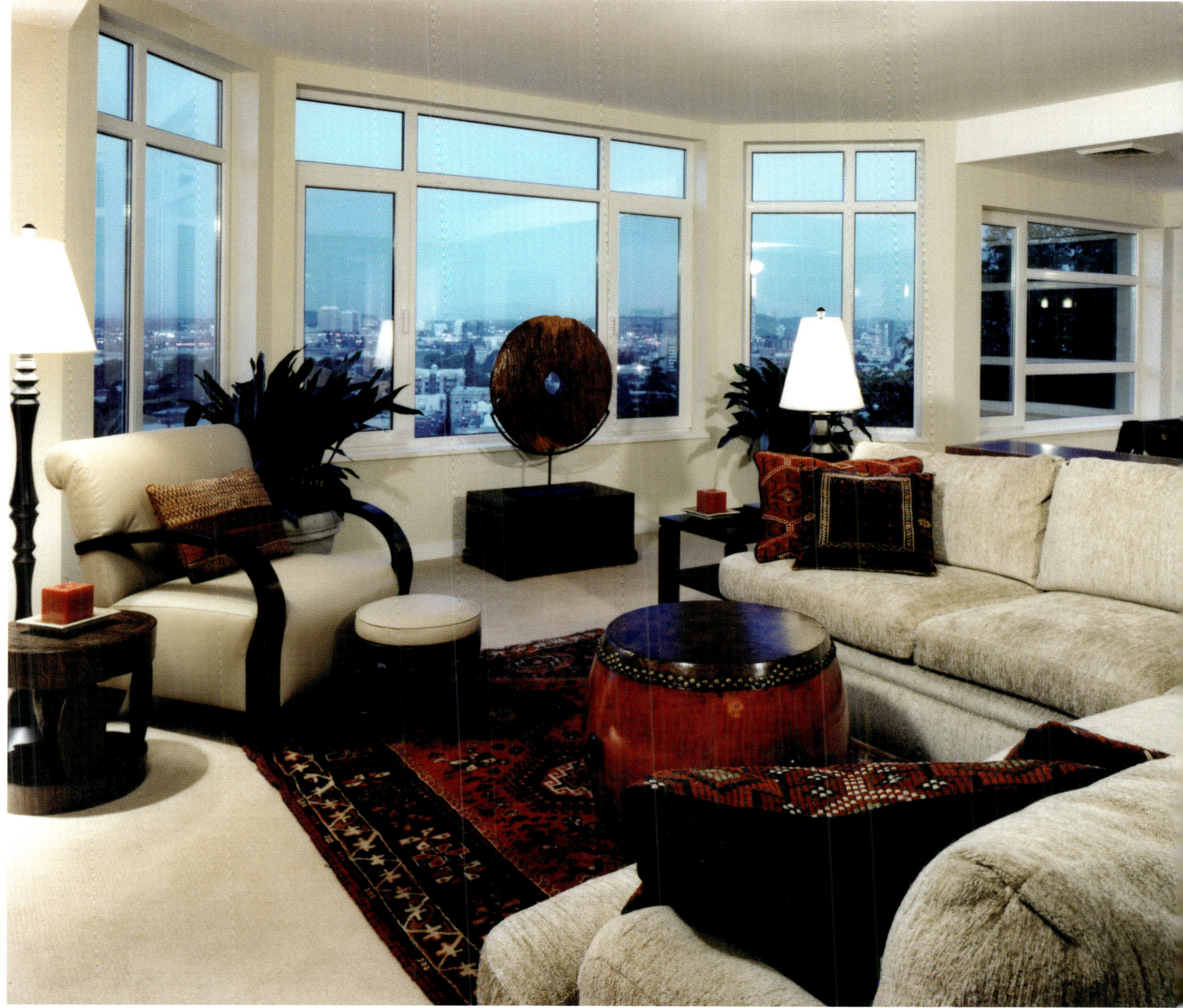

ABOVE
This room was designed so that it could be an extention of his home office when he was seeing clients in his residence. It was designed to entertain friends and family as well.

FACING PAGE LEFT
The owner requested a more informal living space for both family use and for informal entertaining. The custom bar was detailed so that it was integrally tied to the wood paneling that continues into the family room. The runner was selected to add warmth to the limestone hallway and accentuate the warmth of the cherry panels.

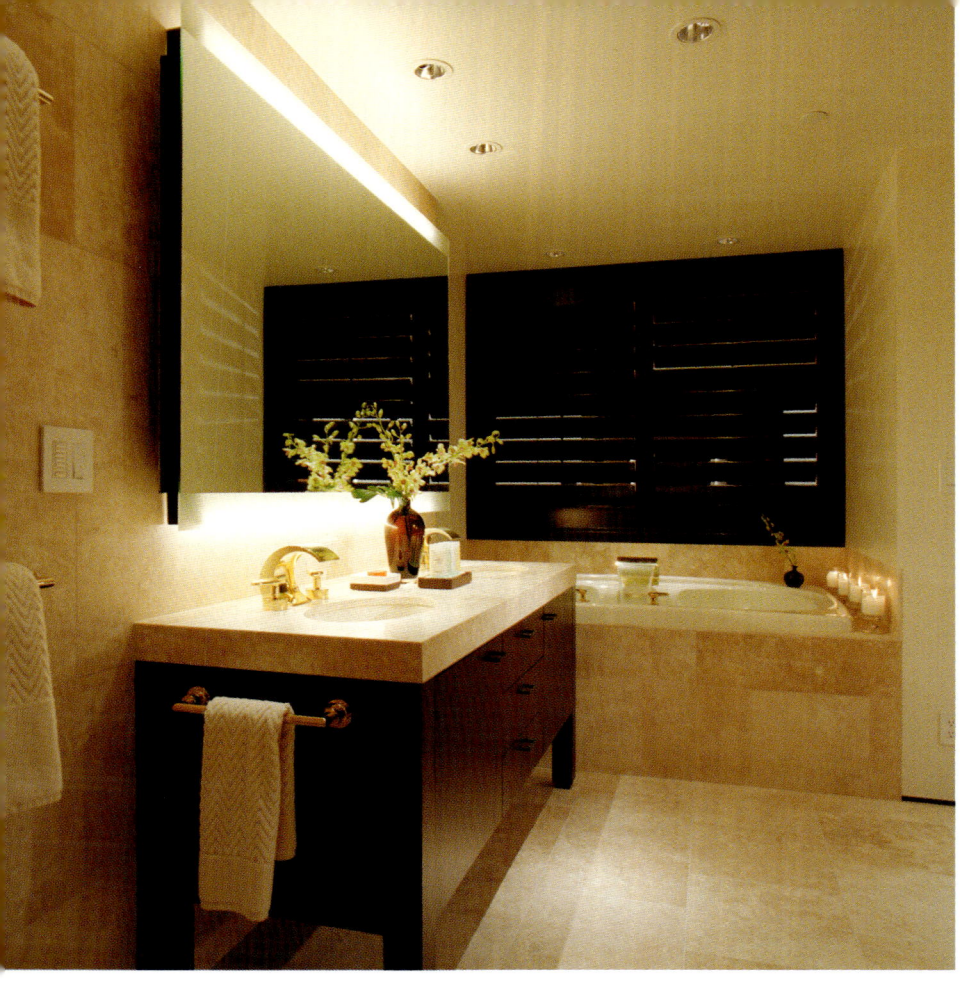

Carol loves working with color and material. She is blessed with an intuitive sense of the way that light influences both of these realms, as well as an innate sense of proportion and the play of light and shadow in the architectural spaces she is working in. Her designs often feature beautifully detailed custom furnishings and window coverings utilizing beautiful fabrics, accessories and artwork all positioned to catch and play with the light in a space.

The design community has recognized Carol's accomplishments with accolades and awards. So far, she has amassed nearly a dozen design awards, including the Best of Show for the Nike World Headquarters/North Campus Project and a Showboats International Award, for Best Semi-Displacement Motor Yacht over 40 Meters. Her yacht designs have also been featured in many publications, including *ShowBoats International*, *Boat International USA*, *Power and MotorYacht* and *Yacht International*. Her residential work has been published in *Portrait of Portland*.

While Carol is honored by the awards and accolades, she feels the true testament to her skills is the client's response to her work. For her, the best compliment came from a client who said, "We used to go out all of the time. But now we just want to stay at home, because you've created such a comfortable environment."

And that, Carol says is her goal. Whether she's designing corporate office spaces, homes or yachts, she wants the end result to draw her clients in–and keep them there.

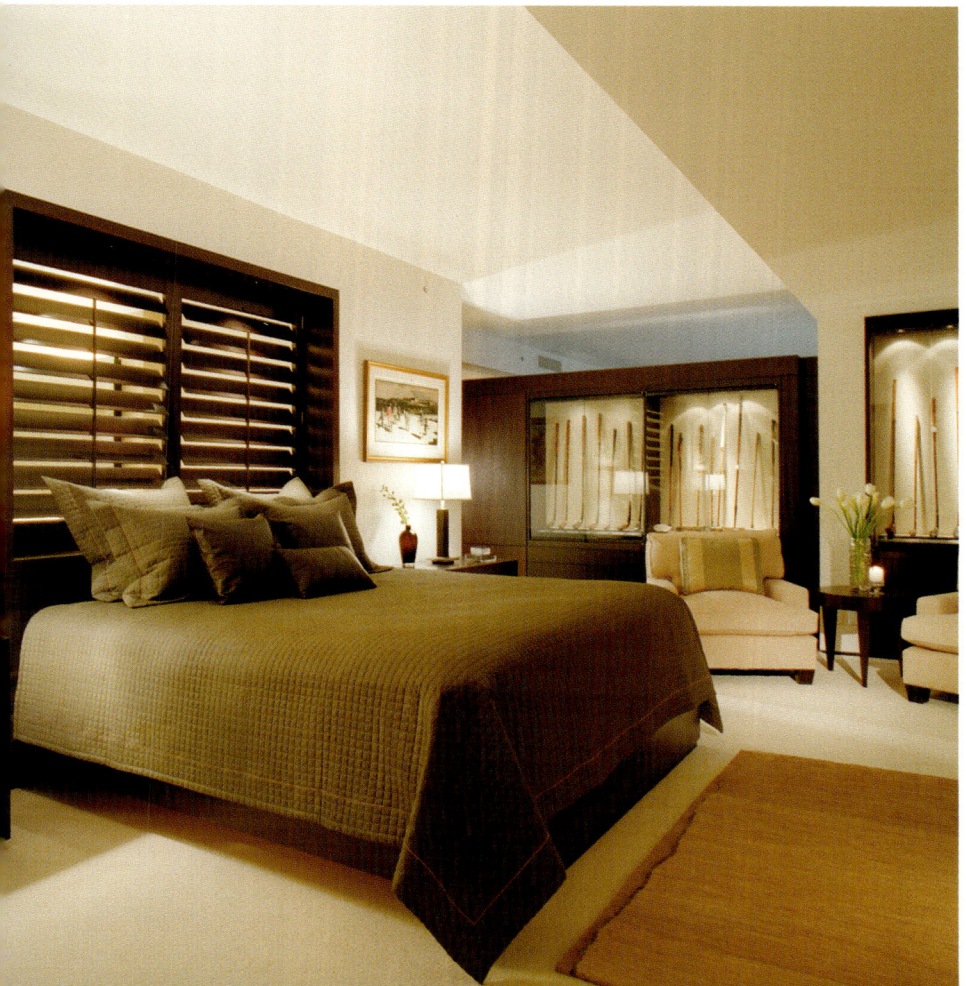

TOP
The guest bath incorporates the clean, modern understated lines of all the display cases throughout the residence. The owner requested an elegant and understated environment for his guests.

BOTTOM
The design for this urban based high rise condominium was based upon the owner's desire to have a home office and guest quarters that were surrounded by his extensive golf club and historic memorabilia collection. He wanted a clean, contemporary environment that would make the collection the focal point of the residence.

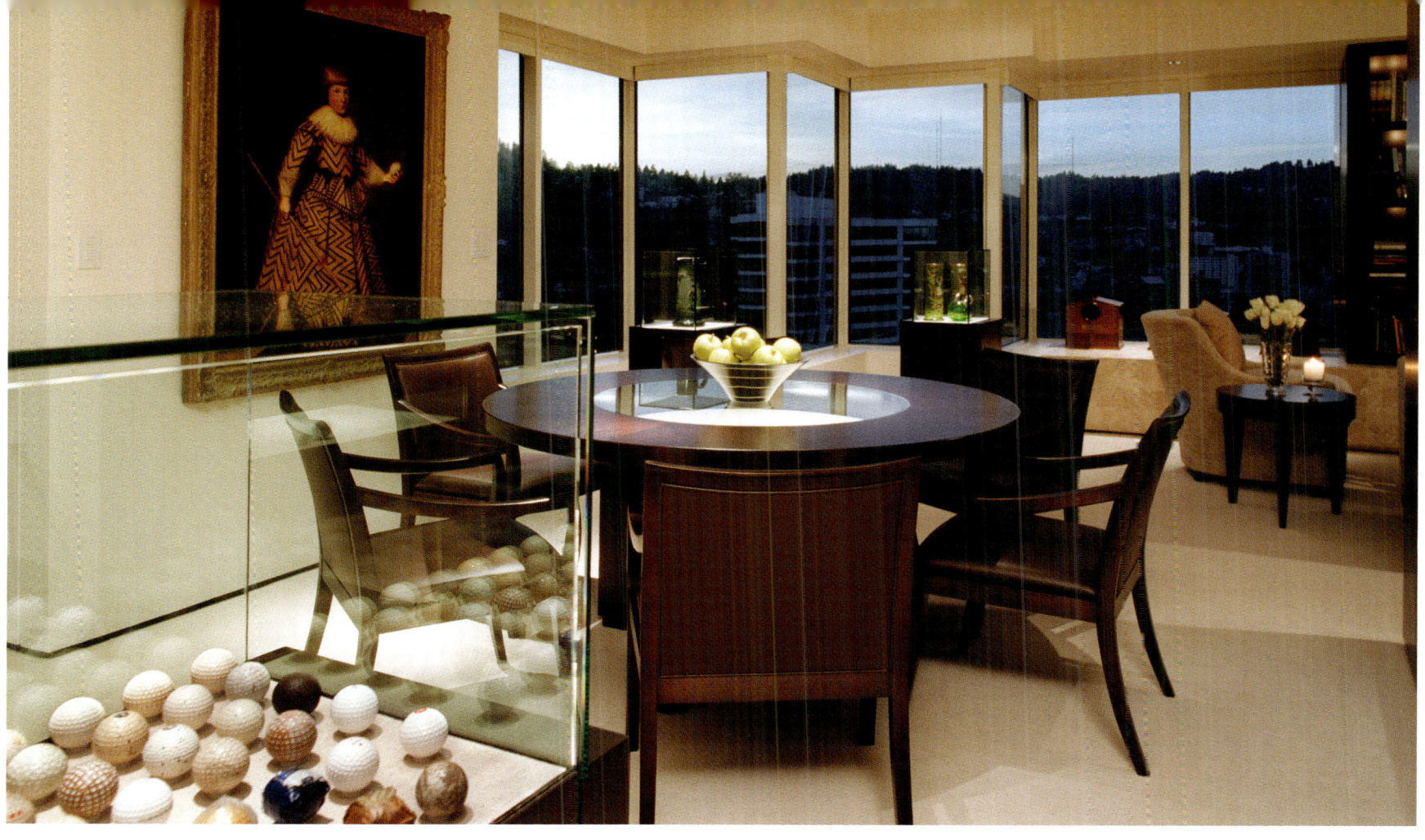

ABOVE
This area was designed for both meetings when the space is being used as an office and for entertaining when guests are staying in the residence. The residence has a full catering kitchen for special events.

More about Carol...

WHAT PERSONAL INDULGENCE DO YOU SPEND THE MOST MONEY ON?

Accessories and orchids for my home.

YOU CAN TELL I LIVE IN THE PACIFIC NORTHWEST BECAUSE I...

Wear black and regularly patronize a Starbuck's coffee shop.

WHAT IS THE BEST PART OF BEING AN INTERIOR DESIGNER?

Creating interior environments for clients that express their individual style. I feel truly blessed to work with interesting clients, beautiful furnishings, materials, lighting, art and accessories every day.

IF YOU COULD ELIMINATE ONE DESIGN/ARCHITECTURAL/BUILDING TECHNIQUE OR STYLE FROM THE WORLD, WHAT WOULD IT BE?

Deconstructivism. I find it brutal and lacking grace or beauty.

WHAT ONE ELEMENT OF STYLE OR PHILOSOPHY HAVE YOU STUCK WITH FOR YEARS THAT STILL WORKS FOR YOU?

Keep the design simple, understated and classic.

Carol Williamson + Associates
Carol Williamson
315 SW Fifth Avenue
Portland, Oregon 97204
503.222.2330
Fax 503.222.7122
www.cwainteriors.com

The Publishing Team

Panache Partners LLC is in the business of creating spectacular publications for discerning readers. The company's hard cover division specializes in the development and production of upscale coffee-table books showcasing world-class travel, interior design, custom home building and architecture, as well as a variety of other topics of interest. Supported by a strong senior management team, professional associate publishers, and a top-notch creative team of photographers, writers, and graphic designers, the company produces only the very best quality of these keepsake publications. Look for our complete portfolio of books at www.panache.com.

We are proud to introduce to you the Panache Partners team below that made this publication possible.

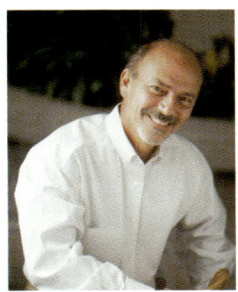

Brian G. Carabet
Brian is co-founder and owner of Panache Partners. With more than 20 years of experience in the publishing industry, he has designed and produced more than 100 magazines and books. He is passionate about high quality design and applies his skill in leading the creative assets of the company. "A spectacular home is one built for entertaining friends and family because without either it's just a house … a boat in the backyard helps too!"

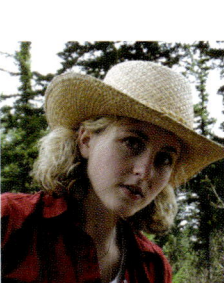

Shanna Germain
Shanna, the book's editor and writer, has worked as a freelance writer in the Pacific Northwest for more than 10 years. When she's not wrangling words, she spends time reading in front of the fireplace in her adorable 1950s home, hiking and biking through the amazing Oregon wilderness and exploring her passions for bluegrass tunes, mixed-media art and locally crafted microbrews and mochas.

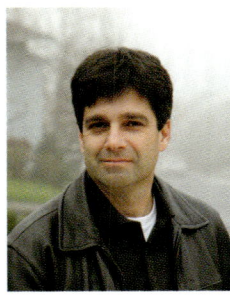

David Papazian
David is one of the most experienced architectural and location photographers in the Northwest. His work has appeared in magazines such as *Sunset*, *Oregon Home and Architectural Record*. To David, a spectacular home is all about exquisite balance between a dramatic structure and the furnishings that inspire those who live in and visit the residence.

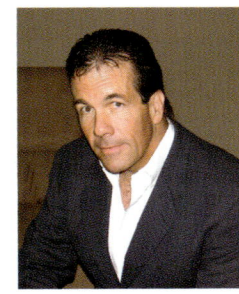

John A. Shand
John is co-founder and owner of Panache Partners and applies his 25 years of sales and marketing experience in guiding the business development activities for the company. His passion toward the publishing business stems from the satisfaction derived from bringing ideas to reality. "My idea of a spectacular home includes an abundance of light, vibrant colors, state-of-the-art technology and beautiful views."

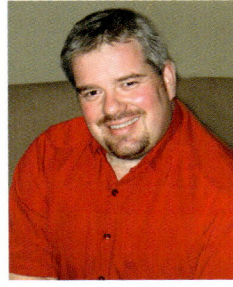

Richard Rayburn
Rich is the Executive Publisher of the Western Region for Panache Partners. He has over 15 years of sales leadership and marketing experience in publishing and advertising. His passion for Spectacular Homes comes from the energy and diversity he encounters in the design community everyday. "A spectacular home is one that from the moment you enter, draws you in and with proper use of form and function creates an environment that embodies the concept of home for those who live in it."

Additional Acknowledgements
Associate Publisher— Karen Fleckenstein
Project Management— Carol Kendall and Beverly Smith.
Graphic Designers— Michele Cunningham-Scott, Emily Kattan and Mary Elizabeth Acree.
Production Coordinators—Kristy Randall, Jennifer Lenhart, Laura Greenwood and Elizabeth Gionta.

PHOTOGRAPHY CREDITS

Page	Designer Name	Photographer
119	Carolyn Allman	Sol Visual Development / Tim Tidball
11	Christine Archer	David Papazian
17	Kathleen Bohlken	Francis Zera
21	DeAnne Brenneis	David Papazian / Roger Turk
125	Lori Brock	Derek & Kim Budd / Rich Derfler / David Papazian
23	Debbie Cahill	David Papzian
27	Gregory Carmichael	Alex Hayden
29	Bonnie Crawford	Francis Zera
35	Michelle Dahl, Sandy Holstead	Dominic Arizona Bonuccelli
131	Erin Davis, Arlene Lord & Stephanie Ness	John Jensen
133	Keri Davis	David Papazian
137	Melody Emerick	Rick Keating / Rebecca Mack / David Papazian / Fred & Holly Stickly
39	Dana Foster	Steve Lindemann / Michael Walmsley
43	Ann Gordinier	John McKinney / Roger Turk / Francis Zera
47	Mary Hanson	David Papazian
53	Fran M. Hazel	Gregg Krogstead
55	Michele Heidt	Philip Cacka / David Papazian
59	Larry Hooke	Dan Langley
65	Tami Jones	David Papazian
67	Cynthia Mennella	Fred Lindholm
71	Cheryl Monroe	John McKinney
75	Craig Norberg	Benjamin Benschneide / Craig Norberry / Bob Weyrick
143	Kathie Pozarich	David Papazian / Robert George Photography
77	Linda Schoener's	Kay Walsh
83	Kylee Shintaffer	David Papazian
89	Ted Tuttle	Scott Van Dyke / Paul Warchol
95	Diane Wainhouse & Val Scalzo	Chapters Photography / Heller Luxury Homes / John Gussman Photography
99	David Weatherford	Roger Turk
149	Carol Williamson	David Papazian / Rich Strode
105	Kathleen Williams	Kirk Swink / Roger Turk
111	Ann Jones-Wilson	Roger Turk

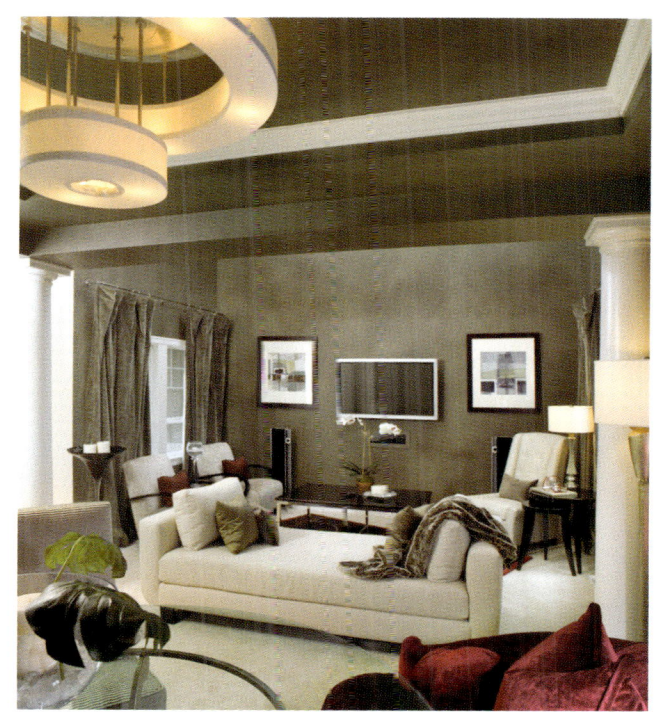

DESIGNER MICHELLE DAHL & SANDY HOLSTEAD, page 35

Index of Designers

Carolyn Allman 119
C. Allman Design Group

Christine Archer 11
Christine Archer Interiors

Kathleen Bohlken 17
Kathleen Bohlken Interior Design

DeAnne Brenneis 21
The John Brenneis Architects, Inc. P.S.

Lori Brock 125
Brock Designs

Debbie Cahill 23
Debbie Cahill Interior Design, LLC

Gregory Carmichael 27
Gregory Carmichael Interior Design

Bonnie K. Crawford 29
BCDG Bonnie Crawford Design Group

Michelle Dahl 35
Belle Grey Interior Design, LLC

Erin Davis 131
Mosaik Design

Keri Davis 133
Keri Davis Design

Melody Emerick 137
Emerick Architects P.C.

Dana T. Foster 39
DTF Design, Inc.

Ann Gordinier 43
A. Gordinier Interiors, Inc.

Mary Hanson 47
LIBERTY 123, LLC

Fran M. Hazel 53
Fran M. Hazel Design Interiors

Michele Heidt 55
Heidt & Oldfield Design

Sandy Holstead 35
Belle Grey Interior Design, LLC

Larry Hooke 59
Larry Hooke Interior Design

Tami Jones 65
Tami Jones Interior Design

Arlene Lord 131
Mosaik Design

Cynthia Mennella 67
Cynthia Mennella Design

Cheryl K. Monroe 71
Monroe Design & Development Co.

Stephanie Ness 131
Mosaik Design

Craig Norberg 75
Norberry Tile

Kathie Pozarich 143
KP Design Group

Val Scalzo 95
Heartland Interiors Inc.

Linda Schoener 77
Schoener's Interiors

Kylee Shintaffer 83
Kylee Shintaffer Design

Ted Tuttle 89
Ted Tuttle Interior Design

Diane Wainhouse 95
Heartland Interiors, Inc.

David Weatherford 99
Weatherford Antiques & Interiors

Carol Williamson 149
Carol Williamson + Associates

Kathleen Williams 105
Design by Kathleen Williams, Inc.

Ann Jones-Wilson 111
Jones-Wilson Designs

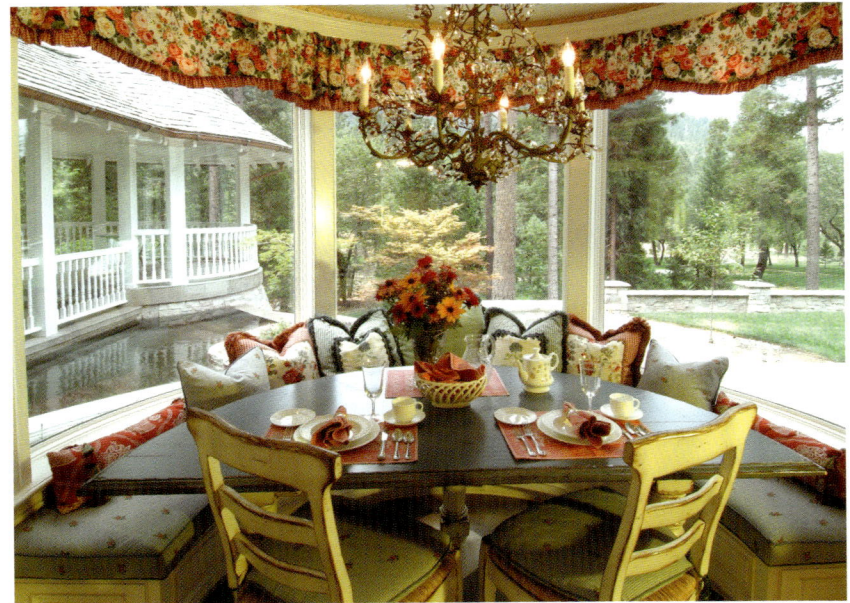

DESIGNER CAROLYN ALLMAN, C. ALLMAN DESIGN GROUP, page 119

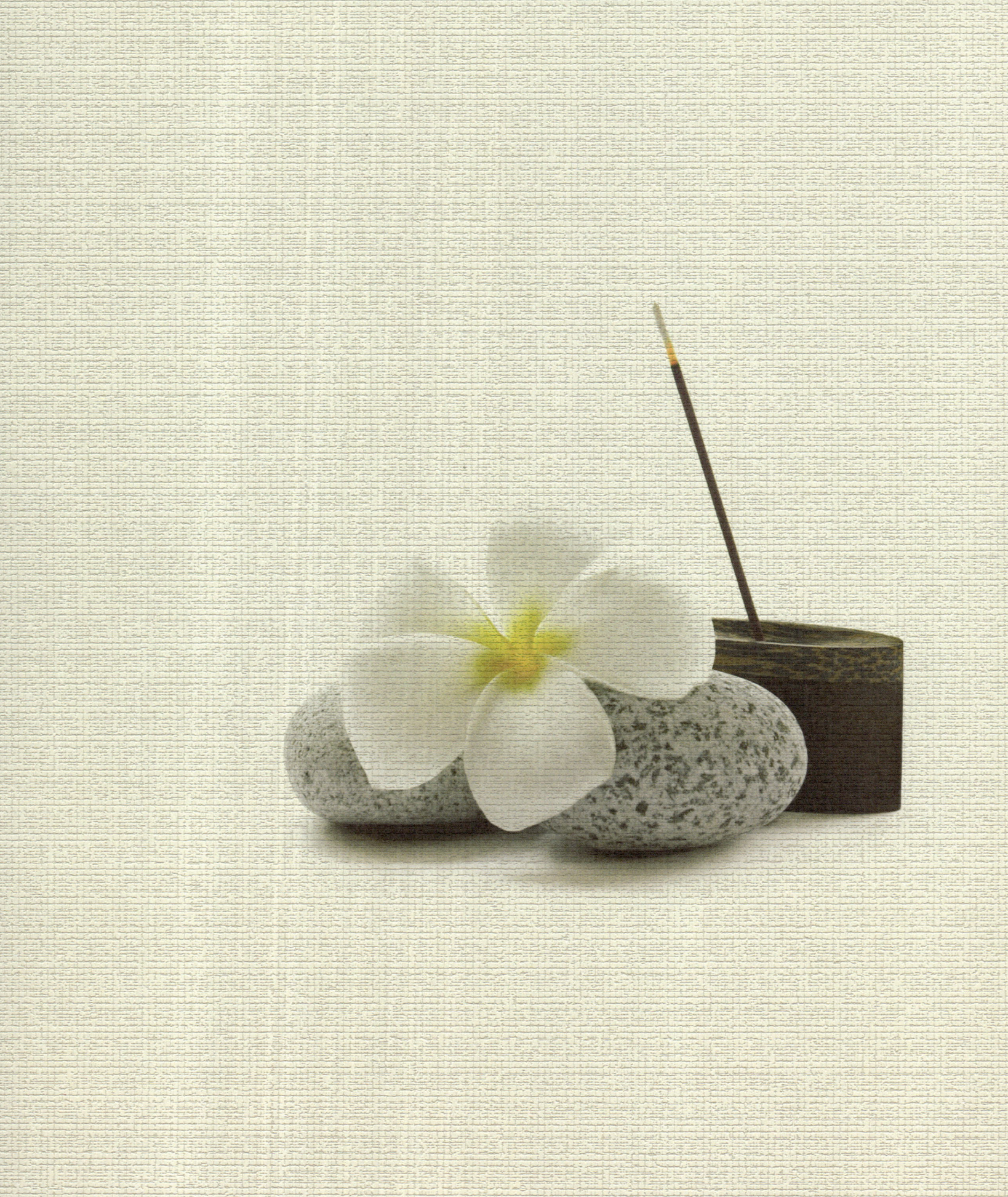